DIGITALIZATION IN TOURISM

Advances in Hospitality and Tourism

DIGITALIZATION IN TOURISM

Hulya Akdemir Cengiz, PhD
Seza Zerman, PhD
Aysegul Acar, PhD
Faizan Ali, PhD
Editors

AAP | APPLE ACADEMIC PRESS

First edition published 2027

Apple Academic Press Inc.
1265 Goldenrod Circle, NE,
Palm Bay, FL 32905 USA

760 Laurentian Drive, Unit 19,
Burlington, ON L7N 0A4, Canada

CRC Press
2385 NW Executive Center Drive,
Suite 320, Boca Raton FL 33431

4 Park Square, Milton Park,
Abingdon, Oxon, OX14 4RN, UK

Apple Academic Press exclusively co-publishes with CRC Press, an imprint of Taylor & Francis Group, LLC

Library and Archives Canada Cataloguing in Publication

CIP data on file with Canada Library and Archives

Library of Congress Cataloging-in-Publication Data

CIP data on file with US Library of Congress

ISBN: 978-1-77964-476-3 (hbk)
ISBN: 978-1-77964-477-0 (ebk)

DOI: 10.1201/9781779644770

About the Book Series: Advances in Hospitality and Tourism

Editor-in-Chief

Mahmood A. Khan, PhD
Professor, Department of Hospitality and Tourism Management,
Pamplin College of Business,
Virginia Polytechnic Institute and State University,
Falls Church, Virginia

This series offers readers valuable information and reports on research developments and advances in the rapidly growing area of hospitality and tourism. Each publication in this series presents state-of-the-art information on specialized topics of current interest. The books in this series are edited or authored by experts in their respective fields. These one-of-a-kind publications are valuable resources for academia as well as for hospitality and tourism professionals.

The series has published titles on myriad specialized topics. The series editor welcomes book proposals on the following and other themes in the field:

- Ecotourism and Green Tourism
- Wildlife Tourism
- Sports Tourism
- Wine and Beverage Tourism
- Sustainability in Tourism
- Hospitality and Tourism Education
- Destination Tourism
- Heritage Tourism
- Rural Tourism
- Medical and Wellness Tourism
- Hospitality and Tourism Management and Human Resources
- Hospitality and Tourism Marketing and Consumer Behavior
- Tourism of Specific Populations (Women, Seniors, Millennials, Religious, etc.)

- Event Tourism
- Island Tourism
- Economic Community Development and Tourism
- Smart Technology in the Hospitality and Tourism Industry

BOOKS IN THE SERIES

Brand Co-Creation Tourism Research: Contemporary Issues and Challenges
Editor: Raouf Ahmad Rather, PhD

Capacity Building Through Heritage Tourism: An International Perspective
Surabhi Srivastava, PhD

Chinese Outbound Tourism 2.0
Editor: Xiang (Robert) Li, PhD

Digitalization in Tourism
Editor: Hulya Akdemir Cengiz, PhD, Seza Zerman, PhD,
Aysegul Acar, PhD, and Faizan Ali, PhD

Dynamics of Heritage Management and Tourism Development: Trends, Practices, and Approaches
Editors: Surabhi Srivastava, PhD, and Ruchika Kulshrestha, PhD

Dynamics of the Tourism Industry: Post-Pandemic and Post-Disaster Perspectives and Strategies
Editors: Gül Erkol Bayram, PhD, and Anukrati Sharma, PhD

Ecotourism and Sustainable Tourism: From Principle to Practice in the New Millennium
Editors: Kelly S. Bricker, PhD, and Jacqueline Kariithi, PhD

Event Tourism in Asian Countries: Challenges and Prospects
Editors: Shruti Arora, PhD, and Anukrati Sharma, PhD

Evolving Paradigms in Tourism and Hospitality in Developing Countries: A Case Study of India
Editor: Bindi Varghese, PhD

Food Safety: Researching the Hazard in Hazardous Foods
Editors: Barbara Almanza, PhD, RD, and Richard Ghiselli, PhD

Halal Tourism: Achieving Muslim-Friendly Tourism Destinations
Editors: Hüseyin Pamukçu, PhD, Ömer Akgün Tekin, PhD, and Shruti Arora, PhD

Himalayan Mountain Tourism: Toward Sustainable Adventure Tourism
Editors: Satish Chandra Bagri, PhD, and Junaid K. C., MBA

Hospitality Marketing and Consumer Behavior: Creating Memorable Experiences
Editor: Vinnie Jauhari, PhD

Labor in the Tourism and Hospitality Industry: Skills, Ethics, Issues, and Rights
Abdallah M. Elshaer, PhD, and Asmaa M. Marzouk, PhD

Management Science in Hospitality and Tourism: Theory, Practice, and Applications
Editors: Muzaffer Uysal, PhD, Zvi Schwartz, PhD, and Ercan Sirakaya-Turk, PhD

Managing Sustainability in the Hospitality and Tourism Industry: Paradigms and Directions for the Future
Editor: Vinnie Jauhari, PhD

Medical Tourism and Wellness: Hospitality Bridging Healthcare (H2H)©
Editor: Frederick J. DeMicco, PhD, RD

Medical Travel Brand Management: Success Strategies for Hospitality Bridging Healthcare (H2H)
Editors: Frederick J. DeMicco, PhD, RD, and Ali A. Poorani, PhD

Medical, Dental, and Wellness Tourism: A Post-Pandemic Perspective
Mary Schreiber Swenson, PhD, and Amit Bansal

Post-COVID Tourism and Hospitality Dynamics: Recovery, Revival, and Re-start
Editors: Umendra Narayan Shukla, PhD, and Sharad Kumar Kulshreshtha, PhD

Poverty Alleviation through Tourism Development: A Comprehensive and Integrated Approach
Robertico Croes, PhD, and Manuel Rivera, PhD

Purpose-Driven Tourism: The Intersection of Cultural Cuisine, Gender Equality, and Sustainable Community Building
Editors: Andrea Edurne Jiménez Ruiz, PhD, and Shivam Bhartiya, PhD

Small Island and Small Destination Tourism: Overcoming the Smallness Barrier for Economic Growth and Tourism Competitiveness
Robertico Croes, PhD

Strategic Management for the Hospitality and Tourism Industry: Developing a Competitive Advantage
Vincent Sabourin, PhD

Strategic Winery Tourism and Management: Building Competitive Winery Tourism and Winery Management Strategy
Editor: Kyuho Lee, PhD

Sustainability, Social Responsibility, and Innovations in Tourism and Hospitality
Editor: H. G. Parsa, PhD; Consulting Editor: Vijaya "Vi" Narapareddy, PhD; Associate Editors: SooCheong (Shawn) Jang, PhD, Marival Segarra-Oña, PhD, and Rachel J. C. Chen, PhD, CHE

Sustainable Tourism Development: Futuristic Approaches
Editor: Anukrati Sharma, PhD

Sustainable Viticulture: The Vines and Wines of Burgundy
Claude Chapuis

The Future of Events: Trends, Technologies, and Stakeholder Engagement
Editors: Narendra Kumar, PhD, Swati Sharma, PhD, and Bruno Barbosa Sousa, PhD

The Hospitality and Tourism Industry in ASEAN and East Asian Destinations: New Growth, Trends, and Developments
Editors: Jinlin Zhao, PhD, Lianping Ren, D.HTM, and Xiangping Li, PhD

The Hospitality and Tourism Industry in China: New Growth, Trends, and Developments
Editor: Jinlin Zhao, PhD

The Indian Hospitality Industry: Dynamics and Future Trends
Editors: Sandeep Munjal and Sudhanshu Bhushan, PhD

Tourism and Hospitality Education: Progress, Challenges, and Prospects
Abdallah M. Elshaer, PhD, and Asmaa M. Marzouk, PhD

Tourism in Central Asia: Cultural Potential and Challenges
Editors: Kemal Kantarci, PhD, Muzaffer Uysal, PhD, and Vincent Magnini, PhD

Tourism in Türkiye: A Comprehensive Overview and Analysis for Sustainable Alternative Tourism
Editor: Ahmet Salih İKİZ

Tourist Behavior: Past, Present, and Future
Editors: Narendra Kumar, PhD, Bruno Barbosa Sousa, PhD, and Swati Sharma, PhD

Wilderness of Wildlife Tourism
Editor: Johra Kayeser Fatima, PhD

Women and Travel: Historical and Contemporary Perspectives
Editors: Catheryn Khoo-Lattimore, PhD, and Erica Wilson, PhD

About the Series Editor-In-Chief

Mahmood A. Khan, PhD
Professor, Department of Hospitality and Tourism Management, Pamplin College of Business, Virginia Tech's National Capital Region Center, USA

Mahmood A. Khan, PhD, is a Professor in the Department of Hospitality and Tourism Management, Pamplin College of Business at Virginia Tech's National Capital Region Center for the past 33 years. Before joining Virginia Tech, he was Professor at the University of Illinois, Urbana-Champaign, for nine years. He joined the newly formed department in 1987 as the first Assistant Department Head and then served as the department head for over a decade. He went to northern Virginia to establish a graduate program and currently serves as the director of the program.

He has authored books on different subjects in hospitality management. He serves as executive editor for book series, *Advances in Hospitality & Tourism Management*, which has published nearly 40 books to date under different research topics. In addition, he has numerous chapters in books and monographs. He has attended over 100 different conferences and chaired sessions and served as keynote speaker. He has served as consultant to selected major international corporations and was invited as expert witness in many legal cases.

Dr. Khan has traveled extensively to 36 countries serving in different capacities, including offering workshops, training, and research, as well as seminars on various topics. He has served as Fulbright senior fellow and has worked on several projects offered by the USAID in Armenia and Cyprus. He has offered management certification training programs in Saudi Arabia, Lebanon, Cyprus, Malaysia, and Armenia, in addition to graduate and undergraduate courses in services management. He held Brahim's Chair in Hospitality Management at the UPM (Universiti Putra Malaysia) and served as the founding board member at the Cesar Ritz College of Hospitality Management in Switzerland. He is a fellow of the Academy of Nutrition and Dietetics and served as a Registered Dietitian. He was awarded Honorary Citizenship and key to the city of Baton Rouge, Louisiana.

He has received the Steven Fletcher Award for his outstanding contribution to hospitality education and research. He is also a recipient of John Wiley & Sons Award for lifetime contribution to outstanding research and scholarship; Donald K. Tressler Award for scholarship; and Cesar Ritz Award for scholarly contribution. He received an Outstanding Doctoral faculty award from the Pamplin College of Business. He has served on the Board of Governors of the Educational Foundation of the International Franchise Association, on the Board of Directors of the Virginia Hospitality and Tourism Association, as a Trustee of the International College of Hospitality Management and as a Trustee on the Foundation of the Hospitality Sales and Marketing Association's International Association. He is a member of several professional associations.

About the Editors

Hulya Akdemir Cengiz, PhD
Assistant Professor, Safranbolu Faculty of Tourism,
Karabuk University, Karabuk, Türkiye

Hulya Akdemir Cengiz, PhD, is an Assistant Professor in the Safranbolu Faculty of Tourism, Karabük University, Türkiye. She completed her bachelor's degree at Eskişehir Osmangazi University, Türkiye, in 2007 and gained industry experience in sales and marketing roles at various companies in Türkiye and USA. She completed her master's degree in business administration at Karabuk University, Türkiye, followed by a PhD at the same university. Her research interests focus on tourism marketing, digital marketing, and consumer behavior. She has publications in various journals, and she presented papers in conferences across the world. She is also a member of the International Council on Hotel, Restaurant, and Institutional Education (ICHRIE). In terms of teaching experience, she has taught undergraduate and graduate courses such as tourism management, tourism marketing, service marketing, customer relationship management, sales management, and research methods and ethics. In 2022, the researcher was awarded a postdoctoral fellowship by TUBITAK, a national research funding agency in Turkey. She spent a year in the United States working on a project focused on "The Effects of Virtual and Augmented Reality Technologies on Hotel Customers' Memorable Tourism Experiences."

Seza Zerman, PhD
Assistant Professor, Safranbolu Faculty of Tourism,
Karabuk University, Karabuk, Türkiye

Seza Zerman, PhD, works as an Assistant Professor at the Safranbolu College of Tourism, Karabuk University, Türkiye. After graduating from the College of Political Sciences, Ankara University, in Türkiye, she studied for her master's at the Rochester Institute of Technology, USA, in Hospitality and Tourism Management, and for her PhD at Oklahoma State University, USA, in Hospitality Administration. She teaches hospitality marketing, sustainable tourism, contemporary hospitality issues, and storytelling in tourism both at the undergraduate and graduate levels. She has several publications on sustainable tourism, local food and street food marketing, social media marketing, and storytelling in hospitality. Her research project, "Storytelling in Tourism: The Impacts of Story Items and Mental Simulation on Storytelling Intention," has recently been approved by The Scientific and Technological Research Council of Türkiye as a nine-month project to be conducted in the United States of America in 2025. She is a member of the International Council on Hotel, Restaurant, and Institutional Education (ICHRIE) and has presented several papers at ICHRIE, EuroCHRIE, and APacCHRIE conferences across the world.

Aysegul Acar, PhD
Associate Professor, Safranbolu Faculty of Tourism,
Karabuk University, Karabuk, Türkiye

Aysegul Acar, PhD, is an Associate Professor in the Department of Recreation Management of the Safranbolu Faculty of Tourism at Karabük University, Türkiye, where she joined as a Research Assistant in 2015. Dr. Acar's research interests are in finance, management and organization, marketing in the tourism industry, and alternative tourism types. She has authored or co-authored over 15 international refereed journal articles, international conference papers and presentations, and book chapters. Regarding her teaching experience, she has taught financial management, sustainable tourism, tourism marketing, and introduction to hospitality and tourism courses at Karabük University. She received her doctoral degree from Istanbul University in January 2020. Her dissertation focus was on corporate social responsibility, brand equity, and the financial performance of hospitality and tourism establishments. She also holds a Master of Science degree in hospitality management from Istanbul University and earned her Bachelor of Science degree in tourism management from Boğaziçi University, Türkiye. Her research project, "Integration of Bloomberg Terminal as an Experiential Learning Tool into Tourism and Hospitality Education," was approved by The Scientific and Technological Research Council of Türkiye as a 12-month project to be conducted in the United States of America in 2023. She is a member of the International Council on Hotel, Restaurant, and Institutional Education (ICHRIE).

She completed a one-year postdoctoral fellowship at Northern Arizona University, followed by another one-year postdoctoral fellowship at the University of South Florida.

Faizan Ali, PhD
Professor, J. E. Cairnes School of Business & Economics, University of Galway, Ireland

Faizan Ali, PhD, is a Professor at the J.E. Cairnes School of Business & Economics at the University of Galway, Ireland, and a renowned expert in contemporary research methodologies related to consumer behavior and human-computer interaction in the hospitality and tourism industry. A scholar, teacher, and mentor, Dr. Ali was ranked among the top 2% of scientists worldwide and was recognized as a Highly Cited Researcher in 2022 and 2023 by Clarivate Analytics. He has published over 130 research papers and book chapters, presented at more than 75 conferences, and has received nearly 17,000 citations. Dr. Ali also serves as an editor and editorial board member for several leading hospitality and tourism journals.

Contents

Contributors

Aysegul Acar
Associate Professor, Safranbolu Faculty of Tourism, Karabuk University, Karabuk, Türkiye

Emel Adamis
Associate Professor, Department of Tourist Guidance, Vocational School of Iznik, Bursa Uludag University, Bursa, Türkiye

Navidreza Ahadi
Lecturer, College of Business, Law and Social Sciences University of Derby, Derby, UK

Faizan Ali
Professor, J. E. Cairnes School of Business & Economics, University of Galway, Galway, Ireland

Laiba Ali
Post Doctoral Researcher, IRC for Finance and Digital Economy, KFUPM Business School, King Fahd University of Petroleum and Minerals, Dhahran, Saudi Arabia.

Sadia Afrin Ananya
PhD Candidate, Adelaide University, Adelaide, Australia

Nesrin M. Bahcelerli
Professor, Near East University, Faculty of Tourism, Tourism Research Center, Nicosia, North Cyprus

Hulya Akdemir Cengiz
Assistant Professor, Safranbolu Faculty of Tourism, Karabuk University, Karabuk, Türkiye

Hakan Cengiz
Professor, Faculty of Business Administration, Karabuk University, Karabuk, Türkiye

Gulsel Ciftci
Associate Professor, Faculty of Applied Sciences, Trakya University, Edirne, Türkiye

Edmira Cakrani
Associate Professor, Western Balkans University, Tirana, Albania

Rina Cakrani
Simon Fraser University, Vancouver, Canada

Enriko Ceko
Head of Business Administration & IT Department, Canadian Institute of Technology, Tirana, Albania

Mustafa Dogan
Associate Professor, Department of Tourism Management, Faculty of Tourism, Batman University, Batman, Türkiye

Marco A. Gardini
Professor, Faculty of Tourism, Kempten University, Kempten, Germany

Sarah Hussain
Professor, Department of Tourism and Hospitality Management, Faculty of Management Studies, Jamia Millia Islamia, New Delhi, India

Onur Icoz
Associate Professor, Aydin Adnan Menderes University, Faculty of Tourism, Aydin, Türkiye

Saima Kareem
Doctoral Researcher, Department of Tourism and Hospitality Management, Faculty of Management Studies, Jamia Millia Islamia, New Delhi, India

Muhammad Khizar Hayat Naeem
Doctoral Researcher, School of Management, Harbin Institute of Technology, China

Peter O'Connor
Professor, College of Business and Law, Adelaide University, Adelaide, Australia

Mahmoud Ibraheam Saleh
Lecturer, Tourism Studies Department, Faculty of Tourism and Hotel Management, Capital University, Cairo, Egypt

Esra Topcuoglu Schoen
Assistant Professor, Department of Hospitality and Tourism Management, Indiana University Kokomo, Kokomo, Indiana, USA

Miray Urkmezer
Assistant Professor, Beykoz Vocational School of Logistics, Beykoz University, İstanbul, Türkiye

Yanqing Wang
Associate Professor, School of Management, Harbin Institute of Technology, China

Pola Q. Wang
Senior Lecturer, School of Hospitality and Tourism, Auckland University of Technology, Auckland, New Zealand

Sonia Lim Ern Yi
Independent Researcher

Geraldine Anne Tan Wern-Yi
Lecturer, School of Hospitality, Tourism & Culinary Arts, University of Wollongong (UOW), Shah Alam, Selangor, Malaysia

Seza Zerman
Assistant Professor, Safranbolu Faculty of Tourism, Karabuk University, Karabuk, Türkiye

Abbreviations

ACCC	Australian Competition and Consumer Commission
ADPPA	American Data Privacy Protection Act
AI	artificial intelligence
AIA	Artificial Intelligence Act
AKA	Algorithmic Accountability Act
AR	augmented reality
BCI	brain-computer interfaces
BMI	brain-machine interfaces
CAGR	compound annual growth rate
CAVs	connected and self-driving vehicles
CCPA	California Consumer Privacy Act
CCPPA	Canadian Consumer Privacy Protection Act
CEO	chief executive officer
CMA	Competition and Markets Authority
CMO	chief marketing officer
CRM	customer relationship management
CRS	central reservation system
CRS	common reporting standard
CRSs	computer reservation systems
DBMS	database management systems
DMA	Digital Markets Act
DMOs	destination marketing organizations
DOI	diffusion of innovation
EC	European Commission
EDRi	European Digital Rights
EHR	electronic health record
EU	European Union
E-WOM	electronic word-of-mouth
FMI	future market insights
FTC	Federal Trade Commission
GDA	Global Distribution Accounts

GDP	gross domestic product
GDPR	General Data Protection Regulation
GDS	Global Distribution System
GPS	Global Positioning System
HES	Historic Environment Scotland
HR	human resources
HSMAI	Hospitality Sales and Marketing Association International
IBE	internet booking engine
ICF	International Classification of Function
ICT	information and communication technology
IMC	integrated marketing communications
IoMT	Internet of Medical Things
IT	information technology
ITS	intelligent transportation system
LiDAR	light detection and ranging
LVCVA	Las Vegas Convention and Visitor Authority
MaaS	mobility-as-a-service
ML	machine learning
MR	mixed reality
NFC	near field communication
NFTs	nonfungible tokens
NH	network hospitality
NTO	national tourism organization
OECD	Organization for Economic Co-operation and Development
OTA	online travel agency
PMS	property management system
POS	point of sale
PWDs	persons with disabilities
QR code	quick-response code
RLVs	reusable launch vehicles
RMS	revenue management system
SDG	Sustainable Development Goals
SEO	search engine optimization
SMA	social media analytics
SMEs	small and medium-sized enterprises

SMI	social media influencers
SMTEs	small and medium-sized tourism enterprises
SNS	social network sites
STD	smart tourism destinations
TAM	technology acceptance model
THOs	tourism and hospitality organizations
TOE	technology-organization-environment
TPB	Theory of Planned Behavior
TRA	Theory of Reasoned Action
UCPD	Unfair Commercial Practices Directive
UGC	user-generated content
UNWTO	United Nations World Tourism Organization
USD	United States dollar
UTAUT	Unified Theory of Acceptance and Use of Technology
VR	virtual reality
WEF	World Economic Forum
WHO	World Health Organization
WTTC	World Travel & Tourism Council
WWOOF	World Wide Opportunities on Organic Farms

Preface

Digital technologies are making changes in tourism faster than ever before. In just the past couple of years, they have transformed how businesses operate, how travelers engage in destinations, and how services are delivered. This book is all about exploring these thrilling changes and giving readers a closer look into the dynamic world of tourism today.

In this book, we cover a wide range of topics, from how tourism businesses are adapting in the digital age to the rise of the digital traveler. We focus on digital leadership and strategic management in tourism enterprises as they work to overcome digital maturity challenges. Furthermore, we delve deeply into the implications of digitalization for sustainable tourism, cultural heritage, and crisis management, with an eye toward future technologies and innovations, such as artificial intelligence and social media. This investigation aims to shed light on the emerging business models and ethical considerations associated with a digitalized world, providing a glimpse into the future of tourism.

This book is a cumulative result of several committed researchers. Let me take this opportunity to express my deepest gratitude to our chief editor, Mahmood A. Khan, whose guidance and support have been invaluable throughout the preparation process. My collaboration with him started with an international research project and proved intellectually enriching and personally rewarding. I also want to thank my co-editors for their hard work and commitment to making this book possible. Working with my co-editors has been both enriching and inspiring. Their continuous support throughout this process is also highly valued. Finally, I would also like to thank the contributing authors who have shared their knowledge in this volume. Without their input, the production of this book would not have been possible. Their different standpoints contributed to adding width and depth to our exploration of digitalization in tourism.

As tourism continues to change due to continuous technological changes, I do hope that this book will serve as a valuable source of information for scholars and practitioners to advance the knowledge on how digitalization influences this field and to create further research and innovation.

—Hulya Akdemir Cengiz, PhD

CHAPTER 1

Introduction to Digitalization in Tourism: Overview and Organization of the Content

HULYA AKDEMIR CENGIZ[1,*], SEZA ZERMAN[1], AYSEGUL ACAR[1], and FAIZAN ALI[2]

[1]*Safranbolu Faculty of Tourism, Karabuk University, Karabuk, Türkiye*

[2]*J. E. Cairnes School of Business & Economics, University of Galway, Galway, Ireland*

*Corresponding author

ABSTRACT

This chapter serves as an introduction to the book "Digitalization in Tourism," providing a comprehensive overview of the transformation digitalization has brought to the tourism sector and a conceptual framework for the topics explored in detail in the subsequent chapters. It is crucial to view digitalization not simply as a technological advancement, but as a strategic and organizational shift affecting everyone in the tourism industry. Digital transformation has significantly transformed tourism operations, marketing approaches, and visitor experiences. This chapter highlights these changes while also highlighting the significant role digital technologies play in the travel and tourism industry. The purpose and contributions of each chapter are outlined, providing an overview of the book's content. This chapter, along with the subsequent chapters, provides a conceptual framework and foundation for exploring the various dimensions of digitalization in tourism.

Digitalization in Tourism. Hulya Akdemir Cengiz, Seza Zerman, Aysegul Acar, and Faizan Ali (Eds.)

DOI: 10.1201/9781779644770-1

1.1 INTRODUCTION

The tourism industry is changing quickly, thanks to the rise of digital technologies that are significantly altering its landscape like never before. Digitalization plays a crucial role in tourism, influencing every aspect of the industry, from destination marketing to the interactions tourists have with their surroundings. This chapter stands out as an essential examination of the crucial impact that digital technology has on contemporary tourism.

The topic of digitalization in tourism has recently become of interest to researchers. In particular, the impact of digitalization on tourism has accelerated following the COVID-19 pandemic (Skare et al., 2021; Lu et al., 2022). In the literature, researchers emphasize the importance of digitalization in tourism from various perspectives. Digitalization affects many areas, from local economic revenues to tourists'behavior and attitudes. Digital technology products have emerged as key elements in revitalizing the tourism industry and enhancing the competitive power of companies (Yuce et al., 2020; Cranmer et al., 2021). Numerous studies highlight that digital products increase tourist satisfaction (Lou et al., 2017; Lee and Kim, 2021) and strengthen the intention to visit (Cranmer et al., 2021).

Pencarelli (2020) emphasizes the rise of technologies and their impacts on the competitiveness of tourism enterprises; therefore, it is very important to undertake a deep analysis of the digital revolution for tourism. The industry players must be aware that changing consumer behavior and expectations requires innovation and adaptation to digitally transformed platforms. Adaptation to digital tools not only contributes to the survival of tourism companies but also to efficiency, engagement, and sustainability.

Why is this book important now? We witness a paradigm shift where digital innovation challenges the old ways of considering tourism and redefines them. Artificial intelligence, virtual reality (VR), and blockchain are not just ideas of the future; they are the realities of the present that shape the way we travel. Recent studies, such as the research conducted by Lo and Cheng (2020), have explored the impact of VR and augmented reality (AR) on tourism. These studies specifically examine how VR and AR technologies attract visitors and significantly enhance their engagement throughout their stay (Omran et al., 2024). Recent studies have examined the effectiveness of VR and AR in attracting visitors.

With digital technologies embedded even further in hospitality services, we expect future research to be centered on this domain profoundly. This book is intended to bring the attention of researchers to the vast potential for innovation and enhancement of hospitality services through digitalization, and hence to trigger a wave of research that will look deeply at the way these technologies will continue to shape the tourism industry.

In addition, the continuous global digitalization process gives more grounds to update strategic management in the tourism sector. As Aras and Buyukozkan (2023) pointed out, higher digital maturation calls for a revision of strategic orientations toward agile, responsive, customer-oriented, and technology-adaptive ones. The contribution has a place in leading one through this complicated and dynamic environment; it allows seeing not only the question of "how" and "what" but also the "why" of digital adoption in tourism.

Synthesizing these insights, this book relates not only to changes but also foresees future trends and foresight at the strategic level into how the industry could change. The careful compilation of chapters here forms a scaffold for the reader to begin conceptualizing how digital tools transform experiences, operational efficiencies, and marketing strategies. Ultimately, this is an exploration of equipping industry professionals and academics alike with the knowledge to lead rather than react to digital advances in tourism.

1.2 CONTRIBUTION OF THIS BOOK

United Nations World Tourism Organization states that emerging technologies and digital transformation indicate the beginning of the Fourth Industrial Revolution, ushering in a new period where digitalization will influence individuals and organizations in an unexpected and surprising way.

Digital movement revolutionized decision-making processes both in micro and macro levels in all industries, and hospitality and tourism industries are no exception to this rapid evolution. This transformation translates a new wave of job profiles, meaning reduced work for employees so that they can focus on delivering excellence in service; and new direction of consumer behavior, meaning more information for travelers and tourists that helps them to find diverse and organized knowledge to manage their travel experience.

This quick transformation, on the other hand, raised some concerns, such as the boundaries, ethical aspect, and legal and social responsibilities within the digital world. To address the rapid transformation and concerns, this book is a humble attempt to provide comprehensive viewpoint and opinion on digital era of tourism from different dimensions, such as, travelers and businesses, availability and confidentiality of digital data, digital adaptation, digital challenges, and so forth.

This book has contributions devoted to understanding the diverse aspect of digitalization in tourism not only by focusing on digital transformation and revolution but also by considering the novel business models, management of potential crises, and the ethical and responsibility dimensions.

In summary, this book is expected to be beneficial for individuals and institutions both in academia and in industry to understand digitalization comprehensively and behave and operate accordingly.

1.3 OVERVIEW OF THE CONTENT

Digitalization in Tourism is essential reading for anyone interested in tourism and digitalization. The singular aim of this book of scholarly text is to stimulate and engage readers in the fast-changing, complex, and increasingly interdisciplinary nature of tourism studies, and to serve as a catalyst for future intellectual, academic, and professional-driven research agendas. It is believed that the integration of tourism studies with digitalization will undoubtedly contribute to the development of the tourism field both in practice and in theory. Therefore, each chapter of this book, which consists of 17 chapters, concentrates on specific facets of digitalization by offering valuable insights for industry professionals, academicians, and students who want to excel in the tourism industry. A summary of the chapters included in this timely book is discussed as follows:

Chapter 2, *The Impact of Digitalization on Tourism Businesses* by **Onur Icoz** aims to explore the effects of digital transformation on tourism businesses and other players, such as transportation, accommodation, and food and beverage sub-sectors, in the tourism markets that are becoming members of these systems and chains. To determine the major effects of digital technologies, this chapter assumes that all tourism activities emerge from a tourism distribution system and tourism value chain, and hence digital technologies then convert these procedures to digital tourism distribution systems and a tourism value chain.

Chapter 3, *Digital Leadership: Reflections on the Digital Maturity of the Tourism Industry* by **Marco A. Gardini** explores the digital maturity of the tourism industry by focusing on four key areas: strategy, leadership, competencies, and organization. While digitalization presents significant opportunities, many tourism companies lack comprehensive strategies, focusing more on operational improvements than long-term digital goals. Leadership plays a critical role in fostering a digital culture and ensuring that companies build the necessary skills and organizational structures to navigate digital transformation successfully. Without strategic digital leadership, tourism companies risk falling behind in an increasingly competitive digital landscape.

Chapter 4, *Digital Traveler* by **Seza Zerman** reviews the positive impacts of digital tools on individuals' travel decisions as well as the negative impacts of technology since the long-term impacts of technology on the society and individuals are not clearly documented. Digital-free holiday concept, a growing market as a solution to mitigate the negative impacts of technology, is also discussed in this chapter as a novel and effective approach.

Chapter 5, *Digitalization and Sustainable Tourism* by **Nesrin M. Bahcelerli** explores how technological advancements, particularly digitalization, are reshaping the tourism industry with a focus on sustainability. It highlights how digital tools, like online platforms, data analytics, artificial intelligence, and virtual/AR enhance access to information, optimize resource use, and improve guest experiences. These innovations are critical in reducing tourism's negative environmental impacts while promoting sociocultural and economic sustainability. This chapter emphasizes the need for integrating digital technologies into tourism management to minimize over-tourism and environmental damage while ensuring fair economic distribution. It also cautions against potential challenges, such as unsustainable travel habits, urging businesses to align digital transformation with sustainability goals.

Chapter 6, *Digitalization in Cultural Heritage Preservation* by **Muhammad Khizar Hayat Naeem** and **Yanqing Wang** explores how digital technologies, like 3D scanning, photogrammetry, and LiDAR are transforming the preservation of cultural heritage. These tools enhance documentation, archiving, and reconstruction of heritage sites, making them more accessible and engaging through virtual and AR. This chapter emphasizes the role of digital archiving and database systems in facilitating collaboration and public access to cultural resources. Case studies, such as the Louvre's virtual tours and Machu Picchu's 3D mapping illustrate successful digital preservation efforts. It also addresses future trends, including the use of AI and IoT, while highlighting challenges, such as data privacy, security, and accessibility. In conclusion, the authors stress the importance of responsible and equitable digitalization to ensure that cultural heritage is preserved and made accessible to all, with a focus on sustainability and collaboration.

Chapter 7, *Digital Destinations: Unraveling the Impact of Social Media on Modern Tourism Dynamics* by **Pola Q. Wang** explores how social media has revolutionized the tourism industry by transforming destination marketing and traveler behavior. It highlights the role of platforms, like Instagram, Facebook, and Tripadvisor in facilitating dynamic and personal engagement with potential tourists through user-generated content and mobile technologies. This chapter discusses influencer marketing's impact on shaping consumer perceptions and examines ethical concerns, such as misinformation and privacy issues. Additionally, it emphasizes the potential of social media in promoting sustainable tourism practices and emerging trends, including AI-driven personalization and VR. The analysis provides valuable insights for academics, practitioners, and policymakers on navigating the challenges and opportunities presented by social media in the tourism sector.

Chapter 8, *A Discussion on Intelligent Technologies and Artificial Intelligence (AI) in Tourism Industry* by **Mustafa Dogan** and **Emel Adamis** aims to provide an overall picture of smart technologies, AI, and the tourism industry, including its intersection with sub-sectors; and to discuss the opportunities and limitations for humanity and our possible future with AI. The authors argue, it has not been possible for the tourism, travel and hospitality industries to remain outside the wheel of development and change since it is also one of the leading sectors contributing to global economy.

Chapter 9, *Innovation in Tourism and Hospitality Amidst Geopolitical Tensions: Digital Warfare* by **Mahmoud Ibraheam Saleh** proposes a new conceptual framework that bridges political science, information warfare, and tourism literature together to contribute to the current theoretical understanding of the causal interactions between geopolitical disputes, digitalization, and their impacts on tourism risk and innovation since there is a lack of research on the connection between geopolitical tensions escalation, emerging forms of digital warfare between states, and their influence on innovation in tourism.

Chapter 10, *The Future of Travel Technology: Foundations and Conceptual Underpinnings* by **Navidreza Ahadi, Saima Kareem,** and **Sarah Hussain** attempts to unravel the intricacies of the facilitation and endorsement of the transformative journey ahead as the dawn of the technological revolution has the potential to significantly transform and reinvent the future possibilities for travel industry. This chapter also presents implications for various stakeholders, including enthusiasts, industry professionals, researchers, and policymakers, and proposes future research directions to further advance the knowledge in the field.

Chapter 11, *The Future of Travel Technology: Applications and Future Directions* by **Laiba Ali** mainly aims to provide insights on possible future advances in travel technology for various stakeholder's perspectives, to design effective experiences that strongly matches with travelers' desires and preferences since technology should be considered together with advancement as well as social aspects, such as variety of groups, as aging population, PWDs together with the other industries, such as health care and communication.

Chapter 12, *The Network Hospitality and Tourism* by **Sonia Lim Ern Yi** and **Geraldine Anne Tan Wern-Yi** aims to conceptually examine network hospitality's evolution, definitions, and types. This chapter explores the impact of digitizing tourism through the lens of network hospitality, illustrating how travel and tourism businesses can optimize their operations.

Chapter 13, *Digital Marketing Strategies for Tourism Businesses: An Overview of Digital Marketing Strategies for Tourism Industry Members* by **Esra Topcuoglu Schoen** provides an overview of digital marketing strategies in the tourism field from different perspectives and emphasizes the importance of digital marketing for both tourism organizations and for customers. This chapter explains the way digital marketing works for tourism, the considerable change in customer behavior in the digital age, best practices in digital marketing, common digital marketing tools used by tourism organizations, digitalization in marketing research, opportunities and challenges in digital marketing, and digital marketing careers.

Chapter 14, *Customer-Centric Digitalization: The Key to Shaping the Future of Medical Tourism* by **Miray Urkmezer** and **Hakan Cengiz** aims to examine the developments occurring in the rapidly evolving field of medical tourism. This chapter analyzes the emergence of digital transformation within medical tourism and potential future trends. Additionally, it aims to highlight the increasingly empowered position of medical tourists as consumers in the market.

Chapter 15, *Crisis Management in the Digital Age* by **Gulsel Ciftci** aims to provide a comprehensive understanding of why crisis management has become such a crucial part of the tourism sector in the digital age. This chapter examines key crisis management features that must be considered to protect tourism from adverse events and ensure long-term success.

Chapter 16, *Ethics and Responsibility in Digital Tourism* by **Edmira Cakrani, Rina Cakrani,** and **Enriko Ceko** addresses the ethical concerns related to big data usage in tourism and hospitality. As smart tourism advances, the massive collection of personal data raises privacy issues, especially in personalized services. This chapter highlights the importance of data ethics and governance, calling for transparent and responsible data management. It emphasizes the need for protecting consumer privacy while using data for business benefits. A proposed framework for ethical data governance encourages building trust with stakeholders through fair and transparent practices. In conclusion, as tourism relies more on big data, businesses must prioritize ethical standards to safeguard consumer privacy and maintain trust.

Chapter 17, *Digital Adoption in Tourism: Challenges and Solutions* by **Sadia Afrin Ananya** and **Peter O'Connor** explores the slow adoption of ICT by Small and Medium-sized Tourism Enterprises (SMTEs), despite its critical role in enhancing competitiveness and efficiency. Barriers include financial constraints, lack of technical expertise, and resistance to change. This chapter uses models like TAM, UTAUT, and the TOE framework to analyze key factors, such as perceived usefulness, organizational readiness, and external support. To overcome challenges, it suggests democratizing technology, improving digital literacy, and fostering innovation within tourism businesses. Strong leadership and external support are vital for SMTEs to successfully integrate digital tools and stay competitive in an increasingly digital marketplace.

In conclusion, we would like to thank all the authors for their valuable contribution to the production of this book. Their timely, relevant, and insightful approach to the topics offers essential information for students, scholars, industry professionals, and any individuals who are interested in digitalization in hospitality and tourism industry.

KEYWORDS

- **artificial intelligence**
- **augmented reality**
- **blockchain**
- **digitalization**
- **data analytics**
- **tourism**
- **virtual reality**

REFERENCES

Aras, A., & Büyüközkan, G. (2023). Digital transformation journey guidance: A holistic digital maturity model based on a systematic literature review. *Systems, 11*(4), 213. https://doi.org/10.3390/systems11040213

Cranmer, E., Urquhart, C., Dieck, M. C., & Jung, T. (2021). Developing augmented reality business models for SMEs in tourism. *Information & Management, 58*(8), 103551. https://doi.org/10.1016/j.im.2021.103551

Lee, W., & Kim, Y. (2021). Does VR tourism enhance users' experience? *Sustainability, 13*(2), 806. https://doi.org/10.3390/su13020806

Lo, W. H., & Cheng, K. L. B. (2020). Does virtual reality attract visitors? The mediating effect of presence on consumer response in virtual reality tourism advertising. *Information Technology & Tourism, 22*, 537–562. https://doi.org/10.1007/s40558-020-00190-2

Lou, L., Tian, Z., & Koh, J. (2017). Tourist satisfaction enhancement using mobile QR code payment: An empirical investigation. *Sustainability, 9*(7), 1186. https://doi.org/10.3390/su9071186

Lu, J., Xiao, X., Xu, Z., Wang, C., Zhang, M., & Zhou, Y. (2022). The potential of virtual tourism in the recovery of the tourism industry during the COVID-19 pandemic. *Current Issues in Tourism, 25*(3), 441–457.

Omran, W., Ramos, R. F., & Casais, B. (2024). Virtual reality and augmented reality applications and their effect on tourist engagement: A hybrid review. *Journal of Hospitality and Tourism Technology, 15*(4), 497-518.

Pencarelli, T. (2020). The digital revolution in the travel and tourism industry. *Information Technology & Tourism, 22*, 455–476. https://doi.org/10.1007/s40558-019-00160-3

Skare, M., Ribeiro Soriano, D., & Porada-Rochon, M. (2021). Impact of COVID-19 on the travel and tourism industry. *Technological Forecasting and Social Change, 163*, 120469. https://doi.org/10.1016/j.techfore.2020.120469

Yuce, A., Arasli, H., Ozturen, A., & Daskin, M. (2020). Feeling the service product closer: Triggering visit intention via virtual reality. *Sustainability, 12*(16), 6632. https://doi.org/10.3390/su12166632

PART I
The Digital Revolution in Tourism: Conceptual Approaches

CHAPTER 2

The Impact of Digitalization on Tourism Businesses

ONUR ICOZ

Aydin Adnan Menderes University, Faculty of Tourism, Aydin, Türkiye

ABSTRACT

Information and communication technologies (ICTs) and digitalization considerably accelerate the transactions among parties in every market where tangible and intangible products are produced and consumed. These effects may arise through fast communication, easy access to information sources, instant monetary payments, delivery of messages to potential buyers, and product customization. Tourism, as a service-dominant industry also has long been benefiting from the merits of digital technologies, from designing products to delivering them through digital distribution channels. The tourism industry consists of various types of businesses from small-sized operations to large size multinationals under the three pillars covering the indispensable parts of the tourism industry as transportation, accommodation, and food and beverage sub-sectors. In order to determine the major effects of ICTs and digital technologies, this chapter assumes that all tourism activities emerge from a tourism distribution system and tourism value chain, and hence digital technologies then convert these procedures to digital tourism distribution systems and a tourism value chain. For this reason, this chapter aims to study the effects of digital transformation on tourism businesses and other players in the tourism markets that are becoming members of these systems and chains.

Digitalization in Tourism. Hulya Akdemir Cengiz, Seza Zerman, Aysegul Acar, and Faizan Ali (Eds.)

DOI: 10.1201/9781779644770-3

2.1 INTRODUCTION

Technological transformations and innovations have a significant effect on our daily lives, and they are felt in every facet of our lives. These changes are widely seen in both the production and consumption phases of goods and services in the economy. Hence, tourism is also considered as one of the sectors where technological progress is being rapidly adapted throughout the 21st century.

Undoubtedly, the labor force is the area where technological transformation has the lowest effect since tourism is known as a labor-intensive sector that creates employment opportunities compared to many other industries or sectors. Therefore, this sector is attractive and beneficial to the countries that have high unemployment rates.

The effects of technological transformation, especially after 1990, on tourism-related sectors have been seen in every aspect of tourism markets, from traveling individuals to tourism services providers, with the obvious contribution of globalization. Digital technologies have been the major reason for the huge growth of the tourism sector, with over 1.5 billion annual international travelers, by accelerating the tourism industry after the 1990s.

Technological innovations and digital technologies have become an important part of tourism and hospitality services, and have been adopted by various tourist attractions, hotels, transportation, as well as other related service providers (Khatri, 2019). Smart tourism applications are now being installed and spread through the strategic use of innovative digital technology systems, and the tourism and hospitality industry has been a pioneer in the adoption of such innovations (Li et al., 2017). In hotel business, every department uses technological applications to make their staff work more effectively and efficiently and to adapt to the digitalized tourist. Otherwise, it would not be possible to survive using traditional methods in a world where technology is rapidly advancing (Rosenbaum and Wong, 2015). For this reason, the basic purpose of this chapter is to study the effects of digital technologies on these businesses that form the supply side of tourism markets.

2.2 DIGITAL TECHNOLOGIES IN THE TOURISM VALUE CHAIN

Today, there is a digital ecosystem where the role of digital platforms that connect activities to each other is becoming increasingly significant.

Digital platforms, which are important elements of this system, are defined as ecosystems that allow users to perform a series of activities and facilitate value creation (Kenney and Zysman, 2015). According to the definition of the World Economic Forum, digital ecosystems consist of *users, government bodies,* and *business firms* that come together through media industries and telecommunication systems in information and communication technology (ICT) environments (WEF, 2007). When this concept is adapted to the tourism industry, the digital ecosystem in tourism consists of the relationships between live entities, such as *service providers, intermediaries, travelers, public bodies*, and *non-living entities,* such as *tools, connections, content, and contact points* (Neidhardt and Werthner, 2018).

Beckendorff et al. (2014, p. 24) explained the main entities that are taking part in digital tourism ecosystem. In their publication, they classified the basic elements and functions of the system, indicating the level of relationship between them. The relationship between digital tourism ecosystem environmental elements and the four basic functions is labeled as strong or weak contributions based on the nature of the relationship. According to the authors, there are 6 basic elements of the digital tourism ecosystem which can be listed as:

1. Primary players (*service providers, brokers, travelers, and visitors*).
2. Sources of information access (*social networks, forums, Wiki's, blogs, photo, and video sharing*).
3. Tools (*portable computers, smart TVs, mobile devices, kiosks, and smart watches*).
4. Connections (*cable broadband, NFC, GPS, media, andprotocols*).
5. Contents (*text, image, video, maps, navigation, dynamic content, and user-generated content*).
6. Contact points *(web sites, search engines, mobile apps, e-mail, phone, and face to face interaction*).

The authors, at the same time, listed the four basic digital ecosystem functions as: (a) *information,* (b) *purchasing*, (c) *experience*, and (d) *sharing*. They also identified that *information* and *purchasing* functions are strongly affected by almost all elements of the digital ecosystem, while *experience* and *sharing* functions are weakly affected by most of these elements. The most effective elements for experience and sharing functions are social networks, media broadcasts, mobile devices, and face-to-face interactions.

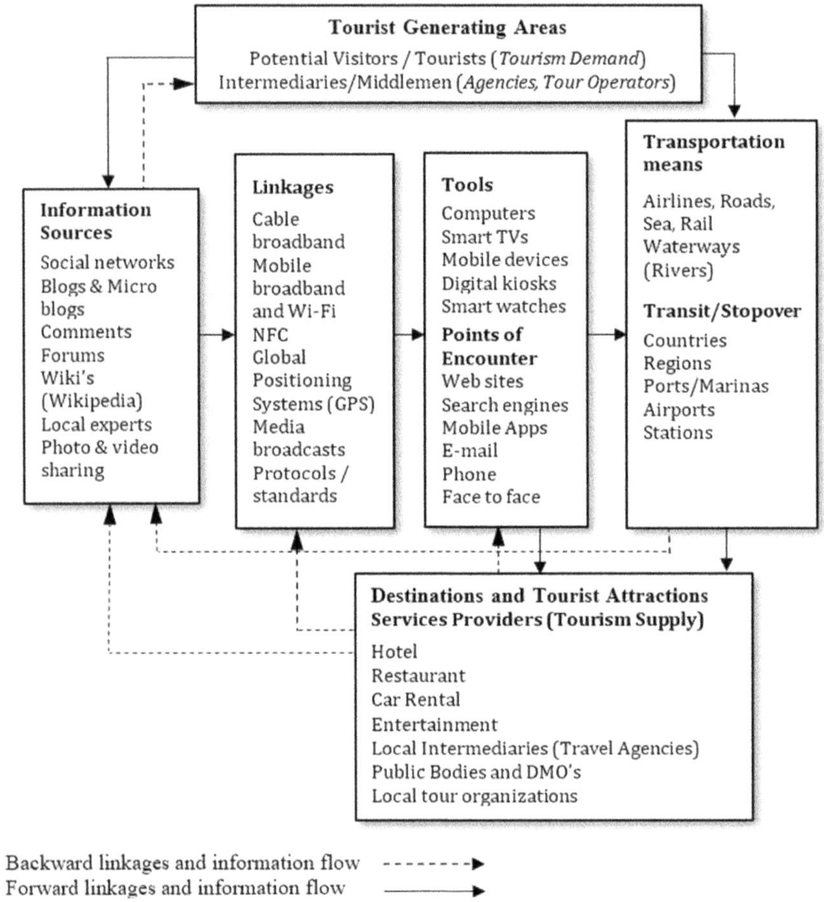

FIGURE 2.1 Relationships and linkages in digital tourism ecosystem.

Source: Icoz (2021, 109).

Figure 2.1 is another representation of the relationships in this system and explains the operation of the elements in the digital tourism ecosystem, *information flow/action* processes, and their *relationships* with each other. The elements on the left side of the figure represent the main tourist information sources, while the tourism service providers are functioning as feeder elements. The basic tools of this information flow and actions are the devices through which digital processes are carried out and the networks that enable such flow.

In the digital tourism ecosystem, traditional travel intermediaries, tour operators, and travel agencies are subject to compete against online travel intermediaries and service providers' websites (Edvardsson et al., 2010). Accommodation and transportation companies also have to compete with sharing economy players within this system, which has been integrated into the internet through platforms, and tends to grow very rapidly within the ecosystem (Heo, 2016). The most dynamic aspect of the digital tourism ecosystem is distribution function, and the main characteristics of digital distribution are explained in the following section.

2.3 DIGITAL DISTRIBUTION SYSTEMS IN TOURISM

In the 1990s, the conventional tourism distribution system went through a significant change with the widespread use of the Internet in tourism businesses. While traditional tourism distribution systems have long been dominated and oriented by travel intermediaries, this dominance has been considerably broken by digital technologies. Owing to the internet connections, potential tourists can easily access tourism services and purchase them directly through digital platforms, and they can find the best services among variety of options.

The travelers who can use digital distribution systems have great flexibility in terms of their choice of services, bookings, and purchases. However, the layers of customers and businesses relationships have also increased in parallel to these changes. For example, the inclusion of Global Distribution Systems and internet search engines has accelerated the procedures and increased the number of alternatives.

Figure 2.2 shows how digital technology tools have taken their place in digital tourism distribution systems, and digital tourists can reach service providers directly in three ways: (a) *via internet search engines*, (b) *using information they gained from social media*, and (c) *making their reservations on internet booking sites*. Another similar method is the fact that users can make their bookings through internet travel agencies. However, in this system, customers may be forced to pay some commissions to digital agencies.

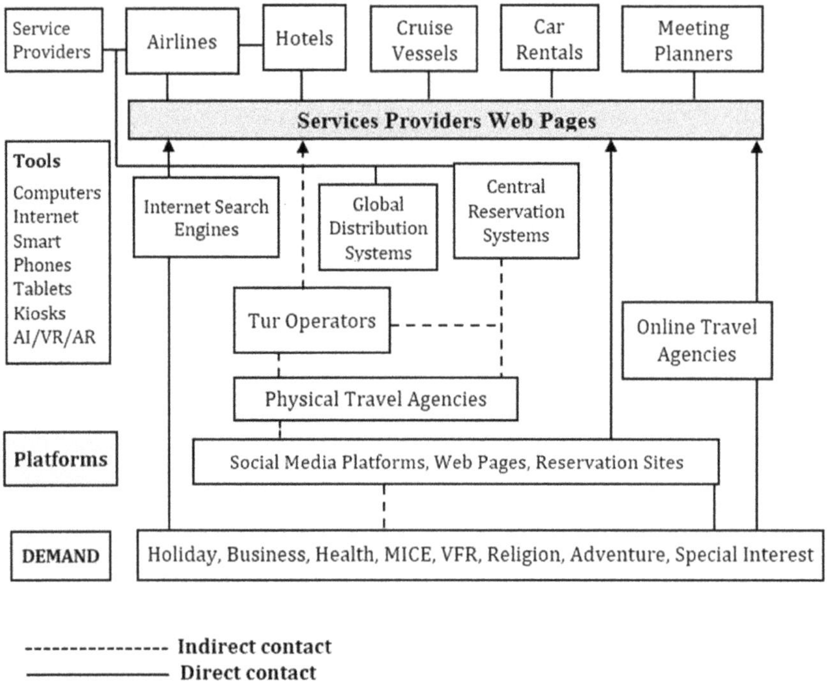

FIGURE 2.2 The digital tourism distribution system.

Source: Icoz (2021, 113).

The most significant role of digital travel intermediaries displayed in Figure 2.2 is to provide fast communication and an instant purchasing process. In the digital tourism distribution system, travel intermediaries can organize tour packages through ICT and digital platforms, and they are able to organize these packages through dynamic packaging systems. In this process, "*dynamic packaging*" that can be created by service providers has the potential to provide opportunities and advantages for travel intermediaries in the following fields (Bilbao et al., 2010):

1. Determining tourists' needs
2. Choosing potential commercial partners
3. Organizing commercial transactions
4. Creating complex products
5. Generating new tourism profiles
6. Forecasting economic, social, and technological conditions

7. Creating new value chains for tourism products
8. Determining potential e-commerce opportunities

2.4 DIGITAL TRANSFORMATION IN TOURISM DISTRIBUTION SYSTEMS

During the past 60 years, the tourism distribution system underwent significant digital transformations. In the 1960s and 1970s, as airline companies continued to sell their flight tickets and bookings with the inclusion of travel agencies into their computerized reservation systems (CRSs), these CRSs evolved into Global Distribution Systems (GDSs) operated by airline companies in the1980s, and as these systems became independent, other firms apart from airline companies also entered into the system in the 1990s. In the 2000s, tourism operators and travelers had an opportunity to connect with each other independently through the effective use of the Internet. In the 2010s, new generation global distribution companies and Meta-search engines entered the system, granting visitors the access to unlimited service alternatives. At the same time, all types of service providers also had the opportunity to reach potential buyers all over the world.

The successive and complementary services in tourism are accepted as the rings of a value chain consisting of the services produced by companies in tourism distribution system. For this reason, digital technologies and specifically the Internet have made significant contributions to creating the tourism value chain described as follows (Houghton, 2007):

1. Service providers can reduce intermediary costs by offering the opportunity to sell their products directly to the final customer.
2. With the inclusion of internet travel intermediaries into the system, a new type of intermediation is emerging.
3. With the adaptation of innovative systems, such as customer relationship management (CRM) via the Internet, many opportunities to improve customer relationship emerge.
4. Traditional travel intermediaries that have been negatively affected by the inclusion of the internet have become more customer-oriented and more concentrated on niche markets in order to survive.

Air transportation represents the fastest transformation to digital technology in tourism distribution systems. This is already a leading tourism sector in the context of digital technology applications. Online ticketing, electronic boarding passes, automated boarding registration at airports, and similar applications are the most well-known digital services. On the other hand, among the other three major players of the sector: as accommodation, intermediation, and catering industries, hotels are known as the fastest growing sector following the airline industry in terms of digital transformation. The main reason for this speed is the fact that the accommodation industry, led by chain hotels, has practiced digital technologies principally in their central reservation systems and later followed by other functional areas. Research on this subject provides information explaining the situation of these three sub-sectors for the implementation of innovations and adaptation of information technologies to their operational processes (Muneta and Lopez, 2013). According to the results of this research, as the use of digital technology makes considerable contributions, such as competition, efficiency, increase in market share, and product and process innovation for these sectors, the two most effective businesses are hotels and travel agencies. The use of digital technologies in the sub-sectors of tourism is explained in the following sections.

2.4.1 DIGITAL TECHNOLOGIES IN TRAVEL INTERMEDIATION

With the use of the internet and information technologies in the travel industry, there have undoubtedly been significant transformations in the travel intermediation, and digital technology has become an important component of travel middlemen's business. With technological developments, new forms of intermediaries, such as cyber-intermediaries, e-intermediaries, and virtual travel agencies have emerged (Buhalis and Licata, 2002; Kracht and Wang, 2010).

Digital travel agency platforms are safe for consumers, and tourists use digital and artificial intelligence-supported platforms in their travel planning processes (Topal and Ucar, 2018). Travel agencies use cloud-based software as strategic tools to allow potential tourists to select content that they can access on board via the airline's web pages before departure. On the other hand, tour operators also use cloud solutions to increase potential tourist engagement by integrating their websites with social media platforms. Online travel intermediaries use information that they obtain from direct promotions and loyalty programs to attract more tourists (Toh et al., 2011).

The major digital travel intermediation models that have emerged in the system are listed as follows (Beckendorff et al., 2014, p. 76):

1. *Online travel agencies*: These agencies operate all the transactions by selling their services to visitors through GDSs. These agencies can provide considerable discounts through volume purchasing from service providers (Prieto, 2019). Some agencies also specialize in tracking last-minute discounts and passing them on to customers.
2. *Meta search engines*: These are web platforms that do not make direct bookings to final customers for service providers; rather they offer the most affordable prices and facilities to clients by scanning the web pages of almost all travel agencies or airline companies.
3. *Aggregators*: These companies bring together the available inventories from multiple GDSs and make them available to other firms. The well-known aggregator in this category is ITA that was purchased by Google (itasoftware.com).
4. *Trip planner web sites*: These sites specialize on destinations and create personalized travel packages that meet the expectations of customers, and they sometimes allow users to book their own individual products.
5. *Affiliates*: These firms market products created by OTAs and charge commissions as fees. Some affiliates may charge fees based on the number of clicks.
6. *Group/volume purchase sites*: These companies provide services based on discounts when a certain number of groups are reached. In this system, final prices are determined by bargaining with both the service provider and the customer.
7. *Opaque sites*: These web travel companies sell inventory that is deemed as "hard to sale" by their service providers at significant discounts. In this system, the seller is not known until the purchase is made and they work as a type of auction site.
8. *Travel products evaluation sites*: These websites represent Meta search engine features and work as web travel companies that

aggregate reviews or commends about travels (blog.hubspot.com, travelonline.com).

These digital travel sites with reservation and purchasing functions provide the following advantages for the customers:

1. User friendly site design
2. Multilingual options
3. Availability on mobile applications
4. Illustrative lists showing all services
5. Booking options for transportation
6. Daily updated prices

In order to support the back of the house automation systems, some travel agencies also use systems, such as "*business source planning*" in the areas of productivity, reporting, customer satisfaction, forecasting, service provider relations, and so forth.

2.4.2 DIGITAL TECHNOLOGIES IN TOURISM TRANSPORTATION

In many parts of the world, travel and transportation services are provided entirely through digital technologies. Transportation services, such as railways, car rentals, buses, sightseeing tours, and air tickets are all connected to computers, and therefore accurate information management is possible.

With the development of tourism, various forms of transportation have emerged, and technological advances in transportation have led to the expansion of tourism (Page, 2009). Digital technologies have brought about significant changes in the travel industry today, and these technologies can increase the efficiency of transportation networks and reduce disruptions (Vijayakumar and Mehendiratta, 2011). Studies on the automation of customer-related transactions, especially in airline transportation, were initiated shortly after the Second World War by the American Airlines company, which was later replaced by the "*Sabre*" brand name CRS system developed by IBM and released in 1960.

Airlines have long been the advanced users of ITCs for many years, leading in areas, such as reservation systems. In particular, web environments have enabled airline companies to sell their services directly to their passengers, thus providing significant reductions in the commissions paid to intermediaries and other operational expenses of the businesses, and allowing these companies to improve their relationships with customers through frequent flyer programs. Similar developments have also been witnessed in the case of cruise-lines, railways, and car rental businesses (Houghton, 2007).

Not only the airlines but also other transportation companies are undoubtedly the businesses where ITCs are heavily used. For example, railways, car rental companies, bus companies, and cruise-lines all have adapted to this technology to some extent. The main reason for this latency is the requirement for high capital investments in information technologies in the initial stages.

Travel agencies and tour operators, as the most important business partners of airline companies, have been the first stakeholders in GDSs over time. For this reason, there is an extensive interaction and cooperation between travel intermediaries and GDSs. In this respect, the main purpose of GDSs is to provide airline flight schedules, ticket fees, availability and reservation status information, and transactions to intermediaries through a central distribution system. The basic functions of GDSs were described by Beckendorff et al. (2014, p. 59) as the followings:

1. *Space availability information*: The system provides comparative information about room or seat availability at a certain time among connected service providers.
2. *Reservation demands*: The infrastructure of the GDS system is available 24/7 and has sufficient transaction capacity.
3. *Passenger information*: Each reservation is processed with a PNR that contains information about the passengers, including their names, addresses, phone numbers, e-mail accounts, reservation period, seat preferences, as well as some special requests.
4. *Fares and conditions*: Airline reservation systems have comprehensive databases, including reservation and payment periods, pre-payments, cancelations, and blocked dates. Fares are determined by yield management that generates dynamic pricing.
5. *Electronic ticketing and itinerary management*: Today, there are almost no printed tickets for transportation means and there is no need to carry them to travel, instead, all tickets are digitally issued and recorded/saved. In most cases, only the PNR codes are sufficient to travel.

Besides these basic functions of GDSs, there are some customer-based secondary functions, such as reservations for additional services (car rentals etc.), travel insurances, integrated travel management, decision support systems, financial reports, accounting, invoicing, credit and debt management, e-commerce tools, institutional travel management, and some company-based services on the back of the house functional areas, such as digital accounting systems, human resources, customer relation management, inward-outward-internal communication, tracking commissions and consensus on transactions, and so forth (Beckendorff et al., 2014, p. 69).

At the beginning of the 19th century, trains were the main indicator of technological innovation in the developed economies, and therefore railways are known as the second transportation category adapting to new technology. The enormous investments are still being made in high-speed rail systems all around the world with the help of ICTs as well (Pagliara and Mauriello, 2019). The next transportation category is cruise lines, some of which use artificial intelligence to better serve to their customers (iata.org/whatwedo).

In addition to the abovementioned services, digital technologies have also brought innovations to the transportation industry. For example, the creation of "*virtual offices,*" customer service without personal contact, the use of digital communication technologies for live communication from a distance, mobile payments, unified travel documents, the use of mobile applications for obtaining transport services, data processing, gathering and analysis, gathering of data on transport flows, use of "*big data*" technology, reorganization and automation of transportation organization systems, customer participation in production (*co-creation*), automation and robotics for traffic control, prediction of traffic conditions, development of autopilot support systems, provision of logistics services, creation of digital platforms focused on booking tickets, searching for freight carriers and determining the most convenient route (Mashkina et al., 2021), and so forth can be given as some of these innovations.

2.4.3 DIGITAL TECHNOLOGIES IN THE ACCOMMODATION SECTOR

The adaptation of ICTs to the accommodation sector started at the beginning of the 1970s and is still continuing to evolve. Technology in hotels is widely used in two functional areas as, (a) at managerial and operational level, and (b) in the rooms for guest services (Cobanoglu and Berezina, 2010). Both areas have vital importance for their long-term survival and competitiveness in the market. Therefore, "*expert information systems*" and "*decision support systems*" as information management systems that can be used in this field are suggested to managers of this business to adapt their managerial processes (Beckendorff et al., 2014, p. 249). Decision-support systems can be used as efficient revenue management system by determining the most appropriate prices (room rates) for hotel rooms. Through these systems, long-term sales forecasts, demand analyses, and market conditions evaluations could be possible. Based on sales forecasts, the most appropriate room pricing can be determined by comparing inventory and space availability.

The main reasons for using digital technologies in hospitality services, include improving operations, differentiation, increasing productivity, increasing revenues, and reducing costs. The proliferation of smart technologies in the hospitality industry provides a modern tool for improving management performance, operational efficiency, co-creating customized and memorable customer experiences, and spreading marketing information (Neuhofer et al., 2014). According to Ivanov et al. (2017), robots, artificial intelligence systems, and service automation systems have the potential to completely fulfill all operations performed by the front office department and increase the cost efficiency of businesses in the long term.

Hotel guests expect comfort and quality service during their stay. To meet these expectations, some technological innovations are being used by hoteliers who are aware of the currently available key digital technologies, such as biometric and audiovisual technologies, wearable devices, and smart digital agents (Stankov et al., 2019). In practice, these applications can enrich tourists' experiences in planning their daily itineraries, finding nearby services tailored to their personal interests, and providing a wide range of useful information to make their accommodations unique from other competitive offers (Kirillova and Chan, 2018). Many hospitality businesses use digital technology to support their business operations by recognizing the potential of technology to provide important benefits in operational, technical, and strategic management. On the other hand, international hotel chains adopt the latest technologies to create a high-tech image, because such technology is believed to improve financial performance. Managers believe that technology reduces manpower and time spent on operations and improves service quality (Buhalis and Law, 2008). Moreover, according to Naumov (2019), with the spread of artificial intelligence applications in the tourism industry, the need for qualified and educated workforces will increase as well.

Digital technology usage in the functional areas of hotels is still developing, and new technologies are coming to the forefront. The new technology products of Intelity technology firm can be given as an example for the matter involved (intelity.com). The firm has produced a product called interactive customer experience, and through this product, such services as the hotels' guest relations department, room service, valet parking, dinner reservations, and spa services can be accessed via an internet-connected device. By means of the same device, non-hotel reservations, such as theaters, restaurants, golf courses, and airlines in the area can also be accessed, and the device also includes a tracking system to prevent theft. The firm also performs functions, such as check-in/check-out, room key locks/unlocks, payments, identity checks, room status controls, menu changes, inventory control, ticketing, and so forth, through digital platforms in hotels (Law et al., 2013). More detailed use and authorization issues to these technologies in hotel businesses are grouped as follows depending on the functional areas (intelity.com).

1. *Effective organization of daily work schedules in the enterprise*: Quick resolution of customer complaints, planning of preventive maintenance, and execution of operations.
2. *Effective content management with quick updates*: All content can be managed from a single center. For example, changes on the food and beverage menu items, real-time inventory management and summary updates, and so forth.
3. *Faster collection of business information*: Based on accurate and actionable data, it is possible to make well-directed decisions to develop processes.
4. *Effective guest marketing by interacting with guests at the right time*: It is possible to use multiple channels to reach the target audience when they are most interested.
5. *Digital menus and dinners in the room with orders*: Providing convenient, purely contact-free dining experiences for guests by replacing hard-to-clean printed menus and in-person service delivery.

6. *Ongoing feedback from guests by monitoring their satisfaction*: Having instant feedback from guests through digital devices, and monitoring increases in guest dissatisfaction, if any.
7. *Managing mobile devices*: Keeping the connected devices up to date and ensuring the continuity of the guests' stays carefree and without any interruption.
8. *Partnerships and integrations with seamless system integration*: In order to make the guest experience management system in hotels simple, and to build a connected technology cluster, the integration of all these processes from property management systems, point of sales, and other services reservation systems is necessary.

Different digital technologies are widely used in the functional service areas of accommodation establishments. For example, washable RFID chips allow management to instantly determine the inventory of such materials in warehouses and on hotel floors by being placed on towels, bathrobes, banquet tablecloths, and other washable linens in hotel rooms (USA Today, 2011).

Digital hospitality has an impact on the guest experience to induce transformation dynamics, to generate a fruitful context on the frontline through human enhancement technologies, and encourage guest acceptance and impact on the guest experience. In this context, digital technologies can provide the following contactless payment advantages for guests and businesses management (intelity.com);

For the hotel guests:

1. Directly passing through without waiting in queues at reception
2. Hassle-free check-in/out via mobile devices
3. Mobile/digital keys for room locks
4. Secure sharing of digital keys
5. Easier payment processes

For the management:

1. Reduced front office workload
2. Priority for safety
3. Increased free time for employees
4. Eliminating the cost of physical key production
5. Exclusion of all physical keys

Regarding the use of technology in hotels, a recent study conducted in Germany is a good source to show the level of technology used in the German hotel industry (info.hotelhero.tech). This research also reveals the technological resources hotel guests use during their travel. Accordingly, the decision stages of the guests and the sources of information at these stages are as summarized in Table 2.1. In the table, it can be seen that there are many areas where digital technologies are used in the accommodation industry. This situation stands out as some technologies that are either shared by both parties at different stages of travel are used in the same process.

TABLE 2.1 The Use of Technology for the Hotel Services in Germany.

Stages	Information Sources Used by the Guests	Information Sources Used by Hotels
Inspiration	Instagram YouTube Facebook Snapshot Printed/web media Word of mouth	
Search: *Determination of travel budget*	Tripadvisor Google My Business Google Maps Google Hotels/Trivago/Kayak Travel blogs/forums Guides	Meta-search management platform
Booking: *For travel and accommodation*	Brand.com Internet travel agencies	Distribution channel management Reservation search engine Direct reservation tool Web chat Voucher management tool
Pre-stay/travel: *Planning the transportation and activities*	Guest portal/applications e-mail SMS WhatsApp/Facebook Messenger GetYourGuide	Guest portal/applications Upselling tool Instant messaging tool Customer relationship management system

TABLE 2.1 *(Continued)*

Stages	Information Sources Used by the Guests	Information Sources Used by Hotels
During stay/visit: *Experiencing*	Check-in terminal Guest portal/applications/in room tablet SMS WhatsApp/Facebook Messenger Instagram/Snapchat	Check-in terminal Guest portal/applications/in room tablet Property management systems Digital keys Instant guest messaging tool Employees tools to work with
Post-stay/travel: *Evaluation of the travel and sharing experiences with others*	Tripadvisor Google reviews/comments Internet travel agencies comments Instagram/Facebook/Snapchat Hotel researches on guest comments	Tripadvisor Customer relationship management system Online brand/name management system
After coming home	Loyalty programs Instagram/Facebook/Snapchat	Loyalty programs Customer relationship management

Source: Reprinted from Hotelhero (2020, p. 17). https://info.hotelhero.tech/de/hotel-tech-markt-deutschland-2020.

On the abovementioned report, there are digital technologies which accommodation establishments use in their functional areas. The functional areas are listed in Table 2.2.

TABLE 2.2 Functional Areas in Hotel Businesses and the Digital Technologies.

Functional Areas	Digital Technologies
The areas of interaction/ communication with customers	Instant messaging In room tablet and guest applications Digital check-in/out kiosks Visitor feedback
Operational areas and background duties	Cloud based property management systems Employee work/collaboration areas Sales points Reporting

TABLE 2.2 *(Continued)*

Functional Areas	Digital Technologies
Marketing	Direct reservation tools
	Meta search
	Customer relationship management
	e-brand management
	Upselling
Distribution	Voucher tool
	Rate shopping
	Distribution channel manager
	Customer relationship management, Internet Booking engine
	Revenue management systems

Source: Reprinted from Hotelhero (2020, p. 22, p. 17). https://info.hotelhero.tech/de/hotel-tech-markt-deutschland-2020.

With the advancement of Internet of Things (IoT), hotel management and services are evolving as smart environments. The "smart hotel" concept appeared 15 years ago, but has gained attention recently, and is rapidly evolving globally (Jeremen et al., 2016). Smart hotel applications are of great importance to the hospitality industry (Lai and Hung, 2018). In this context, the term "smart hotel" means that internet-connected technologies are integrated to simplify daily operations and add value for all stakeholders (Buhalis and Leung, 2018). In addition, smart hotels frequently use technologies, such as IoT, cloud computing, artificial intelligence, smart devices, and big data to provide consumers with sophisticated service experiences and higher levels of customization (Xu, 2018).

Research on the use of smart technologies in the accommodation sector has showed that customer expectations regarding such technologies do not differ much, no matter how hotels are classified (Bilgihan et al., 2016). The availability of digital technologies, which are widely seen in the above-average quality hotels, does not mean that the hotel is a smart one. A comprehensive list of the technologies that smart hotels offer to their guests is presented in Table 2.3.

TABLE 2.3 In-Room Technologies in Smart Hotels.

Technology	Definition
Voice thru IP	Using Internet protocols instead of analog media
Pay per-view TV	Digital video delivery through a pay-based television platform
Voice message	Telephone-based service that allows callers to leave voice messages
In-room accessible plugs	Conveniently mounted electrical plugs for hotel guest access
High-speed internet access	Internet connection at speeds of 1–100 Mbps
In-room safety	Electronic safe box that can be opened using a digital card or code
In-room control panel	IoT technology can enable the lights, heating, air conditioning, and even curtains to be controlled remotely
Battery charging unit	A device that can charge the batteries of various devices, such as wireless chargers
Electronic lock systems	Access to security via electronic media (magnetic stripe, smart card, RFID, and NFC)
In-room play systems	In-room entertainment system
In-room fitness and exercise systems	Special devices for physical exercise
In-room electronic video check-out	A television interface that provides quick account review, account balance, and check-out
Web-based room service	The system can check the current menu and place an order by typing the web address or scanning at QR code
Customized experiences through social media messages	Guests can connect to hotel staff via popular social media platforms
Service robots	There are robots capable of handling materials for housekeeping services
Smart bathrooms	Shower heads with voice assistance feature in bathrooms. Shower systems that detect body temperature, adjust room temperature, and reduce water consumption
In-room tablet computers	It is possible to promote hotel events, rebook special products, and implement customer loyalty programs
More environmentally sensitive linens and other materials	Cotton-quality polyester fabrics developed to prevent water consumption waste that can be melted and turned into fabric
Interactive maps on the wall	Interactive wall maps in hotel rooms can provide guests with real-time information

TABLE 2.3 *(Continued)*

Technology	Definition
Monitoring data-based customer preferences	Information about customers' choices can be collected in guest rooms without compromising their privacy. For example, the most listened radio stations and watched TV channels can be determined using smart speakers
Smart mirror	Smart mirrors in rooms can be transformed into an interactive digital concierge services and a panel where room facilities can be controlled by touch

Source: Adapted from Cobanoglu and Berezina, (2010), RevFine (2020), LoungeUp (2020), Socialtables. (2020).

Hotels can create smart systems by using different internal and external technology resources or tools. The most important technology for this system is the creation of sensors and artificial intelligence network through IoT, the use of big data in order to support a number of decision-making processes, and the establishment of smart hotel management systems by using the internal data of businesses. Additionally, cloud technologies that store hospitality industry-specific data, not only collect statistics and related activities from the hospitality and tourism industry but also allow access to this data without time and space limitations.

Analyzing and processing downloaded data from cloud technology requires many basic processes. These involve, transforming the data concerning processes and applications obtained from tourism businesses, sharing information with the sector, storing the data of companies and individuals, ensuring data compatibility and consolidation, integrating and managing big data, creating and managing the data view, and sending necessary data to the data warehouse of relevant organizations for business analysis (Buhalis and Leung, 2018). Table 2.4 presents some examples of smart applications using IoT technology in the functional areas of hotels.

Finally, the use of robot technology in this business is in its early stages; however there are some examples in certain sectors. Hilton Worldwide Hotels' use of artificial intelligence-based robots to obtain information from hotel guests and use this information to tailor the guest experience to the customer is one of the first examples of such an application. Nowadays, robots are used in the check-in and check-out processes of many hotels around the world. The most popular example was the Henn Na Hotel in Japan, which is not open anymore, where robot receptionists

TABLE 2.4 Use of Internet of Things in the Functional Areas of Hotels.

Internet of Things Zones/Divisions	Internet of Things Types/Sensors	Functions
Inside the hotel		
Guest rooms	Motion sensors	The energy management system adjusted to guest presence and position in the room.
	Voice sensors	Sound activation checking in-room devices, such as curtains, lights, and room heat.
		Measuring room temperature during guest stays to ensure a comfortable atmosphere.
	Door locks	Mobile application functioning keyless card for door locking systems.
	Wearable sensors	Sensors observing the guest's health while exercising.
Restaurant and lobby	Position sensors Promotion signal light	Sensors identifying the presence of registered members and applications sending welcome messages or event invitations.
Facilities	Convenience signal light	Room availability notifications to hotel guests.
Warehouse	Inventory label	Determination of product profile and location. Examining expiration date and stock level.
Outside the hotel		
Building	Thermal sensors	Sensors adjusting energy management system and outside temperature measurement.
	Luminary sensors	Sensors detecting sunlight and adjusting the louvers and brightness.
Roadside	Traffic sensors	Sensors detecting parking space and traffic conditions.
Social network	Content sensors	The system monitoring the content of hotel-related social networks and user-generated content sites, and alerting the manager to get quick feedback.
		Guest stay history can be obtained from internal big data for management review.
PEST (political, economic, social, technological) data	Contextual data extractor	Systems extracting PEST contextual data from around the world and storing them in hospitality big data.

Source: Adapted from Buhalis and Leung (2018).

with artificial intelligence work and carry guests' luggage with their robotic arms (Ivanov and Webster, 2020). Similarly, at the Marriott hotel in Belgium, the robot called "Mario" can speak 19 languages, deliver room cards to guests, and provide information to guests about the hotel's services and more (Hazarhun and Yilmaz, 2020).

2.4.4 DIGITAL TECHNOLOGIES IN THE FOOD-SERVICE INDUSTRY

The food and beverage industry, as one of the three main pillars of the tourism sector along with the transportation and accommodation sectors, also uses digital technologies to the maximum possible extent. There are many new digital technology applications for restaurant businesses. These operations use digital technology both to allow customers to order something and for their own organizational and operational purposes through in-house applications (Hazarhun and Yilmaz, 2020).

In-house technologies in the food and beverage sector are widely used in three basic areas: (a) point-of-sale systems in customer contact areas and background activities, (b) restaurant management systems, and (c) systems in the field of marketing-customer relationships (Beckendorff et al., 2014, p. 246). The first of these systems consists of order entry terminals, cashier stations, manager workstations, and printers, and these systems ensure the effectiveness and efficiency of distribution from the kitchen to the table. This is also a network of server terminals that controls taking orders, transmitting these orders to the kitchen and bar, issuing customer accounts, timing the processes, and sending interactive payments to guest folios. POS systems are also used to collect credit card approvals, sales data, preliminary costing, and menu engineering for background activities. While pre-costing systems determine the weight of raw material and labor costs in production, menu engineering is useful to determine the optimal product-price mix (Beckendorff et al., 2014, p. 247).

Restaurant management systems are used in purchasing, inventory control, menu control, and product costing. Electronic procurement systems enable working with raw material supplier companies in the most efficient way and contribute greatly to product cost analysis and pricing (Beckendorff et al., 2014, p. 248). As an example, Panera Bread has transformed its 400 cafeterias into easy ordering and fast delivery model. At this company, customers can place orders using iPad-equipped kiosks for delivery to their tables. This model was developed in response to customer complaints about long order lines (Dyron, 2015).

The food and beverage sector is a service-based production style that is largely based on manual labor and produces food by transforming agricultural products and is consumed in a short time. For this reason, it is quite natural that information technologies are concentrated more on production. The main production-oriented technology usage areas in this sector are listed as follows (Cavusoglu, 2019):

1. Point-of-sales and integrated payment systems
2. Business intelligence/information systems
3. Front of the house operation systems
4. Inventory management applications
5. Accounting and finance software
6. Workforce management systems, employee monitoring, and recruitment programs
7. Customer relationship management
8. Institutional reporting and real-time reporting systems
9. Personal digital assistants and daily reporting systems
10. Kitchen management systems
11. Integrated cost control
12. Cloud-based applications
13. In-house intranet
14. Emergency and risk systems

Digital technologies at customer contact points are generally seen in web page information, reservation, promotion, marketing, ordering, and payment systems. A company's website is undoubtedly the direct tool for effective marketing. On the other hand, GPS systems, Foursquare and other restaurant search-based applications, and social media platforms are accepted as indirect digital marketing tools in this sector. Big data, IoT, artificial intelligence, autonomous robots, digital menus, robotic workers providing services of chef, waiter, waitress, bartender, and barista services, as well as augmented reality (AR) applications are tools and systems that can be used in the food services industry, providing the advantage of transforming these operations into a smarter business (Zhang et al., 2020).

In addition to abovementioned systems, information kiosks, digital menu services, and virtual reality applications are also frequently preferred technologies that can be used by food service operations (Sahin, 2020). Businesses that want to go beyond the traditional service model, offer food that is presented in different designs and flavors created using 3D printers rather than familiar products (Li et al., 2020). In businesses that want to offer different experiences, 3D virtual displays allow customers to visit the environment, see places, and dish them in advance, and make reservations and orders. Examples of foods to be produced by 3D printers, include pasta, pizza, cakes, and desserts of different designs. The most important advantages of 3D technology can be listed as, production in line with customer expectations, more creative/innovative production, and cost-effective production by preventing unnecessary material use and waste.

The rapid development of restaurant technologies provides various opportunities to meet consumers' changing expectations and demands in terms of product preparation, presentation, and promotion. Compared to printed menus, digital menu systems offer various benefits features, such as three-dimensional images, videos, animations, and entertainment (Sahin, 2020).

AR simulations, which are used in many industries, include a set of applications that allow guests to have fun while preparing their meals (Hwang et al., 2012). For food and beverage businesses, it is important to follow technology with an innovative approach to gain competitiveness in an ever-changing and developing market (Cankul et al., 2018). Technological innovations, which play an important role in the process from customer ordering to food preparation and presentation, have emerged as powerful tools to enhance and personalize the experience provided by AR applications. Businesses can integrate AR applications into their menus using QR codes, while providing customers with quantitative features, such as raw materials, calories, and nutritional values for the food (Winter, 2011).

2.5 CONCLUSION

Technology, specifically digital technology is shaping our lives, relationships, and production styles and processes, and it will continue to affect and change all societies and economies. As Dolnicar (2014) stated in her presentation, we need technology to measure the extent of a problem, monitor development over time, identify progress, identify degradation, gain insight, determine benchmarks, and best practices, and change human behavior with/without technology. Like many other economic sectors, tourism businesses also benefit greatly from technology, in terms of their production processes, marketing activities, and management of physical and human assets. Technological innovations and transformations can be seen in tourism as product-based (virtual tours) and process-based innovations (check-in/out). On the other hand, tourism is known as a labor-intensive production field and requires more face-to-face interaction with customers. Nowadays, face-to-face interactions are turning toward interactions through digital devices and technologies that do not require direct encounters. However, one of the basic principles of the services sector is to pay more attention to some critical times when there are interactions between employees and customers. These critical times are known as "moments of truth" and during these moments, any mistake cannot be compensated by the service provider. However, digital technologies facilitate these interactions and assist both parties by making the procedures faster, easier, and avoiding any error as much as possible. The result is higher customer satisfaction and more profitable work environments for tourism businesses.

Artificial intelligence is not a core subject of this chapter; however, we will witness this ultimate digital technology phenomenon more in our daily lives. Additionally, artificial virtual realities are impressive tools for places where they are used as part of tourism services. The related concept of "Industry 4.0" is used to explain "artificial intelligence and IoT," which also emphasizes the concept of autonomous machines and virtual environments. The most distinctive feature of the technological transformation defined as Industry 4.0 is the change that occurs physically in the form of machines, rather than physical elements, such as electronics, communication, informatics, information technologies, the Internet, software, big data, QR Codes, cloud computing, GPS, IoT, AI, 3D printers, and so forth. For this reason, Industry 4.0 can be described as a predominantly soft and cyber-technological revolution.

In conclusion, digital technologies and services can be observed in every aspect of the tourism sector in varying dimensions, and tourism-related services are provided entirely through digital technologies. Tourism businesses as the main service providers should be prepared for these changes proactively to survive in the sector, gain competitive advantage, and to effectively meet ever-changing customer needs and expectations.

KEYWORDS

- **business source planning**
- **digital tourism eco-system**
- **digital transformation**
- **digital distribution systems**
- **ICTs**
- **smart hotel**
- **tourism services providers**

REFERENCES

Beckendorff, P.J, Sheldon, P. J., & Fesenmaier, D. R. (2014). *Tourism information technology*, 2nd ed, CABI Tourism Texts. Gutenburg Press.

Bilbao, S., Lejarazu, A., & Herrero, J. (2010). Dynamic packaging semantic plat-form for tourism intermediaries, in: information and communication technologies in 2010. In U. Gretzel, R. Law & M. Fuchs (Eds.). *Proceedings of the International Conference* (pp. 617–628), Lugano, Switzerland, Feb. 10–12.

Bilgihan, A., Smith, S., Ricci, P., & Bujisic, M. (2016). Hotel guest preferences of in-room technology amenities. *Journal of Hospitality and Tourism Technology, 7*(2), 118–134.

Buhalis, D., & Leung, R. (2018). Smart hospitality—Interconnectivity and interoperability towards an ecosystem. *International Journal of Hospitality Management, 71*, 41–50.

Buhalis, D., & Law, R. (2008). Progress in information technology and tourism management: 20 years on and 10 years after the Internet—The state of e-Tourism research. *Tourism Management, 29*(4), 609–623.

Buhalis, D., & Licata, M. C. (2002). The future e-Tourism intermediaries. *Tourism Management, 23*(3), 207–220.

Cankul, D., Doğan, A., & Sönmez, B. (2018). Yiyecek-içecek işletmelerinde inovasyon ve artırılmış gerçeklik uygulamaları. *İşletme Araştırmaları Dergisi, 10*(3), 576–591.

Cavusoğlu, M. (2019). An analysis of technology applications in the restaurant industry, *Journal of Hospitality and Tourism Technology, 10*(1), 45–72.

Cobanoğlu, C., & Berezina, E. (2010). Importance-Performance Analysis of In-Room Technology Amenities in Hotels, In: Information and Communication Technologies in 2010. Gretzel, U., Law R. and Fuchs, M. (Eds.). *Proceedings of the International Conference* (pp.25–39). Lugano, Switzerland.

Dolnicar, S. (2014). How technology could help shape environmental sustainability of tourism over the next 30 years, ENTER2024–31st e-Tourism Conference, IFITT, 17–19/01/2024, Izmir, Türkiye.

Dyron M. (2015). Flour on his shoes, CEO spotlight. In R. Shaich & Panera Bread (Eds.), *Barron's: The Dow Jones Business and Financial Weekly*, XCV, No. 8 (February 23), 38–39.

Edvardsson, B., Gustafsson, A., Kristensson, P., & Witell, L. (2010). Service innovation and customer co-development. In P. P. Maglio, C. A. Kieliszewski, & J. Spohrer (Eds.), *Handbook of service science* (pp. 561–577). Springer.

Hazarhun, E., & Yılmaz, D. (2020). Restoranlarda Dijital Dönüşüm: Touch Restoran Örneği-Gastroia: *Journal of Gastronomy and Travel Research, 4*(3), 384–399.

Heo, C. Y. (2016). Sharing economy and prospects in tourism research, *Annals of Tourism Research, 58*, 166–170.

Houghton, J. W. (2007). Online delivery of tourism services: Developments, issues, and challenges. In W. Pease, M. Rowe, & M. Cooper (Eds.), *Information and communication technologies in support of the tourism industry* (pp.2–25). Idea Group Publishing.

Hwang, J., Yoon, S. Y., & Bendle, L. J. (2012). Desired privacy and the impact of crowding on customer emotions and approach-avoidance responses: Waiting in a virtual reality restaurant. *International Journal of Contemporary Hospitality Management, 24*(2), 224–250.

İçöz, O. (2021). *Tourism and technology: Technological transformation in tourism in the historical process.* Detay Publishing (*Turizm ve Teknoloji; Tarihsel Süreçte Turizmde Teknolojik Dönüşüm,* Detay Yayıncılık—in Turkish), Ankara.

Ivanov, S., & Webster, C. (2020). Robots in tourism: A research agenda for tourism economics. *Tourism Economics, 26*(7), 1065–1085. https://doi.org/10.1177/1354816619879583.

Ivanov, S. H., Webster, C., & Berezina, K. (2017). Adoption of robots and service automation by tourism and hospitality companies. *Revista Turismo & Desenvolvimento, 27*(28), 1501–1517.

Jeremen, D., Jędrasiak, M., & Rapacz, A. (2016). The concept of smart hotels as an innovation on the hospitality industry market-case study of Puro Hotel in Wrocław. *Zeszyty Naukowe Uniwersytetu Szczecińskiego Ekonomiczne Problemy Turystyki, 36*(4), 65–75. Doi:10.18276/EPT.2016.4.36–06.

Kenney, M., & Zysman, J. (2015). Choosing a future in the platform economy: The implications and consequences of digital platforms, In: *Kauffman Foundation New Entrepreneurial Growth Conference*, Discussion Paper Amelia Island Florida—June 18/19.

Khatri, I. (2019). Information technology in tourism & hospitality industry: A review of ten years' publications. *Journal of Tourism and Hospitality Education, 9*, 74–87.

Kirillova, K., & Chan, J. (2018). "What is beautiful we book": Hotel visual appeal and expected service quality. *International Journal of Contemporary Hospitality Management, 30*(3), 1788–1807.

Kracht, J., & Wang, Y. (2010). Examining the tourism distribution channel: Evolution and transformation. *International Journal of Contemporary Hospitality Management, 22*(5), 736–757.

Lai, W. C., & Hung, W. H. (2018). A framework of cloud and AI based intelligent hotel. In *Proceedings of the 18th International Conference on Electronic Business* (pp.36–43). ICEB, Guilin, China, December 2–6.

Law, R., Leung, D., Au, N., & Lee, H. A. (2013). Progress and development of information technology in the hospitality industry: Evidence from Cornell Hospitality Quarterly. *Cornell Hospitality Quarterly, 54*(1), 10–24.

Li, Y., Hu, C., Huang, C., & Duan, L. (2017). The concept of smart tourism in the context of tourism information services. *Tourism Management, 58*, 293–300.

Li, X., Xu, X., Song, L., Bi, A., Wu, C., Ma, Y., ... & Zhu, B. (2020). High internal phase emulsion for food-grade 3D printing materials. *ACS Applied Materials & Interfaces,12*(40), 45493–45503.

Mashkina, N. A., Belyaeva, E. S., Obukhova, A. S., & Belyaeva, O. V. (2021). Digitalization of the transport industry in the context of globalization of the world economy. In: *SHS Web of Conferences* (Vol. 92, p.05020). EDP Sciences.

Merten, P. S. (2007). The transformation of the distribution process in the airline industry empowered by information and communication technology, In W. Pease, M. Rowe, & M. Cooper (Eds.), *Information and communication technologies in support of the tourism industry* (pp. 76–114). Idea Group Publishing.

Muneta, M., & Lopez, A. (2013). ICT impact on tourism industry, *International Journal of Management Cases, 15*(2), 84–91.

Naumov, N. (2019). The impact of robots, artificial intelligence, and service automation on service quality and service experience in hospitality. In *Robots, artificial intelligence, and service automation in travel, tourism and hospitality* (pp.123–133). Emerald Publishing Limited.

Neidhardt, J., & Werthner, H. (2018). IT and tourism: Still a hot topic, but do not forget IT. *Information Technology and Tourism, 20*, 1–7. doi.org/10.1007/s40558–018–0115-x.

Neuhofer, B., Buhalis, D., & Ladkin, A. (2014). A typology of technology-enhanced tourism experiences. *International Journal of Tourism Research, 16*(4), 340–350.

Page, S. (2009). Transportation and tourism: A symbiotic relationship? In *the SAGE handbook of tourism studies* (pp.371–395). Sage Publications.

Pagliara, F., & Mauriello, F. (2019). The effects of investments in new transport technologies such as HSR on the tourism industry. *The Open Transportation Journal, 13*(1), 35–40.

Prieto, M. (2019). The state of online travel agencies. https://me-dium.com/traveltechmedia/the-state-of-online-travel-agencies-2019. Access: 15.08.2023

Rosenbaum, M. S., & Wong, I. A. (2015). If you install it, will they use it? Understanding why hospitality customers take "technological pauses" from self-service technology. *Journal of Business Research, 68*(9), 1862–1868.

Şahin, E. (2020). An evaluation of digital menu types and their advantages. *Journal of Tourism & Gastronomy Studies, 8*(4), 2374–2386.

Stankov, U., Filimonau, V., & Slivar, I. (2019). Calm ICT design in hotels: A critical review of applications and implications. *International Journal of Hospitality Management, 82*, 298–307.

Toh, R. S., Raven, P., & DeKay, F. (2011). Selling rooms: Hotels vs. third-party websites. *Cornell Hospitality Quarterly, 52*(2), 181–189.

Topal, İ., & Uçar, M. K. (2018). In tourism, using artificial intelligence forecasting with Tripadvisor data: Year of Türkiye in China. In: *International Conference on Artificial Intelligence and Data Processing* (IDAP), September (pp.1–5). IEEE.

USA Today (2011). Some hotels use RFID chips to keep linens from checking out, July 30. https://www.wtsp.com/article/home/. Access: 20.09.2023.

Vijayakumar, N., & Mehendiratta, G. (2011). Role of ICT in sustainable transportation-focus on reducing traffic congestion.

WEF (2007). World Economic Forum, Digital Ecosystem Convergence between IT, Telecoms, Media and Entertainment: Scenarios to 2015. https://www.weforum.org/reports. Access: 15.10.2023.

Winter, M. (2011). *Scan-me everybody's guide to the magical world of QR codes*. Westsong Publishing.

Xu, X. (2018). Research on the construction and development of smart hotel from the perspective of serving customers. In: *2nd International Conference on Education Science and Economic Management* (pp. 975–978). Atlantis Press.

Zhang, X., Yang, S., Srivastava, G., Chen, M. Y., & Cheng, X. (2020). Hybridization of cognitive computing for food services. *Applied Soft Computing, 89*, 106051.

Web Sources

http://www.iata.org/whatwedo/. Access: 10.02.2024

https://blog.hubspot.com/service/customer-review-sites. Access: 12.02.2024

https://info.hotelhero.tech/de/hotel-tech-markt-deutschland-2020. Der Deutche Hotel Technologie - Markt 2020. Access: 17.12.2023

https://intelity.com/hospitality-platform/. Enable a Contactless Hospitality, Explore the future, Guest experience. Access: 05.01.2024

https://www.itasoftware.com/. Access: 12.12.2023

https://www.loungeup.com/en/2017/12/01/top-3-smart-room-technology-impress-guests/. Access: 21 November, 2023

https://www.revfine.com/smart-room. 7 Ways to Transform a Hotel Room Into a Smart Room. Access: 15.01.2024.

https://www.socialtables.com/blog/hospitality/in-room-technology-trends/. In Room Hospitality Technologies. Access: 14.01.2024.

https://www.travelonline.com/product-review. Access: 10.02.2024

CHAPTER 3

Digital Leadership: Reflections on the Digital Maturity of the Tourism Industry

MARCO A. GARDINI

Faculty of Tourism, Kempten University, Kempten, Germany

ABSTRACT

Digital maturity models represent analytical frameworks designed to systematically assess the digital capabilities and readiness of organizations or entire industries. Within the scholarly discourse, the notion of "digital maturity" has emerged as a conceptual lens through which the current state of a firm's digital transformation can be evaluated, while simultaneously offering a foundation for the formulation of strategic orientations and decision-making processes. Although varying in scope and level of abstraction, most models converge around four core dimensions in the context of organizational assessments: strategy, leadership and corporate culture, competencies and skills, and organizational structure. The subsequent analysis applies these dimensions to the tourism industry, with the aim of identifying critical areas of concern that are pivotal to enabling and accelerating digital transformation within the sector.

3.1 INTRODUCTION

The ongoing advancement of digitalization and artificial intelligence is fundamentally transforming the tourism industry and has increasingly become a central focus within both tourism research and practical

Digitalization in Tourism. Hulya Akdemir Cengiz, Seza Zerman, Aysegul Acar, and Faizan Ali (Eds.)

DOI: 10.1201/9781779644770-4

applications (Gretzel, 2022; Egger, 2022; Buhalis et al., 2019). Remarkably, digitalization is hitting large parts of the tourism industry at its weakest and strongest points at the same time. Tourism, traditionally understood as an information and service business (Buhalis 2003; Poon, 1993), benefits on the one hand from the expanded possibilities of digital information processing/transmission and its historically developed expertise in utilizing information in an economically efficient way, but on the other hand, it is losing its information sovereignty, that is, the possibility of making information exclusively and internally available at low transaction costs. This development, combined with the fact that only a limited number of tourism enterprises can be classified as "born digitals," has significantly altered the industry's power dynamics over the past two decades. Structural shifts and increasing competition across various segments of the tourism sector—manifested in phenomena, such as lower entry barriers, intensified competitive rivalry, industry restructuring, substitution threats, processes of dis- and reintermediation, heightened consumer power, and increased market transparency—underscore this transformation (Pencarelli, 2020; Buhalis et al., 2019). The rapid pace of change, particularly over the last twenty years, is exemplified by the rise of numerous companies with no prior involvement in tourism, which, through purely digital business models, have bypassed the analog stage and now challenge incumbent providers across multiple competitive and operational dimensions. Prominent examples, include Booking, Google, and Airbnb within the accommodation sector.

To date, only a few traditional actors from the various sub-sectors of the tourism industry have been able to formulate and implement effective strategic responses to these disruptive, digitally-driven business models. Many established companies still lack a forward-looking, systematic digitalization approach that would enable them to effectively navigate evolving market and organizational demands. While digitalization and artificial intelligence are increasingly perceived as opportunities rather than threats by most industry stakeholders, current digital initiatives tend to be reactive, operationally confined, or isolated in nature. These efforts often fall short of constituting a coherent and integrated digitalization strategy with clearly articulated objectives aimed at transforming conventional tourism offerings into digitally enabled, and thus more sustainable business models (Gardini and Sommer, 2023). This chapter aims to clarify where tourism currently stands in terms of digitalization, and thus attempts to answer the question of the digital maturity of the tourism industry, that is, how strongly digitalization is culturally, strategically, and structurally anchored in tourism organizations.

3.2 DIGITAL LEADERSHIP AND DIGITAL MATURITY

Digital leadership is generally understood as the strategic and operational management of organizational systems and stakeholder relationships through the comprehensive utilization of digital technologies, with the objective of enhancing both the efficiency and effectiveness of a company's internal processes and external interactions (Wirtz, 2021). Despite the increasing relevance of digital leadership in the context of digital transformation, numerous empirical studies have consistently classified the tourism industry—and the majority of tourism enterprises—as exhibiting below-average levels of digitalization and digital maturity over an extended period (Deutsche Telekom, 2022; Demary and Goecke, 2021; Ghandi et al., 2016; Strategy and PwC, 2013). A look into the past shows that the origins of digitalization in tourism were promising. The potential of digitalization was notably recognized early on by airlines. The Sabre Corporation, founded by American Airlines in the early 1960s, could soon process flight bookings electronically in larger numbers. In Germany, tourism services became bookable on a larger scale, particularly with the START system in the 1970s. These booking systems were further developed and expanded into global distribution systems (GDS), which, in addition to flight bookings, increasingly made other tourism services bookable, from accommodation providers to tour operators, mobility service providers and insurance companies (Schulz et al., 2015, p. 215ff.). Due to the specific nature of tourism as an information business, some areas of tourism (e.g., airlines, travel agencies) have been pioneers in the realization and implementation of technology and platform-driven business models (Bieger and Beritelli, 2018), which raises the question of when and why the leading role as an information intermediary between tourism supply and demand got lost.

The tourism industry appears to remain in an early or experimental phase of the digital era, suggesting that digitalization within the sector is still in its formative stages. While the digital environment presents numerous opportunities, it is characterized by a scarcity of established standards and consistent patterns. As a result, the fundamental questions and challenges addressed by both academic research and industry practice in the context of digital transformation and digital maturity remain largely unchanged. A striking example of this persistence is the continued relevance of basic digital hygiene factors—such as online bookability and digital visibility—as critical issues in tourism digitalization, even more than three decades after the commercial emergence of the Internet in 1991 (Online Birds, 2023; BTE Tourismus- und Regionalberatung, 2022). It is currently apparent that the majority of players in the tourism industry only, to a limited extent, display the necessary entrepreneurial and technological skills or prerequisites to manage a successful digital transformation along fundamental internal and external performance dimensions (i.e., booking engine, customer journey design, touchpoint management, customer relationship management, reputation management, etc.) (Egger, 2022; Hotelhero, 2020; Roland Berger 2019; h2c, 2019; Input Consulting, 2018; Gardini, 2017a; Ghandi et al., 2016).

Hence, the transformation dynamics of digitalization and artificial intelligence require a critical examination of the digital maturity level of the tourism industry in order to identify the most important challenges on the path to digital transformation in tourism. Within the academic discourse, the concept of *digital maturity* has evolved as a key analytical construct for evaluating the current state of an organization's digital transformation efforts, while simultaneously serving as a basis for formulating strategic orientations and future action plans. According to Chanias and Hess, digital maturity refers to "the status of a company's digital transformation" and captures "what a company has already achieved with regard to transformation efforts" (Chanias and Hess, 2016, p. 4). Digital maturity models or digitalization indices, therefore, serve as tools for systematically examining and evaluating the digital competence of industries or companies, as well as for incrementally improving digital capabilities, processes, structures, or frameworks within businesses and organizations. Businesses can leverage the results of digital maturity assessments to compare their performance with other companies or competitors, identify their digital strengths and weaknesses across all business or service processes, and prioritize digital initiatives with the greatest potential impact. The higher the maturity level, the more likely a company is to be flexible and agile in responding to and implementing digital innovations and business models. Companies with high digital maturity are more capable of effectively moderating digital change processes and distributing decision-making processes across different management levels, thereby fostering awareness and a shift in mindset regarding digital transformation challenges within the organization. A variety of digital maturity models have been developed across both academic and industry contexts (Proff et al., 2021; Thordsen et al., 2020; Remane et al., 2017). While these models differ in their structure, scope, and level of abstraction, they generally converge around four core dimensions that are commonly used in organizational digital audits and capability assessments. These dimensions include:

1. *Strategy,* addressing suitable goals and digital solutions to successfully shape the business model and long-term company development.
2. *Leadership and corporate culture*, involving normative orientation, attitudes, and appropriate thinking and behaviors crucial for harnessing digital potentials.
3. *Competencies and skills*, emphasizing digital intelligence required to achieve digital goals using suitable systems, tools, digital skills, and technologies.
4. *Organization*, considering the right structures, processes, and people to successfully implement the digital strategy.

Subsequently, along these four dimensions, the digital maturity of the tourism industry will be examined, highlighting current problem areas deemed essential on the path of digital transformation in tourism. It's important to note that the observations discussed here are necessarily generalizing and selective in nature and may not explicitly align with the individual operational realities of particular companies. Nevertheless, these observations represent a condensed essence of prevailing patterns of perception, findings, and conclusions from contributions in both academic research and business practice, underscoring the necessary action required in the context of digital transformation processes in the tourism industry.

3.2.1 DIGITAL STRATEGY: WHAT IS YOUR STRATEGY?

Historically, tourism companies have focused extensively on increasing operational efficiency. They have grown larger, faster, more productive, and more effective—essentially striving to enhance their efficiency in existing processes. As is well understood, efficiency means doing things "right," a fundamental skill that companies and entrepreneurs must master. However, in his seminal work *"What is Strategy?"*, Michael Porter (1996) argued nearly 30 years ago that operational excellence, while crucial, does not constitute a strategy and cannot substitute for one ("operational effectiveness is not a strategy"). In the context of digital transformation, many tourism companies have found themselves overly focused on technological solutions, often at the expense of a customer-centric approach. As a result, tactical decisions are often prioritized over strategic considerations (Gardini, 2021a, 2021b; Furr and Shipilov, 2021). This mirrors the well-established adage in digital transformation management that *"strategy, not technology, drives digital transformation"* (Kane et al., 2015). However, this approach has proven problematic, as numerous studies across industries have shown that the majority of digital transformation initiatives fail to achieve their intended outcomes. This trend has been consistently highlighted in research for many years (Davenport and Westerman, 2018; Martin, 2018; Piccoli, 2008). For instance, in 2019, US companies allocated an estimated USD 1.3 trillion to digital transformation efforts, of which approximately USD 900 billion was deemed wasted due to insufficient foresight and an excessive focus on technology (Tabrizi et al., 2019).

It appears that the technological and operational aspects of digital transformation continue to dominate the discourse, overshadowing the more critical strategic question of how digitalization can create long-term value for both companies and customers. There remains a lack of clarity about whether the potential for digital change is so profound and transformative that it fundamentally challenges the operational models of tourism companies and reshapes the economic structures within which they operate. In this context, Porter (2001) was quick to emphasize that the view of digital technology, particularly internet-based technologies, must be framed through a strategic lens. He argued that digital opportunities should be evaluated by their strategic added value, rather than merely as tools to improve operational efficiency: *"...see the Internet for what it is: an enabling technology—a powerful set of tools that can be used wisely or unwisely, in almost any industry and as part of almost any strategy. We need to ask fundamental questions: Who will capture the economic benefits the Internet creates? Will all the value end up going to customers, or will companies be able to reap a share of it? What will be the Internet's impact on industry structure? Will it expand or shrink the pool of profits?*

And what will be its impact on strategy? Will the Internet bolster or erode the ability of companies to gain sustainable advantage over competitors?" (Porter, 2001, p. 64). While the COVID-19 pandemic has catalyzed a shift in awareness and spurred a digitalization drive within the tourism sector, the strategic and cultural dimensions of digital transformation are still underappreciated by many in the industry. As Pencarelli (2020, p. 467) notes, *"The survival of traditional enterprises is seriously threatened by the new playbook rules established by digitalization. Consequently, these business entities are called to innovate and re-think the business model they have been using thus far to create value for tourists and to achieve satisfactory performance levels."*

In addition to operational efficiency, the other key competency that distinguishes successful companies from less successful ones is effectiveness—defined as the ability to do the "right thing." However, identifying what constitutes the "right thing" for a company is inherently context-dependent, as it is influenced by the goals and objectives set by the company itself. This presents the most essential and foundational question that any entrepreneur or company must answer. In the digital age, a strategic response is necessary, yet tourism companies frequently struggle to develop a clear and coherent understanding of what they should pursue and what they should avoid: *"Operationally urgent questions that are unimportant for securing the future supersede strategically important but non-urgent questions."* This phenomenon, known as Graham's law of planning, outlines a management dilemma that is considered typical for many companies—especially small and medium-sized enterprises. In many tourism companies, there is a noticeable overemphasis on operational and tactical elements of business management, often at the expense of strategic planning and coordination. This situation leads to the phenomenon in which companies are *"too busy 'running the business' to strategically manage it"* (Rodwell and Shadur, 2007, p. 53). The industry's traditionally strong product and sales orientation exacerbates this issue, as many tourism companies find it difficult to pivot toward a more strategic, long-term approach (Gardini, 2017b).

Successful companies, however, are adept at balancing both operational efficiency and strategic effectiveness, as both are essential for achieving superior corporate and marketing performance. The tension between operational and strategic orientations, as well as the challenge of integrating both analog and digital corporate activities, extends across various organizational domains. To address these challenges, a return to a clear, market- and customer-centered focus is imperative (mission/purpose). This requires the consistent alignment of corporate activities with the company's long-term developed resources, ensuring that these capabilities are non-imitable, company-specific, non-substitutable, and capable of creating value in the market. As Frehse (2006), Goutier and Schmidt (2003), and Porter (2004) assert, these resources should generate additional benefits perceived by customers, thereby creating a sustainable competitive advantage.

The evolving competitive landscape in various market and customer segments within the tourism industry, driven by digitalization, has opened up new strategic opportunities for service providers. These opportunities pertain to how companies engage with their customers as they transition toward becoming "smart" or digitally-oriented tourism enterprises. This shift occurs within the context of the interaction between artificial and natural intelligence (Haux et al., 2021), the ongoing analogization and digitalization of business operations (Bichler et al., 2019), and the strategic behaviors that arise from these changes—such as standardization versus individualization, mechanization versus humanization, and externalization versus internalization (Gardini, 2025, 2022). One way to navigate these complexities is by leveraging the dimensions of analogization and digitalization to create a portfolio that identifies four general strategic directions. The choice of strategy depends on the company's objectives, its target customer base, and its positioning within the broader competitive landscape. These directions can serve as guiding frameworks for understanding the balance between the "tech" and "touch" dimensions of tourism in the digital era (Gardini, 2025) (Figure 3.1):

1. *Integrative strategy (high-touch and high-tech)*

   In this approach, digitalization and artificial intelligence are harnessed to deliver highly individualized, intensive, and unique customer experiences. The goal is to create an *"intelligent"* environment that fosters targeted, interpersonal, and relationship-oriented interactions between customers and companies, fully exploiting the technological capabilities available to enhance the customer journey.

2. *Human-centered strategy (high-touch)*

   In response to the growing trend of digitalization and mechanization, a countervailing force of analogization is emerging, as some customers express a desire to *"escape from technology"* (Gretzel et al., 2015, p. 185). The high-touch strategy focuses on placing people, rather than technology, at the core of the experience. It seeks to create a *"social"* environment that promotes authentic, real-life interactions, emphasizing social connection, collaboration, time sovereignty, and a break from the everyday digital world to offer meaningful and quality customer experiences.

3. *Technology-centered strategy (high-tech)*

   Here, digitalization, mechanization, and automation are the driving forces behind the business model. The strategy places technology, rather than human interactions, at the forefront. The objective is to build a *"technical"* environment that maximizes the potential of digital tools and applications to deliver personalized, technologically enriched customer experiences.

4. *Cost-centered strategy (low-tech and low-touch)*

   This approach does not focus on maximizing technological potential but rather on optimizing it for cost-efficiency. The strategy aims to create a *"rational"* environment through standardization, rationalization, automation, and externalization. By substituting human labor with technological solutions, companies can reduce costs, offer price advantages, and achieve efficiency gains from both the company's and customers' perspectives.

At this juncture, it becomes imperative for each tourism enterprise to initiate and cultivate a digital transformation process that is tailored to its unique organizational history, identity, and prevailing strategic vision. The central strategic question that tourism companies and organizations must address is whether this transformation should proceed as an evolutionary progression or take the form of a disruptive, revolutionary shift. This dilemma is not a novel one, nor is it exclusively a consequence of digitalization; rather, it reflects a longstanding tension in strategic management between sustaining established operations and embracing innovation—between optimizing existing capabilities (efficiency) and pursuing new opportunities (effectiveness). In this context, the concept of organizational ambidexterity has gained prominence in scholarly discourse as a framework for understanding the inherent challenges of digital transformation

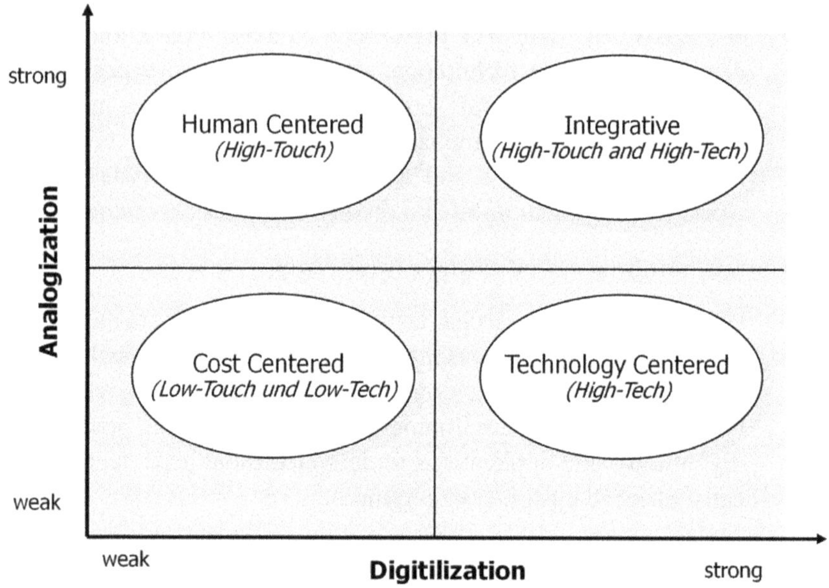

FIGURE 3.1 Analogization and digitalization as competitive dimensions in the tourism industry.

Source: Gardini (2022, p. 453).

(Raisch et al., 2009; O'Reilly and Tushman, 2004). Organizational ambidexterity refers to a firm's ability to simultaneously exploit existing competencies and explore new opportunities. From a strategic perspective, this dual capability enables firms to expand and optimize their core business operations (exploitation) while concurrently developing innovations and new business models (exploration) to maintain competitiveness in a rapidly evolving, digital environment (Kollmann, 2020; Duwe, 2018).

However, in the strategic development process, it is crucial to recognize that digitalization and digital transformation in tourism do not necessarily require radical or disruptive change. Sustainable business models and innovations are often the product of intelligent adaptation rather than wholesale reinvention. In many cases, digital transformation in tourism should not be conceptualized as the reflexive substitution of physical or material components with digital alternatives. Rather, it requires a careful and context-sensitive calibration that preserves the value of analog elements where appropriate. Furthermore, transformation does not always entail a complete strategic overhaul; instead, it may involve the purposeful application of digital technologies to better address existing customer needs, enhancing or reimagining customer experiences in ways that are both satisfying and inspiring (Furr and Shipilov, 2021).

A best practice example of a digital leadership approach is provided by the French hotel group Accor. Shortly after taking office as the new CEO of hotel group Accor in August 2013, Sebastien Bazin was attributed with the following quote: "The last 40 years, 90% of our efforts have been focused on brand and product, the next 40 years, 90% will be focused on digital, clients and data!" Since this statement, the group has undergone a remarkable strategic transformation, from a hotel group with more functional hotel offerings to a hospitality ecosystem that currently unites more than 50 brands and companies (hotels, clubs, restaurants, co-working, tech start-ups, sharing, etc.) around the Accor umbrella brand. Through the interplay of brand families grouped around lifestyle (25hours, Mama Shelter, JoandJoe, Mondrian, Delano, etc.), luxury (Sofitel, Raffles, Fairmont, Banyan, etc.), economy (Ibis, Ibis Styles, Ibis Budget) and numerous other individual brands, as well as additional services and shops, the aim is to create a unique brand world in which customers can live out their individual wishes at any time, in almost any place (Accor Live Limitless). The strategy centered around the customer relationship, brand relevance, and the analog and digital product experience enables Accor, like no other company in the global chain hotel industry, to accompany customers throughout the entire travel process, to relate to them, to provide them with tailor-made offers in real-time from the Accor brand world, and thus to bind them ever more strongly to the Accor ecosystem, which currently makes the company a digital leader in the international hotel industry (Gardini, 2021a, 2021b).

3.2.2 DIGITAL LEADERSHIP AND LEADERSHIP CULTURE

Tourism companies can only convince customers in the digital age if they offer them significant benefits (Wirtz, 2021; Gardini, 2019). Success for these companies doesn't come solely from offering digital rather than analog products or services. Instead, it stems from embracing market-oriented management as a leading principle. This involves clearly defining the benefits that the digitalization of their activities brings to both customers and the company (Hennig-Thurau et al., 2014). The focus on the customer remains essential in the digital era. Understanding the new (old) needs, motivation landscapes, and behavioral patterns of customers provides a crucial framework for addressing strategic and operational challenges. This understanding is vital for the success or failure of tourism companies in the digital age. However, if marketing is increasingly understood less as a leadership philosophy and the "born digitals" in tourism lack marketing knowledge while the protagonists of the "old economy" lack understanding of digital technologies, then digital in tourism will also fall short of its potential. Therefore, it seems that in many areas of digitalization, both internally and externally in tourism companies, there is still considerable potential for optimization on the way to digital excellence or digital leadership: *"Let's face it, marketing missed its last slot. Digital technology should have given marketers unprecedented powers—the power to understand customers; the power to increase returns; the power to shape the C-suite agenda. Naturally, the CMO stature should have risen. Marketing should have finally become the central function. It didn't come that way. Too many top CMOs still haven't found their power formula. Too many marketers got lost in digital tactics. And too many CEOs still don't get why customer focus matters. Slot missed"* (Barta, 2020).

Why is this so? Shouldn't digitalization fulfill the long-awaited dream of all tourism professionals? To be able to offer the right product to the transparent customer at anytime, anywhere, at the right price? *"Fundamentally, it's because most digital technologies provide possibilities for efficiency gains and customer intimacy. But if people lack the right mindset to change and the current organizational practices are flawed, digital transformation will simply magnify those flaws"* (Tabrizi et al., 2021: p. 120). The bottleneck on the way to a digital company is, therefore, the top executives or owners and the prevailing corporate or management philosophy and leadership culture with them. The cultural-intellectual adaptation that companies and their actors must make is characterized by the strongly divergent characteristics of traditional and digital leadership philosophies and styles (see Table 3.1), which emphasize that digital transformation cannot be managed technologically but must focus on the cultural process and the human being (Tokarski et al., 2021; Frankiewicz and Chamorro-Premuzic, 2021; Goran et al., 2017). People remain—especially in the digital age—meaning seekers. Assuming that companies are made by humans for humans, each company must accordingly define and convey its specific purpose and entrepreneurial purpose if it wants to present its diverse stakeholders with an understandable and comprehensive perspective (Gardini, 2021a, 2021b; Gnamm et al., 2018).

From a strategic and organizational perspective, the tension between traditional and digital mindsets constitutes both a systemic and cultural challenge for large parts of the tourism industry (Laesser et al., 2021). Sectors such as hospitality, gastronomy, and leisure or cultural enterprises are often characterized by a historically low affinity for digital technologies. This can be attributed to persistently low levels of digital maturity and productivity among many stakeholders, which in turn stem from a critical or even dismissive stance toward the adoption of new information and communication technologies (O'Connor, 2021; Borkmann, 2020; Sigala, 2014). This reluctance is often rooted in a prevailing mental model that positions digitalization and hospitality as conceptually opposed. Within this mindset, digital transformation is perceived not merely as a challenge to operational practices but as a fundamental contradiction to the self-perception of hoteliers and restaurateurs as hosts. In this view, digitalization threatens the core identity of an industry that has traditionally defined itself as a "people business" (Gardini, 2022). This conflict is further reinforced by structural characteristics typical of the tourism sector, including the predominance of small and medium-sized enterprises and the prevalence of owner-managed or family-run businesses. These identity-defining elements, which have long been considered strengths of the industry, are now being called into question by the digital imperative. As a result, many actors within the industry are experiencing what can be described as an identity crisis, manifesting in fears of both internal cultural disruption and a perceived erosion of external brand or service authenticity.

TABLE 3.1 Traditional vs Digital Mindset.

Traditional Mindset	Digital Mindset
Intransparency	Transparency
Result orientation	Process orientation
Expert knowledge	Community knowledge
Care	Speed
Hierarchy	Equality
Continuity	Agility
Secrecy	Candidness
Security	Experimentation
Tradition	Change

The starting point for cultural and identity-based transformation processes remains difficult—if not inherently problematic—for many tourism companies. While there is an increasing openness and willingness within the industry to engage with new digital technologies and methods—particularly in the context of digital business models and digital distribution—many organizations still feel inadequately prepared for the demands of a digital future (Thomas, 2024; Laesser et al., 2021; Schuler, 2019) or fall short of their own expectations (Borkmann, 2020; Berger, 2019). In many cases, the pace of economic and technological development is far ahead of the psychological readiness and cultural adaptability of key stakeholders. Furthermore, the digital research and innovation ecosystem in the tourism sector—as well as technology adoption and employee digital competence—continues to lag significantly behind other industries (Demary and Goecke, 2021; Hotelhero, 2020). Digitalization, in this context, confronts the tourism sector at two of its most vulnerable points: the persistent absence of systematic innovation management and the chronic underdevelopment of professional human resource strategies. These challenges are compounded by a long-standing image crisis faced by tourism employees, alongside leadership cultures and management practices that are often deeply misaligned with the demands of digital transformation. Commonly described leadership styles in the industry remain conservative, hierarchical, patriarchal, and insufficiently oriented toward employee empowerment and collaboration (Francis and Baum, 2018; Gardini, 2016; Kusluvan et al., 2010). This disconnect is particularly problematic in light of the expectations of younger generations—particularly generations Y and Z—who not only expect a digitally fluent corporate environment but also value lifestyle flexibility, participative leadership, and purpose-driven work. These generations seek more than just technological modernization; they demand a redefined workplace culture centered on work-life balance, meaningful contribution, and personal fulfillment (Schlotter and Huber, 2020; Maas, 2019).

If digitalization is indeed a central element of corporate strategy—one that permeates and transforms every level of a business—then both academic literature and business practice are in agreement: "Digitalization is a top management issue" (Kollmann, 2020; Gnamm et al., 2018). Successful leaders in tourism—be they individuals, enterprises, or institutions—tend to possess a clear sense of strategic intention: they know what they want, what they do not want, and what they are willing to invest to achieve their goals. A renewed focus on *purpose*—a concept increasingly at the center of normative management discourse—has emerged as a response to this challenge. Purpose is a holistic synthesis of a company's vision, mission, core values, and cultural principles. It asks foundational questions such as: "Why do we exist?", "What do we stand for?", and "What defines our identity?" (Esch, 2021; McKinsey, 2020; Quinn and Thakor, 2018). Expressions such as "corporate DNA," "the soul of the company," or "philosophical heartbeat" are often used to describe this concept. Accordingly, the creation of meaningful and identity-based value—both internally for employees and externally for customers—must become a core focus of digital leadership and marketing agendas. From a leadership perspective, this necessitates a normative, identity-driven approach to digital transformation—one that begins with the cultural and philosophical foundations of each individual tourism organization, whether a destination, hotel, travel agency, or restaurant. The ultimate goal is to foster a consistent, market-oriented, and customer-centric understanding of the company, one that transcends binary notions of digital versus analog and instead embraces a unified, purpose-driven identity (Gardini, 2021a, 2021b).

3.2.3 *DIGITAL INTELLIGENCE: ARE YOU SMART ENOUGH?*

In the context of digitalization, every tourism company must consequently question which competencies and skills it needs to develop and possess to survive in the digital world or adapt to digital transformation. Following the commonly accepted intelligence definition from psychology, stating that intelligence reflects the ability to learn from experience, solve problems, and adapt to new situations (Myers, 2015), a hallmark of intelligent companies in the era of digital transformation seems to be making innovation and adaptability core competencies (Stoll and Dorn, 2021). This ability, referred to as digital intelligence, is not only a matter of the discussed digital mindset but also a question of the means by which this core competency can be built. Two central aspects come into focus: firstly, the question of the suitable systems, tools, and technologies a company needs to confront digital transformation and achieve its goals, and secondly, the digital expertise of the involved stakeholders, meaning the employees' ability to handle these new digital tools and possibilities. The discourse on the digital intelligence of tourism companies or the relevance of digital intelligence is largely conducted under the term "smart tourism" in scientific literature (Liu et al., 2023; Chen et al., 2021; Ye et al., 2020; Ardito et al., 2019; Jovicic, 2019; Wise and Heidari, 2019; Gretzel and Scarpino-Johns, 2018). A smart tourism, according to Gretzel et al. (2016), relies on core technologies, namely Information and Communication Technology (ICT), mobile communication, cloud computing, virtual reality, and artificial intelligence (AI). "Smartness" or the development of digital intelligence is not merely an operational issue but tightly linked to the strategic orientation of the company. Hence, the deployment of suitable systems, tools, technologies, and skills is not about the specific singular functionality in a particular application context, but particularly involves the extent to which technology and the ability to apply it, contribute to supporting new forms of collaboration and value creation across the entire company. This not only facilitates adaptation to digital transformation but also leads to increased innovation, customer benefits, and competitiveness. In this sense, digital intelligence serves as a transmission belt for achieving company goals, where standards for new technologies and skills must align with customer benefits, multifunctionality, connectivity, integration, and synchronization for a holistic and strategic understanding of the digital and analog performance and value chain of a company to succeed (Gardini and Sommer, 2023; Liu et al., 2023).

The diversity of potential applications, along with the dynamics and heterogeneity of the described digital landscape or ecosystem (Schaffer et al., 2021), pose significant challenges for many actors in the tourism industry. This includes numerous participants, rapidly growing computing capabilities, an expanded range of data generation and processing (e.g., big/open data, blockchain, cloud computing, data mining), enhanced information and communication technologies (e.g., Internet, broadband, mobile technology), the network effects of social media (Facebook, TikTok, Instagram, etc.), mobile hardware and software technologies (e.g., apps, tablets, smart phones, wearables), and the aforementioned AI (e.g., generative AI, conversational AI, Internet of Things, virtual reality). In the hotel industry, essential technical equipment includes PMS systems, booking engines, channel management, revenue management, rate shopping tools, and online reputation tools for the majority of larger establishments. However, newer digital technologies, such as chatbots, digital keys, self-check-in tools, cloud PMS systems, or systems for digital organizational efficiency currently have a lower adoption rate in the hotel industry (Hotelhero, 2020; Roland Berger, 2019). Additionally, virtual/mixed reality applications, robotics, or more sophisticated systems for intelligent hotel rooms are worldwide not yet widely present on the industry's digital agenda (Lee et al., 2021; Borkmann et al., 2019; Bowen and Morosan, 2018).

The example of data management may exemplify the current challenges and expansion of "smartness" or "digital intelligence" in the tourism industry. In a core area of digitalization—the purposeful handling of data—the complexity of the challenge is still underestimated in many parts of the industry. Considering that the raw material for any digital or AI information is data, the quality, availability, and processing of this data inevitably play a crucial role in digitalization. This applies both at the macro level, involving infrastructure (e.g., big data, open data), and at the micro level, involving the competition and market dynamics among various players in tourism (e.g., CRM, customer data management, data warehouse). For instance, at the macro level, the issue of open data in tourism, despite numerous promising approaches to establish open and comprehensive data hubs, has stagnated for years. Efforts are still ongoing to create suitable conditions (Schmucker and Reif, 2021; BTE, 2022). This observation corresponds to the current state of data management at the operational level of tourism service providers. Assuming that the "heart" of a tourism company's data management lies in aligning and synchronizing information, systems, and data sources toward a long-demanded "single customer view" (Stone et al., 2003), the majority of actors in the tourism industry, beyond standardized loyalty programs, are far from displaying a professional and centralized customer data management (Toedt, 2021; Grimaldi et al., 2020; Gardini 2017b; Pucciani and Murphy, 2011).

If the "smartness" or digital intelligence of a tourism company is measured by whether the systems, tools, technologies, and capabilities used are suitable for increasing customer satisfaction and the quality of the traveler or guest experience—as is often implicitly assumed in the literature on smart tourism (Gretzel, 2022; Neuhofer et al., 2015) but often not necessarily the case in reality (Bichler et al., 2019; Bolton et al., 2018)—then many tourism companies seem to have a significant need to catch up in terms of their digital capabilities to develop or deliver an individualized and personalized customer experience, thus conveying a unique and superior customer experience. This is not only because many tourism companies find it challenging to understand and identify their analog and/or digital "key customer journeys" (Rawson et al., 2013) and "experiential touchpoints" (Kim and So, 2022), but particularly due to technological problems and expertise deficits in customer-related data management. Outdated system landscapes, the complexity and fragmentation of deployed technologies, and lacking integration and migration mechanisms in many tourism companies lead to an inefficient IT configuration that often does not comply with current data protection regulations. In the hotel industry, for example, many systems required for hotel operations, from PMS, RMS, and CRS to IBE, CRM, and POS, are often not or only marginally interconnected, resulting in data quality issues. In larger hotels, up to 30 different (incorrect/redundant) guest profiles may exist, which are of little use for marketing automation or individualized customer experiences and relationships (Toedt, 2021; h2c, 2019). *"Despite the 'R' in CRM and the $11 billion spent on CRM software annually, many companies don't understand customer relationships at all...In study after study, we find that consumers are frequently frustrated by companies' inability to meet their relationship expectations"* (Avery et al., 2014, p. 73f.). Beyond "classic" CRM applications or automated marketing and sales systems (omnichannel, marketing/data automation, etc.), more advanced systems for capturing customer-relevant and behavior-oriented data (e.g., machine/deep learning, web/predictive analytics, data mining, big data solutions, etc.) highlight, that it is not so much the technological possibilities that limit the digital intelligence of tourism companies but, especially, deficient knowledge bases in digital know-how at managerial and operational levels and the resulting limited digital competence of tourism actors.

Despite its tradition as an information business, a significant portion of the tourism industry still lacks digital affinity, digital skills, and digital competence. This assessment doesn't only concern individual company sectors, functions, or individuals; it extends across the majority of tourist organizations and companies at all hierarchical levels (Carlisle et al., 2021; Borkmann et al., 2020). The digitalization process not only requires a transformation or adaptation of educational profiles in tourism across both academic and non-academic areas but also compels stakeholders to define digital competence and skills specific to their companies, deemed necessary at different hierarchical levels. A critical factor in the digital maturity of tourism companies is particularly the digital competence of leaders. The greater strategic relevance of the digital realm and the associated change process necessitate crucial support at the decision-making level; without this backing, the digital transformation is unlikely to succeed. Every tourism company must ponder the skills and competencies required for a digital leader to recognize digital potentials and develop the company within the framework of digital transformation (Kollmann, 2020). In this context, Carlisle et al. (2021) emphasize that in tourism education, the focus should not primarily be on showcasing the specific capabilities of new technologies but rather on understanding the fundamental effects of digitalization on tourism: *"Educational programs in tourism should not drift away too far from their home ground and should primarily be dealing with the effects of digitization on the socio-economic, commercial, managerial, sustainable, and ethical aspects of tourism—instead of focusing on technology as such (e.g., machine learning, programming, software development, artificial intelligence)."*

3.2.4 DIGITAL ORGANIZATION: SAME SAME BUT DIFFERENT?

The digital or "digitized" tourism organization forms the foundation of a successful digital transformation. Therefore, digitalization becomes the primary task of today's corporate leadership. It involves exploring how tourism companies can leverage the potential of digital technologies for their own evolution, ensuring economic resilience and continued growth in the digital era (Rheinhardt, 2020). Particularly crucial is the ability to enable structures, processes, and people to operate agile and flexibly. In the realm of digitalization, the focus is on utilizing data to make better and faster decisions, shifting decision-making to smaller, cross-functional teams, and developing iterative and swift approaches. This mindset should not be limited to a handful of functions and protagonists but should involve a broad spectrum of corporate processes, structures, and employees. This includes fostering creative partnerships with external entities to expand necessary skills and create an environment that nurtures the development of new ideas (Kollmann 2020; Dorner and Edelman, 2015). For tourism companies of all sizes and industries, the emphasis should not only be on defining a digital strategy and leadership concept, outlining digital product and service offerings but also advancing the digitalization and interconnection of corporate processes with a focus on desired operational efficiency. Ultimately, ensuring the digital intelligence of the organization through a suitable customer-centric information and data concept is essential (Davenport and Redman, 2021; Biesel and Hame, 2018).

A customer-centric digitalization strategy necessitates a restructuring of the organizational structure and decision-making pathways. Given the significance of digitalization and the responsibility of employees for a compelling customer experience, this restructuring should not only affect the organization as a whole but particularly the structural and procedural relationships of marketing, IT, and HR. It underscores the need for enhanced digital competency and emphasizes the relevance of a customer-centric integration and reorganization of marketing/sales, IT, and HR to achieve sustainable competitive advantages in both analog and digital marketing efforts. The fact that diverse cultures and mindsets within the company converge here, requiring joint efforts for customer benefit, satisfaction, and loyalty, poses a challenging task for top management (Gardini, 2021a, 2021b). The consistent development of new structures, processes, and competencies around the central drivers of customer value (product experience, brand relevance, quality of customer relationships) is considered essential even in the digital age (Gardini, 2019). However, significant strategic and organizational questions regarding value creation, competence and role distribution, cooperation, and responsibility culture, as well as information and result in sovereignty in digital tourism management, remain unresolved and need to be individually addressed by each company (Dawar and Bendle, 2018; Kreutzer et al., 2017; Swaan Arons et al., 2014). In the digital marketing reality of tourism, new and unfamiliar problems and challenges arise. For instance, questions emerge about who conceptually, content-wise, and organizationally oversees the digital and/or analog customer journey or the total customer experience concerning cost, quality, and time process drivers. Immediately associated with this is the decision on who should be responsible for customer data, customer profitability, or customer value. This raises the question of whether it is advisable in the digital age to appoint a chief technology officer or chief digital officer and how organizational and information hierarchies between marketing, operations, HR, and information technology (IT) should be shaped in the future regarding the optimization of digital and analog marketing efforts (Gardini, 2019; Rust et al., 2010).

In this regard, it is crucial for many tourism companies to redefine organizational interfaces and structures, consolidating them in alignment with a customer-centric approach. Despite this imperative, most tourism companies still struggle to embrace process orientation as a structuring determinant for experience management. This challenge persists despite the fact that the customer journey inherently overlays the functional organizational structures of many companies in its content-conceptual orientation. The endeavors of marketing to make the customer the central focal point of organizational design and development often face strong opposition from departmental egos, silo thinking, and misallocated control mechanisms. Younger, smaller, and owner-led tourism companies may potentially have adaptation and implementation advantages over tourism corporations and system operators. The granularity of the tourism industry, represented by small and medium-sized or owner-managed structures, offers a high degree of strategic and operational flexibility and agility in decision-making. However, cultural barriers, knowledge gaps, and financial constraints, especially in the digital transformation, hinder small and medium-sized companies in the tourism sector (Laesser et al., 2021).

When structures, processes, and competencies change, the nature of leadership and collaboration in the "new" digitized organization also evolves. This aspect is extensively discussed in academia and practice under the term "new work," addressing future-proof and digital work environments. New work, more of a trend term than a specific concept or model, is widely used in the context of digitalization without necessarily being digitally connected to its origin by philosopher Frithjof Bergmann (Schermuly, 2020). Apart from basic principles, like freedom, self-responsibility, meaning, development, and social responsibility, a multitude of new work measures are discussed in the literature, such as decentralization and flexibilization of work, flat hierarchies, agile project work, holacracy, and so forth. The digital transformation significantly propels the "new work" philosophy, enabling new forms of work and diverse flexibility paths. Networking, collaboration, and agility emerge as the new key principles in a transforming digital and virtual work environment. Digitalization accelerates the increasing blurring of boundaries between work and life. Notably, the COVID-19 pandemic has led to the dissolution of the traditional workday, exemplified by the widespread adoption of remote work. These experiences have led to changes on both the company and employee sides, prompting a reevaluation of organizational issues in many tourism companies. Consequently, the structures, processes, and competencies of tourism work environments need to be renegotiated in a company-specific manner (Borkmann et al., 2020).

Whether such transformation processes ultimately benefit or harm the company's performance will be determined on a company-specific basis. It depends on the business model, company size, digital maturity, cultural prerequisites, and, importantly, the approach that appears suitable from the company's perspective to advance the digital agenda without losing sight of the customer. Tourism companies willing to shift their mindset from a purely technology-oriented approach (inside out) to a customer-centric approach (outside in)—and to organize themselves with all the consequences around customer needs—are likely to win the competition for customers (Markey, 2020; Esch and Kochann, 2019).

3.3 CONCLUSION

In light of the discussed aspects, it becomes increasingly evident that the future viability of many tourism service providers will be determined by their ability to actively manage technological disruption and transform traditional tourism offerings into digitized, and thus sustainable business models. To succeed amid such profound environmental shifts, a strategic orientation is indispensable—one that aims to sharpen customer focus through targeted digital initiatives and innovation. Technology, in this context, must always serve as a means to an end: its deployment should be guided by the goal of generating substantial added value for customers and securing the long-term competitiveness and resilience of the organization. Despite the pronounced heterogeneity of the tourism industry—with its wide array of sub-sectors and business models (e.g., hospitality, gastronomy, transport, travel agencies, and intermediaries)—a common observation persists across the sector: the strategic and cultural dimensions of digital transformation are still underestimated by many stakeholders. While traditional industry actors increasingly display openness toward new technologies and digital working methods, the pace of economic and technological change continues to outstrip the psychological and mental readiness of those responsible for shaping this transformation. This discrepancy underscores one of the key strategic challenges for the future: the necessity for tourism companies to develop a holistic and organization-wide understanding of both digital and analog management. Rather than remaining confined to individual projects, tools, or analysis methods, digital transformation must become embedded as a core capability of the organization. Only then can companies move from being passive recipients of technological trends to active drivers of company-specific digitalization processes—thus positioning themselves to remain relevant and competitive in a dynamic marketplace.

To attain such a position of *digital leadership*, technological competence alone is not sufficient. What is required is a fundamental intellectual and cultural shift that demands openness, adaptability, and commitment across all organizational levels. Digital transformation changes not only the technological foundations of work but also the nature of leadership and collaboration itself. As new roles emerge and traditional positions become obsolete or are fundamentally redefined, tourism faces an acute need for educational reform, reskilling, and systematic knowledge management to avoid stagnation due to talent shortages and obsolete qualification structures (Samala et al., 2020). Indeed, the digital maturity of an organization is closely tied to the digital maturity of its people. Therefore, the human dimension of digital transformation is a decisive factor in the long-term success of tourism enterprises. Alongside technological infrastructure and organizational processes, it is the employees—through their competencies, mindset, and readiness to engage with change—who ultimately determine whether the industry can not only keep pace with digital developments but actively shape and lead them.

KEYWORDS

- **customer-centric approach**
- **digital maturity**
- **digital transformation**
- **digital intelligence**
- **strategic effectiveness**
- **smartness**
- **tech and touch**

REFERENCES

Ardito, L., Cerchione, R., Del Vecchio, P., & Raguseo, E. (2019). Big data in smart tourism: Challenges, issues and opportunities. *Current Issues in Tourism, 22*(15), 1805–1809.

Avery, J., Fournier, S., & Wittenbraker, J. (2014). Unlock the mysteries of your customer relationships are you connecting with consumers the way they want you to? *Harvard Business Review, 92*(7/8), 72–81.

Barta, T. (2020, June 15). *The time for marketing is now (again)*. https://thomasbarta.com/the-time-for-marketing-is-now-again/.

Bichler, B., Pikkemaat, B., & Peters, M. (2019). Analogisierung als Folge zunehmender Digitalisierung im Tourismus. In T. Bieger, P. Beritelli, & C. Laesser (Hrsg.), *Schweizer Jahrbuch für Tourismus 2018/2019* (85–98). ESV.

Bieger, T., & Beritelli, P. (2018). Dienstleistung 4.0—Der Tourismus als Lead-Industrie? In M. Bruhn & K. Hadwich (Hrsg.), *Service Business Development* (pp. 587–601). Springer Gabler.

Biesel, H., & Hame, H. (2018). *Vertrieb und Marketing in der digitalen Welt*. Springer Gabler.

Bolton, R. N., McColl-Kennedy, J. R., Cheung, L., Gallan, A., Orsingher, C., Witell, L., & Zaki, M. (2018). Customer experience challenges: Bringing together digital, physical and social realms. *Journal of Service Management, 29*(5), 776–808.

Borkmann, V. (2020). Future Hotel—*Das Smarte Resiliente Hotel*. Fraunhofer Verlag.

Borkmann, V., Brecheisen, M., Endress, C., Strunck, S., & Rief, S. (2020). *FutureHotel—Zukunftsfähige Arbeitswelten im Gastgewerbe*. Fraunhofer Verlag.

Borkmann, V., Stolze, D., & Bruns, C. (2019). *Future Hotel—Das intelligente Hotelzimmer.* Fraunhofer Verlag.

Bowen, J., & Morosan, C. (2018). Beware hospitality industry: The robots are coming. *Worldwide Hospitality and Tourism Themes, 10*(6), 726–733.

BTE—Tourismus- und Regionalberatung (2022). *DMO DigitalMonitor: Stand der Digitalisierung in deutschen Destinationen*. Berlin u.a.

Buhalis, D. (2003). *eTourism: Information technology for strategic tourism management*. Financial Times Prentice Hall.

Buhalis, D., Harwood, T., Bogicevic, V., Viglia, G., Beldona, S., & Hofacker, C. (2019). Technological disruptions in services: Lessons from tourism and hospitality. *Journal of Service Management, 30*(4), 484–506.

Carlisle, S., Ivanov, S., & Dijkmans, C. (2021). The digital skills divide: Evidence from the European tourism industry. *Journal of Tourism Futures*, Vol. ahead-of-print No. ahead-of-print. https://doi.org/10.1108/JTF-07-2020-0114.

Chanias, S., & Hess, T. (2016). How digital are we? Maturity models for the assessment of a company's status in the digital transformation. Management Report/Institut für Wirtschaftsinformatik und Neue Medien, 2, 1–14.

Chen, S., Tian, D., Law, R., & Zhang, M. (2021). Bibliometric and visualized review of smart tourism research. *International Journal of Tourism Research*, Vol. ahead-of-print. DOI: 10.1002/jtr.2501.

Davenport, T. H., & Redman, T. C. (2021). Digital transformation comes down to talent in four key areas. *Harvard Business Review*, Special Issue, Summer, S. 139–141.

Davenport, T. H., & Westerman, G. (2018). Why so many high-profile digital transformations fail. https://hbr.org/2018/03/why-so-many-high-profile-digital-transformations-fail.
Dawar, N., & Bendle, E. (2018). Marketing in the age of Alexa. *Harvard Business Review, 96*(3), 80–86.
Demary, V., & Goecke, H. (2021). Digitalisierung der Branchen in Deutschland—eine empirische Erhebung. *Wirtschaftsdienst, 101*(3), 181–185.
Deutsche Telekom. (2022). *Digitalisierungsindex Mittelstand 2020/2021: Der digitale Status quo des deutschen Mittelstands.* Bonn.
Dörner, K., & Edelman, D. (2015). *What 'digital' really means.* McKinsey & Company.
Duwe, J. (2018). *Beidhändige Führung: Wie Sie als Führungskraft in großen Organisationen Innovationssprünge ermöglichen.* Springer Gabler, Berlin • Heidelberg. DOI: 10.1007/978-3-662-55856-0.
Egger, R. (2022). *Applied data science in tourism—Interdisciplinary approaches, methodologies, and application.* Springer.
Esch, F. J., & Kochann, D. (2019). *Kunden begeistern mit System.* Campus.
Esch, F. R. (2021). *Purpose und vision.* Campus.
Francis, H., & Baum, T. (2018). HR transformation within the hotel industry: Building capacity for change. *Worldwide Hospitality and Tourism Themes, 10*(1), 86–100.
Frankiewicz, B., & Chamorro-Premuzic, T. (2021). Digital transformation is about talent, not technology. *Harvard Business Review*, Special Issue, Summer 2021, 134–136.
Frehse, J. (2006). Erfolgsfaktoren im internationalen Markenmanagement von Hotelunternehmen: Ein integrativer Ansatz unter Berücksichtigung der Ressourcenorientierung. *Jahrbuch der Absatz- und Verbrauchsforschung, 2*, 140–154.
Furr, N., Shipilov, A. (2021). Digital doesn′t have to be disruptive. *Harvard Business Review*, Special Issue, Summer, 93–99.
Gardini, M. A. (2016). Zukunft Personal—Personal der Zukunft: Plädoyer für eine neue personalpolitische Agenda im Tourismus. In T. Bieger, P. Beritelli, & C. Laesser (Hrsg.), *Schweizer Jahrbuch für Tourismus 2015/2016* (99–113). ESV.
Gardini, M. A. (2017a). Evolution oder Revolution—Tourismusmarketing in der digitalen Welt. In M. Landvogt, A. Brysch, & M. A. Gardini (Hrsg.), *Tourismus—E-Tourismus—M-Tourismus: Herausforderungen und Trends der Digitalisierung im Tourismus, Schriften zu Tourismus und Freizeit* (pp. 43–52). ESV.
Gardini, M. A. (2017b). Leadership und Exzellenz im Tourismusmarketing: Was Tourismusunternehmen leisten müssen! In M. A. Gardini (Hrsg.), *Marketingexzellenz im Tourismus: Konzepte—Fallstudien—Best Practices* (pp. 9–38). ESV.
Gardini, M. A. (2019). Marketing goes digital—Schöne neue Welt im Tourismusmarketing? In T. Bieger, P. Beritelli & C. Laesser (Hrsg.), *Schweizer Jahrbuch für Tourismus 2018/2019* (131–148). ESV.
Gardini, M. A. (2021a). *Leadership im Marketing.* Springer Gabler.
Gardini, M. A. (2021b). Beyond purpose: Von der Haltung zur Handlung. *Markenartikel, 83*(10), 100–103.
Gardini, M. A. (2022). *Marketing-Management in der Hotellerie* (4. Aufl.). DeGruyter.
Gardini, M. A. (2025). A balancing act—Developing a digital leadership strategy between digital and analogue worlds in the tourism and hotel industry. *International Marketing Journal of Culture and Tourism,* 6, 14–21.

Gardini, M. A., & Sommer, G. (2023). Digitalisierung im Tourismus—Tradition muss laufen lernen! In Gardini, M. A., Sommer, G. (Hrsg.), *Digital Leadership im tourismus: Digitalisierung und Künstliche Intelligenz als Wettbewerbsfaktoren der Zukunft* (pp. 3–41). Springer Gabler.

Ghandi, P., Khanna, S., & Ramaswamv, S. (2016). Which industries are the most digital (and why). *Harvard Business Review, 94*(1), 2–6.

Gnamm, J., Kalmbach, R., & Schertler, M. (2018). *Von der Vision zur Transformation: Digitalisierung ist Chefsache.* Bain & Company.

Goran, J., LaBerge, L., & Srinivasan, R. (2017). *Culture for a digital age*. McKinsey & Company.

Gouthier, M., & Schmid, S. (2003). Customers and customer relationships in service firms: The perspective of the resource-based view. *Marketing Theory*, *3*(1), 119–143.

Gretzel, U., Zhong, L., & Koo, C. (2016). Application of smart tourism to cities. *International Journal of Tourism Cities*, *2*(2).

Gretzel, U. (2022). The Smart DMO: A new step in the digital transformation of destination management organizations. *European Journal of Tourism Research, 30*, doi.org/10.54055/ejtr.v30i.2589.

Gretzel, U., & Scarpino-Johns, M. (2018). Destination resilience and smart tourism destinations. *Tourism Review International, 22*, 263–276.

Gretzel, U., Sigala, M. & Xiang, Z. et al. (2015). *Smart tourism: Foundations and developments. Electronic Markets, 25*, 179–188.

Grimaldi, M., Ciasullo, M. V., Troisi, O., & Castellani, P. (2020). Data-based value co-creation in smart service systems: A reinterpretation of customer journey. *International Journal of Business and Management, 15*(6), 212–121.

h2c (2019). *The state of CRM and guest data management*. Ratingen.

Haux, R., Gahl, K., Jipp, M., Kruse, R., & Richter, O. (2021). *Zusammenwirken von natürlicher und künstlicher Intelligenz*. Springer Nature.

Hennig-Thurau, T. v. d. Esche, J., & Wege, E. (2014, Sept). Marketing in der digitalen Welt. *Harvard Business Manager,* 34–43.

Hotelhero. (2020). *Der deutsche Hotel Technologiemarkt 2020*. Berlin.

Jovičić, Dobrica Z. (2019). *From the traditional understanding of tourism destination to the smart tourism destination. Current ISSUES in Tourism, 22*(3), 276–282.

Kane, G. C., Palmer, D., Phillips, A. N., Kiron, D., & Buckley, N. (2015). Strategy, not technology, drives digital transformation. *MIT Sloan Management Review, 14*, 1–25.

Kim, H., & So, K. K. F. (2022). Two decades of customer experience research in hospitality and tourism: A bibliometric analysis and thematic content analysis. *International Journal of Hospitality Management, 100*, 2022. doi.org/10.1016/j.ijhm.2021.103082.

Kollmann, T. (2020). *Digital Leadership: Grundlagen der Unternehmensführung in der Digitalen Wirtschaft*. Springer Gabler.

Kreutzer, R. T., Neugebauer, T., & Pattloch, A. (2017). *Digital business leadership.* Springer Gabler.

Kusluvan, S., Kusluvan, Z., Ilhan, I., & Buyruk, L. (2010). The human dimension—A review of human resources management issues in the tourism and hospitality industry. *Cornell Hotel and Restaurant Administration Quarterly, 51*, 171–214.

Laesser, C., Schegg, R., Bandi Tanner, M., Liebrich, A., Gasser, F., Ogi, R., Stuber-Berries, N., & Fux, M. (2021). *Digitalisierung im Schweizer Tourismus: Progress Report.* Bericht im Auftrag des Staatssekretariats für Wirtschaft SECO.

Lee, Y., Lee, S., & Kim, D. Y. (2021). Exploring hotel guests' perceptions of using robot assistants. *Tourism Management Perspectives, 37*, 100781. doi.org/10.1016/j.tmp.2020.100781.

Liu, J., Hall, C., Zhu, C., & Cheng, V. (2023). Redefining the concept of smart tourism in tourism and hospitality. *Anatolia,* 1–13. 10.1080/13032917.2023.2282712.

Maas, R. (2019). *Generation Z für Personaler und Führungskräfte*. Hanser.

Markey, R. (2020). Are you under evaluating your customers? *Harvard Business Review, 98*(1/2), 42–50.

Martin, J.-F. (2018). *Unlocking success in digital transformations.* https://www.mckinsey.com/~/media/McKinsey/Business%20Functions/Organization/Our%20Insights/Unlocking%20success%20in%20digital%20transformations/Unlocking-success-in-digital-transformations.ashx#:~:text=Transformations%20are%20hard%.

McKinsey (2020, Nov). *More than a mission statement: How the 5Ps embed purpose to deliver value*. McKinsey & Company.

Myers, D. G. (2015). *Psychologie* (3. Aufl.). Springer.

Neuhofer, B., Buhalis, D., & Ladkin, A. (2015). Smart technologies for personalized experiences: A case study in the hospitality domain. *Electronic Markets, 25*(3), 243–254.

O'Connor, P. (2021). Digital transformation: The blurring of organizational boundaries in hotel distribution. In Gardini, M. A., Ottenbacher, M., & Schuckert, M. (Hrsg.), *The Routledge companion to international hospitality management* (pp. 142–151). Routledge.

O'Reilly, C. A., & Tushman, M. L. (2004). The ambidextrous organization. *Harvard Business Review, 82*(2), 74–81.

Online Birds. (2023). *Hotel digital score Branchen-report 2023.* München.

Pencarelli, T. (2020). The digital revolution in the travel and tourism industry. *Information Technology & Tourism, 22*(3), 455–476.

Piccoli, G. (2008). Information technology in hotel management: A framework for evaluating the sustainability of IT-dependent competitive advantage. *Cornell Hospitality Quarterly, 49*(3), 282–296.

Poon, A. (1993). *Tourism, technologies and competitive strategies*. CAB International.

Porter, M. E. (1996). What is strategy? Harvard Business Review, *74*(11/12), 37–54.

Porter, M. E. (2001). Strategy and the Internet. *Harvard Business Review, 79*(3), 63–78.

Porter, M. E. (2004). Competitive *s*trategy: Techniques for *a*nalyzing *i*ndustries and *c*ompetitors. Free Press.

Proff, H., Ahrens, C., Neuroth, W., Proff, H., Knobbe, F., Szybisty, G., & Sommer, S. (2021). *Accelerating Digitalization—Chancen der Digitalisierung erkennen und nutzen.* Springer Gabler.

Pucciani, K., & Murphy, H. C. (2011). An investigation of data management and property management systems in hotels. *Tourism and Hospitality Management, 17*(1), 101–114.

Quinn, R. E., & Thakor, A. V. (2018). Creating a purpose driven organization. *Harvard Business Review, 96*(4), 78–85.

Raisch, S., Birkinshaw, J., Probst, G., & Tushman, M. L. (2009). Organizational ambidexterity: Balancing exploitation and exploration for sustained performance. *Organization Science, 20*(4), 685–695.

Rawson, A., Duncan, E., & Jones, C. (2013). The truth about customer experience. *Harvard Business Review, 91*(9), 90–98.

Remane, G., Hanelt, A., Wiesboeck, F., & Kolbe, L. M. (2017). *Digital maturity in traditional industries-an exploratory analysis*. ECIS, 25th. European Conference on Information Systems (ECIS), June 2017, Guimarães.

Rheinhardt, K. (2020). *Digitale Transformation der Organisation: Grundlagen, Praktiken und Praxisbeispiele der digitalen Unternehmensentwicklung.* Springer Gabler.

Rodwell, J. J., & Shadur, M. A. (2007). Strategy as a configuration of activities: Evidence that strategy absence exists. *Strategic Change, 16*(1–2), 43–55.

Roland Berger (2019). *Hotellerie 4.1—Digitalisierungsstudie*. München.

Rust, R. T., Moorman, C., & Bhalla, G. (2010). Rethinking marketing. *Harvard Business Review, 88*(1/2), 94–101.

Samala, N., Katkam, B. S., Bellamkonda, R. S., & Rodriguez, R. V. (2020). Impact of AI and robotics in the tourism sector: A critical insight. *Journal of Tourism Futures, 8*(1), 73–87.

Schaffer, N., Engert, M., Sommer, G., Shokoui, J., & Krcmar, H. (2021). The digitized ecosystem of tourism in Europe: Current trends and implications. In W. Wörndl, C. Koo & J. L. Stienmetz (Hrsg.), *Information and communication technologies in tourism* (pp. 352–364.) Springer.

Schermuly, C. C. (2020, Dec). Wann New Work funktioniert und wann nicht. *Harvard Business, Manager, H.12*, 22–29.

Schlotter, L., & Hubert, P. (2020). *Generation Z—Personalmanagement und Führung.* Springer Gabler.

Schmücker, D., & Reif, J. (2021). The big data illusion. *Zeitschrift für Tourismuswissenschaft, 13*(2), 157–166.

Schuler, A. (2019). Hindernisse. Herausforderungen. Chancen. *Tourismus Digital, DTV-Magazin*, pp. 4–7.

Sigala, M. (2014). E-hospitality and technology. I. S. Pantelidis (Hrsg.), *The Routledge handbook of hospitality management* (pp. 287–301). Routledge.

Stoll, S., & Dörn, S. (2021). *Digitale Intelligenz—Das Betriebssystem für Digitale Revolutionäre*. Springer.

Stone, M., Foss, B., Henderson, I., Irwin, D., O'Donnell, J., & Woodcock, N. (2003). The quality of customer information management in customer life cycle management. *Journal of Database Marketing & Customer Strategy Management, 10*(3), 240–254.

Strategy&PwC (2013). *Measuring industry digitalization: Leaders and laggards in the digital-economy.* https://www.strategyand.pwc.com/gx/en/insights/2002-2013/measuring-industry-digitalization/strategyand-measuring-industry-digitalization-leaders-laggards-digital-economy.pdf

Schulz, A., Weithöner, U., Egger, R., & Goecke, R. (Eds.). (2014). *eTourismus: Prozesse und Systeme: Informationsmanagement im Tourismus*. Walter de Gruyter GmbH & Co KG.

Swaan Arons, M., Driest, F., & Weed, K. (2014). The ultimate marketing machine. *Harvard Business Review, 92*(7–8), 55–63.

Tabrizi, B., Lam, E., Girard, K., & Irvin, V. (2019). Digital transformation is not about technology. *Harvard Business Review, 13*(March), 1–6.

Tabrizi, B., Lam, E., Girard, K., & Irvin, V. (2021). Digital transformation is not about technology. *Harvard Business Review*, Special Issue, Summer, 120–122.

Thomas, G. (2024). Challenges and trends of digital innovation in the tourism sector: Contemporary literature review. *Open Journal of Business and Management, 12*, 179–190. https://doi.org/10.4236/ojbm.2024.121013

Thordsen, T., Murawski, M., & Bick, M. (2020). How to measure digitalization? A critical evaluation of digital maturity models. In M. Hattingh, M. Matthee, H. Smuts, L. Pappas, Y. Dwivedi, & M. Mäntymäki (Hrsg.), *Responsible design, implementation and use of information and communication technology*, I3E 2020. Lecture Notes in Computer Science, Vol. 12066. Springer. https://doi.org/10.1007/978-3-030-44999-5_30.

Toedt, M. (2021). *Wer ersetzt das PMS?* Whitepaper. Daily point.

Tokarski, K. O., Kissling-Näf, I., & Schellinger, J. (2021). Digital Business in der Praxis. In J. Schellinger, K. O. Tokarski, I. Kissling-Näf (Hrsg.), *Digital business: Analysen und Handlungsfelder in der Praxis* (pp. 1–13). Springer Gabler.

Wirtz, B. W. (2021). *Digital business and electronic commerce: strategy, business models and technology*. Springer.

Wise, N., & Heidari, H. (2019). Developing smart tourism destinations with the internet of things. In *Big data and innovation in tourism, travel, and hospitality: Managerial approaches, techniques, and applications* (pp. 21-29). Singapore: Springer Singapore.

Ye, B. H., Ye, H., & Law, R. (2020). Systematic review of smart tourism research. *Sustainability, 12*, 3401. DOI: 10.3390/su12083401.

CHAPTER 4

Digital Traveler

SEZA ZERMAN

Safranbolu Tourism Faculty, Karabuk University, Karabuk, Türkiye

ABSTRACT

Digital technologies and digital tools have revolutionized the tourism industry, offering variety of digital support for physical travel, and digital opportunities for tourism experience. This chapter examines the travelers, who are now able to utilize technology for physical tourism experience as well as for digital travel options while they are physically not mobile. This technology brings its own downsides; thus, digital free holidays are now options of alternative tourism. This chapter also addresses the digital opportunities that are available for travelers as well as digital-free alternatives when technology becomes harmful in1 physical, social, and mental aspects.

4.1 INTRODUCTION

It is now commonly agreed that tourism is a fundamental industry for countries and regions with a broad economic impact. World Travel & Tourism Council's (WTTC) latest annual research shows:

1. In 2023, the travel & tourism sector contributed 9.1% to the global GDP; an increase of 23.2% from 2022 and only 4.1% below the 2019 (pre-COVID) level,

Digitalization in Tourism. Hulya Akdemir Cengiz, Seza Zerman, Aysegul Acar, and Faizan Ali (Eds.)

DOI: 10.1201/9781779644770-5

2. In 2023, there were 27 million new jobs, representing a 9.1% increase compared to 2022, and only 1.4% below the 2019 level,
3. Domestic visitor spending rose by 18.1% in 2023, surpassing the 2019 level,
4. International visitor spending registered a 33.1% jump in 2023 but remained 14.4% below the 2019 total (WTTC, 2024).

In addition to the contribution of tourism to the countries, travelers benefit from tourism activities; accordingly, from tourist's perspective, travel motivations are various, such as:

1. Relaxation needs,
2. Stimulation (safety and security) needs,
3. Self-esteem and development needs,
4. Fulfillment needs,
5. Relationship needs (Pearce and Lee, 2005).

These motivations can trigger not only physical travel but also any other travel-related activities, such as information seeking, or experience sharing. In fact, tourism is "home-away-back- home" activity (Tjostheim and Waterworth, 2022, p. 5). It is now part of personal life of majority and when a traveler leaves a place, they leave a part of their identity and adopt another one (Tjostheim and Waterworth, 2022, p. 5). This departure is not only physical; it can be digital departure, if, and when the travelers utilize current technology to be digitally mobile depending on their own choice. They can either prefer physical travel and utilize technology to stay connected with their origin, or technology can be a tool for their digital travel. Fan et al. (2019) state, within the tourism industry, tourists now have the power to decide when and how they connect their home and environment, and what content they share with their connections.

Either physical or digital; tourism overall is an experience. It has been almost three decades since Pine and Gilmore (1999) introduced the term experience economy in 1998, by explaining the process starting from commodities, goods, services, and finally shifting to an experience. The authors also argue that the concept of experience is going beyond common tangible activities, such as theme parks and theaters (Pine and Gilmore, 1998). In the context of tourism, experience is defined as a comprehensive construct, which is different from everyday activities; the dynamic nature brings recognition of increasing importance of concepts, such as consumer involvement, co-creation, and technological implementations in tourism experience (Neuhofer et al., 2014). Accordingly, the tourism experience evolved overtime and went beyond theme parks to create themed environments through digital tools.

Recently, technology is in every aspect of individual's everyday lives. For example, remote experts and digital assistants are now offered as two essential technology-based models to support customers' immediate needs (Parise et al., 2016); recently Xbox and PlayStation games provide an option that can be played in a tourist mode (Tjostheim and Waterworth, 2022, p. 97). It has been just a decade that Amazon transformed the customer experience and introduced Mayday in 2013, which lets users 24/7 interactively communicate with a remote tech-support with one-click on any problem with their tablets. For the company that support was almost the same experience as having an actual tech support near customers. This innovation provided an insight for the future of the impact of technology on customer experience. Such assistance and technology used in hospitality industries as well, virtual fitness instructors as a virtual concierge, where the trainers are available 24/7, wherever the individuals are around the world (Parise, et al., 2016). The industry of tourism had already been utilizing the advantages of technology, and closely applied latest developments starting from development of the Internet (Buhalis and Law, 2008). Modern tourism marketing is currently built on digital information (Nemec Rudez, 2023). Accordingly, the contemporary tourism is built around a new type of traveler, called "digital traveler." This type of travelers either utilize digital tools and technology to create, experience, and share a tourism activity; or even without physical mobility they experience the tourism activity digitally via the tools, such as augmented reality or virtual reality. Thus, this chapter addresses the possible opportunities brought by digitalization, the advantages of this digital movement, as well as the other side of the coin, the drawbacks of these technologies. Accordingly, as a tool to mitigate the negative impacts, digital free holiday concept is also addressed.

4.2 DIGITAL TRAVEL

Visual aspects are the core consumption part of tourism activity, and this is called "the tourist gaze" as Urry (1990) refers. These visuals evolved to virtual dimension, accordingly, virtual tourism and virtual reality in tourism started in 1990s (Tjostheim and Waterworth, 2022, p. 5). Due to the recent technological advances, digital interaction is now available, and tourist can also connect with their online social contacts, such as family members, friends, colleagues/clients, peer travelers and other travelers (Fan et al., 2019). Since the Internet and the new media reshaped touristic experience and weakened the boundaries of place (Fan et al., 2019), now the travelers can remain connected to their origin destination and connections; or regardless the physical places and destinations, they can be mobile and travel digitally.

4.2.1 DIGITAL TRAVEL AS AN ALTERNATIVE FOR PHYSICAL TRAVEL

Digital travel, while the individual is physically stationary, is a promising option in the tourism industry. In case physical travel is difficult, impossible, or even prohibited, digital travel will be the substitute and mitigate the negative impact of social isolation (Tjostheim and Waterworth, 2022). The alternative of physical travel is not a new phenomenon. The postcards, gifts, or even cameras can be reminders of a destination as they mentally take the traveler to a certain destination as tourism is not solely a new place experience but rather an emotional phenomena of social connections and togetherness (Urry and Larsen, 2011). Thus, physical travel is not the only option for tourism experience as emotional and social connections are possible through various tools.

Music, on the other hand, proposed as another imaginative means of travel as certain music types represent certain destinations. For example, Connell and Gibson (2004) approached the alternative travel concept from the perspective of music and proposed that music enabled travelers digitally travel to destinations without physical travel. Digital travel, before the tools, such as phones, tablets, and VR technology, was possible via music as a vicarious pleasure even in 1950s. According to Connell and Gibson (2004), in 1950s and 1960s, majority of the albums aimed to "capture" the sound from long distance enabling the individual's vicarious travel to variety of holiday destinations, which was the core of virtual tourism. Different forms of music were essentially served as the metaphors of being somewhere with the distant pleasure of remote journeys.

This kind of tourism, then, was important to make travel possible even virtually, whereas physical travel was difficult due to the economic and social conditions of post-war times.

In 1970s, after the rapid development in physical mass tourism, music continued to create the sense of space, and recreate the impression of certain spaces. Unlike in the 1950s, this creation and recreation brought new-age esthetic and ideology. The design of the music provided transport to other spaces; these trips were to outer spaces in a cozy sensual environment. This kind of travel was not to actual places but rather to inner spaces. Music is able to emphasize the mystical life of traditional people, their link to their origins and specific instrument, which addresses the connection motivation of travel and tourism (Connell and Gibson (2004). For example, the exotic image of the natives of a destination on album covers were seen as the reminders of the travels to the West. In addition, as majority of music consumers in 1950s were men, gender depiction was essential part of these destinations and their presentation. In terms of destination and its representation, Hawaii was admired as an exotic destination for the travelers in the United States, whereas the Mediterranean coast was a trendy destination for Britain. By 1960s, Greek islands had the similar role for the rest of the world (Connell and Gibson, 2004). In short, starting from souvenirs and postcards as stated by Urry and Larsen, (2011), physical travel was substituted. Music, starting from 50s and 60s, built the very first example of digital travel providing local characteristics of a destination, and substituting the physical travel.

In addition to mental transportation to another destination through postcards, souvenirs, and even music, when the physical travel was impossible, or demanding; another world-wide phenomenon forced people to experience alternative travel means to physical destination: COVID-19 pandemic. The pandemic had a dramatic and strong impact on hospitality and tourism industry. Travel choices, service sectors, cultural institutions, and events were also affected as these sectors are closely related components of the industry. During the pandemic, the attitudes and behaviors on replacement of physical and virtual dimensions changed dramatically, the travel and tourism industry also experienced a dramatic shift and digital activities became new normal rather than being exceptional. Virtual visits to museums, broad-casted concerts, and events became common activities in the travel industry (Tjostheim and Waterworth, 2022, pp. 95, 129).

Addressing the intangible means of travel, such as mental transportation, tourism experience, and motivations cannot be explained from one single perspective or solely from the tangible frame. Fan et al. (2019) revealed that consistently with other studies, travel motivations are dynamic and multilevel. Thus, it can be concluded that hedonic needs would be the core as well as utilitarian needs; and intangible experiences are the part of the overall experience as well as tangible and physical experiences. Obviously virtual experiences cannot purely reproduce the sense of physical place; however, they produce substantial deception of the place (Tjostheim and Waterworth, 2022, p. 80). In their seminal work, Hirschman and Holbrook (1982) introduced the hedonic consumption term. "Hedonic consumption designates those facets of consumer behavior that relate to the multisensory, fantasy, and emotive aspects of one's experience with product" (p. 92), "hedonic consumption refers to consumers' multisensory images, fantasies, and emotional arousal in using products. This configuration of effects may be termed hedonic response" (p. 93). In their work, the authors refer multisensory dimension as the experience building on taste, sound, and visual images. Introducing these hedonic aspects had an impact on travel and tourism industry in various ways: First, any tourism experience should be elaborated through intangible benefits; and second as long as the hedonic expectations are met, physical travel might not be the only option to achieve satisfaction of travel. In other words, digital travel can be an alternative for physical travel, which requires a strategic consideration from the perspective of travelers and service providers.

4.3 THE TWO STAKEHOLDERS OF DIGITAL TRAVEL

The digital revolution created a radical shift in our world and requires scholars, managers, and citizens to understand this new phenomenon from a new perspective (Pencarelli, 2020). In other words, technological advancements require collaboration of stakeholders; for example, Known Traveler Digital Identity initiative by the World Economic Forum aims to bring together individuals, governments, travel industries, and other agents in a global approach to ensure safe and smooth travel (Serra and Leong, 2020). Thus, the two main stakeholders of digital travel are examined in detail in this chapter. Namely, travelers, who utilize technology for their travel as well as using technology to digitally travel while they are at their original destination; and the service providers who deliver customized digital services for travelers as well as taking the advantage of digital opportunities to obtain and process data and feedback.

4.3.1 DIGITAL TRAVELERS

Digital traveler can be approached in two ways; one, digital traveler is the one who is not traveling physically but digitally via digital tools, such as virtual reality, augmented reality, and so forth. According to Tjostheim and Waterworth (2022, pp. 73, 74), the major difference between physical and digital travel is the presence of travelers' physical body at the original destination. Although there are some similarities, physical and digital travel are significantly differing; however, experience of place can be similar; as digital experience can become spatial if, and when the virtual place can trigger physical senses. Place attachment is one of the essential terms in the context of tourism, and it is the bond between the traveler and a certain place. From the digital travel perspective, place attachment is closely connected to digital experience specially for the places well-known by the travelers (Tjostheim and Waterworth, 2022, pp. 73, 74).

Digital travel and digital traveler refer to different concepts, and digital traveler is not necessarily or always the agent of digital travel. By utilizing recent developments that enabled visual trips without physical trips to many places, such as museums, stadiums, and cities, digital travel is an alternative for physical travel, in case of traveling to a place or destination is prohibited, becomes difficult, or impossible (Tjostheim and Waterworth, 2022, p. 1). Digital traveler, on the other hand should be approached in two distinct ways; one, traveler that is physically still and travels via technological advancements, such as VR, AI; two, the traveler physically travels utilizing variety of digital tools, such as seeking information, sharing information, and co-creating the experience via the tools of technology.

Perhaps, digital technologies, such as VR, is not meant to be a substitute for physical travel but just another form of travel and cannot be evaluated as more or less satisfactory than its physical counterpart (Slater and Sanchez-Vives, 2016). However, regardless the travel type, digital travel-related information is inseparable aspect of tourism marketing initiatives (Nemec Rudez, 2023). Accordingly, while travelers diversify their travel choices utilizing some tools, it becomes essential to integrate technology to the actual travels. Simultaneously, UNWTO also recognized the importance of technology within the industry and regenerate tourism to incorporate technology and innovation, and sustainability. Accordingly, attempts were made to adopt digital tools (UNWTO, 2021). Technological developments change the way travelers as well as the hospitality and tourism organizations behave, especially in interacting with travelers (Yallop et al., 2023). To successfully manage the interaction with travelers; the typology and characteristics are essential to observe and evaluate wisely. One of the broadest segmentations was proposed by Fan and colleagues. Based on the findings of their study, tourist online social contact typology can be examined under the following six groups:

Disconnected immersive traveler: Motivated by self-improvement, understanding the others experiencing local culture,

1. Digital detox traveler: Motivated by understanding the others, experiencing local culture, self-reflect, emptying oneself, enhancing companion bond,
2. Diversionary traveler: Motivated by relaxation, experiencing local culture, escape from daily life, recovery,
3. Dual zone traveler: Motivated by relaxation, experiencing local culture, natural scenery; escape from the daily life, enhancing companion bond, enjoying life, cuisine, understanding the others,
4. Daily life controller: Motivated by relaxation and recovery,
5. Social media addict: Motivated by relaxation, recovery, experiencing local culture, natural scenery (Fan et al., 2019).

The authors also revealed six types of travelers based on their preferences and placed them under four categories. In their study, the travelers evaluated based on their online or face to face contact choice as follows:

1. High online contact high face to face contact: dual zone traveler.
2. Low online contact low face to face contact: diversionary traveler.
3. High online contact low face to face contact: social media addict and daily life controller.
4. High face to face contact low online contact: digital detox and disconnected immersive traveler (Fan et al., 2019).

These classifications are essential to understand the motivations and behavior of customers and their relation to technology. Additionally, the choice of online and face to face contact is not strict grouping as individual choices are time and context dependent. The preferences can change based on the group the individual is traveling with, the motivation and reason of travel, the destination, and so forth. Therefore, digital travel is the flexible choice for travelers depending on internal and external motivations. The individual side of a digital traveler would be understood better together with some individual definitions since the advance progress brought new segments and definitions to understand, monitor, and accommodate in the modern world. The following groups are now in the core of the digital environment and are essential to understand for future steps of the industry.

Digital natives: Cambridge Dictionary defines digital natives as "a person who is very familiar with digital technology, computers, and so forth; because they have grown up with them" (Cambridge Dictionary, 2024). Accordingly, these groups should be approached as the core of the technological practices. The primary characteristics of this group are being very eager and flexible to try, adapt, and switch to any novel service, product, and idea. As this group considers technology and technological devices as inevitable part of their lives, the industry should provide online component for any product or service that they provide. Digital immigrants: According to Cambridge Dictionary, "a person who started using digital technology, computers, the Internet, and so forth during their adult life but did not grow up using them" are considered as digital immigrants (Cambridge Dictionary, 2024). Thus, compared to digital natives, it can be argued that digital immigrants are reluctant and less flexible, in terms of technology and its adaptation in their plans such as travel. For digital immigrants' travel promotional materials, the options should be in a way that encourage face to face interaction with locals, share the local shops, and provide an environment to meet other travelers that would work to attract travelers (Fan, et al., s 2019). In short, while digital natives are generally fast, young, future oriented, multitasking, playful, digital, action-focused, and constant connection seekers; digital immigrants are slow, seniors, past oriented, logical, serious, analog, knowledge based, and isolation seekers (Bayne and Ross, 2007). As it is not easy to segment the travelers based on one single characteristic, the distinction between digital immigrants and digital natives is not crystal-clear. Thus, the digital travelers can be the member of both segments. Even more, due to their flexibility and mobility, digital natives can be volunteers to temporarily disconnect and seek other experiences for their travel plans.

Digital nomads are a different segment from short term business and leisure tourists; digital nomadism is location-independent remote working style and new form of tourist mobility (Zhou et al., 2024). They are the new generation who have a location-independent and self-determined life, and who no longer have financially secure nine-to-five jobs (Muller, 2016). Digital nomads generally combine remote work and travel. The only fundamental need of this segment of travelers is stable internet connection (Lopez, 2024). Digital nomad is now a widely accepted term, insomuch Lonely Planet offers a list of convenient destinations for remote workers on its webpage (Balsam, 2024). Lifting starting from the pandemic now remote work created the process even more; however, according to Willment (2020), remote workers are not motivated by the motivation of experiencing new place, new cultures, and new lifestyles, where these motivations are the core of digital nomads. These groups are in the core of technological decisions. For example, digital immigrants are late adapters of the technology, accordingly, should be considered in technology-intense services, such as service robots used in restaurants. The industry that's why has a critical role to clearly define its relationship with technology.

4.3.2 SERVICE PROVIDERS AND POLICY MAKERS

The main promises of tourism such as the popularity of a destination and place-branding is not in the control of the tourism industry, rather managed by the travelers and tourists (Urry and Larsen, 2011). Thus, compared to traditional media era, when the owner of the information was the service provider, the travelers are now more powerful as the co-creator, or even as the owner of the information. Accordingly, it is now even more important for service providers to monitor the digital activities of digital travelers to shape and re-shape; create and re-create their offerings and services. As Urry and Larsen (2011) argue, the difference of service providers and travelers is fluid in mobile environments and places are comprehensively connected. This connection separates and unites the host and guest simultaneously. The reason for separation is that now, the service provider is not the only source of information as it used to be in the traditional media era. The information can be obtained from other travelers even in a more objective aspect, through any digital channels and tools. Thus, service providers and policy makers are the other side of digital travel to create, provide, and constantly revise the digital offerings for the travelers.

Technology connects consumer and demand, and industry and businesses through technological innovation (Navio-Marco et al., 2018). The current digital eco-system utilizes information and use of digital data as an essential source of competitive advantage (Pencarelli, 2020). In addition, the promise of technology brings variety of options for business owners to please the customers and travelers because the world we live in now is hyperconnected (Schell, 2022, p. 93). For example, through their own mobile apps, hotels are able to provide customized services before, during, and after customers' stay (Parise et al., 2016). In addition, customers' orders can be facilitated conveniently, product recommendations among customers can be managed promptly, and product advisors can be substituted by chatbots. Additionally, cost of hotels can be reduced by minimizing the customer service workload, and timely and prompt response can be possible (Ali et al., 2023).

For service providers and business owners, digitalization is essential as it changes barriers to entry, shapes transparency and competition, and reshapes distribution channels, in addition to tourism being one of the biggest categories to sell the service and products over the Internet (Navio-Marco et al., 2018). Providing digital aids, such as digital assistance, not only assists the customer but also salespeople. In the cases where digital assistance is available, salespeople's role shifts to advisors rather than information providers (Parise et al., 2016). In short, technology, especially information communication technologies is vital for the stakeholders in operative, structural, strategic, and marketing levels (Neuhofer et al., 2014).

Technology and digitalization also are essential for the service providers and businesses to manage big data, and customers' and or competitors' information. Tourism activities inherently require tourism and hospitality organizations to share travelers' data with other stakeholders, which brings concerns about data security and privacy (Yallop et al., 2023). Although research shows that almost 80% of customers are voluntarily sharing their personal information with the retailer, user value versus privacy tradeoff still is an essential concern to manage (Parise et al., 2016). This concern is a minor sign of the problematic aspect of digital tools and services. Therefore, it is essential to cautiously consider that trust is an essential aspect for use of technology. In their work, Ali et al. (2023) proposed that four main variables, namely, relevance, credibility, usefulness, and intelligence significantly impact the trust for the technological tools, such as chatbots. The authors further elaborate on the terms in detail:

Relevance: Within the context of conversation with the tools, responses by the tools should effectively address and appropriately match with the request.

Credibility: Credible resources generally exhibit expertise, high level of believability, and trustworthiness.

Usefulness: It is essential for the tools to provide valuable, beneficial, and essential assistance or information in a timely and well-organized context.

Intelligence: Cognitive and general mental functions, such as problem solving and reasoning are essential aspects.

In short, these four dimensions, relevance, credibility, usefulness, and intelligence are essential for businesses to focus on to manage their relationships with digital travelers. In other words, these are the dimensions that connect service providers and travelers within the industry. The digital revolution scenario requires various clarifications in managerial and theoretical aspects; one of which is defining or redefining the public good rules of web, and the boundaries and use of information by the companies, such as Google and Facebook (Pencarelli, 2020). The above-mentioned four dimensions also can help to set boundaries for individuals, companies, and policy makers. Like the individual aspect brought some specific terms, such as digital natives, digital immigrants, and digital nomads, the available and accessible technology, technological tools and devices, and possible travel options through physical or virtual reality comprehensively bring other broad terms from the perspective of service providers. One of these terms is smart tourism. According to Pencarelli (2020), smart tourism now refers not only technological but also social and economic developments covered and shaped by technology, such as big data, and in Tourism 4.0, digital technologies significantly impact the travelers' behavior before, during, and after the trip; and transforms traditional travelers into smart tourists and/or digital travelers (Pencarelli, 2020). Thus, digital tools are not only utilized to provide alternatives and options for digital travelers but also successfully and sustainably manage the impacts of tourism within the smart tourism perspective. Digital travelers now access not only practical information, such as booking or check-in, but also seek a variety of options, such as sustainable destinations and green hotels. Thus, digital travelers are now the agents of smart tourism, considering the social, economic, and environmental impacts of their choices and behaviors.

In addition to information seeking phase, after the trip and in the post-consumption phase, digital tourists utilize blogs/websites to attach more meaning to the experience with a more thoughtful way of retelling the experience and their story. The digital traveler then becomes a storyteller, creating his/her personal brand and building expertise for their followers (Pencarelli, 2020). Digital media enables the digital traveler to share their experience through telling their tourism stories (Bassano et al., 2019). Digital storytelling then becomes another theme for digital travelers to communicate their experiences; a development the industry must monitor and manage. The digital stories are essential for the businesses to obtain necessary information and volunteer feedback of the travelers. Boje (2019) argues that the digital age is the time that storytelling has been replaced by discourse. Thus, it is even more important for the businesses to wisely monitor digital storytelling practices to remain competitive. The finding of the study by Neuhofer et al. (2014), shows that it is not sufficient to examine technology as the generic facilitator of an experience. Instead, it should be examined if technology is central or peripheral to the experience. After years from this statement, no-technology is one of the options for travelers and digital free options should be added to the topics to technology-related research.

This chapter mainly examines the digitalization and its impacts and applications in the industry. However, as stated above, how central the technology is to a particular experience is the essential question to answer, as in some cases, technology-free options are needed by travelers. Also, the overuse and over dependence of technology might create significant hurdles. Thus, digitalization brings its own solution and offerings for over-dependence and long-term negative impacts. Voluntarily limiting technology use or, not using any technological device in certain context and certain amount of time is one of the new trends to deal with the negative impacts of technology. Accordingly, digital free or digital detox holidays are offered as a new approach to technology-intense market, as a niche product market. Jiang and Balaji (2022) state, it is essential to consider the fact that while previous studies approached technology non-use phenomenon as a problem to be solved; the current literature considers the term as a volunteer and deliberated choice. Unlike other activities of technology non-use, digital detox is conscious, voluntary, temporary, and place and time specific activity.

4.4 FLIP SIDE OF THE COIN: CHALLENGES OF DIGITAL TRAVEL AND DIGITALIZATION

The strategic adaptation of information and communication technologies in tourism industry is not new (Buhalis, 1998). What is new and unexpected is, acknowledging the two sides of the coin; on one hand technology intense character of the industry, on the other hand the drawback of technology leading the travelers, searching variety of options where they can voluntarily limit their dependence with technology. Despite many benefits, advantages, and positive impacts, the technology comes with its own drawbacks. For example, the negative long-term impacts of technology on various areas, such as well-being is not known clearly (Li et al., 2020); and physical, mental, and social problems are already associated with technology (Jiang and Balaji, 2022). Technology adaptation has been the focus of tourism research; however, negative impacts of technology, especially dominant use of smartphone and social media is a relatively new topic (Li et al., 2020). After years Urry and Larsen examine tourist gaze in detail (Urry and Larsen, 2011); new terms such as "distracted gaze" labels detrimental impacts of misuse of technology in tourist experience (Li et al., 2020). Since, digital experience, culture, and identity are closely interconnected (Schell, 2022:137), it is challenging to detect the various negative and positive impacts of technology. In addition, there are enough evidence that compared to physical interaction, virtual activities and interactions can be hectic and demanding (Tjostheim and Waterworth, 2022, p. 3) and disconnecting from technology on a holiday could potentially contribute to travelers' psychological sustainability (Floros et al., 2021).

The motivations of a traveler for vacation are stated above and technology in general provides convenient platforms for these motivations. To mitigate any actual or possible impacts of technology, alternative tourism types are getting popular. Digital free holidays are now alternatives for the digital travelers who voluntarily take a break and practice tourism experience where digital tools are limited or even do not exist for limited time and in a specific context. The impact of technology is twofold. In addition to its advantages and convenience, it also brings the danger of digital addiction. Digital detox, is now considered as the countermovement of intense technology practice (Schell, 2022, p. 83) and it is explained as: "a period of time during which you do not use mobile phones, computers, and so forth, because you usually use these devices too much" (Cambridge Dictionary). Schell (2022, p. 83) defines the term as "a periodic disconnect from social or online media to reduce stress and to focus on physical relationships in the real world." It is now an alternative for digital travelers if and when they decide to take a break or seek alternative travel options.

To provide an alternative for the digital travelers who are intensely engaging with technology and seek an alternative to pause this close relationship, digital free tourism and digital free holidays are getting common in the industry. Digital detox is the encouragement and desire to disconnect from online or digital media for a longer or shorter period. Although the motivation is rarely to disconnect permanently, digital detox is a sign that constant connectivity is experienced as negative and worth resisting (Syvertsen and Enli, 2020). A digital detox also refers to a period of time, when a person refrains from using tech devices, such as smartphones, televisions, computers, tablets, and social media sites. "Detoxing" from digital devices is often considered as a tool to focus on real-life social interactions without distractions. By forgoing digital devices, at least temporarily, people can let go of the stress that stems from constant connectivity (Cherry, 2023). Hotels and destinations now offering digital detox or "mobile fasting" programs where the guests are required to leave their electronic devices in various destinations, such as Paris and Maldives (Jiang and Balaji, 2022). Digital free tourism is a concept describing spaces where use of digital technology is deliberately limited, such as by cancelling internet or mobile phone signals. This concept was first introduced in academic research in 2009 (Schell, 2022:138, 141). Digital detox holiday is a voluntary choice of travelers to spend their holiday without internet and no-or limited electronic devices (Jiang and Balaji, 2022). It is essential to consider that instead of temporary resistance, mindful rejection of digital devices is more beneficial (Schell, 2022). As many other concepts and terms exist in the tourism field, there is no common definition, and no single name is assigned for the concept. The concept is explained in the literature with various names such as:

1. Unplugged tourism
2. Digital free tourism
3. Disconnected tourism
4. Digital-free travel (Ozdemir and Goktas, 2021).

Regardless the name, the concept provides similar alternatives for digital travelers. Volunteer disconnection, alternative travel activities, ensuring well-being, mitigating the negative impact of technology are the options that digital free holidays provide to digital travelers.

4.5 CONCLUSION AND FUTURE DIRECTIONS

In their work on digital technology and its impact on customer experience, Parise et al. (2016) argued that it is not effective to compare online and physical shopping and chose one. Instead, richer customer experience can be achieved by a rich understanding of complex mix of touchpoints, engagement in personalized and emotional context, and understanding both in-store and online behavior. Additionally, as "the dose makes the poison," moderate use of technology increases well-being, while high and low exposure tends to decrease well-being. Against common concerns, digital technology itself does not directly affect well-being or mental health; it has its own pros and cons that individuals should and could shape (Hoehe and Thibaut, 2020). Hoehe and Thibaut (2020) also argue that in terms of digital technology use and its impacts on mental health or well-being problems, it is not the case in general, but it is the individual that shapes the size of the impacts. Individual differences, such as family, education, and social background, the available support systems are vital for the effect. Thus, although this chapter addresses digitalization and its importance, as well as digital-free alternatives, the focus is not promoting one option over another. Instead, this chapter argues that digital travel and digital traveler should be approached and examined comprehensively. Likewise, Neuhofer and Buhalis (2012) also argued that it is essential to develop a holistic perspective rather than recognizing single technologies. For this reason, digital travelers should be considered within the industry where digital pause is available to them through innovative service providers who offer high technology as well as options of no-technology. Recent developments create a substitute for the interaction of host and guest, and it has not been clearly proposed whether these developments improve or worsen the overall tourist experience (Pencarelli, 2020). In fact, Slater and Sanchez-Vives (2016), emphasize that alternative technological tools, such as VR are not substitute but alternative of travel experience. Thus, two sides of technology (intense technology and no-technology or technological break) should be understood comprehensively to accommodate digital travelers. Either digital native, digital immigrant, or digital nomads, all groups are closely connected technology; but also want flexibility to manage or even pause their relationship. Thus, the industry, service providers, and policy makers should not only invest in high technological infrastructure but also invest in establishments that offer variety of technology disconnected activities.

4.6 FUTURE WORK

It is vital to investigate which segment utilizes which kind of digital information to fully benefit customer segmentation and reach out the targeted segment (Nemec Rudez, 2023). Thus, it is essential to investigate the digital traveler group not only in terms of generations (ages) but also in terms of other characteristics, such as their lifestyles, remote workers, digital nomads, and so forth. In addition to the intense technology need of digital travelers, future studies should investigate particular times without technology.

Neuhofer et al. (2014) provide significant contribution to the literature by providing experience hierarchy pyramid where they classify four groups of experience in terms of technology use: conventional experience, technology assisted experience, technology enhanced experience, and technology empowered experience. Utilizing the essential grouping of technology use, future research on technology- free or technological detox holidays should be considered from the perspective of experience hierarchy pyramid of Neuhofer et al. (2014). In addition, there are still concerns on profitability of the service providers (Schell, 2022, p. 143). Thus, the economic aspects and its impact on competitive advantage from financial perspective should be examined as well for digital travelers' activities.

KEYWORDS

- **digital detox**
- **digital natives**
- **digital nomads**
- **digital travel**
- **hedonic consumption**
- **mobile fasting**
- **physical travel**

REFERENCES

Ali, F., Yasar, B., Ali, L., & Dogan, S. (2023). Antecedents and consequences of travelers' trust towards personalized travel recommendations offered by ChatGPT. *International Journal of Hospitality Management, 114*, 103588.

Balsam, J. (2024, Jan 31). Lonely planet. https://www.lonelyplanet.com/articles/best-countries-for-remote-working

Bassano, C., Barile, S., Piciocchi, P., Spohrer, J. C., Iandolo, F., & Fisk, R. (2019). Storytelling about places: Tourism marketing in the digital age. *Cities, 87*, 10–20.

Bayne, S., & Ross, J. (2007, Dec). The "digital native" and "digital immigrant": A dangerous opposition. In *Annual Conference of the Society for Research into Higher Education (SRHE)* (Vol. 20).

Boje, D. M. (2019). Storytelling organization is being transformed into discourse of digital organization. *Management, 22*(2), 336–356.

Buhalis, D. (1998). Strategic use of information technologies in the tourism industry. *Tourism management, 19*(5), 409-421.

Buhalis, D., & Law, R. (2008). Progress in information technology and tourism management: 20 years on and 10 years after the Internet—The state of eTourism research. *Tourism Management, 29*(4), 609–623.

Cherry, K. (2023). How to do a digital detox. https://www.verywellmind.com/why-and-how-to-do-a-digital-detox-4771321

Connell, J., & Gibson, C. (2004). Vicarious journeys: Travels in music. *Tourism Geographies, 6*(1), 2–25.

Fan, D. X., Buhalis, D., & Lin, B. (2019). A tourist typology of online and face-to-face social contact: Destination immersion and tourism encapsulation/decapsulation. *Annals of Tourism Research, 78*, 102757.

Floros, C., Cai, W., McKenna, B., & Ajeeb, D. (2021). Imagine being off-the-grid: Millennials' perceptions of digital-free travel. *Journal of Sustainable Tourism, 29*(5), 751–766.

Hirschman, E. C., & Holbrook, M. B. (1982). Hedonic consumption: Emerging concepts, methods and propositions. *Journal of marketing, 46*(3), 92–101.

Hoehe, M. R., & Thibaut, F. (2020). Going digital: How technology use may influence human brains and behavior. *Dialogues in Clinical Neuroscience, 22*(2), 93–97.

https://dictionary.cambridge.org/dictionary/english/digital-detox?q=digital++detox

https://dictionary.cambridge.org/dictionary/english/digital-nomad.

Jiang, Y., & Balaji, M. S. (2022). Getting unwired: What drives travellers to take a digital detox holiday? *Tourism Recreation Research, 47*(5–6), 453–469.

Li, J., Pearce, P. L., & Oktadiana, H. (2020). Can digital-free tourism build character strengths? *Annals of Tourism Research, 85*, 103037.

López, A. M. (2024, Mar 1). Digital nomads—Statistics & facts. https://www.statista.com/aboutus/our-research-commitment/2501/ana-m-lopez retrieved

Müller, A. (2016). The digital nomad: Buzzword or research category? *Transnational Social Review, 6*(3), 344–348.

Navío-Marco, J., Ruiz-Gómez, L. M., & Sevilla-Sevilla, C. (2018). Progress in information technology and tourism management: 30 years on and 20 years after the internet-Revisiting Buhalis & Law's landmark study about eTourism. *Tourism Management, 69*, 460–470.

Nemec Rudež, H. (2023). What features of digital travel-related information is generation Z looking for? *Tourism and Hospitality Management, 29*(4), 495–504.
Neuhofer, B. and Buhalis, D. (2012). Understanding and managing technology-enabled enhanced tourist experiences. Paper presented at the 2nd Advances in Hospitality and Tourism Marketing and Management Conference, 31st May to 3rd June 2012, Corfu Island, Greece.
Neuhofer, B., Buhalis, D., & Ladkin, A. (2014). A typology of technology-enhanced tourism experiences. *International Journal of Tourism Research, 16*(4), 340–350.
Ozdemir, M. A., & Goktas, L. S. (2021). Research trends on digital detox holiday: A bibliometric analysis, 2012–2020. *Tourism & Management Studies, 17*(3), 21–35.
Parise, S., Guinan, P. J., & Kafka, R. (2016). Solving the crisis of immediacy: How digital technology can transform the customer experience. *Business Horizons, 59*(4), 411–420.
Pearce, P. L., & Lee, U. I. (2005). Developing the travel career approach to tourist motivation. *Journal of Travel Research, 43*(3), 226–237.
Pencarelli, T. (2020). The digital revolution in the travel and tourism industry. *Information Technology & Tourism, 22*(3), 455–476.
Pine, B. J., & Gilmore, J. H. (1998). *Welcome to the experience economy* (Vol. 76, No. 4, pp. 97–105). Harvard Business Review Press.
Pine, B., & Gilmore, J. H. (1999). *The experience economy.* Boston, MA: Harvard Business School Press.
Pine, B. J., & Gilmore, J. H. (2013). The experience economy: Past, present and future. In *Handbook on the experience economy* (pp. 21–44). Edward Elgar Publishing.
Schell, B. H. (2022). *Digital detox: Why taking a break from technology can improve your well-being.* Greenwood.
Serra, A., & Leong, C. (2020). https://www.weforum.org/agenda/2020/05/this-is-what-travelling-will-be-like-after-covid-19/
Slater, M., & Sanchez-Vives, M. V. (2016). Enhancing our lives with immersive virtual reality. *Frontiers in Robotics and AI, 3*, 74.
Syvertsen, T., & Enli, G. (2020). Digital detox: Media resistance and the promise of authenticity. *Convergence, 26*(5–6), 1269–1283.
Tjostheim, I., & Waterworth, J. A. (2022). The psychosocial reality of digital travel: Being in virtual places (p. 152). Springer Nature.
UNWTO (2021). https://www.untourism.int/news/digital-tools-to-revitalize-tourism
Urry, J. (1990). *The tourist gaze: Leisure and travel in contemporary societies.* Sage Publications.
Urry, J., & Larsen, J. (2011). *The tourist gaze 3.0*, 3rd ed. Sage Publications.
Willment, N. (2020). The travel blogger as digital nomad: (Re-) imagining workplace performances of digital nomadism within travel blogging work. *Information Technology & Tourism, 22*(3), 391–416.
World Travel Tourism Council (2024). https://wttc.org/research/economic-impact
Yallop, A. C., Gică, O. A., Moisescu, O. I., Coroş, M. M., & Séraphin, H. (2023). The digital traveller: implications for data ethics and data governance in tourism and hospitality. *Journal of Consumer Marketing, 40*(2), 155–170.
Zhou, L., Buhalis, D., Fan, D. X., Ladkin, A., & Lian, X. (2024). Attracting digital nomads: Smart destination strategies, innovation and competitiveness. *Journal of Destination Marketing & Management, 31*, 100850.

PART II
Digital Transformation and Sustainable Tourism Strategies

CHAPTER 5

Digitalization and Sustainable Tourism

NESRIN M. BAHCELERLI

Near East University, Faculty of Tourism, Tourism Research Center, Nicosia, North Cyprus

ABSTRACT

Technological developments cause some changes in the tourism sector, as in every sector. Innovations are needed in our world where the relationship between technology and tourism keeps evolving. These innovations have shifted to an international dimension with the influence of globalization. Thanks to the increase in technological opportunities, the spread of the Internet, and online sites, people can now meet their needs in a short time. In sustainable tourism, diversity in tourism activities has gained importance as the demands and expectations of tourists increase. In this regard, it would be appropriate to define and explain the concept of information before examining the importance of the production, use, distribution, and exchange of information in the formation and development of the destination and in the production, marketing, and development of the tourism product. In the next stage, it is crucial to determine what the goals of sustainable tourism are in order to establish what kind of effects information and technology will have on achieving these goals. This chapter aims to examine the contribution of digitalization to sustainable tourism and its application areas.

5.1 INTRODUCTION

The sustainable components of protecting the natural environment and cultural heritage are linked to the growth of tourism in the modern world.

Digitalization in Tourism. Hulya Akdemir Cengiz, Seza Zerman, Aysegul Acar, and Faizan Ali (Eds.)

DOI: 10.1201/9781779644770-7

Numerous locations have begun to reduce the detrimental effects of tourism on the environment and on social and cultural aspects of the local community. Rather than focusing on mass tourism development, today's tourism development often adapts to the growth of alternative or special interest tourism (Streimikiene et al., 2021). The improvement of the natural and cultural environments' carrying capacity as well as the advancement of local residents' welfare are encouraged by this stage of tourist development. Destinations must evaluate the carrying capacity of natural and cultural ecosystems to match tourists' expectations, which go beyond the physical items available, driven by the motivation, developing awareness, and maturity of tourists who prefer this special interest tourism (Martinez et al., 2019).

Tourism is considered as a labor-intensive sector, and therefore needs to have accountability in terms of sustainability on both local and global scales. The sustainable tourism method requires the most effective and efficient use of existing resources and opportunities by anticipating long-term changes in line with the principles in order to achieve the purpose of sustainable tourism. Sustainable tourism is defined as a form of production in which environmental values, society, and culture are carried out by taking advantage of developments in the three dimensions of sustainability: economic, environmental, and sociocultural impacts. It is argued that sustainable tourism can meet both local and international needs of the existing tourism industry, while protecting the environment, promoting future opportunities, and taking the long-term impact of tourism on local communities, and the local and international economy into account. In a region that attaches importance to information and information technologies and has developed knowledge and skills, it will be possible to ensure responsible use of tourism resources, satisfied tourists, and the transfer of these resources to future generations.

5.2 SUSTAINABLE TOURISM

Sustainable tourism development can be achieved by ensuring that the utilization of various resources does not exceed their capacity for renewal. The principles of sustainable tourism development, as outlined by Harris et al. (2012), include the following: protecting environmental quality, benefiting both local communities and tourists, maintaining the connections between tourism and the environment, fostering harmony between local populations and their surroundings, creating dynamic conditions appropriate for the carrying capacity, and ensuring collaborative efforts among all stakeholders to achieve sustainable development goals (Lu and Nepal, 2009).

Sustainable tourism can contribute to better public health, the economy, and welfare of local communities. As the foundational element of tourism, the sustainability of tourism should not merely be a platitude without pledges from several stakeholders to preserve the natural, socioeconomic, and cultural sustainability of society. Three factors are involved in the development of sustainable tourism: social, economic, and environmental (Postma et al., 2017; Higgins-Desbiolles, 2018).

5.2.1 DIMENSIONS OF SUSTAINABILITY AND TOURISM

Krajnc and Glavic (2005) noted that numerous studies discuss the dimensions of sustainability alongside social, economic, and environmental indicators. They emphasized that the "social, competitive, and economic" dimensions are often explored to enhance the practical guidance provided by the sustainability framework. The principle of sustainability is based on the sociocultural, economic, and environmental impact dimensions of the tourism sector, and ensures that the relationship between these three dimensions is balanced. (Kristensen and Mosgaard, 2020). In the literature, it has been observed that the social and cultural dimensions of the sustainability concept are addressed separately or can be addressed together. Numerous societal segments pay close attention to these three dimensions. Protecting the natural resources necessary for sustainability, as well as building environment, wildlife, agriculture, and natural surroundings, is important. Nonetheless, tourism needs substantial backing from an economic and sociocultural perspective to benefit the locals, improve their quality of life, protect local culture, and maintain their standard of living (Janker and Mann, 2020).

5.2.1.1 ENVIRONMENTAL DIMENSION

When the concept of environmental dimension of sustainability is analyzed, it is understood that it is a concept related to the natural environment, including human activities. At the same time, it is emphasized that the most important aspect of the multidimensional sustainability concept is the environment (Choi and Ng, 2011). Catlin et al. (2017) define environmental sustainability as "sustaining/maintaining natural capital" and establishes environmental sustainability according to the following three rules:

1. To help prevent the degradation of waste discharged by any activity without reducing the future absorption capacity of the local environment or minimizing the benefits it provides.
2. To create renewable resources in environmental sustainability; organic systems regenerate specific resources. They house the produced resources in harvesting environments and ensure that they are operational with income from non-renewable resources to sustain these resources and make them available for use.
3. To achieve a high level of sustainable benefit through renewable resources.

The increasing production and consumption frenzy in people's daily lives causes the limited resources to be depleted more rapidly. In this regard, especially the protection of non-renewable energy resources has become more important. With the increasing production and globalization after the industrial revolution, people's living standards have increased and the increase in consumption has caused some problems on the environment. However, in recent years, with the increasing pressure on the environment, climate change, and decline in resources, the value of the environmental dimension has started to increase (Kuhlman and Farrington, 2010). At this point, the need for alternative energy sources is felt day by day. Realizing this situation, businesses and nations have started to turn to renewable energy sources. Renewable energy utilized from natural resources does not cause any harm to nature. These energy sources, which renew themselves rapidly and do not deplete, are seen as a savior model for future generations. Sectors such as tourism, which are in close relationship with nature, need transformation for a structure suitable for renewable energy sources. Businesses and countries make important decisions about the environment in order to be realized. Although people and businesses are aware of this situation, it is sometimes neglected because the economic gain factor is at the forefront. In fact, environmental sustainability when done correctly should harmonize economic gains with people and nature (Boar et al., 2020).

5.2.1.2 SOCIAL DIMENSION

Difficulties in conceptualizing social sustainability stem from the fact that there is no clear distinction between analytical, normative, and political aspects and people may prefer one over the other (Janker and Mann, 2020). One of the reasons for this problem already lies in the broad and diverse social meaning of the word, which has an analytical and normative meaning. The most common definition of social sustainability is a positive state in communities and the process by which it can be achieved. This definition includes the following principles (Lozano, 2020):

1. The principle of equal access to key services
2. The principle of intergenerational equality
3. The principle of a system of relations that values different cultures
4. The principle of political participation of citizens, especially at local level
5. The principle of a sense of community
6. A system that communicates awareness of social sustainability
7. The principle of creating mechanisms through which the community can fulfill its needs as far as possible
8. The principle of political advocacy for needs that cannot be met by the community

Approaches to the social dimension of sustainability are as diverse as the economic dimension. Social sustainability refers to the extent to which social values, social identities, social relations, and social institutions can continue into the future. It is stated that maintaining society's integrity and capacity for cooperation is necessary for social sustainability. Individual needs like those for education, health, welfare, nutrition, housing, and cultural expression should be met by the social dimension (Mies and Gold, 2021). Especially over the last decade, there has been an intense focus worldwide on economic sustainability. While this focus has led to prosperity for some segments of society, the majority still faces significant challenges in surviving. The concept of social sustainability, though frequently discussed in academic circles and public discourse, lacks a universally accepted definition. This ambiguity has led to some critical scrutiny. Generally, social sustainability is understood to encompass equality, welfare, and the balance between sociocultural groups over time, as well as the continuity of quality-of-life indicators from one generation to another. This equality is based on sustainability in areas, such as education, health, welfare, elimination of gender discrimination, and safe and quality life (Fischer et al., 2020).

5.2.1.3 ECONOMIC DIMENSION

The economic dimension of sustainable development aims to ensure welfare across all societal sectors, maintain optimal production costs, support the viability of all initiatives, and promote the long-term decentralization of their continuity (Kristensen and Mosgaard, 2020). For neoclassical economists, economic sustainability is the preservation of capital. Financial sustainability can be said to exist if there is no reduction between income and consumption, and if it progresses steadily. It is critical to analyze the internal and external factors affecting firms in the context of economic sustainability. Accordingly, businesses' financial performance, their intangible asset management, their influence on the economy, their social and environmental consequences, and their management of these effects should all be considered when implementing sustainability management (Abad-Segura and Gonzalez-Zamar, 2021). An economy that maximizes general well-being while minimizing resource use and environmental harm is ideal and sustainable. For an economy to be genuinely sustainable, the rate of resource use must not exceed the planet's capacity for renewal (Daly, 1990; United Nations Environment Programme [UNEP], 2021).

5.3 DIGITALIZATION

According to Schallmo and Tidd (2021), one of the key themes transforming society and enterprises both now and in the future is digitalization. Digitalization is a systemic phenomenon that permeates all contemporary visual communication technology. This system operates on a digital coding system, as opposed to traditional media, and allows for multi-layered interaction and rapid communication. This system plays a significant role in the moving image art because of this, as evidenced by the fact that a visual message is made up of digital codes. Many different concepts come to the agenda with the digitization process. Specifically, new experiences in the evolution of visual communication are ushering in a new era (Ritter and Pedersen, 2020). One of the key technological elements of the new media era is the idea of "digitalization," also known as "digitization," which is the process of integrating information and communication technology into the media landscape. Traditional reporting techniques are changing because of digitalization, which makes it possible for information to freely circulate among various communication platforms (Mentsiev et al., 2020).

The term of digitalization might be regarded as the most significant technological advancement that has facilitated recent advancements across various domains. Considering this, digitization is the process of transforming analog messages—words, images, characters, and so forth—into signals that can be electronically processed, stored, and transmitted in discrete pulses. Digitizing messages allows for their easy combination—audio, image, and text—and allows for the integration of information that was previously unattainable. Digitalization has far-reaching implications outside of the telecom industry. Compiling text, video, and audio into one document allows for a multitude of computer-based multimedia applications. Furthermore, digitalization has led to the digitization of all forms of communication, including computers, radios, televisions, music, phones, and photographs (Lichtenthaler, 2021).

5.4 DIGITALIZATION IN TOURISM

With the effect of globalization, several changes have occurred in the structure of the tourism sector. In the past, sea-sand-sun and recreational activities were at the forefront among the purposes of visiting a destination within the scope of tourism activities. Technological advances and global competitive environment have increased the importance of innovations in the sector. The increasing use of the Internet and the widespread use of online marketing channels have enabled businesses to provide effective, efficient, low-cost, and quality services to people (Hadjielias et al., 2022). In the age of technology in the tourism sector, the need for information has become more evident. Having up-to-date information about a destination that has not been visited before and the experiences of people who have visited it are important factors that tourists take into account during the preference phase. The use of online travel agencies instead of traditional travel agencies is one of the global changes in the tourism sector. Online travel agencies that offer accommodation reservations, flight tickets, and access to up-to-date information about the destination have become popular (Talwar et al., 2023).

Tourism establishments and tourists follow technology-oriented developments in the sector. The gaining importance of service understanding according to individual characteristics is a situation that tourism businesses take into consideration in order not to fall behind their competitors. Tourism businesses that want to stand out by differentiating from their competitors have started to benefit from new technological developments (Johnson, 2023). Some of the technological developments that will mark the future are the Internet of Things (IoT), cloud computing, artificial intelligence technologies, big data, augmented reality, virtual reality, and face recognition technology (Samara et al., 2020).

Internet of Things (IoT): The concept of IoT is used to describe the spread of internet connectivity and computing capability to various objects and devices (Mulani and Pingle, 2016). It defines the concept of the IoT as an open and comprehensive network of smart objects that have the capacity to automatically organize themselves, share information, provide data and resources, react in face situations, move, and make changes in the environment (Madakam, 2015). The starting point of this concept, which Kevin Ashton (Ashton, 2009) pronounced for the first time in 1999, is accepted as the system developed by a group of academicians in 1991 to see the amount of coffee in the coffee machine (Stafford-Fraser, 1995; Kutup, 2011).

Augmented virtual reality: Augmented reality (AR), a remarkable technological advancement, continues to expand across various sectors, including the hospitality industry. Within this industry, visitors can use an app to access comprehensive information about sightseeing opportunities at their location, thereby enhancing their experience. These apps overlay relevant information—such as precise location, historical context, nearby dining options, and more—directly onto the user's smartphone camera view, effectively transforming the app into a personal tour guide. Moreover, hotels are leveraging AR to offer immersive experiences, enabling potential guests to virtually explore the premises and its surroundings. Additionally, some hotels provide interactive maps in their rooms, allowing travelers to discover extensive details about their immediate environment (Ivasciuc, 2020).

One of the most exciting technical advancements of the future is virtual reality (VR), which allows for the creation of various experiences through the use of computer-mediated imagery and graphical settings. Potentially, there are an infinite number of tourism experiences that VR can simulate (Musa et al., 2022). VR has emerged as an important development in hotel technology with the marketing of services and rooms. Virtual hotel tours are an excellent example of this immersive trend. Many professionals believe that this type of hotel technology will become mandatory in the not-too-distant future.

Data and analytics: IoT integrations, sensors, mobile applications, and application analytics provide a continuous stream of data that simplifies many aspects of life. While the sheer volume of big data may not be overwhelmingly detailed, it effectively enables the adaptation of strategies to meet user needs and preferences, enhancing operational efficiency and increasing revenues. Furthermore, all this data can also be leveraged for improved prevention and forecasting (Yallop and Seraphin, 2020).

Artificial intelligence (AI): AI's ultimate objective is to give visitors a more smooth and well-planned experience from start to finish. This can be accomplished in several ways: gathering and analyzing visitor information, determining the preferences of the user to construct a customized lodging package, targeted and successful marketing strategies, the capacity to assess a promotional campaign's efficacy in advance, and customizing every aspect of the visitor experience. Although AI has just lately become widely available, it already plays a significant role in hotel technology. As the prevalence of customers' seeking unique experience grows, their expectations are seen as more legitimate (Kontogianni et al., 2022).

Big data: One of the newest "catch phrases" is big data. Gathering, analyzing, sharing, and responding to this data is critical for hotels. This is particularly crucial for large properties capable of accommodating thousands of visitors each month, where efficient management and guest satisfaction are key to operational success. By combining the information they collect themselves and that available online, hotels are able to use big data in relation to their revenue management strategy, adopting appropriate sales and marketing approaches, and identifying offers that may be suitable for specific travelers or hotel guests (Gurgu et al., 2021).

5.5 DIGITALIZATION AND SUSTAINABLE TOURISM

Digitalization is the new playmaker that integrates more and more in our lives every day and is the technology that changes the ways of thinking and shaping things. It brings new dimensions to businesses along with providing growth strategies. Digitalization transfers the information flow of objects, visuals, and sounds through a fast and spontaneous signal channel. As a result, the digital representation—specifically, the digital image for an object and the digital format for a signal—is referred to as digitization. This initial definition of digitization describes the process of creating a representation of something in the physical world in another form of media (Talwar et al., 2023). The result of this first definition of digitization is defined as the creation of a representation of something in the physical world in another form of media (Talwar et al., 2023).

The possibilities of a different definition of digitization: The degree to which a society's goals of growth development and value creation are realized through technology. A definition based on value and income expands the idea of digitization as it goes beyond managing knowledge about objects to create new value based on the characteristics of digital information. Instead of thinking about transactions and systems, thinking about the array of technologies that can play a role in value creation: mobile phones, telemetry, social preferences, big data, metadata, analytics, behavior, expression, cloud infrastructure, and so forth, represent part of the emerging digital economy and future sources of value (Saseanu et al., 2020).

In the digitally sound scenario, trends such as mobile internet, IoT, and big data are creating greater opportunities in all areas. From here, businesses are using such techniques to optimize their resources and costs, and to develop more knowledge about enterprise technologies and processes. The social environment has helped to bring people together and places them on a common digitalization platform. This brings economic stability due to cost efficiency and numerous growth opportunities. Therefore, this approach aims at overall growth and brings us closer to sustainable development (Agostini et al., 2020).

Digitalization in the context of sustainable tourism refers to the integration of digital technologies and strategies to enhance the sustainability of the tourism industry. This includes leveraging digital tools and platforms to minimize negative environmental impacts, promote sociocultural authenticity, and ensure equitable distribution of economic benefits. Digitalization contributes to sustainable tourism in different ways. The first of these is information and communication technologies. Digital platforms provide easier access to the target market and facilitate the flow of information. On the other hand, through digital platforms, guests can make online bookings and access a multitude of information (Fossen and Sorgner, 2021).

Destination management organizations (DMOs) use digital tools for planning, monitoring, and management. Geographic information systems (GIS) and data analytics help optimize tourism flows, minimize overcrowding in sensitive areas, and reduce environmental pollution. VR and AR offer an immersive experience that reduces the need for physical travel. By allowing people to explore destinations virtually, these technologies can help reduce over tourism and protect sensitive ecosystems (Estevao et al., 2020).

Digitalization enables remote working and collaboration, reducing the need for business travel and the associated carbon footprint. Sustainable tourism companies can use digital communication tools to attract customers, partners, and employees without traveling long distances. Digital technology enables real-time monitoring of environmental indicators, visitor numbers, and socioeconomic impacts. With this information, stakeholders can assess the effectiveness of sustainability initiatives, identify areas for improvement, and report on progress toward achieving the Sustainable Development Goals. Social media and online platforms offer opportunities for local communities to engage with tourists, share their culture, and promote sustainable practices. Digital marketing campaigns can raise awareness of community-based tourism initiatives and encourage support from travelers (Castro et al., 2021).

Digitalization and sustainable tourism are of increasing importance in today's tourism industry. Research shows that digital technologies have the potential to transform the tourism experience and can also play a critical role in achieving sustainable tourism goals. In particular, digital tools, such as social media, mobile technology, and cloud computing facilitate access to travel planning, bookings, destination information, and tourism services, while allowing tourists to learn about sustainable travel options and contribute to the conservation of natural resources (Rodrigues et al., 2023). Furthermore, digital technologies can help tourists experience local cultures and environmental sensitivity in destinations. However, it should be kept in mind that digitalization also brings some challenges for sustainable tourism. For example, excessive flow of tourists may increase with the spread of digital marketing and reservation systems, which may damage local ecosystems and cultural textures. Therefore, the tourism industry should consider the principles of sustainability in the process of digitalization and use digital technologies for the protection of natural and cultural resources, the well-being of society, and the needs of future generations. In this context, an in-depth examination of the relationship between digitalization and sustainable tourism and the development of appropriate strategies is critical for the future of the tourism industry (Scriosteanu et al., 2022).

Overall, digitalization plays a crucial role in advancing sustainable tourism by promoting transparency, facilitating responsible decision-making, and encouraging collaboration among stakeholders. By harnessing the power of digital technologies, the tourism industry can move toward a more sustainable and resilient future (Loureiro and Nascimento, 2021).

5.6 CONCLUSION

Digitalization and sustainable tourism represent an important transformation in the tourism industry. The use of digital technologies in the tourism sector offers many opportunities to enhance travel experiences, optimize operations, and reduce environmental impact. Sustainable tourism aims to minimize the negative impacts of tourism by protecting natural and cultural resources, improving the well-being of communities and local economies, and encouraging visitors to understand local cultures.

Digital technologies include many tools that tourists use to make travel plans, make bookings, and receive information while traveling. These can take various forms, including online booking platforms, travel apps, mapping and navigation services, VR tours, and others. These technologies can serve sustainable tourism goals, such as suggesting more sustainable transport options to reduce the carbon footprint when traveling or contributing to local environmental initiatives. Furthermore, synergies can be found between digitalization and sustainable tourism. For example, smart city technologies can track tourists' movements and help them manage resources more effectively to minimize environmental impact. Furthermore, digitalization can support the equitable distribution of tourism revenues and local development by connecting more closely with local communities.

However, digitalization can also have negative impacts on sustainable tourism. For example, an overflow of tourists can damage natural and cultural sites, and digital marketing can encourage unsustainable travel habits. Therefore, the tourism industry should strive to integrate digital technologies with sustainability principles and maintain a balance. This means protecting natural and cultural resources and considering the well-being of local communities while improving tourism experiences.

KEYWORDS

- **carrying capacity**
- **digitalization**
- **information and communication technologies**
- **local ecosystems**
- **sustainable tourism**
- **special interest tourism**
- **social sustainability**

REFERENCES

Abad-Segura, E., & González-Zamar, M. D. (2021). Sustainable economic development in higher education institutions: A global analysis within the SDGs framework. *Journal of Cleaner Production, 294*, 126133. https://doi.org/10.1016/j.jclepro.2021.126133

Agostini, L., Galati, F., & Gastaldi, L. (2020). The digitalization of the innovation process: Challenges and opportunities from a management perspective. *European Journal of Innovation Management, 23*(1), 1–12. https://doi.org/10.1108/EJIM-01-2019-0001

Ashton, K. (2009). That 'Internet of Things' Thing: In the real world, things matter more than ideas. *RFID Journal.* 22 (7), 97–114 .

Boar, A., Bastida, R., & Marimon, F. (2020). Relationships between the sharing economy, sustainability and sustainable development goals: A systematic literature review. *Sustainability, 12*(17), 6744. https://doi.org/10.3390/su12176744

Castro, G. D. R., Fernandez, M. C. G., & Colsa, A. U. (2021). Unleashing the convergence amid digitalization and sustainability towards pursuing the Sustainable Development Goals (SDGs): A holistic review. *Journal of Cleaner Production, 280*, 122204. https://doi.org/10.1016/j.jclepro.2020.122204

Catlin, J. R., Luchs, M. G., & Phipps, M. (2017). Consumer perceptions of the social vs. environmental dimensions of sustainability. *Journal of Consumer Policy, 40*, 245–277. https://doi.org/10.1007/s10603-017-9356-x

Choi, S., & Ng, A. (2011). Environmental and economic dimensions of sustainability and price effects on consumer responses. *Journal of Business Ethics, 104*, 269–282. https://doi.org/10.1007/s10551-011-0908-8

Daly, H. E. (1990). Toward some operational principles of sustainable development. *Ecological Economics*, *2*(1), 1–6. https://doi.org/10.1016/0921-8009(90)90010-R

Estevao, J., Carneiro, M. J., & Teixeira, L. (2020). Destination management systems' adoption and management model: Proposal of a framework. *Journal of Organizational Computing and Electronic Commerce, 30*(2), 89–110. https://doi.org/10.1080/10919392.2020.1726446

Fischer, D., Brettel, M., & Mauer, R. (2020). The three dimensions of sustainability: A delicate balancing act for entrepreneurs made more complex by stakeholder expectations. *Journal of Business Ethics, 163*, 87–106. https://doi.org/10.1007/s10551-018-3993-y

Fossen, F. M., & Sorgner, A. (2021). Digitalization of work and entry into entrepreneurship. *Journal of Business Research, 125*, 548–563. https://doi.org/10.1016/j.jbusres.2020.02.020

Gurgu, E., Zorzoliu, R. I., Pistol, L., Gurgu, I., Ungureanu, C., & Nae, G. (2021). The relationship between big data-driven technologies and performance management strategies applied to companies in the hospitality, tourism & travel industry. *Annals of Spiru Haret University. Economic Series, 21*(4), 97–136. https://doi.org/10.26458/2146

Hadjielias, E., Christofi, M., Christou, P., & Drotarova, M. H. (2022). Digitalization, agility, and customer value in tourism. *Technological Forecasting and Social Change, 175*, 121334. https://doi.org/10.1016/j.techfore.2021.121334

Harris, R., Williams, P., & Griffin, T. (Eds.) (2012). *Sustainable tourism*. Routledge.

Harris, R., Griffin, T., & Williams, P. (2017). *Sustainable tourism* (2nd ed.). Routledge. https://doi.org/10.4324/9781315768194

Higgins-Desbiolles, F. (2018). Sustainable tourism: Sustaining tourism or something more? *Tourism Management Perspectives, 25*, 157–160. https://doi.org/10.1016/j.tmp.2017.11.017

Ivasciuc, I. S. (2020). Augmented reality and facial recognition technologies: Building bridges between the hospitality industry and tourists during pandemic. *Bulletin of the Transilvania University of Brasov. Series V: Economic Sciences*, *13*, 75–92. https://doi.org/10.31926/but.es.2020.13.62.2.4

Janker, J., & Mann, S. (2020). Understanding the social dimension of sustainability in agriculture: A critical review of sustainability assessment tools. *Environment, Development and Sustainability, 22*(3), 1671–1691. https://doi.org/10.1007/s10668-018-0261-1

Johnson, A. G. (2023). Why are smart destinations not all technology-oriented? Examining the development of smart tourism initiatives based on path dependence. *Current Issues in Tourism, 26*(8), 1282–1294. https://doi.org/10.1080/13683500.2023.2173109

Kontogianni, A., Alepis, E., & Patsakis, C. (2022). Smart tourism and artificial intelligence: Paving the way to the post-covid-19 era. In *Advances in Artificial Intelligence-based Technologies: Selected Papers in Honour of Professor Nikolaos G. Bourbakis* (Vol. 1, pp. 93–109). Springer. https://doi.org/10.1007/978-3-030-81096-5_9

Krajnc, D., & Glavič, P. (2005). How to compare companies on relevant dimensions of sustainability. *Ecological Economics, 55*(4), 551–563. https://doi.org/10.1016/j.ecolecon.2004.12.011

Kristensen, H. S., & Mosgaard, M. A. (2020). A review of micro-level indicators for a circular economy–Moving away from the three dimensions of sustainability? *Journal of Cleaner Production, 243*, 118531. https://doi.org/10.1016/j.jclepro.2019.118531

Kuhlman, T., & Farrington, J. (2010). What is sustainability? *Sustainability, 2*(11), 3436–3448. https://doi.org/10.3390/su2113436

Lichtenthaler, U. (2021). Digitainability: The combined effects of the megatrends digitalization and sustainability. *Journal of Innovation Management, 9*(2), 64–80. https://doi.org/10.24840/2183-0606_009.002_0006

Loureiro, S. M. C., & Nascimento, J. (2021). Shaping a view on the influence of technologies on sustainable tourism. *Sustainability, 13*(22), 12691. https://doi.org/10.3390/su132212691

Lozano, R. (2020). Analysing the use of tools, initiatives, and approaches to promote sustainability in corporations. *Corporate Social Responsibility and Environmental Management, 27*(2), 982–998. https://doi.org/10.1002/csr.1860

Lu, J., & Nepal, S. K. (2009). Sustainable tourism research: An analysis of papers published in the *Journal of Sustainable Tourism. Journal of Sustainable Tourism, 17*(1), 5–16. https://doi.org/10.1080/09669580802396761

Madakam, S. (2015). Internet of things: Smart things. *International Journal of Future Computer and Communication, 4*(4), 250. https://doi.org/10.7763/IJFCC.2015.V4.395

Martínez, J. M. G., Martín, J. M. M., Fernández, J. A. S., & Mogorrón-Guerrero, H. (2019). An analysis of the stability of rural tourism as a desired condition for sustainable tourism. *Journal of Business Research, 100*, 165–174. https://doi.org/10.1016/j.jbusres.2019.03.037

Mentsiev, A. U., Engel, M. V., Tsamaev, A. M., Abubakarov, M. V., & Yushaeva, R. S. (2020). The concept of digitalization and its impact on the modern economy. In *International Scientific Conference "Far East Con" (ISCFEC 2020)* (pp. 2960–2964). Atlantis Press. https://doi.org/10.2991/aebmr.k.201102.418

Mies, A., & Gold, S. (2021). Mapping the social dimension of the circular economy. *Journal of Cleaner Production, 321*, 128960. https://doi.org/10.1016/j.jclepro.2021.128960

Mulani, T. T., & Pingle, S. V. (2016). Internet of Things. *International Research Journal of Multidisciplinary Studies, 2*(3).

Musa, M., Rahman, P., Kang, Z. R., & Hossain, S. F. A. (2022). Technology application in the Chinese tourism industry. In *Technology application in tourism in Asia: Innovations, theories and practices* (pp. 219–239). Springer. https://doi.org/10.1007/978-981-19-1527-4_12

Postma, A., Cavagnaro, E., & Spruyt, E. (2017). Sustainable tourism 2040. *Journal of Tourism Futures, 3*(1), 13–22. https://doi.org/10.1108/JTF-10-2016-0023

Ritter, T., & Pedersen, C. L. (2020). Digitization capability and the digitalization of business models in business-to-business firms: Past, present, and future. *Industrial Marketing Management, 86*, 180–190. https://doi.org/10.1016/j.indmarman.2019.11.019

Rodrigues, V., Eusébio, C., & Breda, Z. (2023). Enhancing sustainable development through tourism digitalisation: A systematic literature review. *Information Technology & Tourism, 25*(1), 13–45. https://doi.org/10.1007/s40558-023-00212-y

Samara, D., Magnisalis, I., & Peristeras, V. (2020). Artificial intelligence and big data in tourism: A systematic literature review. *Journal of Hospitality and Tourism Technology, 11*(2), 343–367. https://doi.org/10.1108/JHTT-10-2018-0105

Saseanu, A. S., Ghita, S. I., Albastroiu, I., & Stoian, C. A. (2020). Aspects of digitalization and related impact on green tourism in European countries. *Information, 11*(11), 507. https://doi.org/10.3390/info11110507

Schallmo, D. R., & Tidd, J. (2021). *Digitalization.* Springer International Publishing. https://doi.org/10.1007/978-3-030-69360-5

Scriosteanu, A., Barbu, C. M., & Criveanu, M. M. (2022). Sustainable tourism in the current European context. In *Managing risk and decision making in times of economic distress* (pp. 17–36). Emerald Publishing Limited. https://doi.org/10.1108/978-1-80071-533-320211004

Streimikiene, D., Svagzdiene, B., Jasinskas, E., & Simanavicius, A. (2021). Sustainable tourism development and competitiveness: The systematic literature review. *Sustainable Development, 29*(1), 259–271. https://doi.org/10.1002/sd.2124

Talwar, S., Kaur, P., Nunkoo, R., & Dhir, A. (2023). Digitalization and sustainability: Virtual reality tourism in a post-pandemic world. *Journal of Sustainable Tourism, 31*(11), 2564–2591. https://doi.org/10.1080/09669582.2023.2206491

United Nations Environment Programme (UNEP). (2021). *Making peace with nature: A scientific blueprint to tackle the climate, biodiversity and pollution emergencies.* Nairobi: UNEP. https://www.unep.org/resources/making-peace-nature

Yallop, A., & Seraphin, H. (2020). Big data and analytics in tourism and hospitality: Opportunities and risks. *Journal of Tourism Futures, 6*(3), 257–262. https://doi.org/10.1108/JTF-05-2019-0033

CHAPTER 6

Digitalization in Cultural Heritage Preservation

MUHAMMAD KHIZAR HAYAT NAEEM* and YANQING WANG

School of Management, Harbin Institute of Technology, China

*Corresponding author

ABSTRACT

This chapter investigates the relationship between digitalization and cultural heritage, namely, its preservation, involvement, and sustainability implications. It begins by discussing the importance of cultural heritage and its issues before delving into merging digital technologies with conventional preservation methods. The report examines best practices and upcoming trends by looking at digital documenting approaches, virtual reconstruction, and case studies such as the Louvre Museum and Machu Picchu. Furthermore, it discusses the relevance of accessibility, data protection, and community engagement in digitization efforts, emphasizing inclusive approaches that empower various stakeholders. It also investigates the possibilities of digital tools like smartphone apps, virtual tours, and augmented reality to improve tourist experiences and cultural appreciation. The study emphasizes digitalization's revolutionary potential in cultural heritage tourism by addressing future directions and difficulties, such as policy recommendations, the influence of developing technologies, and partnership opportunities. Finally, it emphasizes the importance of responsible implementation, equitable access, and collaboration to ensure that digitalization positively contributes to preserving and promoting our shared cultural heritage while fostering sustainability and enriching experiences for current and future generations.

Digitalization in Tourism. Hulya Akdemir Cengiz, Seza Zerman, Aysegul Acar, and Faizan Ali (Eds.)

DOI: 10.1201/9781779644770-8

6.1 INTRODUCTION

Cultural heritage has centuries-long roots, as individuals and civilizations have been drawn to investigate and celebrate their cultural legacy. Pilgrimages to religious sites, grand tours of classical antiquity, and expeditions to discover lost civilizations are just a few examples of humanity's persistent love of history (Rudgley, 2000). However, it was not until the later half of the 20th century that cultural heritage tourism emerged as a distinct and increasingly prominent segment of the larger tourism business. Cultural heritage tourism has grown due to increasing awareness of its importance and the need to preserve it for future generations (Kim et al., 2021). Technological advancements have increased public access to cultural assets, allowing travelers to explore remote sites and interact with indigenous tribes.

In recent years, digitalization has emerged as a significant instrument for preserving and promoting cultural heritage, and transforming how we document, interpret, and experience the past (Mendoza et al., 2023; Sabarirajan et al., 2024). From three-dimensional (3D) scanning and virtual reality (VR) (Büyüksalih et al., 2020) to digital databases, chatbots, and mobile applications (Ahmad et al., 2024; Turner et al., 2018), digital technologies provide novel answers to the difficulties confronting cultural heritage sites and the tourism industry.

This chapter will investigate the junction of digitalization in cultural heritage preservation, revealing digital technology's enormous impact on preservation efforts and visitor experiences. It will explore how digital tools are transforming cultural heritage conservation, ranging from advanced documentation approaches to novel interpretive methodologies. Furthermore, this chapter will look at how digitalization is changing the landscape of cultural heritage preservation by increasing accessibility, engagement, and sustainability. Through case studies and research, it will provide insights into best practices, difficulties, and future directions for using digitization to protect and promote our shared cultural heritage.

6.2 TRANSFORMING DIGITALIZATION IN CULTURAL HERITAGE PRESERVATION

Digitalization has transformed cultural heritage preservation by introducing cutting-edge approaches and technologies for recording, archiving, and rebuilding heritage locations and artifacts. Here, we investigate the different ways of digitalization in cultural heritage preservation.

6.2.1 DIGITAL DOCUMENTATION TECHNIQUES: 3D SCANNING, PHOTOGRAMMETRY, AND LIDAR

Digital documentation techniques have transformed the area of cultural heritage preservation, giving cutting-edge technologies for recording, analyzing, and visualizing heritage locations and artifacts with unparalleled precision. The most popular digital documentation techniques are 3D scanning, photogrammetry, and LiDAR (light detection and ranging). Here, we go over each of these strategies in detail.

6.2.1.1 3D SCANNING

3D scanning, sometimes called laser scanning or surveying, uses laser technology to acquire exact 3D measurements of objects and situations (Büyüksalih et al., 2020; Templin and Popielarczyk, 2020). The method typically includes the following steps:

(a) Laser scanning involves using a laser beam to scan an object's surface.
(b) Generating a point cloud of XYZ coordinates.
(c) This data is then processed to create a mesh, a digital representation of the object's surface geometry.
(d) High-resolution images or textures can be layered on the mesh for photorealistic reproduction.
(e) 3D scanning has various applications in cultural heritage preservation, including digitalizing cultural artifacts, documenting heritage sites, and creating virtual reconstructions for tourists to explore and interact with restored heritage places.

6.2.1.2 PHOTOGRAMMETRY

Photogrammetry is a method of creating 3D models using overlapping images of an object or location (Ch'ng et al., 2019). It involves image acquisition, processing, 3D reconstruction, and texture mapping. It has applications in cultural heritage preservation, such as cultural artifact documentation, reconstructing heritage sites and architectural buildings, and allowing researchers, educators, and the public to explore and interact with heritage places. This process helps identify similar features and match points between images, ensuring an accurate representation of the object or scene.

6.2.1.3 LIDAR

LiDAR is a remote sensing technology that utilizes laser pulses to build precise 3D maps of objects and environments (Li et al., 2023). LiDAR technology involves laser scanning, data processing, and 3D modeling to create detailed topographic maps of cultural heritage sites and landscapes. It allows structural analysis of buildings, monuments, and archaeological sites, providing information about their state and integrity. LiDAR also aids in site mapping and monitoring, allowing researchers and conservationists to track changes over time and plan conservation actions. Digital documentation techniques like 3D scanning, photogrammetry, and LiDAR have transformed cultural heritage preservation by enabling precise digital representations of heritage objects.

6.3 DIGITAL ARCHIVING AND DATABASE MANAGEMENT SYSTEMS

Digital archiving and database management systems (DBMS) play an essential role in cultural heritage preservation because they provide centralized platforms for storing, organizing, and accessing digital documentation of heritage locations, artifacts, and related information (Bisták et al., 2021). These systems provide scholars, conservationists, educators, and the general public access to rich cultural heritage resources, facilitating study, education, and public outreach. In this section, we look at the most essential components of digital archiving and DBMS in cultural heritage preservation.

6.3.1 STORAGE AND ORGANIZATION

Digital archiving systems store and preserve cultural heritage items such as 3D models, photos, videos, documents, and information (Tsipi et al., 2023).

These systems are intended to handle massive amounts of data, ensuring that digital assets are safely kept and conveniently accessed over time. DBMS make digital archives easier to organize and maintain, allowing for structured data storage, retrieval, and manipulation. DBMS enables users to create, update, and query databases that contain information about heritage places, artifacts, provenance, conservation treatments, research findings, and other relevant data.

6.3.2 *ACCESSIBILITY AND SEARCHABILITY*

Digital archiving systems offer user-friendly interfaces and search features to make cultural heritage resources more accessible. Users can search for specific assets or information using keywords, filters, and advanced search tools, allowing for quick retrieval of relevant content (García-Santiago and Olvera-Lobo, 2017). DBMS allow users to organize and categorize digital assets using metadata, tags, and schemes. Metadata provides descriptive information about digital assets, such as title, creator, date, location, subject, and keywords, allowing users to find and access relevant content.

6.3.3 *PRESERVATION AND LONG-TERM ACCESS*

Digital archiving systems use preservation measures to maintain the integrity and accessibility of digital materials. It includes data redundancy, backup methods, encryption, authentication, and version control techniques to prevent data loss, corruption, and unauthorized access (Butler et al., 2022). Database management solutions aid data preservation by allowing data movement, format conversion, and metadata preservation procedures. These solutions keep digital assets accessible and usable, even as technology advances and hardware and software platforms change.

6.3.4 *COLLABORATION AND SHARING*

Digital archiving systems promote collaboration and knowledge exchange among academics, environmentalists, educators, and the general public. Users can exchange digital assets, research findings, and best practices with colleagues and stakeholders, which promotes multidisciplinary collaboration and community participation (Jacob and Nóbrega, 2021). Database management solutions facilitate collaborative processes by incorporating access controls, permissions, and versioning procedures. These capabilities allow numerous users to collaborate on shared databases, contribute data, and collaborate on research projects while maintaining data integrity and security.

6.3.5 INTEROPERABILITY AND INTEGRATION

Digital archiving and database management solutions are compatible with other software tools and platforms for cultural heritage preservation. It enables seamless integration of digital archives with various systems, including content management systems, geographic information systems, and VR environments (García-Marco et al., 2020; Paskaleva and Azorin, 2010). Interoperability allows users to use current tools and infrastructure, communicate data across platforms, and incorporate digital assets into various applications and workflows. It encourages creativity, efficiency, and scalability in cultural heritage protection activities.

6.4 VIRTUAL RECONSTRUCTION AND AUGMENTED REALITY APPLICATIONS

Virtual reconstruction and augmented reality (AR) apps are transformative digital tools that change how we preserve and interpret cultural material. Virtual reconstruction entails digitally recreating historical locations, architectural buildings, and cultural landscapes using archaeological evidence, historical documentation, and academic research (Chong et al., 2022). These reconstructions provide information about cultural sites' look, layout, and function from various historical periods. They strive for historical accuracy, using professional knowledge and archaeological finds to ensure accurate representation. Furthermore, virtual reconstructions offer immersive experiences that enable users to traverse, explore, and interact with rebuilt surroundings in real-time. Users can interact with history in dynamic and engaging ways by using virtual tours, educational games, and multimedia exhibits, which enhance awareness and appreciation of cultural heritage.

AR applications add digital content to the actual environment, enhancing visitors' experiences at historical sites and museums. AR technology delivers contextual information and interpretations of heritage locations and artifacts, helping people comprehend and engage. Users can view historical images, films, audio recordings, and written information layered on tangible objects, which enhances their learning experience. AR applications also provide interactive experiences, allowing users to control virtual items, browse historical reconstructions, and participate in storytelling activities. This interactivity encourages curiosity, creativity, and active learning, appealing to a wide range of consumers.

These digital tools will substantially impact cultural heritage protection, interpretation, and involvement. Virtual reconstructions allow researchers, educators, and the general public to investigate and comprehend cultural sites and artifacts in novel and engaging ways (Chong et al., 2022). They contribute to research by visualizing historical contexts and architectural elements, making communicating findings to a wide range of audiences easier. AR applications improve engagement and outreach by attracting and capturing visitors through interactive and immersive experiences. Museums, heritage sites, and cultural organizations use AR technology to produce interesting exhibitions, tours, and educational programs that promote curiosity and respect for cultural heritage.

Furthermore, virtual reconstruction and AR apps improve accessibility and inclusivity in cultural heritage events (Chong et al., 2021). These digital tools make experiences more accessible to a wide range of audiences, including those with disabilities, language problems, and limited mobility. Users can tailor online experiences to their tastes, hobbies, and accessibility requirements, ensuring that cultural heritage is accessible to everyone. Cultural heritage organizations can use digital technology to expand their reach, engage new audiences, and encourage future generations to respect and protect our shared cultural legacy. As digital technologies advance, virtual reconstruction and AR will play a more significant role in defining the future of cultural heritage preservation and education.

6.5 CASE STUDIES: EXAMPLES OF SUCCESSFUL DIGITAL PRESERVATION PROJECTS

Several effective digital preservation projects have substantially impacted tourism by improving visitor experiences, promoting cultural assets, and reaching a larger audience (Conway, 2010; Masnadi et al., 2023). Here are some notable case studies.

1. **Google Arts & Culture** collaborates with cultural organizations globally to digitize and showcase artworks, artifacts, and heritage locations. Google Arts & Culture provides users with immersive and interactive interactions with global cultural heritage via high-resolution photos, 3D models, virtual tours, and curated displays. For example, users can visit the historic ruins of Machu Picchu (Payntar, 2022), the complex carvings of Angkor Wat (Siregar, 2021), and the iconic masterpieces of the Louvre Museum from the comfort of their own homes (Evrard and Krebs, 2018). By making cultural assets available to a worldwide audience, Google Arts & Culture encourages travel and cultural inquiry.

2. **The Vatican Museums** provides a virtual tour of their holdings, allowing visitors to explore the galleries, chapels, and courtyards from anywhere worldwide (Verde and Valero, 2021). Users can view high-resolution masterpieces like Michelangelo's Sistine Chapel ceiling and Raphael's Stanze di Raffaello using interactive multimedia material. The virtual tour offers a thorough and immersive view of the Vatican Museums, enabling people to plan future excursions to Rome to see these masterpieces. Furthermore, the virtual tour expands the accessibility of the Vatican's collections, making them available to people who may be unable to visit in person owing to physical disabilities or travel restrictions.

3. **Historic Environment Scotland (HES)** offers digital materials to promote tourism and highlight Scotland's cultural heritage. Visitors can experience historic places, including Edinburgh Castle, Stirling Castle, and Skara Brae, via online platforms such as the HES website and mobile apps, which provide virtual tours, interactive maps, and multimedia guides (Millican et al., 2017). These digital tools provide visitors with helpful information about Scotland's history, architecture, and archaeology, helping them better understand and appreciate its cultural heritage. Furthermore, the availability of digital information encourages travelers to visit historic locations in person, where they can gain personal experience with Scotland's legacy.

4. **The Acropolis Museum** in Athens provides a virtual tour that allows visitors to view exhibits and galleries remotely. Users can learn about the history and significance of the Parthenon sculptures and other ancient artifacts on display in the museum via high-resolution photos, 360-degree panoramas, and multimedia content (Poulaki et al., 2021). The virtual tour engages and informs viewers interested in Greek history and archaeology, inviting them to visit the Acropolis Museum and other cultural destinations in Athens during their trip.

These case studies demonstrate the importance of digital preservation projects in tourism promotion by offering immersive, educational, and accessible experiences with cultural heritage. These programs encourage travel, artistic exploration, and enjoyment of varied historical destinations by utilizing digital technology to present artworks, artifacts, and historic buildings. Furthermore, they increase access to cultural heritage, allowing people worldwide to interact with and learn about heritage sites and artifacts regardless of their geographic location or travel restrictions. Overall, digital preservation projects are important in improving tourist experiences and promoting cultural heritage tourism globally.

6.6 DIGITAL TOOLS FOR ENHANCING VISITOR EXPERIENCES

6.6.1 MOBILE APPLICATIONS

Mobile applications have developed as vital tools for improving tourist experiences in cultural heritage tourism, with a wide range of features and functions that enrich exploration, learning, and engagement with heritage sites and artifacts. Here is a detailed look at mobile applications for cultural heritage tourism.

6.6.1.1 ACCESSIBILITY AND CONVENIENCE

Mobile applications offer tourists easy access to information, maps, and multimedia content about heritage sites via smartphones or tablets (Camilleri et al., 2023). This accessibility allows tourists to explore cultural attractions independently, eliminating the need for guided tours or physical guidebooks. Tourists can easily download and install heritage tourism apps from app stores, allowing them to access valuable resources before, during, and after their trips to heritage sites.

6.6.1.2 INTERACTIVE MAPS AND NAVIGATION

Cultural tourism applications often include interactive maps and navigation tools to assist users in navigating cultural sites, finding points of interest, and scheduling visits efficiently (Camilleri et al., 2023). These maps frequently feature markers, trails, and checkpoints to direct tourists along predetermined routes or thematic tours. Users can obtain detailed information about each area of interest, such as historical context, architectural significance, and multimedia content, which helps them understand and appreciate the site.

6.6.1.3 AUDIO GUIDES AND AR

Audio guides and AR are popular in historical tourism apps, offering narrated tours of locations, museums, and artifacts (Tsepapadakis and Gavalas, 2023). These audio guides provide compelling storytelling, historical context, and expert commentary to enhance visitors' experiences and develop deeper connections with cultural heritage. Furthermore, several apps use AR technology to superimpose digital content on the physical environment, improving users' comprehension and involvement with heritage places through immersive experiences.

6.6.1.4 MULTIMEDIA CONTENT AND VIRTUAL TOURS

Heritage tourism applications commonly use multimedia information, including high-resolution photos, films, 3D models, and virtual tours, to highlight heritage places and artifacts in greater depth (Iacovino et al., 2020). Users can explore interactive exhibitions, watch digital reconstructions, and immerse themselves in virtual worlds that bring history to life. Virtual tours enable users to see heritage places remotely, providing panoramic views of galleries, exhibitions, and architectural highlights, increasing access to cultural heritage for those unable to attend in person.

6.6.1.5 PERSONALIZED EXPERIENCES AND RECOMMENDATIONS

Some heritage tourism apps provide personalized experiences based on user interests, choices, and demographics (Konstantakis et al., 2020). These apps can give personalized routes, points of interest, and targeted content based on users' profiles and behavior by employing data analytics and user profiling. Personalization elements increase tourist engagement and satisfaction by catering to specific tastes and learning styles, increasing the overall cultural heritage tourism experience.

6.6.1.6 GAMIFICATION AND INTERACTIVE ACTIVITIES

Gamification and interactive activities are widely used in historical tourism apps to increase visitor engagement and motivation (Marques et al., 2023). These apps may incorporate interactive quizzes, scavenger hunts, challenges, and incentives that inspire users to visit historical locations, solve riddles, and participate in educational activities. Gamified experiences encourage active learning, curiosity, and enjoyment, attracting visitors of all ages and backgrounds.

Overall, mobile apps for cultural heritage tourism improve visitor experiences by giving easy access to information, interactive maps, multimedia material, personalized suggestions, and gamified activities. These apps enable visitors to explore heritage places autonomously, learn about history and culture, and interact with cultural heritage in immersive and meaningful ways. As technology advances, mobile applications will continue to develop and improve the cultural heritage tourism experience, instilling curiosity, forging relationships, and protecting our shared history for future generations.

6.6.2 VIRTUAL TOURS AND INTERACTIVE EXHIBITS

Virtual tours and interactive exhibits have transformed how visitors interact with cultural heritage sites, museums, and exhibitions, providing immersive and informative experiences that cross physical and geographical borders (Kamariotou et al., 2021). Here's a detailed look into virtual tours and interactive exhibitions in cultural heritage tourism.

6.6.2.1 VIRTUAL TOURS

Virtual tours use digital technology to replicate realistic experiences of historical sites, allowing viewers to explore them remotely from anywhere in the world. The key aspects of virtual tours are:

1. High-quality imaging: Virtual tours frequently include high-resolution photos or 360-degree panoramic views, giving users a thorough and accurate representation of historical locations, museums, and exhibitions.
2. Users can use straightforward controls to navigate virtual tours, moving effortlessly around different places, zooming in on specific details, and switching between viewpoints.
3. Audio guides and spoken commentary may be included in virtual tours to provide context, historical background, and insights into the significance of specific artifacts or architectural details.
4. Multimedia enhancements: Some virtual tours include multimedia components like videos, animations, and interactive hotspots that provide additional information, enriching the user experience and enhancing engagement.

6.6.2.2 INTERACTIVE EXHIBIT

Interactive exhibitions use digital technology to create interactive experiences that engage visitors and promote learning and exploration. Key features of interactive exhibitions are:

1. Hands-on activities: Interactive exhibitions frequently feature hands-on activities, touchscreens, and displays, allowing visitors to control things, examine concepts, and interact with multimedia information.
2. Gamification features: Some interactive displays use gamification features like quizzes, riddles, challenges, and incentives to encourage visitors to participate, learn, and compete while exploring cultural heritage themes.
3. AR and VR: Advanced interactive exhibits may combine AR and VR technology to superimpose digital content on the actual

surroundings or to create immersive virtual experiences that transfer visitors to other periods or locales.

4. Customization and personalization: Interactive exhibits may offer customization options or personalized experiences that cater to visitors' interests, preferences, and learning styles, allowing them to tailor their experience to suit their individual needs.

6.6.2.3 EDUCATIONAL BENEFITS

Virtual tours and interactive exhibits provide educational opportunities for people of all ages and backgrounds (Cheng, 2022; Kuna et al., 2023). These include the following:

1. Enhanced learning: Virtual tours and interactive displays help visitors learn and appreciate cultural heritage themes, artifacts, and historical events by offering access to multimedia content, historical context, and expert commentary.
2. Hands-on activities, gamification, and multimedia upgrades promote active engagement and participation, fostering curiosity, critical thinking, and problem-solving abilities.
3. Accessibility and inclusivity: Virtual tours and interactive exhibitions can be viewed remotely, making cultural heritage more accessible to people who cannot visit heritage sites in person due to physical, financial, or geographical limitations. Furthermore, digital platforms can be created to accommodate varied learning styles, languages, and access needs, assuring inclusion for all visitors.

6.7 CHALLENGES AND OPPORTUNITIES

6.7.1 ACCESSIBILITY AND DIGITAL DIVIDE CONCERNS

Accessibility and digital divide concerns pose substantial difficulties in digitalizing cultural heritage preservation, necessitating careful study and proactive efforts to promote inclusivity and equitable access for everyone (Doğan and Jelinčić, 2023). These concerns cover various issues, including technological access, skills, and impediments that may prevent some persons or groups from fully participating in digital cultural heritage activities.

One of the most pressing challenges is unequal access to technology and digital resources across groups (Van Dijk, 2020). The digital divide is the difference between those with access to computers, the internet, and other digital technology and those without. This disparity can be influenced by socioeconomic class, geographic location, age, handicap, and educational background. Individuals from marginalized communities, rural places, or economically poor origins may lack access to reliable internet connectivity, digital equipment, or the skills required to traverse digital platforms successfully. As a result, people may face challenges in accessing online exhibits, virtual tours, and educational resources about cultural heritage. Furthermore, Van Dijk (2020) explains in his book that accessibility concerns go beyond physical access to technology and include issues like usability, design, and accommodating varied demands. To ensure that individuals with disabilities, such as those with visual, auditory, motor, or cognitive impairments, can use digital platforms and information, accessibility principles must be considered. This could include offering alternative formats for material, such as audio descriptions, captions, and screen readers, assuring compatibility with assistive technology, and adhering to online accessibility standards. Cultural sensitivity and language diversity must also be considered to ensure digital experiences are inclusive and welcoming to people from all backgrounds.

Addressing accessibility and digital divide challenges in digitalizing cultural heritage tourism and its preservation necessitates collaboration between cultural heritage organizations, technology developers, policymakers, and community stakeholders (Jamil, 2021). Strategies for fostering inclusion and equal access could include:

1. Digital inclusion efforts: Developing programs and efforts to increase digital literacy, skill training, and access to technology in underserved communities, including collaborations with libraries, community centers, and educational institutions (Giglitto et al., 2023).
2. Universal design: Using universal design principles in the creation of digital platforms and content to ensure accessibility and usability for people with a variety of needs and abilities (Karovska Ristovska and Minov, 2022).

3. Community engagement: Community engagement entails working with local communities and stakeholders to understand their needs, preferences, and access hurdles and co-creating digital solutions tailored to their specific contexts and difficulties (Roque, 2022).
4. Collaboration and partnerships: Hirsenberger et al. (2019) articulate that working with technology companies, accessibility experts, and advocacy groups will create new solutions and best practices for solving accessibility and digital divide issues in cultural heritage tourism.
5. Policy and Regulation: Advocating for policies and regulations that promote digital rinclusion, accessibility standards, and equal access to technology resources, including funding initiatives, tax incentives, and legislation to support digital equity initiatives (Boodaghi et al., 2022).

By prioritizing accessibility and digital inclusion in digitalizing cultural heritage tourism, organizations may ensure that digital cultural heritage experiences are accessible, inclusive, and enriching for all tourists, regardless of background or ability. This commitment to fairness and accessibility improves the visitor experience and promotes social inclusion, diversity, and empowerment in the cultural heritage sector.

6.7.2 DATA PRIVACY AND SECURITY ISSUES

Data privacy and security concerns are important factors in digitalizing cultural heritage preservation since they entail gathering, storing, and administrating sensitive visitor information and digital assets (Vuković and Štefanac, 2023). These challenges include a variety of concerns about personal data protection, compliance with privacy legislation, and mitigating cybersecurity threats associated with the use of digital technology for historical interpretation and tourism. One of the most pressing problems is preserving visitor privacy and the ethical use of personal data obtained through digital platforms and interactions. Cultural heritage organizations frequently collect visitor data for various objectives, including tickets, bookings, marketing, and personalized experiences. Personal identifiers such as names, contact information, demographic information, and behavioral data may be acquired via website analytics or mobile applications.

Protecting sensitive data against unauthorized access, misuse, or breaches is critical for maintaining visitor confidence and complying with privacy rules such as the General Data Protection Regulation (GDPR) in the European Union and the California Consumer Privacy Act (CCPA) in the United States.

Furthermore, data privacy considerations apply to third-party services, cloud storage, and data sharing agreements, which may require transferring visitor data to other vendors or partners (Vuković and Štefanac, 2023). Cultural heritage organizations must enter data processing agreements with third-party service providers to protect visitor privacy and comply with legal requirements. Furthermore, transparency and informed consent are critical components of data privacy. Visitors should be informed about how their data will be used, who will have access to it, and how they can exercise their rights to access, rectification, or deletion.

Addressing data privacy and security concerns in digitalizing cultural heritage tourism necessitates a holistic approach that includes technology, governance, and compliance controls. Key solutions for managing data privacy and security concerns may include:

1. Data protection policies: Create detailed data protection policies and procedures outlining how visitor data will be gathered, processed, stored, and secured following applicable privacy rules (Borissova, 2018).
2. Privacy by design: incorporating privacy concepts and data protection safeguards into the design and development of digital platforms, applications, and services to reduce privacy risks and increase user confidence (Kosmas et al., 2020).
3. Staff training and awareness: Offering training and awareness programs to staff members involved in data handling, cybersecurity, and compliance to ensure they understand their obligations and best practices for preserving visitor privacy and data security (Black, 2018).
4. Incident response planning: Creating incident response plans and processes to address data breaches, cyberattacks, and other security issues, such as notification procedures, forensic investigations, and remediation strategies (Psaroudakis et al., 2021).
5. Compliance monitoring: Regularly monitoring and auditing data processing activities to ensure compliance with privacy regulations, industry standards, and organizational policies, as well as

conducting privacy impact assessments to identify and mitigate privacy risks associated with new initiatives or technologies (Guilfoyle and Mitchell, 2015).

Organizations that prioritize data privacy and security in the digitalization of cultural heritage tourism can build visitor trust, protect sensitive information, and ensure the responsible use of digital technologies to improve visitor experiences and preserve cultural heritage for future generations.

6.8 INTEGRATION OF DIGITAL TECHNOLOGIES WITH TRADITIONAL PRESERVATION METHODS

6.8.1 COMPATIBILITY AND INTEROPERABILITY

Compatibility and interoperability challenges include assuring compatibility and interoperability between new digital tools and traditional preservation techniques (TK, 2022). Cultural heritage experts must navigate the complications of combining modern tools like 3D scanning, photogrammetry, and VR with traditional documenting, restoration, and conservation methods. Achieving seamless integration necessitates careful planning, training, and adaptation to ensure digital technology supplements conventional techniques rather than undermine preservation efforts.

6.8.2 INFRASTRUCTURE AND CAPACITY BUILDING

Integrating digital technology with traditional preservation methods requires investment in infrastructure, equipment, and experience for data collecting, processing, and management (Kamran, 2022). Cultural heritage organizations must obtain specialized hardware and software for digital preservation efforts and train staff members to operate and maintain these technologies successfully. Furthermore, improving data storage, archival, and curation infrastructure is required to manage the vast volumes of digital data generated by preservation efforts while ensuring long-term accessibility and preservation.

6.8.3 OPPORTUNITIES FOR ENHANCED DOCUMENTATION AND INTERPRETATION

Despite obstacles, digital technologies and traditional preservation methods can improve cultural heritage recording, interpretation, and presentation (Alma'aitah et al., 2020). Digital techniques enable capturing high-resolution 3D models, detailed photogrammetric reconstructions, and immersive virtual environments, which provide significant insights into cultural buildings and artifacts. These digital representations can be utilized for study, education, and public engagement, making knowledge more widely available and encouraging appreciation for cultural heritage.

6.8.4 FACILITATING COLLABORATION AND ENGAGEMENT

Digital technology enables collaboration, knowledge exchange, and interdisciplinary research in the cultural heritage industry and beyond (Blake, 2018). By digitizing heritage assets and making them available online, cultural heritage organizations can engage with scholars, educators, and the general public worldwide, allowing for remote exploration, analysis, and interpretation. Furthermore, digital platforms and virtual displays enable interactive storytelling, community participation, and co-creation of cultural narratives, allowing a wide range of stakeholders to participate in heritage preservation and interpretation initiatives.

6.9 HARNESSING DIGITALIZATION FOR SUSTAINABLE TOURISM PRACTICES

Harnessing digitalization for sustainable tourism practices includes utilizing digital technology and techniques to reduce environmental effects, enhance sociocultural benefits, and ensure economic sustainability in the tourism business (Hoang et al., 2023). This strategy tries to balance the requirements of visitors, local people, and the environment, ensuring that tourism operations are sustainable, responsible, and beneficial to all stakeholders. Here's a detailed look at how digitization might be leveraged for sustainable tourism practices:

1. Environmental conservation: Digital technologies can help reduce the environmental impact of tourism activities. For example, internet booking systems and mobile applications simplify travel

planning and eliminate the need for paper-based products like brochures and tickets, reducing waste output and resource usage (Cai et al., 2021). Furthermore, digital tools allow for monitoring and managing tourist flows, which help limit the effects of overpopulation, habitat deterioration, and pollution in sensitive natural areas. Furthermore, VR and AR experiences provide alternatives to physical travel, allowing visitors to enjoy sites remotely while lowering carbon emissions from transit.

2. Cultural preservation and community empowerment: Digitalization can empower local populations by facilitating cultural expression, heritage interpretation, and economic engagement in tourism operations (Suardana et al., 2022). Local artists, guides, and entrepreneurs can expose their cultural heritage, products, and services to a worldwide audience via digital platforms such as community-based tourism websites and online marketplaces. It promotes cultural diversity and economic inclusion. Furthermore, digital storytelling projects, interactive displays, and virtual tours help to spread cultural information and practices, encouraging people to learn and appreciate different cultures. By including local communities in tourist decision-making processes and revenue-sharing mechanisms, digitalization can ensure that tourism benefits are dispersed equitably and contribute to destination communities' sustainable development.

3. Economic resilience and innovation: Digitalization promotes economic resilience and innovation in the tourism industry by increasing market competitiveness, expanding revenue streams, and encouraging entrepreneurship (Shen et al., 2022). Tourism businesses can use digital marketing techniques, social media campaigns, and online booking platforms to reach new audiences, attract customers, and respond to changing market trends. Furthermore, digital channels, such as crowdfunding websites and peer-to-peer sharing platforms, make it easier to fund and develop sustainable tourism projects, including eco-friendly hotels, community-based initiatives, and responsible tour operators. Furthermore, digital technologies such as big data analytics and artificial intelligence (AI) provide valuable insights into consumer behavior, market demand, and sustainability indicators, allowing

businesses and destinations to make data-driven decisions and optimize resource allocation for long-term outcomes.

4. Education and awareness: Digitalization promotes education and understanding sustainable tourism practices among stakeholders such as travelers, industry professionals, legislators, and local communities (Kisusi and Masele, 2019). Websites, smartphone applications, and online courses are examples of digital platforms that provide easily available and interactive learning resources on themes including responsible travel, environmental conservation, and cultural heritage preservation. Furthermore, social media platforms, blogs, and virtual events enable knowledge sharing, conversation, and collaboration among various stakeholders, boosting awareness of sustainable tourism concerns and driving positive behavior change. By leveraging digitalization for education and awareness campaigns, the tourist sector can enable people to make educated decisions, adopt sustainable travel practices, and become ambassadors for responsible tourism in their communities.

To summarize, digitizing for sustainable tourism practices necessitates a comprehensive and collaborative approach incorporating environmental, social, and economic factors into tourist planning, management, and development. The tourism industry can help achieve the United Nations Sustainable Development Goals (SDGs) by leveraging digital technologies and strategies to reduce environmental impact, promote cultural preservation, foster economic resilience, and educate stakeholders. It will ensure that tourism remains a force for positive change and sustainable development in the coming years.

6.10 CASE STUDIES: BEST PRACTICES IN DIGITALIZATION OF CULTURAL HERITAGE PRESERVATION

6.10.1 THE LOUVRE MUSEUM: DIGITIZATION INITIATIVES AND VIRTUAL TOURS

The Louvre Museum, one of the world's largest and most visited museums, has launched substantial digitalization initiatives to improve access and engagement with its massive collection of artworks and artifacts (Evrard and Krebs, 2018). Through collaborations with technological companies and digital platforms, the Louvre has created virtual tours that allow visitors to experience its galleries and exhibitions remotely. These virtual tours provide high-resolution photos, 360-degree views, and full descriptions of artworks, creating an immersive and instructive experience for internet visitors. Furthermore, the Louvre has digitized a large collection, making it available via online databases, mobile applications, and digital archives. By embracing digitalization, the Louvre Museum has increased access to its cultural treasures, reaching audiences worldwide and instilling a love of art and history.

6.10.2 MACHU PICCHU: 3D MAPPING AND CONSERVATION EFFORTS

Machu Picchu, a famous archaeological site and UNESCO World legacy Site in Peru, has introduced innovative 3D mapping and conservation measures to protect its cultural legacy and improve visitor experiences (Masini et al., 2023). Machu Picchu has created detailed 3D maps of the monument and its surroundings using LiDAR technology in collaboration with archaeologists, environmentalists, and technological specialists. These 3D maps aid archaeological study, conservation planning, and environmental monitoring, thereby protecting Machu Picchu from natural disasters, erosion, and visitor impacts. Furthermore, Machu Picchu has introduced sustainable tourism techniques such as visiting limitations, route maintenance, and cultural education programs to balance conservation and tourism development. Machu Picchu ensures long-term preservation through 3D mapping and conservation activities.

6.10.3 THE ACROPOLIS MUSEUM: AR EXHIBITS AND EDUCATIONAL PROGRAMS

The Acropolis Museum in Athens, Greece, utilizes AR technology to improve tourist experiences and promote cultural education (Poulaki et al., 2021). The museum's AR exhibits enable visitors to engage with virtual replicas of ancient Greek sculptures, architectural features, and artifacts. Visitors can use mobile applications and AR devices to see how the Parthenon and other Acropolis monuments appeared in ancient times, providing insight into their historical context and significance. The Acropolis Museum also offers educational programs and seminars incorporating AR technology to engage students and visitors in interactive learning experiences. By mixing AR with traditional museum exhibits and educational activities, the Acropolis Museum improves visitor engagement, promotes cultural understanding, and protects the history of ancient Greek civilization.

6.10.4 PETRA, JORDAN: DIGITAL PRESERVATION AND COMMUNITY ENGAGEMENT

Petra, an archaeological monument and UNESCO World legacy monument in Jordan, has introduced digital preservation projects to protect its cultural legacy and include local communities in conservation efforts (Aburamadan et al., 2021). The Petra Archaeological Park has collaborated with technology businesses and academic institutions to digitize archaeological data, produce digital reconstructions, and build interactive exhibits highlighting the history and relevance of Petra's monuments and artifacts. Petra has also created community participation programs that involve local communities in cultural protection, tourism management, and economic development projects. Petra supports sustainable tourism, cultural exchange, and economic empowerment for local people via digital platforms, including websites, mobile applications, and VR experiences. Petra uses digital preservation and community involvement to preserve and promote its cultural heritage.

6.11 FUTURE DIRECTIONS AND IMPLICATIONS

6.11.1 EMERGING TECHNOLOGIES AND TRENDS IN DIGITAL PRESERVATION

Emerging technologies and trends in cultural heritage will likely affect the future of digitization by providing creative solutions for preservation, interpretation, and visitor engagement. These could include advances in AI, machine learning, and data analytics, which can improve the efficiency and effectiveness of digital preservation operations by automating tasks like artifact detection, metadata tagging, and conservation planning.

VR and AR technologies are predicted to become increasingly immersive and interactive, allowing visitors to engage with cultural heritage in novel ways, such as virtual time travel to historical periods or interactive storytelling experiences. Furthermore, the Internet of Things (IoT) and sensor technologies show promise for real-time monitoring and management of heritage monuments, allowing proactive conservation actions.

6.11.2 POLICY RECOMMENDATIONS FOR GOVERNMENTS AND CULTURAL ORGANIZATIONS

Governments and cultural organizations have an important role in influencing the future of digitalization in cultural heritage tourism by developing policies, providing money, and establishing regulatory frameworks. Policy proposals may include developing standards and rules for digital preservation, data protection, and accessibility to promote consistency and interoperability across digital efforts. Furthermore, governments can encourage investment in digital infrastructure and capacity building through grants, tax breaks, and public–private partnerships. Cultural organizations should priorities digital literacy training for their employees, create ethical rules for data handling and preservation, and participate in collaborative networks to share best practices and resources. Furthermore, governments should address the socioeconomic consequences of digitalization for local populations, ensuring that tourism development is sustainable, inclusive, and fair.

6.11.3 POTENTIAL IMPACT OF DIGITALIZATION ON CULTURAL HERITAGE PRESERVATION

The extensive use of digitalization in cultural heritage preservation can transform the field, opening up new possibilities and problems for maintaining and promoting cultural material. Digital technology can help document, analyze, and interpret cultural places and artifacts, giving scholars fresh insights into their historical relevance and preservation needs. However, digitization creates worries about data privacy, cybersecurity, and authenticity because digital assets are susceptible to theft, manipulation, or misinterpretation. Furthermore, digitalization may exacerbate existing inequities and power imbalances in the cultural heritage sector by limiting access to technology and digital resources for some communities or areas. As a result, digitalization's ethical, social, and cultural ramifications on cultural heritage preservation must be carefully considered to ensure that digital initiatives are implemented responsibly and inclusively.

6.11.4 OPPORTUNITIES FOR COLLABORATION AND KNOWLEDGE SHARING

Collaboration and knowledge exchange are critical for maximizing the benefits of digitization in cultural heritage preservation while tackling shared difficulties across regions and industries. Establishing multidisciplinary research networks, cooperating with technological businesses and academic institutions, and engaging with local communities and indigenous peoples in co-creation processes are all potential avenues for collaboration. Furthermore, knowledge-sharing platforms such as online forums, conferences, and workshops can help digital preservation and tourism professionals communicate best practices, lessons learned, and case studies. By encouraging collaboration and knowledge sharing, stakeholders may use their combined skills and resources to promote digital cultural heritage tourism and preserve the long-term viability of our common cultural legacy for future generations.

6.12 CONCLUSION

In conclusion, the journey through the landscape of digitalization in cultural heritage preservation has revealed profound insights and implications for the future. As we reflect on integrating digital technologies with traditional preservation methods and examining best practices showcased in case studies, it becomes increasingly apparent that digitalization holds transformative potential for the preservation, interpretation, and promotion of cultural heritage. The synthesis of these findings underscores the critical importance of accessibility, community engagement, and equitable access to digital resources in harnessing digitalization to democratize access to cultural heritage.

Looking ahead, the horizon of digitalization in cultural heritage preservation is filled with promise, yet it also presents many challenges that demand attention and proactive strategies. While emerging technologies such as AI, AR, and IoT offer compelling opportunities for innovation and exploration, they also raise significant concerns regarding data privacy, cybersecurity, and the preservation of authenticity. Addressing these challenges requires a multifaceted approach encompassing collaborative efforts, robust policies, and community engagement to ensure digitalization is implemented responsibly and inclusively.

Moreover, as we navigate the future landscape of digitalization in preserving cultural heritage, it becomes evident that ensuring equitable access to digital resources, fostering collaboration, and addressing socio-economic impacts are paramount challenges that demand collective action and steadfast commitment from stakeholders across sectors. By embracing digital technologies and fostering collaboration, stakeholders can unlock new frontiers for preserving, interpreting, and promoting cultural heritage, enriching visitor experiences, advancing conservation efforts, and promoting sustainable tourism practices.

In essence, digitalization stands as a powerful force with the potential to revolutionize cultural heritage preservation, offering boundless opportunities for innovation and transformation. Yet, realizing this potential requires a steadfast commitment to principles of accessibility, authenticity, and sustainability, ensuring that our cultural heritage remains accessible, valued, and well-preserved for the enrichment of present and future generations. As we chart the course forward, let us stay guided by these principles, fostering a future where cultural heritage is cherished, celebrated, and safeguarded for all.

KEYWORDS

- **augmented reality**
- **cultural heritage**
- **digitalization**
- **3D scanning**
- **LiDAR**
- **Louvre Museum**
- **Machu Picchu**

REFERENCES

Aburamadan, R., Trillo, C., Udeaja, C., Moustaka, A., Awuah, K. G., & Makore, B. C. (2021). Heritage conservation and digital technologies in Jordan. *Digital Applications in Archaeology and Cultural Heritage*, *22*, e00197.

Ahmad, M., Naeem, M. K. H., Mobo, F. D., Tahir, M. W., & Akram, M. (2024). Navigating the journey: How Chatbots are transforming tourism and hospitality. In *Design and development of emerging Chatbot technology* (pp. 236–255). IGI Global.

Alma'aitah, W. Z. a., Talib, A. Z., & Osman, M. A. (2020). Opportunities and challenges in enhancing access to metadata of cultural heritage collections: A survey. *Artificial Intelligence Review*, *53*(5), 3621–3646.

Bisták, P., Zachar, J., Rášová, A., Lieskovský, T., Kravjanská, I., Orosová, M., Kročková, K., & Felcan, M. (2021). Archaeological digital archiving in heritage management in Slovakia. *Internet Archaeology*, *58*.

Black, R. (2018). Improving engagement between tourists and staff at natural and cultural heritage tourism sites: Exploring the concept of interpretive conversations. *Tourism Recreation Research*, *43*(1), 82–90.

Blake, J. (2018). Museums and safeguarding intangible cultural heritage–facilitating participation and strengthening their function in society. *International Journal of Intangible Heritage*, *13*(1), 18–32.

Boodaghi, O., Fanni, Z., & Mehan, A. (2022). Regulation and policy-making for urban cultural heritage preservation: A comparison between Iran and Italy. *Journal of Cultural Heritage Management and Sustainable Development.*

Borissova, V. (2018). Cultural heritage digitization and related intellectual property issues. *Journal of Cultural Heritage*, *34*, 145–150.

Butler, G., Szili, G., & Huang, H. (2022). Cultural heritage tourism development in Panyu District, Guangzhou: community perspectives on pride and preservation, and concerns for the future. *Journal of Heritage Tourism*, *17*(1), 56–73.

Büyüksalih, G., Kan, T., Özkan, G. E., Meriç, M., Isın, L., & Kersten, T. P. (2020). Preserving the knowledge of the past through virtual visits: From 3D laser scanning to virtual reality visualisation at the Istanbul Çatalca İnceğiz caves. *PFG–Journal of Photogrammetry, Remote Sensing and Geoinformation Science*, *88*(2), 133–146.

Cai, Z., Fang, C., Zhang, Q., & Chen, F. (2021). Joint development of cultural heritage protection and tourism: The case of Mount Lushan cultural landscape heritage site. *Heritage Science*, *9*(1), 1–16.

Camilleri, M. A., Troise, C., & Kozak, M. (2023). Functionality and usability features of ubiquitous mobile technologies: The acceptance of interactive travel apps. *Journal of Hospitality and Tourism Technology*, *14*(2), 188–207.

Ch'ng, E., Cai, S., Zhang, T. E., & Leow, F.-T. (2019). Crowdsourcing 3D cultural heritage: best practice for mass photogrammetry. *Journal of Cultural Heritage Management and Sustainable Development*, *9*(1), 24–42.

Cheng, K.-H. (2022). Teachers' perceptions of exploiting immersive virtual field trips for learning in primary education. *Journal of Research on Technology in Education*, *54*(3), 438–455.

Chong, H. T., Lim, C. K., Ahmed, M. F., Tan, K. L., & Mokhtar, M. B. (2021). Virtual reality usability and accessibility for cultural heritage practices: Challenges mapping and recommendations. *Electronics*, *10*(12), 1430.

Chong, H. T., Lim, C. K., Rafi, A., Tan, K. L., & Mokhtar, M. (2022). Comprehensive systematic review on virtual reality for cultural heritage practices: Coherent taxonomy and motivations. *Multimedia Systems*, 1–16.

Conway, P. (2010). Preservation in the age of Google: Digitization, digital preservation, and dilemmas. *The Library Quarterly*, *80*(1), 61–79.

Doğan, E., & Jelinčić, D. A. (2023). Changing patterns of mobility and accessibility to culture and leisure: Paradox of inequalities. *Cities*, *132*, 104093.

Evrard, Y., & Krebs, A. (2018). The authenticity of the museum experience in the digital age: The case of the Louvre. *Journal of Cultural Economics*, *42*, 353–363.

García-Marco, F.-J., Galindo, F., Lasala, P., & del Ramo, J. L. (2020). *Advancing the interoperability of the GLAM+ and cultural tourism sectors through KOS: Perspectives and challenges*. Knowledge Organization at the Interface.

García-Santiago, L., & Olvera-Lobo, M.-D. (2017). IPABA checklist for Heritage in Spanish: How to assess visibility and accessibility on the web. *Preservation, Digital Technology & Culture*, *46*(4), 136–148.

Giglitto, D., Ciolfi, L., Lockley, E., & Kaldeli, E. (2023). *Digital approaches to inclusion and participation in cultural heritage: Insights from research and practice in Europe*. Taylor & Francis.

Guilfoyle, D. R., & Mitchell, M. B. (2015). Compliance-based archaeological heritage management and place-based participatory mapping for negotiated outcomes. *Australian Archaeology*, *80*(1), 80–90.

Hirsenberger, H., Ranogajec, J., Vucetic, S., Lalic, B., & Gracanin, D. (2019). Collaborative projects in cultural heritage conservation–management challenges and risks. *Journal of Cultural Heritage*, *37*, 215–224.

Hoang, S. D., Dey, S. K., Tučková, Z., & Pham, T. P. (2023). Harnessing the power of virtual reality: Enhancing telepresence and inspiring sustainable travel intentions in the tourism industry. *Technology in Society*, *75*, 102378.

Iacovino, A., De Paolis, L. T., & Ndou, V. (2020). Technologies to support tourism innovation and cultural heritage: Development of an immersive virtual reality application. *Augmented Reality, Virtual Reality, and Computer Graphics: 7th International Conference*, AVR 2020, Lecce, Italy, September 7–10, 2020, Proceedings, Part II 7.

Jacob, J., & Nóbrega, R. (2021). Collaborative augmented reality for cultural heritage, tourist sites and museums: sharing Visitors' experiences and interactions. In *Augmented reality in tourism, museums and heritage: A new technology to inform and entertain* (pp. 27–47). Springer.

Jamil, S. (2021). From digital divide to digital inclusion: Challenges for wide-ranging digitalization in Pakistan. *Telecommunications Policy*, *45*(8), 102206.

Kamariotou, V., Kamariotou, M., & Kitsios, F. (2021). Strategic planning for virtual exhibitions and visitors' experience: A multidisciplinary approach for museums in the digital age. *Digital Applications in Archaeology and Cultural Heritage*, *21*, e00183.

Kamran, M. (2022). Role of cultural heritage in promoting the resilience of linear/critical infrastructure system with the enhancement of economic dimension of resilience: A critical review. *International Journal of Construction Management*, *22*(7), 1345–1354.

Karovska Ristovska, A., & Minov, N. (2022). *Universal design and cultural heritage. Studia* universitatis hereditati.

Kim, S., Whitford, M., & Arcodia, C. (2021). Development of intangible cultural heritage as a sustainable tourism resource: The intangible cultural heritage practitioners' perspectives. In *Authenticity and authentication of heritage* (pp. 34–47). Routledge.

Kisusi, R. L., & Masele, J. J. (2019). Efficacy of public awareness strategies for promoting existing cultural heritage tourism assets in Dar es Salaam. *Journal of Heritage Tourism, 14*(2), 117–137.

Konstantakis, M., Alexandridis, G., & Caridakis, G. (2020). A personalized heritage-oriented recommender system based on extended cultural tourist typologies. *Big Data and Cognitive Computing, 4*(2), 12.

Kosmas, P., Galanakis, G., Constantinou, V., Drossis, G., Christofi, M., Klironomos, I., Zaphiris, P., Antona, M., & Stephanidis, C. (2020). Enhancing accessibility in cultural heritage environments: Considerations for social computing. *Universal Access in the Information Society, 19*, 471–482.

Kuna, P., Hašková, A., & Borza, Ľ. (2023). Creation of virtual reality for education purposes. *Sustainability, 15*(9), 7153.

Li, Y., Zhao, L., Chen, Y., Zhang, N., Fan, H., & Zhang, Z. (2023). 3D LiDAR and multi-technology collaboration for preservation of built heritage in China: A review. *International Journal of Applied Earth Observation and Geoinformation, 116*, 103156.

Marques, C. G., Pedro, J. P., & Araújo, I. (2023). A systematic literature review of gamification in/for cultural heritage: leveling up, going beyond. *Heritage, 6*(8), 5935–5951.

Masini, N., Romano, G., Sieczkowska, D., Capozzoli, L., Spizzichino, D., Gabellone, F., Bastante, J., Scavone, M., Sileo, M., & Abate, N. (2023). Non invasive subsurface imaging to investigate the site evolution of Machu Picchu. *Scientific Reports, 13*(1), 16035.

Masnadi, I., Rosman, D., Levyta, F., & Adiati, M. P. (2023). Evaluating the visitor satisfaction on cultural heritage digital museum in google arts and culture: A study of Puppet Museum Jakarta. *2023 International Conference on Digital Applications, Transformation & Economy (ICDATE).*

Mendoza, M. A. D., De La Hoz Franco, E., & Gómez, J. E. G. (2023). Technologies for the preservation of cultural heritage—A systematic review of the literature. *Sustainability, 15*(2), 1059.

Millican, K., Dixon, P., Macinnes, L., & Middleton, M. (2017). Mapping the historic landscape: Historic land-use assessment in Scotland. *Landscapes, 18*(1), 71–87.

Paskaleva, K. A., & Azorin, J. A. (2010). Developing integrated e-tourism services for cultural heritage destinations. *International Journal of Services Technology and Management, 13*(3–4), 247–262.

Payntar, N. D. (2022). Archaeological heritage 'on-the-rise': Detecting emerging tourist attractions in Peru using machine learning and geotagged photographs. *Journal of Heritage Tourism, 17*(2), 222–244.

Poulaki, P., Kritikos, A., & Vasilakis, N. (2021). Digital Technology as a means of promoting cultural tourism in Greece–Case Study: Acropolis Museum. *Sustainable Development, Culture, Traditions, 1.*

Psaroudakis, C., Xanthopoulos, G., Stavrakoudis, D., Barnias, A., Varela, V., Gkotsis, I., Karvouniari, A., Agorgianitis, S., Chasiotis, I., & Vlachogiannis, D. (2021). Development of an early warning and incident response system for the protection of visitors from natural hazards in important outdoor sites in Greece. *Sustainability*, *13*(9), 5143.

Roque, M. I. (2022). Storytelling in cultural heritage: Tourism and community engagement. In *Global perspectives on strategic storytelling in destination marketing* (pp. 22–37). IGI Global.

Rudgley, R. (2000). *The lost civilizations of the stone age*. Simon and Schuster.

Sabarirajan, A., Reddi, L. T., Rangineni, S., Regin, R., Rajest, S. S., & Paramasivan, P. (2024). Leveraging MIS Technologies for Preserving India's cultural heritage on digitization, accessibility, and sustainability. In *Data-driven intelligent business sustainability* (pp. 122–135). IGI Global.

Shen, J., Chou, R.-J., Zhu, R., & Chen, S.-H. (2022). Experience of community resilience in rural areas around heritage sites in Quanzhou under transition to a knowledge economy. *Land*, *11*(12), 2155.

Siregar, A. T. (2021). Angkor Wat—A transcultural history of heritage Volume 1: Angkor in France. From Plaster Casts to Exhibition Pavilions. Volume 2: Angkor in Cambodia. From Jungle Find to Global Icon, by Michael Falser. *Bijdragen tot de taal-, land-en volkenkunde/Journal of the Humanities and Social Sciences of Southeast Asia*, *177*(4), 569–571.

Suardana, I. W., Gelgel, I. P., & Watra, I. W. (2022). Traditional villages empowerment in local wisdom preservation towards cultural tourism development. *International Journal of Social Sciences*, *5*(1), 74–81.

Templin, T., & Popielarczyk, D. (2020). The use of low-cost unmanned aerial vehicles in the process of building models for cultural tourism, 3D web and augmented/mixed reality applications. *Sensors*, *20*(19), 5457.

TK, G. K. (2022). Conserving knowledge heritage: opportunities and challenges in conceptualizing cultural heritage information system (CHIS) in the Indian context. *Global Knowledge, Memory and Communication*, *71*(6/7), 564–583.

Tsepapadakis, M., & Gavalas, D. (2023). Are you talking to me? An audio augmented reality conversational guide for cultural heritage. *Pervasive and Mobile Computing*, *92*, 101797.

Tsipi, L., Vouyioukas, D., Loumos, G., Kargas, A., & Varoutas, D. (2023). Digital repository as a service (D-RaaS): Enhancing access and preservation of cultural heritage artifacts. *Heritage*, *6*(10), 6881–6900.

Turner, M., Dowsland, S., Mazel, A., & Giesen, M. (2018). Rock art CARE: A cross-platform mobile application for crowdsourcing heritage conservation data for the safeguarding of open-air rock art. *Journal of Cultural Heritage Management and Sustainable Development*, *8*(4), 420–433.

Van Dijk, J. (2020). *The digital divide*. John Wiley & Sons.

Verde, A., & Valero, J. M. (2021). Virtual museums and Google arts & culture: Alternatives to the face-to-face visit to experience art. *International Journal of Education and Research*, *9*(2), 43–54.

Vuković, M., & Štefanac, T. (2023). Digital cultural heritage, Cybersecurity, and the human factor. *Preservation, Digital Technology & Culture*, *52*(4), 129–141.

PART III
Future Technologies and Digital Innovation

CHAPTER 7

Digital Destinations: Unraveling the Impact of Social Media on Modern Tourism Dynamics

POLA Q. WANG

School of Hospitality and Tourism, Auckland University of Technology, Auckland, New Zealand

ABSTRACT

This chapter explores the impact of social media on the tourism industry, detailing how digital platforms have revolutionized destination marketing and traveler behavior. The transition from traditional marketing methods to interactive digital engagement is examined, highlighting the role of mobile technologies and user-generated content in democratizing travel information. This chapter discusses the significance of social media in destination branding, emphasizing how platforms facilitate more dynamic and personal engagement with potential tourists. It also explores the strategic use of influencer marketing in shaping consumer perceptions and behaviors. Additionally, this chapter addresses the challenges and ethical considerations associated with social media in tourism, including issues of misinformation, privacy concerns, and the promotion of sustainable practices. Emerging trends and future research directions are outlined, emphasizing the importance of leveraging social media analytics and advanced technologies, such as virtual reality and AI-driven personalization to enhance the tourism experience. This comprehensive analysis underscores the evolving landscape of tourism in the digital age and provides insights into navigating the opportunities and challenges presented by social media.

Digitalization in Tourism. Hulya Akdemir Cengiz, Seza Zerman, Aysegul Acar, and Faizan Ali (Eds.)

DOI: 10.1201/9781779644770-10

7.1 INTRODUCTION

The emergence of social media has fundamentally transformed the tourism industry, marking a significant shift from traditional marketing methods to digital platforms. This transformation has been catalyzed by the proliferation of platforms, like Facebook, Instagram, and Tripadvisor, which have fundamentally altered how destinations are marketed and perceived (Hudson and Thal, 2013). The role of these digital platforms extends beyond mere promotional tools. They have become integral in shaping travelers' interactions, behaviors, and expectations. Initially, the tourism sector relied heavily on conventional marketing methods, including print media, broadcast advertising, and travel agencies. However, with the advent of web 2.0, the landscape began to change dramatically especially in the last decade. Social media platforms, characterized by their interactive and user-generated content (UGC), have allowed for a more dynamic form of engagement between travelers, destinations, and travel-related businesses (Boyd and Ellison, 2007). The real-time, interactive nature of these platforms has enabled a more immediate and personal way for users to access information, share experiences, and form connections. Mobile technologies like smartphones and tablets have further accelerated this shift by altering the timing and nature of traveler information consumption (Gretzel and Fesenmaier, 2009). This move to digital platforms reflects a broader trend in consumer behavior toward seeking instant, accessible, and personalized content. Consequently, the tourism industry has had to adapt, developing strategies to engage with consumers on these platforms effectively and innovatively. This shift to digital platforms has not only provided marketing opportunities for the tourism industry but also fundamentally altered the role of travelers. From being passive recipients of information, travelers have become active creators and sharers of content (Wang et al., 2014). This participatory aspect of social media has led to a more democratized form of information dissemination, where peer reviews, user experiences, and shared content significantly influence travel decisions.

The primary objective of this chapter is to explore the transformative impact of social media on the tourism industry, focusing on how digital platforms have revolutionized destination marketing, traveler engagement, and the overall travel experience. This chapter seeks to provide a comprehensive analysis of the shift from traditional marketing methods to digital platforms, highlighting the pivotal role of social media in shaping modern tourism dynamics. By examining the integration of mobile technologies and UGC, this chapter aims to demonstrate how these elements have democratized travel information and empowered travelers to become active participants in the marketing process. Additionally, this chapter explores the strategic use of influencer marketing and its efficacy in influencing consumer behavior and perceptions. Ethical considerations, such as misinformation and privacy concerns are also addressed, emphasizing the need for sustainable and responsible social media practices in the tourism domain. Furthermore, this chapter discusses emerging trends and future research directions, including the use of social media analytics and advanced technologies, like virtual reality (VR) and AI-driven personalization, to enhance the tourism experience. The scope of this chapter extends to providing insights for academics, industry practitioners, and policymakers on navigating the opportunities and challenges presented by social media in the tourism sector. Through a detailed exploration of these themes, this chapter aims to offer a nuanced understanding of the digital transformation in tourism and its implications for the future of the industry.

7.2 EVOLUTION OF SOCIAL MEDIA IN TOURISM

Social media, a term constantly evolving in its definition and application, is broadly understood as a platform for interaction among people, where they create, share, and exchange information and ideas in virtual communities and networks (Zeng and Gerritsen, 2014). Kaplan and Haenlein (2010) describe it as internet-based applications that enable the creation and exchange of UGC, building on the technological foundations of web 2.0. Cohen (2011) compiled 30 definitions, each highlighting different aspects, including the reliance on information technology, the function as a peer-to-peer communication channel fostering content creation and exchange, and the ability to link users into virtual communities, impacting real-life behaviors. Social networking, often discussed in tandem with social media, focuses more on building social networks and relationships among people with shared interests or connections. Social networking is the use of social media primarily to connect and interact with others—groups of people with shared interests—whereas social media refers more broadly to tools and platforms for creating and distributing content (Lachapelle, 2011).

Social media encompasses a wide range of platforms, including social networking sites, consumer review sites, content community sites, wikis, internet forums, and location-based media. It has reshaped social connectivity by integrating various forms of communication, including text, pictures, videos, and audio. Social media platforms are online spaces where individuals can interact and share digital content (Kaplan and Haenlein, 2010). While primarily designed for social interaction, these platforms have evolved into significant advertising channels. This development is crucial for industries like tourism, where marketing strategies are rapidly adapting to new digital realms.

According to Xiang and Gretzel (2010), a relatively small number of domains form the core, dominating the social media landscape within the tourism context. This core group includes websites that travelers frequently visit to share experiences, access reviews, or connect with others in virtual communities. Xiang and Gretzel (2010) categorize social media into three major types: virtual communities (such as iougo.com and lonelyplanet.com), consumer review sites (such as tripadvisor.com and zagat.com), and personal blogs. These categories together constitute the majority of social media sites relevant to travel. Additionally, there are significant contributions from social networking and media sharing sites, though they form a smaller proportion of the overall social media landscape in this context. The most popular social media websites that contain travel-related content are tripadvisor.com, virtualtourist.com, and iguoguo.com in the United States (Xiang and Gretzel, 2010). Chu et al. (2020) reviewed the literature on social media advertising from 2004 to 2019 and concluded that the top three social media platforms reviewed were Facebook, Tripadvisor.com, and Twitter among a number of relevant journals.

7.3 SOCIAL MEDIA AND DESTINATION MARKETING

Research has consistently highlighted the role of social media as a vital marketing tool (Li, 2011; Okazaki and Taylor, 2013; Saxena and Khanna, 2013). The increasing scholarly attention in this field is evident from the diversity of research topics, ranging from the use and impact of advertising on social media to consumer-generated content and electronic word of mouth (Knoll, 2016). Social media's transformational impact on customer service, marketing, and promotion within the tourism sector is a well-recognized theme in recent scholarly discourse. Tourism organizations, including destination marketing organizations (DMOs) are reconfiguring their business models and operations to incorporate social media. Notable examples include Tourism Australia's invitation to operators to promote their services on its extensive Facebook base and the Australian National Online Strategy Committee's development of the "Tourism e-kit", with a significant focus on social media (Tourism Australia, 2012; Tourism Queensland, 2012). However, there is a noticeable variance in social media usage in the tourism sector across countries. For instance, while U.S. DMOs have been proactively incorporating various social media tools, Swiss DMOs have been more reserved.

Researchers have also observed differences in social media use between small-medium enterprises and larger companies in the tourism sector (Pesonen, 2011), with business scale potentially influencing social media success. DMOs face challenges in integrating social media, such as reconciling corporate and social media cultures and adapting traditional management structures to innovative communication tools. The traditional providers of travel-related information are also grappling with the rising significance of social media (Xiang and Gretzel, 2010). Notably, many national tourism organizations (NTOs) have not fully utilized social media for tourism management, with limited presence on platforms like Facebook and underuse of UGC (Stankov et al., 2010).

Recent studies have explored how engagement with social media influences the reception of embedded advertisements. Voorveld et al. (2018) discovered that interactions with different social media platforms yield varied responses to advertisements. Additionally, Johnston et al. (2018) identified a positive correlation between attitudes toward social media advertising and specific social media behaviors. Their work also introduced new perspectives on viral advertising in social media, borrowing concepts from non-advertising media studies. Similarly, Seo et al. (2018) found that narrative transportation significantly influences the effectiveness of viral advertising on social media, particularly when strong interpersonal connections exist between the sender and receiver of the message.

Kaosiri et al. (2019) identified that the UGC on social media not only aids in decision-making but also sets expectations about destinations. Investigating the motivations behind travel knowledge sharing on social network sites, Huang et al. (2010) identified three main drivers: obtaining travel information, disseminating information, and personal documentation.

They also observed privacy concerns and the time-consuming nature of SNS (social networking site) as significant barriers to travel knowledge sharing. The “Share a Coke” campaign, launched by Coca-Cola in 2011 in Australia, stands as a testament to the power of innovative marketing and its unintentional yet significant impact on destination marketing. Initially conceived to bolster Coca-Cola’s market share and consumer engagement, the campaign replaced the iconic Coca-Cola logo on bottles with 150 of the most popular Australian names, encouraging consumers to find bottles with their names or create custom labels at kiosks. As this campaign gained momentum, with the hashtag #Share a Coke flooding social media, an interesting development occurred. People began associating the bottles with various iconic locations and tourist destinations across Australia, sharing their experiences and photos on social media platforms. This incidental promotion of tourism destinations emerged as individuals used personalized bottles as souvenirs and mementos, inadvertently turning them into symbols of their travel experiences. The overwhelming social media buzz generated through this campaign not only led to a significant increase in Coca-Cola’s sales and market share but also promoted Australian tourism spots globally. The campaign’s unexpected success in this dual role, boosting both brand engagement and tourism, was later emulated in other global markets, showcasing the potent combination of personalization and social media in creating viral marketing phenomena and underlining the campaign’s indirect yet effective contribution to destination marketing.

7.4 IMPACT ON TRAVELER BEHAVIOR AND DECISION-MAKING

Over the past decade, social media’s impact on tourism has been a focal point of scholarly research which collectively suggests that social media has fundamentally transformed how tourists source information and make decisions (Dickinger and Mazanec, 2015; Jacobsen and Munar, 2012; Mehraliyev et al., 2019). This impact extends to destination marketing, where platforms, like Facebook, Weibo, Twitter, Instagram, and YouTube are increasingly used to influence destination choices within online communities (Bakr and Ali, 2013). Travel constitutes a journey where individuals leave their daily lives, engage with new environments and cultures, and then return, enriched by their experiences (Gretzel et al., 2006). This journey can be conceptualized into three distinct stages:

pre-trip, during-the-trip, and post-trip. In each of these stages, social media plays a pivotal role in shaping the travel experience.

During the pre-trip stage, travelers engage in planning and preparation, which is increasingly influenced by social media. Platforms like Instagram and Tripadvisor offer a wealth of information and peer reviews, guiding travelers in making informed decisions about destinations, accommodations, and activities (Gretzel et al., 2006). Studies have shown that information source preferences and the use of social media significantly vary in the pre-trip stage, influenced by factors, like destination characteristics and individual decision-making styles. In the during-the-trip stage, the role of social media shifts to real-time information access, communication, and sharing. Mobile technologies enable travelers to interact with their social networks, seek immediate advice, and share experiences as they happen. This real-time engagement profoundly impacts travel behaviors and decision-making processes, enhancing the travel experience through a social and interactive lens (Gretzel and Fesenmaier, 2009). Finally, the post-trip stage sees travelers reflecting on and sharing their experiences more extensively. Social media platforms serve as a repository where travelers can relive their journeys, offer recommendations, and engage with a broader community. This stage reinforces the social construction of travel experiences, as shared narratives contribute to the collective meaning-making process.

Understanding the dynamic use of social media across these stages is crucial and offers insights into traveler behavior and preferences, enabling the development of tailored marketing and communication strategies. The concept of a "media repertoire" is particularly useful here, suggesting that travelers develop unique, stage-specific patterns in their use of social media, influenced by various individual and situational factors (Gretzel et al., 2006).

7.4.1 INFLUENCER MARKETING

Influencer marketing harnesses the potential of individuals with significant social followings to enhance brand awareness and influence consumer behaviors. This marketing strategy, though not a new concept, has gained a renewed momentum with the advent of social media. It involves leveraging the status of opinion leaders, celebrities, and other influential figures to shape consumer attitudes and behaviors, a practice that has been a staple in marketing and tourism for some time (Roy et al., 2021). The dynamics of influencer marketing are well-explained by Kelman's (1961) seminal work, which identified three processes of social influence: compliance, where individuals accept influence for favorable outcomes; identification, where they adopt behaviors to maintain a relationship; and internalization, where the influence aligns with their personal values. This framework provides a foundational understanding of influencer marketing. Additionally, McCracken's (1989) meaning transfer model explains how influencers convey cultural meanings associated with themselves to the brands they endorse, thereby enhancing the brand's credibility and value. Scheer and Stern (1992) further elucidated this with a framework outlining the stages from the influencer's initial attempt to influence the follower to the follower's eventual behavior. These theories underscore the multifaceted nature of influencer marketing and its significant role in shaping consumer choices in the digital age.

The core of influencer marketing lies in the relationship between influencers and their followers, fundamentally involving the transfer and internalization of cultural meanings and values. Kelman's (1961) theory illustrates how individuals adopt behaviors through compliance, identification, and internalization, the latter being crucial as it resonates with personal values. McCracken's (1989) model suggests that celebrities transfer their cultural associations to endorsed brands, embedding the brand within the influencer's cultural fabric. Social media influencers (SMIs) stand out in this landscape, deriving influence from their personal brand, crafted through social media content. Their effectiveness stems from their understanding of social media rhetoric, the needs of their followers, and their ability to engage personally, fostering a sense of community around the brands they promote.

7.4.2 "INSTAGRAMMABLE TOURISM": HOW VISUAL APPEAL SHAPES DESTINATION POPULARITY

Instagram, a visually driven platform, allows users to capture, enhance with filters, and share photos and videos. With over 1.4 billion total users as of 2024 (Statista, 2024), Instagram significantly influences modern tourism. Research has examined how social media affects tourism, focusing on tourist photos (Larsen et al., 2007), the tourist gaze (Dinhopl and Gretzel, 2016), traveler identity (Gretzel, 2018), and destination consumption (Smith, 2018), along with the value generation around tourist experiences (Conti and Lexhagen, 2020). This section explores a critical phenomenon introduced by Instagram: tourism driven by Instagrammability.

Unlike text-centric platforms, such as Twitter and Facebook, Instagram thrives on instant visual appeal rather than deep analysis or discussion. Images on Instagram are primarily designed for immediate visual impact, giving rise to "Instagramism," a concept where users employ specific esthetic strategies to create visually appealing images and curate an esthetically driven identity (Manovich, 2019). This approach aligns with a society that values beautiful images, experiences, and designs as central to both economic and social functions.

For Instagram users, esthetics is crucial to forming and performing their identity. Social media spaces have become arenas for constructing, expressing, and marketing an idealized self. This process of identity formation requires validation from others, where captivating images play a critical role in attracting attention. The regulation of esthetics on Instagram enhances the likelihood of drawing public interest. Consequently, users are motivated to produce sophisticated images to project a stylish persona. Creating visually appealing images involves various strategies, including placing a well-styled self against an attractive backdrop. These backdrops range from everyday settings, like cafes and well-designed apartments to exotic landscapes. Such landscapes serve as signs that bolster individual status and desirability, acting as badges of a branded self and esthetic backdrops for self-promotion. This insight is vital to understanding Instagram-driven tourism. Although tourism has always been visual, the rise of social media has intensified the importance of visual appeal, making it a primary goal of travel.

Travelers increasingly seek out destinations that offer picturesque settings for social media. Instagrammable locations can be any esthetically pleasing place, even if they lack traditional tourist attractions. Esthetically appealing places can gain fame and become popular tourist spots solely based on their visual qualities. Tourism today is increasingly driven by visual consumption, with destinations not only offering products but also curating images that captivate audiences. Tourists meticulously arrange objects, choose color filters, and find the perfect angles before capturing and sharing their photos on social media. This process, known as scenarization, transforms spaces into theatrical settings designed to simulate and enhance reality for tourists.

Scenography, originally a theatrical term, has evolved to create three-dimensional, picturesque representations of spaces (Hann, 2018). This involves more than mere decoration. It's about creating dramatic, narrative-driven environments that engage spectators. The concept of scenery extends from these roots, encompassing not only natural beauty but also artificial constructs designed to attract tourists. Mass tourism often relies on fabricated sceneries to entice visitors, contrasting everyday banality with visually striking settings. Destinations and businesses increasingly use social media to market "Instagrammable" spots, leveraging visually appealing elements, such as striking backgrounds, curated decor, and optimal lighting.

Instagrammable locations, even if artificially enhanced, attract tourists seeking perfect photo opportunities. Examples include South Korea's "life shot" trend, where esthetically appealing spots draw both local and international visitors (Oh, 2020), and Indonesia's Orchid Forest Cikole Lembang, marketed explicitly as an Instagram-friendly destination. Travel bloggers and journalists often compile lists of the most Instagrammable places, highlighting the global trend toward visually curated tourism spots. This phenomenon extends to specially designed sceneries, such as streets adorned with floating umbrellas, which have been replicated worldwide.

In some cases, these Instagrammable sceneries involve deliberate visual illusions, like Bali's Pura Lempuyang Temple, where a mirror creates the appearance of a lake in photos (NZ Herald, 2019). Such settings are crafted primarily for their photographic appeal, underscoring the shift toward visual consumption in modern tourism. These examples illustrate the significant impact of Instagrammable tourism, where the quest for the perfect photo can transform, disrupt, or revitalize destinations. The "life shot" phenomenon demonstrates how visual appeal on social media can drive tourism trends, reshaping the physical and cultural landscapes of travel destinations.

7.5 CHALLENGES AND ETHICAL CONSIDERATIONS

The integration of social media into the tourism industry has brought forth a multitude of transformative opportunities, yet it simultaneously presents a series of significant challenges and issues that need careful consideration and strategic management. Several issues have emerged that are worthy of consideration. Addressing misinformation and privacy concerns in the context of social media use in tourism becomes increasingly complex when considering the phenomenon of lurkers—individuals who consume content without actively engaging. Lurkers often refrain from participation due to apprehensions about exposure and the perceived risks to their privacy. Yet, their perspectives, feedback, and criticism are invaluable for companies seeking to refine their products and services based on authentic consumer insights. Sun et al. (2014) propose strategies to encourage these lurkers to contribute, including offering tangible rewards (external stimuli), boosting users' self-confidence (encouragement), simplifying platform usage (usability improvement), and providing guidance for newcomers through advice from experienced members. It's crucial for the tourism industry to foster an environment that not only combats misinformation and upholds privacy standards but also encourages honest and reliable interaction from all users, including lurkers. Such an environment not only improves the quality and reliability of the information shared but also ensures a more inclusive and representative feedback mechanism, enabling service providers to better understand and cater to the needs and concerns of a broader user base.

From a technical perspective, the language barrier is a significant challenge in this globalized, predominantly English-speaking online world. Tourists and tourism practitioners from non-English speaking countries often find themselves at a disadvantage when using social media for international travel planning or marketing. This suggests a need for multilingual platforms to accommodate both the providers and consumers in the tourism industry. Another technological challenge lies in the limitations of current product search engines, which struggle to effectively utilize information dispersed across various social media platforms. This highlights an area for further research and development in information technology and website design, to improve data management and cross-media information sharing.

From a management perspective, the use of social media in tourism also presents risks. The vast amount of UGC on social media platforms can serve as a potent source of word-of-mouth, which can be both beneficial and detrimental. Negative feedback from dissatisfied customers, if not managed appropriately, can lead to adverse consequences for the tourism industry.

Furthermore, the credibility of UGC has been a point of concern among researchers, given its influence on consumer perceptions and decision-making in tourism (Munar and Jacobsen, 2013). These challenges underscore the need for strategic management and innovative solutions to harness the potential of social media effectively in the tourism sector.

The ethical landscape of influencer marketing in tourism is becoming increasingly complex and further heightened when considering the characteristics of facilitators who play a significant role in shaping audience behaviors and perceptions. Service providers need to design strategies that address users with varied motivations, such as altruism or personal fulfilment. For those inclined toward sharing their travel experiences, continuous encouragement and recognition can be effective. This approach aligns with the growing strategy of leveraging SMIs in the tourism industry. These influencers, through their posts on platforms, like Facebook, Instagram, blogs, and Twitter are shaping audience behaviors and travel decisions (Magno and Cassia, 2018). The ethical implications extend beyond transparency and authenticity in endorsements. There's a need for tourism agencies to identify and collaborate with active contributors who offer valuable travel advice and insights. These influencers, who guide audiences on where to go, eat, or what to do at a destination, wield considerable power in persuading and influencing larger audiences. Ensuring that these influencers operate within an ethical framework is crucial. This includes clear disclosure of sponsored content, promoting sustainable and responsible tourism practices, and maintaining a balance between commercial interests and genuine, trustworthy engagement with their audience. In this way, influencer marketing can be harnessed effectively and ethically, offering benefits not just to service providers and influencers, but also to the wider audience seeking authentic travel experiences.

The complicated relationship between destination authenticity and traveler expectations is deeply influenced by the portrayal of destinations on social media platforms, particularly those like Instagram and YouTube, which prioritize visual appeal. These platforms, by offering a holistic online experience of the destination brand, shape traveler expectations significantly. When brand managers effectively use these platforms to showcase a blend of official content and UGC, they create a perception of the destination that emphasizes its temporal consistency, credibility, and originality. This perception directly impacts traveler expectations, as visitors arrive with preconceived notions of what the destination should be like, heavily influenced by the visual narratives they have consumed online (Jimenez-Barreto et al., 2020).

However, the challenge arises when the curated, idealized online presentation of a destination conflicts with its actual, on-ground reality. This discrepancy can lead to a gap between expectation and experience, potentially resulting in traveler dissatisfaction. Conversely, when the visual content accurately reflects the destination's authentic character, it aligns traveler expectations more closely with reality, enhancing their overall experience. Thus, ensuring the authenticity of the online portrayal is not only crucial for maintaining the destination's integrity but also for managing traveler expectations effectively. By doing so, destinations can foster positive experiences, increase satisfaction, and encourage genuine recommendations, reinforcing the importance of authenticity in the online promotion of tourism destinations.

7.6 EMERGING TRENDS AND FUTURE DIRECTIONS

The exploration of new technologies, such as VR, live streaming, and AI-driven personalization in social media is opening up novel avenues in tourism, transcending traditional boundaries of marketing, entertainment, education, accessibility, and heritage preservation. The integration of VR in tourism is not just a tool for creating immersive marketing experiences; it's reshaping the very nature of tourist experiences. Current research in VR tourism, adopting an inductive approach, expands beyond the previously held view that VR primarily serves to enhance the tourist experience in positive ways (Bogicevic et al., 2019).

The existing research on VR in tourism is divided into two main approaches: constructing conceptual models based on various concepts or using specific theories to test VR applications in tourism contexts. These studies generally conclude that VR can positively mediate any type of tourist experience, making it an effective marketing tool for tourism destinations and companies. However, an area that remains relatively unexplored in VR tourism research is the potential for negative emotional responses. While general tourism literature has recently highlighted the importance of studying negative emotions in tourist experiences (Nawijn and Biran, 2019; Oren et al., 2021), VR tourism studies have yet to address this aspect. Considering negative emotional states is crucial, as they can impact the experience in hedonic contexts or be perceived positively in eudaimonic contexts, especially when the experiences are deemed meaningful by tourists. Therefore, future research in VR and tourism needs to encompass a broader spectrum of emotional responses to provide a more comprehensive understanding of its impact on the tourist experience.

Live streaming through e-commerce platforms has also become a revolutionary online marketing tool. This technique, involving streamers showcasing products and services in real-time online environments, has seen significant application in the tourism sector, known as tourism e-commerce live streaming. Notable examples, include China's Ctrip Group initiating the "Boss Live Session," Japan National Tourism Agency broadcasting its Okinawa campaign via Facebook live, and Tourism Australia's "Live from Aus" streaming Australian travel experiences. Research by Zhang et al. (2021) suggests that live streaming of tourist destinations positively influences tourists' desire to visit the places. The key advantage of live streaming in the context of tourism marketing lies in its capacity for real-time interaction, allowing merchants to engage with multiple consumers simultaneously. This interactivity can enhance consumers' perceptions of product value and foster purchase intentions (Wongkitrungrueng et al., 2020). However, the success of converting viewers into buyers isn't universal. As indicated by Wongkitrungrueng et al. (2020), successful live streaming requires a strategic approach that accentuates the positives of the medium while mitigating the negative impacts of consumer uncertainty. The challenge for many businesses lies in effectively leveraging this medium to meet their marketing objectives, as only a few have mastered the art of converting live streaming viewership into tangible commercial results.

AI-driven personalization in social media tourism, increasingly embraced by consumers for its enhancement of the travel experience, is transforming tourism marketing and management services. The recent trend toward personalized services has led to higher satisfaction rates, as these approaches enable the creation of detailed individual profiles used in targeted marketing (Doborjeh et al., 2021). Personalized modeling, a significant evolution from traditional AI systems, tailors a model for each individual based on data from people with similar traits. This method offers a more accurate classification or prediction of an individual tourist's behavior by focusing on datasets most relevant to them. Unlike global modeling, personalized modeling enhances efficiency by selecting and using a smaller yet more pertinent subset of available data for AI learning algorithms (Kasabov, 2007). Incorporating these AI-driven technologies allows the development of smart tourism platforms that adapt to individual lifestyles and past experiences, offering a curated list of services and creating tailored travel programs for each user. This advanced level of personalization in tourism not only enhances the user experience through more relevant and engaging content but also improves the overall effectiveness of tourism marketing strategies. As AI continues to evolve, its role in shaping personalized, impactful, and satisfying tourism experiences is becoming increasingly significant, marking a new era in how travel destinations and services are marketed and experienced.

Social media has become an important tool in promoting sustainable tourism, leveraging its extensive reach and UGC to foster sustainable practices among tourists. Platforms like Instagram, with its focus on visual appeal, play a significant role in influencing travel behavior and destination choices. The potential of social media to support sustainable tourism is evident in several ways, including awareness raising, behavior modification, and destination management.

Firstly, social media's ability to reach global audiences with minimal effort makes it a powerful medium for spreading awareness about sustainable tourism practices. Studies have shown that UGC on platforms like Instagram can significantly impact tourists' attitudes and behaviors (Reilly and Hynan, 2014). This includes encouraging eco-friendly practices, promoting lesser-known sustainable destinations, and highlighting the importance of preserving natural and cultural heritage (Hysa et al., 2022).

Secondly, social media influences tourist behavior by fostering a culture of sustainability through peer influence and social norms. Tourists often look to social media for travel inspiration and advice, which can be harnessed to promote sustainable behaviors. For instance, influencers and travel bloggers who advocate for sustainable tourism can shape their followers' perceptions and actions, encouraging them to make environmentally responsible travel choices (Kilipiri et al., 2023). This peer influence is critical in creating a ripple effect where sustainable practices become more mainstream.

Additionally, social media offers valuable insights for destination management, helping to balance tourism flows and mitigate over tourism. By monitoring social media activity, destination managers can gather real-time data on tourist preferences and behaviors, allowing for more effective planning and management of tourism resources (Hysa et al., 2022). This data-driven approach helps ensure that tourism development aligns with sustainability goals, promoting long-term ecological and social benefits.

However, despite its potential, the integration of social media into sustainable tourism strategies is still in its infancy, and more empirical research is needed to fully understand its impact (Chatterjee and Dsilva, 2020). There are challenges in ensuring that the messages conveyed are genuinely sustainable and not merely greenwashing. As the industry evolves, a more nuanced approach to leveraging social media for sustainability will be necessary, balancing promotional activities with genuine efforts to promote sustainable tourism practices.

The intersection of social media and tourism continues to evolve, presenting several promising avenues for future research. As digital platforms play an increasingly critical role in shaping travel behavior and destination marketing, understanding their long-term implications and potential benefits becomes essential. One key area for future research is the impact of social media analytics (SMA) on tourism. SMA can provide insights into tourist preferences, behavior patterns, and sentiment, allowing tourism stakeholders to tailor their services and marketing strategies more effectively. Studies have highlighted the importance of various analytical approaches, such as sentiment analysis and social network analysis, in understanding tourist behavior and enhancing the tourism experience (Mukhopadhyay et al., 2023). Future research could explore the integration of SMA with advanced technologies like artificial intelligence to predict trends and customize travel experiences.

Another crucial area is the role of social media in promoting sustainable tourism. While social media's potential to influence sustainable travel behavior is acknowledged, there is a need for more empirical studies to understand how social media campaigns can effectively promote sustainability in tourism. Research could focus on the types of content that most effectively encourage eco-friendly practices and how social media platforms can be used to foster a culture of sustainability among tourists (Hysa et al., 2022). Additionally, the role of influencers in promoting sustainable destinations and practices warrants further exploration. The impact of social media on destination branding is another rich field for future research. Social media platforms have revolutionized how destinations are marketed, enabling more dynamic and interactive branding strategies. Future studies could examine the long-term effects of social media-driven destination branding on tourist perceptions and destination loyalty. Additionally, understanding the challenges and opportunities of using social media for branding in various cultural and geographical contexts could provide valuable insights for global tourism marketing strategies (Rudolf, 2022).

Lastly, the influence of social media on tourist experiences and satisfaction is a significant area for further investigation. As tourists increasingly rely on social media for travel planning and sharing their experiences, understanding how these platforms shape their expectations and perceptions can help improve service delivery in the tourism industry. Future research could explore the psychological impacts of social media on tourists, such as the effects of social media-induced pressure to visit popular destinations and the phenomenon of "Instagrammable" tourism spots (Jain et al., 2022).

7.7 CONCLUSION

The interplay between social media and tourism has revolutionized the industry, shifting from traditional marketing methods to dynamic digital platforms. This transformation has not only altered how destinations are marketed but also how they are perceived and experienced by travelers. Social media platforms, like Facebook, Instagram, and Tripadvisor have become essential tools for destination marketing, influencing traveler behavior and expectations significantly. The interactive nature of these platforms facilitates a more personalized and immediate form of engagement, allowing travelers to become active participants in the dissemination of travel information (Hudson and Thal, 2013; Boyd and Ellison, 2007).

For academics, the evolving landscape of social media and tourism offers a rich field for research. Future studies could delve into areas, such as the impact of SMA on tourism marketing, the role of social media in promoting sustainable tourism, and the psychological effects of social media on traveler behavior. Understanding these aspects can provide deeper insights into how digital interactions shape travel experiences and destination choices, ultimately contributing to the development of more effective and ethical marketing strategies (Mukhopadhyay et al., 2023; Hysa et al., 2022).

Industry practitioners can leverage the insights gained from social media research to enhance their marketing strategies and service delivery. By monitoring social media trends and UGC, tourism businesses can tailor their offerings to meet the evolving preferences of travelers. Additionally, the strategic use of influencers and visually appealing content can help destinations attract and retain tourists, fostering brand loyalty and enhancing overall satisfaction (Manovich, 2019; Kilipiri et al., 2023).

Policymakers play a crucial role in regulating and guiding the use of social media in tourism. Ensuring that digital marketing practices are ethical and sustainable is vital for the long-term health of the tourism industry. Policies that promote transparency, protect user privacy, and encourage sustainable travel behaviors can help mitigate some of the challenges posed by the rise of social media (Chatterjee and Dsilva, 2020).

Navigating the challenges and opportunities presented by social media in tourism requires a collaborative effort from academics, industry practitioners, and policymakers. While social media offers unprecedented opportunities for engagement and promotion, it also poses risks, such as misinformation, privacy concerns, and the potential for unsustainable travel practices. Addressing these issues through research, innovative marketing strategies, and robust policy frameworks will be essential in harnessing the full potential of social media to promote a vibrant, sustainable, and ethical tourism industry.

KEYWORDS

- **destination marketing**
- **influencer marketing**
- **Instagrammable tourism**
- **social media analytics**
- **scenarization**
- **tourism industry transformation**
- **user-generated content**

RERERENCES

Bakr, G. M. W. A., & Ali, I. E. H. (2013). The role of social networking sites in promoting Egypt as an international tourist destination. *South Asian Journal of Tourism and Heritage, 6*(1), 169–183.

Bogicevic, V., Seo, S., Kandampully, J. A., Liu, S. Q., & Rudd, N. A. (2019). Virtual reality presence as a preamble of tourism experience: The role of mental imagery. *Tourism Management, 74*, 55–64.

Boyd, D. M., & Ellison, N. B. (2007). Social network sites: Definition, history, and scholarship. *Journal of Computer-Mediated Communication, 13*(1), 210–230. https://doi.org/10.1111/j.1083-6101.2007.00393.x

Chatterjee, J., & Dsilva, N. R. (2020). The role of social media in promoting sustainable tourism. *Emerald Insight*. Retrieved from https://www.emerald.com/insight/.

Chu, S.-C., Deng, T., & Cheng, H. (2020). The role of social media advertising in hospitality, tourism and travel: A literature review and research agenda. *International Journal of Contemporary Hospitality Management, 32*(11), 3419–3438.

Cohen, H. (2011). 30 Social Media Definitions. Posted by Heidi Cohen on May 9, 2011 in Actionable Marketing Social Media, 101. http://heidicohen.com/social-media-definition/ (accessed February 25, 2013).

Conti, E., & Lexhagen, M. (2020). Instagramming nature-based tourism experiences: A netnographic study of online photography and value creation. *Tourism Management Perspectives, 34*, 100650.

Dickinger, A., & Mazanec, J. A. (2015). Significant word items in hotel guest reviews: A feature extraction approach. *Tourism Recreation Research, 40*(3), 353–363.

Dinhopl, A., & Gretzel, U. (2016). Selfie-taking as touristic looking. *Annals of Tourism Research, 57*, 126–139.

Doborjeh, M., Doborjeh, Z., Merkin, A., Bahrami, H., Sumich, A., Krishnamurthi, R., ... & Kasabov, N. (2021). Personalised predictive modelling with brain-inspired spiking neural networks of longitudinal MRI neuroimaging data and the case study of dementia. *Neural Networks, 144*, 522–539.

Gretzel, U. (2018). Tourism and social media. *The Sage Handbook of Tourism Management, 2*, 415–432.

Gretzel, U., & Fesenmaier, D. R. (2009). Information technology: Shaping the past, present, and future of tourism. In *Tourism management* (pp. 41–64). Elsevier. https://doi.org/10.1016/B978-0-12-374900-6.00003-3.

Gretzel, U., Fesenmaier, D. R., & O'Leary, J. T. (2006). The transformation of consumer behaviour. In D. Buhalis & C. Costa (Eds.), *Tourism business frontiers: Consumers, products and industry* (pp. 9–18). Burlington, Massachusetts: Elsevier.

Hann, R. (2018). *Beyond scenography*. Routledge.

Huang, Y., Basu, C., & Hsu, M. K. (2010). Exploring motivations of travel knowledge sharing on social network sites: An empirical investigation of US college students. *Journal of Hospitality Marketing and Management, 19*(7), 717–734.

Hudson, S., & Thal, K. (2013). The impact of social media on the consumer decision process: Implications for tourism marketing. *Journal of Travel and Tourism Marketing, 30*(1–2), 156–160. https://doi.org/10.1080/10548408.2013.751276.

Hysa, B., Zdonek, I., & Karasek, A. (2022). Social media in sustainable tourism recovery. *Sustainability, 14*(2), 760. https://doi.org/10.3390/su14020760.
Jacobsen, J. K. S., & Munar, A. M. (2012). Tourist information search and destination choice in a digital age. *Tourism Management Perspectives, 1*, 39–47.
Jain, T., Mukhopadhyay, S., Modgil, S., & Singh, R. K. (2022). Social media analytics in tourism: A review and agenda for future research. *Benchmarking: An International Journal, 30*(9), 3725–3750. https://doi.org/10.1108/BIJ-05-2022-0309.
Jiménez-Barreto, J., Rubio, N., Campo, S., & Molinillo, S. (2020). Linking the online destination brand experience and brand credibility with tourists' behavioral intentions toward a destination. *Tourism Management, 79*, 104101.
Johnston, W. J., Khalil, S., Le, A. N. H., & Cheng, J. M. S. (2018). Behavioral implications of international social media advertising: An investigation of intervening and contingency factors. *Journal of International Marketing, 26*(2), 43–61.
Kaosiri, Y. N., Callarisa Fiol, L. J., Moliner Tena, M. Á., Rodríguez Artola, R. M., & Sanchez García, J. (2019). User-generated content sources in social media: A new approach to explore tourist satisfaction. *Journal of Travel Research, 58*(2), 253–265.
Kaplan, A. M., & Haenlein, M. (2010). Users of the world, unite! The challenges and opportunities of social media. *Business Horizons, 53*(1), 59–68. https://doi.org/10.1016/j.bushor.2009.09.003.
Kasabov, E. (2007). Towards a contingent, empirically validated, and power cognizant relationship marketing. *European Journal of Marketing, 41*(1/2), 94–120.
Kelman, H. C. (1961). Processes of opinion change. *Public Opinion Quarterly, 25*, 57–78
Kilipiri, E., Papaioannou, E., & Kotzaivazoglou, I. (2023). Social media and influencer marketing for promoting sustainable tourism destinations: The Instagram case. *Sustainability, 15*(8), 6374. https://doi.org/10.3390/su15086374.
Knoll, J. (2016). Advertising in social media: A review of empirical evidence. *International Journal of Advertising, 35*(2), 266–300. https://doi.org/10.1080/02650487.2015.1021898.Lachapelle, P. (2011). *The use of social networking in community development. CD Practice,* (17), 2–7.
Larsen, J., Urry, J., & Axhausen, K. W. (2007). Networks and tourism: Mobile social life. *Annals of Tourism Research, 34*(1), 244–262. https://doi.org/10.1016/j.annals.2006.08.002.
Li, H. (2011). The interactive web: Toward a new discipline. *Journal of Advertising Research, 51*, 13–26.
Li, X. (2011). Factors influencing user participation in social media marketing. *Computers in Human Behavior, 27*(6), 2128–2137. https://doi.org/10.1016/j.chb.2011.06.011.
Magno, F., & Cassia, F. (2018). The impact of social media influencers in tourism. *Anatolia, 29*(2), 288–290.
Manovich, L. (2019). The aesthetic society: Instagram as a life form. *Data Publics, Routledge, Forthcoming, 2*, 19.
McCracken, G. (1989). Who is the celebrity endorser? Cultural foundations of the endorsement process. *Journal of Consumer Research, 16*(3), 310–321.
Mehraliyev, F., Choi, Y., & Koseoglu, M. A. (2019). Social structure of social media research in tourism and hospitality. *Tourism Recreation Research, 44*(4), 451–465.

Mukhopadhyay, S., Jain, T., Modgil, S., & Singh, R. K. (2023). Social media analytics in tourism: A review and agenda for future research. *Benchmarking: An International Journal, 30*(9), 3725–3750. https://doi.org/10.1108/BIJ-05-2022-0309.

Munar, A. M., & Jacobsen, J. K. S. (2013). Trust and involvement in tourism social media and web-based travel information sources. *Scandinavian Journal of Hospitality and Tourism, 13*(1), 1–19. https://doi.org/10.1080/15022250.2013.764511.

Nawijn, J., & Biran, A. (2019). Negative emotions in tourism: A meaningful analysis. *Current Issues in Tourism, 22*(19), 2386–2398.

NZ Herald (2019, July 10). *Visitors have discovered that a Bali tourist attraction popular with Instagram influencers is actually a fake photo op.* https://www.nzherald.co.nz/travel/visitors-have-discovered-that-a-bali-tourist-attraction-popular-with-instagram-influencers-is-actually-a-fake-photo-op/4IJPLK7K5AA6XYP764F5OLKQQ4/. (accessed on August 7, 2024).

Oh, Y. (2020). Tourism, aesthetic experience, and transformation: A case study on Ihwa Mural village, Seoul. *Annals of Tourism Research, 82*, 102908. https://doi.org/10.1016/j.annals.2020.102908.

Okazaki, S., & Taylor, C. R. (2013). Social media and international advertising: Theoretical challenges and future directions. *International Marketing Review, 30*(1), 56–71. https://doi.org/10.1108/02651331311298573.

Oren, G., Shani, A., & Poria, Y. (2021). Dialectical emotions in a dark heritage site: A study at the Auschwitz Death Camp. *Tourism Management, 82*, 104194.

Pesonen, J. (2011). Social media marketing in tourism: The future of marketing innovation. *Journal of Travel and Tourism Marketing, 28*(4), 443–453. https://doi.org/10.1080/10548408.2011.567425.

Reilly, A. H., & Hynan, K. A. (2014). Corporate communication, sustainability, and social media: It's not easy (really) being green. *Business Horizons, 57*(6), 747–758. https://doi.org/10.1016/j.bushor.2014.07.008.

Roy, S., Dryl, T., & Gil, S. (2021). Leveraging influencers for effective tourism marketing. *Journal of Travel and Tourism Marketing, 38*(7), 643–657. https://doi.org/10.1080/10548408.2021.1982187.

Rudolf, W. (2022). Social media and destination branding in tourism: A systematic review of the literature. *Sustainability, 14*(20), 13528. https://doi.org/10.3390/su142013528.

Saxena, A., & Khanna, U. (2013). Advertising on social network sites: A structural equation modelling approach. *Vision: The Journal of Business Perspective, 17*(1), 17–25.

Scheer, L. K., & Stern, L. W. (1992). The effect of influence type and performance outcomes on attitude toward the influencer. *Journal of Marketing Research, 29*(1), 128–142.

Seo, Y., Li, X., Choi, Y. K., & Yoon, S. (2018). Narrative transportation and paratextual features of social media in viral advertising. *Journal of Advertising, 47*(1), 83–95.

Smith, S. P. (2018). Instagram abroad: Performance, consumption and colonial narrative in tourism. *Postcolonial Studies, 21*(2), 172–191.

Stankov, U., Lazic, L., & Dragicevic, V. (2010). The extent of use of basic Facebook user-generated content by the national tourism organizations in Europe. *European Journal of Tourism Research, 3*(2), 105–113.

Statista (2024). Number of Instagram Users Worldwide from 2019 to 2028 (in millions). https://www.statista.com/forecasts/1138856/instagram-users-in-the-world. (accessed on August 7, 2024).

Sun, N., Rau, P. P. L., & Ma, L. (2014). Understanding lurkers in online communities: A literature review. *Computers in Human Behavior*, *38*, 110–117.

Tourism Australia. (2012). Social Media and Tourism. https://www.tourism.australia.com/en.

Tourism Queensland. (2012). Tourism e-kit: Social Media. https://www.tourismqueensland.com.au/.

Voorveld, H. A. M., van Noort, G., Muntinga, D. G., & Bronner, F. (2018). Engagement with social media and social media advertising: The differentiating role of platform type. *Journal of Advertising, 47*(1), 38–54.

Wang, D., Xiang, Z., & Fesenmaier, D. R. (2014). Smartphone use in everyday life and travel. *Journal of Travel Research.*

Wongkitrungrueng, A., Dehouche, N., & Assarut, N. (2020). Live streaming commerce from the sellers' perspective: Implications for online relationship marketing. *Journal of Marketing Management*, *36*(5–6), 488–518.

Xiang, Z., & Gretzel, U. (2010). Role of social media in online travel information search. *Tourism Management, 31*(2), 179–188. https://doi.org/10.1016/j.tourman.2009.02.016.

Zeng, B., & Gerritsen, R. (2014). What do we know about social media in tourism? A review. *Tourism Management Perspectives, 10*, 27–36. https://doi.org/10.1016/j.tmp.2014.01.001.

Zhang, W., Wang, Y., & Zhang, T. (2021). Can "live streaming" really drive visitors to the destination? From the aspect of "social presence". *Sage Open*, *11*(1). https://doi.org/10.1177/21582440211006691.

CHAPTER 8

A Discussion on Intelligent Technologies and Artificial Intelligence in Tourism Industry

MUSTAFA DOGAN[1] and EMEL ADAMIS[2*]

[1]*Department of Tourism Management, Faculty of Tourism, Batman University, Batman, Türkiye*

[2]*Department of Tourist Guidance, Vocational School of Iznik, Bursa Uludag University, Bursa, Türkiye*

*Corresponding author

ABSTRACT

Countries, societies, industries, universities, educational institutions, security units, and other organizations closely follow swift technological developments to understand and manage the effects of artificial intelligence (AI) on societies, the values it will add to our lives, the social reflections of change and transformation, and the opportunities plus threats that arise in our fast digitalizing world. AI can offer capabilities far beyond human reach through advanced domains, such as machine learning, computer vision, and natural language processing, thereby enabling companies and institutions to automate processes and make better decisions using data. Developments in this field lead to increased investments and rapid advancement of technology around the world, especially following the outbreak of COVID-19. While AI continues to be an area shaping our future, we are also expected to take conscious steps and keep up with the progress in this regard. Not surprisingly, it has not been possible for the tourism, travel, and hospitality industry to remain outside of this wheel of

Digitalization in Tourism. Hulya Akdemir Cengiz, Seza Zerman, Aysegul Acar, and Faizan Ali (Eds.)

DOI: 10.1201/9781779644770-11

development and change since it is also one of the leading sectors contributing to global economy. Therefore, this chapter aims to provide an overall picture of smart technologies, AI, and the tourism industry, including its intersection with sub-sectors, and to discuss the opportunities and limitations for humanity and our possible future with AI.

8.1 INTRODUCTION

We live in an age where progress is reduced to technological development, or where progress and technological development have long been equated. We are in a time where the majority of people believe that technological inventions and developments are the most functional and unlimited expression of human creativity, and that they are for the absolute benefit of society as a whole. Since the 16th century, we have lived through centuries in which the concept of industry entered our lives and historical milestones were gradually crowned with "revolutions." It is clear that these developments accelerated in the 20th century and we entered a technological system integrated with interconnected networks. In the last period, as a cumulative sum and the highest level of all the previous ones, technologies with "humanoid" characteristics-capabilities can be seen as a dimensional metamorphosis in industrial revolutions. Perhaps we are finally creating our own gods, the anthropomorphic beings to which the Sumerians attributed humanoid abilities for their gods.

As stated by Schwab (2016), humanity is going through the fourth industrial revolution, shaped by advancements in emerging technologies in areas, including robotics, artificial intelligence (AI), nanotechnology, quantum computing, the Internet of Things (IoT), fifth-generation wireless technologies, and autonomous vehicles. No doubt, all these will change the way people live, work, and interact. Becoming a bedrock component of the digital transformation taking place in divergent sectors, automation is not only the basic replacement of human labor force by machines, but also a self-sufficient, self-managing system in which machines can perform things without human-led support (Addo and Yagci, 2014). AI, which has become the symbolic address of technological progress today, is a reality that is rapidly entering in all areas of our lives and generating debate.

AI is leading a transformation process that has a significant impact on life, business, education, and our global perspective. Limna et al. (2021)

shortly define it as a *"thinking power created by humans"* which has a great potential of integration in a wide range of sectors today. Research on AI today is mostly focused on the economy, specifically on capital productivity, efficiency, sustainability, marketing, and consumer satisfaction—its benefits—while its impact on employment and labor markets—its negative effects—is more limited. The ethical and legal aspects of AI (Walsh et al., 2019; Gurkaynak et al., 2016; Kopacek, 2012; Veruggio, 2010), and its prospective impact for transforming jobs and required skills (Huang and Rust, 2018) are also areas of research. The application of AI in the tourism and hospitality industry, including key themes, strengths, and restricted aspects (Tussyadiah, 2020), as well as common applications in the tourism sector are potential areas for development and their implications (Doborjeh et al., 2022; Loureiro et al., 2022; Rahmadian et al., 2022; Soliman et al., 2023; Tussyadiah, 2020).

As in other industries and sectors, the integration of automation and AI, which is advancing with controlled and uncontrolled processes, remains a dynamic area of research in tourism. The use of advanced intelligent technologies, such as AI practices in tourism has, or is expected to have, some benefits for consumers and producers, such as comfort, convenience, and savings, but there are also some concerns. Tussyadiah (2020) emphasizes that one of the most important consequences of intensive automation of tourism service ecosystems will be the loss of human interaction offered during the tourism experience. Technological progress, automation, and integration of AI may have a remarkable impact in many areas and at many levels, but a bigger problem is lurking quietly on the sidelines, as it reduces or eventually eliminates the social interface of tourism encounters between the tourists and the others (host and visitor), which essentially involves the socio-cultural dimension of tourism experience. The integration of the tourism industry with AI can extend the "phantasmagoria-fantastic world" that Benjamin (1993) articulated in the "passages," eliminating the potential for contact with reality or the real other.

Moreover, the fact that its predicted shocking effects are concentrated in the labor market, and that the human dimension of this field is fraught with risks on a very large scale, justifies a further interest. The transition of tourism from a labor-intensive to a technology-intensive industry within the service sector will have many predictable and unpredictable consequences. This is where the uncertainty that science is trying to predict is currently concentrated, and we will be involved in the discussions in the following sections. This chapter aims to explore and discuss the relationship between smart technologies and the tourism industry with its relevant sub-sectors. The study contributes to the existing debates in the literature by taking into account different views on the impact of smart technologies on work, job, and basically employment in the tourism industry including risks and opportunities.

8.2 INTELLIGENT TECHNOLOGIES AND ARTIFICIAL INTELLIGENCE

AI is described as the capability to learn, understand, and make judgments and opinions. In this process, analytics technology, big data technology, cloud or cyber technology, and domain knowledge, which are the basic elements of industrial AI, have played a major role. AI systems are defined as systems with human capabilities and intelligence, and it is also said that AI systems exceed human capabilities, recognize their surroundings, and are able to take actions to maximize the chances of success (Bolonkin, 2011; Dobrev, 2012; Say, 2021). The fact that machines exhibit human behaviors, such as language processing-communication, information storage, automatic reasoning, learning, object perception, and object use and movement (Russell and Norvig, 2010) may mean that they have human capabilities. Therefore, AI can be defined as a system thinking and acting rationally like a human.

It can be narrow (Apple-Siri, Open AI-ChatGPT, video games, search engines, social networks, web cookies, online advertising services, data miners, autopilots, traffic control software, automated telephone answering services, audio guides, etc.) or general (human-level AI). Intelligent systems, which can be categorized as general (human-level AI) or super AI (AI superior to humans) (Urban, 2015), can reach the dimension of the most talented and best-equipped super intelligences (Bostrom, 2014) in almost all fields with their creativity, including scientific fields, universal subject mastery, and abilities in social fields, so that the pace of technological and scientific development in many fields of technology and science will not develop at a constant rate, but rather exponentially by increasing its speed (Kurzweil, 2005; Vinge, 2017). This situation indicates that it will become increasingly difficult to follow technological developments, understand the knowledge behind them, and adapt to them (Cagatay, 2019).

This stage is called the technological singularity and is used to describe this hypothetical situation in which the pace of technological development reaches a point where it cannot be followed, adapted, and controlled by today's institutions, methods, tools, and the mental capacity of today's people (Vinge, 2017). Indeed, it is clear that if we allow AI technologies to develop scientific creativity and even social skills, after a certain period of time we will encounter the most riskless type of AI, which is supposed to make humans redundant. Nevertheless, there is a great risk in rigidly opposing change without fully understanding the limits and promises of AI research, and in pursuing change while ignoring the potentially catastrophic consequences for individuals and power centers (Cagatay, 2019).

In October 2023, the president of the United States of America (USA) issued an executive order requiring AI developers to share data with the government. However, the European Union (EU) went further than other countries and approved the world's first AI law on March 13, 2023 with a regulation that AI systems should be supervised by humans, non-discriminatory, safe, transparent, and environmentally friendly (euronews, March 14, 2023). The United Nations unanimously adopted the resolution on the draft law, which was created with the support of 123 countries with the aim of "making AI systems safe at the global level." The resolution, which is not binding on UN member states, forms the basis for the general framework for the development, use, accessibility, and distribution of AI technologies and legal regulations to ensure international security in this field (Anadolu Agency, March 14, 2024). Another notable development is the lawsuit filed against OpenAI, one of the pioneering companies operating in the AI field, by the New York Times for the unauthorized use of its data sources and by Elon Musk, the company's co-founder. Elon Musk accuses OpenAI, which he joined as a non-profit organization with the guarantee that it would be safe and for the benefit of humanity, of turning this founding principle on its head and moving in secret "toward a profit-driven future" with "potentially disastrous consequences for humanity" (euronews, March 3, 2014).

8.2.1 JOB-EMPLOYMENT AND INTELLIGENT TECHNOLOGIES

It is possible to encounter both optimistic and pessimistic views regarding the impact of AI applications on the economy and in particular on employment. The optimistic view claims that AI will uplift the demand for qualified and skilled labor by enhancing human abilities. Due to its dynamic efficiency, AI is expected to have a positively significant impact on the economy and is fast becoming one of the core areas embedded in the industrial targets and strategies of the world's developed countries (Dutton, 2018). Considerable research funding has also been reserved for projects in order to accelerate those countries in the competition for the future big breakthroughs in AI and smart machines (Russell et al., 2015). This means that the faster AI technology improves, the more resources will be accessible to use in technical research areas.

The socio-economic impacts of intelligent automation systems on the tourism industry, local communities, other stakeholders, and the wider economy relate to changes in productivity, when and to what extent travel and hospitality jobs will be replaced by intelligent machines, the consequences for wages, income distribution (inequality), gender issues, and general well-being in tourism destinations. In relation to the workforce, advancement of automation also causes concerns about the diminishing skills and knowledge because of excessive dependence on technology (Lin et al., 2011) and the possibility for a future composition of an unemployed society (Pham et al., 2018). As the pace of technological advance accelerates, the way in which business is conducted and employees work in modern organizations is affected. The focus on processes for employees to follow and implement this change at a similar pace, or even to anticipate future changes, often leads to uncertainty, and this uncertainty can lead to anxiety (Erebak and Turgut, 2021).

Other implications of the emergence of intelligent machines are discussed in the context of the technological singularity, a phenomenon in which uncontrollable and irreversible technological growth and AI become smarter than humans, resulting in the end of human civilization on earth. It is generally argued that AI will replace the human labor force and jobs will be infested by machines created (Huang et al., 2019: 45). Although estimates and studies vary, it has been suggested that 30% of jobs in the United Kingdom, 38% in the United States, 21% in Japan, and 77% in China could be automated in the next decade (Wang and Siau, 2019: 69). With current technology, 30% of all jobs currently performed by humans could be automated (Chui et al., 2017); half of all jobs in the United States could be lost to automation (Schwab, 2016); AI could replace humans in jobs, such as cleaners, security guards, and drivers, which require average skills, and in jobs, such as lawyers, doctors, and engineers, which require high skills (Colvin, 2003).

Job insecurity as a fundamental socio-economic issue has come to the forefront in the AI debate (Erebak and Turgut, 2021), and the threat of losing one's job is recognized as one of the most important concerns worldwide (American Psychological Association, 2013). Nevertheless, it is predicted that AI will face significant challenges in occupations that require complex perceptual skills, creativity, and social intelligence (Walsh, 2018: 637). In summary, the following factors can be predicted as negative impacts of AI and automation:

1. Redundancies and unemployment
2. Reduced human interaction and altered customer experience
3. Technology dependency and loss of human skills

There are a number of assumptions about the main effects of new technologies as part of the employment process. One is the substitution of jobs by AI and the other is the displacement of labor with the emergence of new jobs or tasks. According to the substitution effect, the use of AI has a negative impact on the labor market and creates unemployment. Leontief (1983) emphasized that almost all jobs will be performed by AI within a few years and that unemployment will increase as a result; as a solution, governments can significantly reduce the negative impact through effective redistribution policies. In the displacement effect, there is a shift of employees from one position or previous job to another job or position (Petropoulos, 2018: 119). Frey and Osborne (2013), who believe that this expected effect will support productivity growth, which in turn will lead to an increase in real incomes, and thus the demand for other goods, argue that the disruption effect, which requires a reorganization of labor supply as technology replaces labor, will be offset by an increase in employment as a result of the emergence of new jobs in high productivity sectors. Similarly, Acemoglu and Restrepo (2018) emphasize that in a framework where tasks previously performed by labor are automated and at the same time other new technologies complement labor, labor has a comparative advantage in new and more complex tasks; therefore, technological developments that will substitute labor will also create new jobs and positions, which will enable labor to maintain its position—importance in the medium-long term: "If new jobs and tasks continue to be created, even in the face of rapid automation, employment and the share of the labor force may remain stable in the long run" (Acemoglu and Restrepo, 2018: 1489). On the other hand, it is stated that the unemployment rate resulting from new technologies outnumbers the rate of employment growth created by the economy (Danaher, 2017). The World Bank's 2019 report also has critical findings on this issue stating that while automation displaces some jobs, it also creates new ones demanding urgent attention in human capital especially in developing countries (World Bank Report, 2019).

These recommendations on investing in human capital, lifelong learning, and functional education processes focused on multi-skill development also underline what the future holds. It is also predicted that countries with relatively low human capital investments will be left behind in this race, no matter what they do, and that existing developed countries will have a significant advantage in global competition. It seems that a world order in which unequal development will continue, even if its form changes, will persist. Another dimension may be the amount of energy required by AI or autonomous intelligent systems. Humanity has created supercomputers that exceed the computational capacity of an average human brain, which performs about 10 quadrillion calculations per second; for example, China's Tianhe-2 can perform 34 quadrillion calculations per second while consuming 24 MW of power and occupying 720 m^2 of space, while the human brain, on the other hand, operates with a much smaller power of 20 W, which is about one millionth of the power required by Tianhe-2 (Gurkaynak et al., 2016). In the burning current of global warming and related climate change, it is also seen that the energy needs and costs of AI to be employed instead of humans should be taken into account.

8.3 TOURISM AND INTELLIGENT TECHNOLOGIES

Intelligent systems, digital and automation applications, and AI also bring obvious advantages and risks to the tourism industry. From the perspective of service providers, they can increase productivity, efficiency, cost savings, improve support for tourists, make business decisions more efficient, increase safety and security, create flexible workplaces with synergistic collaboration between employees and intelligent systems, and increase job satisfaction (Huang and Rust, 2018; Kopacek, 2012). Robots used in customer services can offer a better quality customer experience (Kopacek, 2012). Accordingly, Ivanov and Webster (2019a, b) suggest that advances in robotic technologies offer great possibilities for various autonomous aspects of tourism services. Tourism providers have already started using smart machines extensively in their operations in recent years, for example, KLM Airlines introduced an android robot for passenger guiding at Amsterdam Schiphol Airport, followed by a robot with a smart trolley to carry passengers' luggage to the assigned gate in 2018.

Henn na Hotel known as the first robotic hotel was opened in Japan in 2015 and by the end of 2023 had grown into a chain of 22 hotels, including one in the United States, one in South Korea, and one in Japan (Hennna Hotel, 2024). These hotels use dinosaur receptionists, robot porters, cloakroom robots, precision beds, automatic dry cleaners, in-room personal assistants, and holograms. The growth graph of this hotel proves that it is a profitable investment that works commercially and is embraced by consumers. Global online booking systems, such as Booking and Tripadvisor (accessed March 1, 2024) all have a hotel score above 8 based on customer reviews. Robot hotels themselves may influence tourist preference as an element of attraction in today's exceptionalism. In the future, the ability to offer both "robotic" and "human" service may be one of the key elements determining the competitiveness of accommodation businesses.

In line with this trend, hotels around the world are implementing intelligent automation for some of their customer-facing operations, such as check-in, virtual personal assistants, and room delivery robots (Tussyadiah, 2017). The development of the Internet and online booking systems has also enabled some new applications and opportunities, referred to as the "sharing economy." Digital platforms, such as Airbnb (2008) and Uber (2009) are the most prominent examples of this trend. The fact that these US-based companies are now a major competitor and alternative to the traditional players in the sector is also the subject of serious debate. It is well known that these applications, which incorporate and exploit many elements of technological development, offer consumers an alternative opportunity and convenience. These platforms, which are spreading rapidly throughout the world, have intensified competition with the traditional players in the tourism sector, while at the same time broadening the overall range of offers.

Intelligent automation, robots, cobots, AI, and internet-based applications also pose risks for tourism, such as loss of jobs and employment, control risks due to robotic autonomy, challenges regarding security, safety, and privacy conditions (Boyd and Holton, 2018; Huang and Rust,

2018; Kopacek, 2012; Nedelkoska and Quintini, 2018). However, there is another potential impact on tourism. Visitor-host relationships and interactions between tourists and local people in the destination are known to be a factor fostering tourist satisfaction and positive attitudes toward tourism destinations. The human and cultural component of the tourism product, which is labor intensive and an important combination of human, cultural, and natural factors, is likely to be weakened in the coming period. Service workers, who are the most important human element in tourism, have a dual function, both as mediators of place and culture and as providers of services. No matter how high the quality of service that humanoid AI robots or cobots will provide in place of humans, the aspects that are important to tourists, such as culture-locality-intimacy-hospitality, and so forth may be incomplete. A receptionist in an accommodation facility, a ticket agent in a travel agency, a waiter in a restaurant, a guide in a museum may be a humanoid robot, and this may well be profitable for the organizations providing the services, but it can be predicted that the experience, emotion, and meaning perceived by the visitor will definitely be different from today. Although it is not yet clear how new fields and jobs will be shaped for those who will be unemployed as a result of human substitution in these areas, it is clear that they will require much more in terms of qualifications and skills than today and will need to be continually developed:

> *Many jobs today, and many more in the near future, will require specialized skills, a combination of technical knowledge, problem solving, and critical thinking, as well as soft skills such as perseverance, collaboration and empathy. Gone are the days of staying in one job or one company for decades, replaced by the need for workers to be lifelong learners who are likely to have many jobs throughout their careers* (World Bank Report, 2019).

It is clear that if AI reduces or eliminates human contact for visitors (Tussyadiah, 2017), it will make a difference to the experience of social, cultural, ethnic, religious, and other attractions. For a seaside tourist, an all-inclusive tourism experience consisting of the airport, transfer vehicle, hotel, and hotel activities is highly susceptible to automation, and therefore dehumanization. However, for the explorer, the adventurer, the curious, and the independent cultural tourist, interaction with local culture and people is possible even when encountering and using relatively automated services.

AI technology could provide an opportunity for tour operators to offer packaged travel options tailored to customers' personal preferences.

Artificial travel advisors that work like a tour operator to scan different options and offer the most ideal alternatives are also possible. It is clear that AI-assisted travel services, which will be shaped according to tourism types and tourist typologies, will be equipped with mobile, digital applications, big data analytics, and robotic technologies in terms of destinations. How this process between facilitating and guiding travel will affect trends, preferences, and satisfaction remains to be seen in empirical studies.

8.3.1 TRAVEL INDUSTRY AND INTELLIGENT TECHNOLOGIES

We can see that the travel industry was automated much earlier than many other sectors. The travel industry, which includes transport companies, tour operators, and travel agents, was perhaps the first group to integrate technological developments, particularly through airlines. Starting in the 1950s, reservation systems developed by companies, such as American Airlines, United Airlines, and British Airways were later adopted by tour operators and travel agents. At the same time, MARS1, developed by Hitachi for Japan Railways, began to make seat reservations for trains (IPSJ, Japan National Railway, 2024). The transformation of central reservation systems into global distribution systems (Apollo, Travicom, Galileo, Amadeus, Orbitz) was followed by independent internet-based reservation systems/portals (Booking, Expedia, Tripadvisor, Priceline, etc.). In the transport sector, airlines in particular have invested heavily in technology and are now able to reach their customers directly through their websites and mobile applications. The Internet, smart mobile phones, and mobile applications have not only facilitated the sales and marketing processes of large service providers, especially airlines, but have also increased their profitability. These developments, which in particular simplify and facilitate booking and purchasing processes, have had many consequences.

The traditional distribution system, in which all transport companies, in particular airlines, delivered tickets to the final consumer through travel agencies, has been replaced by direct distribution and a structure that eliminates intermediaries. This situation has contributed to the fact that the commissions paid to the intermediaries (travel agencies) on the tickets have remained in the budgets of the transport companies, thus increasing their profits. Although some of this has been reversed with the replacement of physical agencies by internet-based travel portals, small and medium sized representative travel agencies in the "street agency" dimension have experienced major financial problems. The automation of the travel industry has put small travel agencies or service providers in a difficult position in terms of intermediation and commission income, while the large service providers (transport companies and some large tour operators) and online booking portals have been strengthened.

In addition, internet-based online travel portals offering a large scale of services, such as transport, accommodation, tour guiding, food and beverage, car rental, and so forth have largely replaced the traditional functions of tour operators and have had the effect of facilitating and increasing individual travel by reducing the share of organized mass group travel. Automation in this area has also led to monopolization, with a few large service providers dominating the travel and tourism industry worldwide. These eco-systems, which make intensive use of big data and AI technologies, are now effective in guiding preferences and trends and meeting consumer needs.

Airlines have begun to implement intelligent automation in many customer-facing front line operations, such as check-in, virtual personal assistants, and baggage claim. This has caused a remarkable reduction in the number of airline staff at airports and job shifts. Airlines have introduced more self-service options and conveniences, such as easier check-in processes, self-boarding and checkpoints, e-gates, and more. In the field of aviation; the robot "Mini ADA" at Istanbul Airport, "Spencer" at Amsterdam Schiphol Airport, and "Care-E" at Royal Dutch Airlines provide services, such as passenger guidance, baggage transportation, voice directions, and voice response to flight information inquiries (Tussyadiah, 2020).

In addition, companies using big data analytics in their marketing functions are predicting and even targeting the preferences of their potential customers. Although it may be difficult for customers to adapt at first, they do so in a short time and the process is mutually driven. This motivation, which also paves the way for investment, supports capital investment in advanced technology.

8.3.2 HOSPITALITY INDUSTRY AND INTELLIGENT TECHNOLOGIES

It is evident that AI has made its mark in recent years and is one of the most heavily invested technologies, which has caused profound transformation in businesses and sectors of all sizes. Inevitably, the hospitality industry is also one of the key fields for the application of AI.

No doubt that hospitality industry has been operating in a highly-competitive world, where the expectations by consumers are skyscraping. Due to the climb of digitalization, online platforms, social media, guest review sites, and so forth, demanding expectations, such as tailored and fast services, personalized experiences, interactive engagement, and efficiency have gained more importance than ever before. Under recent circumstances, it can be foreseen that AI may exert pivotal role in transformation of the hospitality industry.

A recent study synthesizing the existing literature on AI in tourism by Garcia-Madurga and Grillo-Mendez (2023) has identified the main categories revealing the uses of AI in the tourism industry. Their synthesis of the literature revealed various applications of AI mostly studied by reserachers, from forecasting and operational efficiency to enhancing customer experiences and sustainability. In addition, Huang et al. (2022) suggest a theory-based framework identifying five major types of AI applications in the hospitality and tourism industry, such as search/booking engines, virtual agents/chatbots, robots and autonomous vehicles, kiosks/self-service screens, and AR/VR devices (Figure 8.1). Expert systems, computer vision, natural language processing, and robotic processing automation are the four distinct subfields that make up the unified idea of AI, which is based on machine learning and deep learning (Huang et al., 2022).

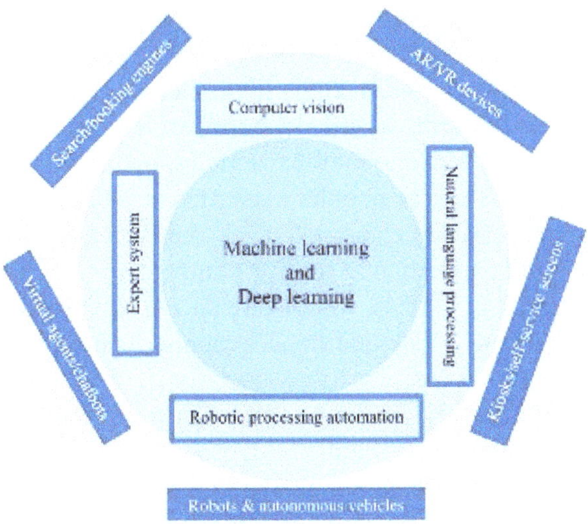

FIGURE 8.1 Five major types of AI applications in the hospitality and tourism industry.
Source: Reprinted with permission from Huang et al. (2022).

Integrating AI-based technologies into the hospitality industry might also mean a changeover in terms of reforming the operational processes including consumer experiences. Equipped with natural language processing abilities, virtual assistants and chatbots serving for instant communication with guests who are in need of support, such as language translation, facial recognition (security measures), and speedy services, replying inquiries, providing real-time recommendations (Ivanov and Webster, 2019) can be some of the examples. AI driven systems are also able to examine the guest data for streamlining the services for better experience ranging from offering best room options to dining experiences, which facilitate guest satisfaction and loyalty, which can be translated as increased service quality (Prentice et al., 2020). In addition, AI helps with predicting analytical algorithms for smart revenue management by foreseeing demand patterns, planning pricing strategies, reducing costs, and so forth (Kong et al., 2023). With a dynamic market landscape, hospitality industry may facilitate guest satisfaction and experience, better performance in business issues in a highly competitive environment through intregrating AI with a transformative vision.

It is obvious that AI has found many niche options to function in hospitality industry. Since the introduction and use of Siri (Apple), Echo and Alexa (Amazon), new experiences provided by businesses through AI has been charming the guests/customers. For example, Alexa could talk to the guests to take control of in-house technology by supporting in-room services, such as lights, temperature, and entertainment. The hospitality industry mostly adopts robotic services which are AI-powered. Robots and autonomous vehicles, patrol, baggage delivery, and cooking systems can be popular examples in addition to self-service kiosks allowing tourists to check-in, check-out, order and pay faster and with fewer errors, and enhance service competency and hedonic motivation (Manzoor et al., 2024). Robots are successfully used in the daily activities of the front office and housekeeping departments (Lukanova and Ilieva, 2019).

Alongside the benefits, in the previous research, some concerns were voiced, such as double-edged challenges, pros and cons of AI applications (Fomby, 2019), potential technological disruptions Buhalis et al. (2019), job displacement and privacy concerns Plikas et al. (2023) regarding the hospitality industry. By drawing attention to the challenges and pressures that the organizations are undergoing for successful automation processes and AI implementation in the hospitality and tourism sector, Jabeen et al. (2022) highlight five key areas to consider for automation and AI: human knowledge, service settings, robotic applications, internal environment of the organization, and institutional environment of the organization. The authors also suggest a framework for navigating those challenges.

8.3.3 MUSEUMS AND INTELLIGENT TECHNOLOGIES

The use of intelligent technologies to replace humans, especially in information services, has begun to be used in the promotion of cultural heritage, especially in museums. Being branches of AI, machine learning and deep learning, as well as AI that can interpret, have been used in the field of information and knowledge for a long time, and the "audio guide" service, which has been used in museums for a long time, has become widespread in many museums, and a new stage has been reached with QR code and mobile application options. Online options for visiting museums online have also become widespread, especially in the post-pandemic period. These applications, which offer remote access with virtual museology, are spreading around the world. Google, in partnership with cultural institutions and artists from many parts of the world, is carrying out projects in this field; Google offers users 1200 museums and exhibition galleries online with the application called Arts and Culture (Romano, 2022). Museums equipped with interactive and augmented reality applications are also enriched with multiple options for museum visitors with different profiles (Dilek et al., 2019). Similar applications have started to be used or may soon be used for archaeological sites, ruins, and cultural heritage sites or assets.

It can be predicted that all this will have a negative impact on the livelihoods of museum staff and tourist guides working in museums and cultural heritage sites. In the "audio tour" and "guided tour" options, although the interactive nature of the guided tour (asking questions and receiving answers) is an advantage, it is clear that this is only an option for group trips and organized tours. As the proportion of independent travel increases, the technological trend is likely to continue. It seems likely that the tourist guide profession, which is reduced to the use of foreign languages and the transfer of information and knowledge, will over time be replaced by intelligent technology and robots. It can be said, however, that the replacement of guides who also perform the function of tour manager in groups or organized tours is difficult for the time being. Nevertheless, it can be said that it will not be difficult at all when AI has the same capabilities as humans and general (AGI) and super (ASI) models are included in our lives.

8.3.4 RESTAURANT INDUSTRY AND INTELLIGENT TECHNOLOGIES

Since the world has become highly interconnected with digitally driven environment and technology, the tourism industry stakeholders and businesses have started to use advanced technologies and AI as a powerful catalyst in order to adapt to efficiency improvement, fluctuant consumer demands, customer experiences, personalized services, new opportunities for improvement, and many more.

The rise of robots and robotic services has been shaping the tourism sector continuously. In the food and beverage departments of accommodation establishments, restaurants, fast food establishments, and various businesses in food and beverage service; the robots undertake human tasks, such as being service personnel, bartender-barmaid, waiter, and assistant chef or chef (Ivanov and Webster, 2019a; 2020). Compared to hotel industry, where AI-supported services are used mostly, it can be said that the use of these applications is more limited and is still less available in restaurants (Liu et al., 2024). Additionally, AI-based systems exert a specific role in many issues covering food safety and (service) quality. For example, Japanese Kura Sushi Company, one of the chain sushi restaurants with more than 500 locations in the world, uses robot chefs in the preparation of sushi by implementing innovative systems and advanced technology (kurasushi.com). Robotic systems and AI-supported machines can prepare meals to the right sizes, track cooking processes, and provide support to kitchen staff. Personalized services supported by AI may exert important roles in restaurant management processes by analyzing customer preferences and habits, providing personalized recommendations based on users' past behavior. A recent study by Zhu (2022) concluded that customers' perception of enhanced interaction quality with a service robot leads to their perception of the robot as user-friendly and beneficial, ultimately boosting their attitudes toward the robot. Consequently, customers feel a deeper connection with the robot and are more inclined to embrace robotic services.

The restaurants have been seeking the options to provide high standards of service by monitoring the food supply chain and ensuring quality control in food preparation processes. Recent developments induced by AI in the restaurant industry cover a wide range from customer service to operational efficiency, from waste management to efficient customer interactions (Zhu, 2022). Product development is another issue that food and beverage industry needs to improve. Gastrograph AI can be given as an example for answering this problem. It is an AI platform used to model human sensory perception and control consumer preferences of food and beverage products. It develops an AI that understands consumers' taste and preference perceptions and offers it to the manufacturer with services, such as new product development, portfolio management, product adaptation, and deep market insights (Cerkez and Kizidemir, 2020).

8.4 CONCLUSION

In the cycle of nature's endless reshuffling, perhaps the utmost achievement of evolution is to ensure the continuity of life (Gurkaynak et al., 2016). In the last 50 years, 68% of all species that have ever existed on Earth have become extinct. As humans are part of the living species, their future is in jeopardy and to a large extent they have caused it. Urban (2015) highlights two main consequences of a possible super AI: the introduction of super AI will either enable immortality for our species or steer the human race toward extinction. It is curious to consider whether human evolution, after the agricultural and industrial revolutions, including climate change, can enter a new phase with the technological revolution. For while humanity has experienced the technological revolution with the civilization it has created and achieved, it has also largely destroyed the most basic conditions for survival, such as climate change, water, and food crises. Technological developments can be both the cause and the result of this evolutionary process.

We are instinctively engaged in an enduring struggle with nature to protect and prolong our existence, and therefore we will either try to eliminate the threats of existence that the systems, tendencies, and structures that produce super-AI may pose to all of humanity when we encounter explicit/implicit threat itself, or we will endeavor to eliminate this potential threat beforehand. However, it is also possible that the speed of technological developments will continue to increase day by day and our speed of following it will not increase in the same way; therefore, the harmony between technological developments and our adaptation to them may deteriorate sooner or later (Cagatay, 2019) to the detriment of humanity. While AI is not a novel study field, research in the tourism industry has grown significantly since 2018 and is considered still in its early stages, which means its increasing prominence is an expected trend (Kong et al., 2023).

Discussions and struggles continue between those who do not want the development process of AI to be controlled by rules, such as ethics, law, and so forth, or by areas, such as trade and competition, those who do, and those who think that it is not very possible to control it even if one wanted to. It may not be possible to restrict an area which, although risky, has considerable potential for "progress-development-profitability" in this and the next age. The next generations will experience and see what this rapid exponential process will bring and take away.

KEYWORDS

- **artificial intelligence**
- **automation**
- **big data analytics**
- **employment-labor**
- **humanoid**
- **intelligent technologies**
- **tourism industry**

REFERENCES

Acemoglu, D., & Restrepo, P. (2018). *Artificial intelligence, automation and work*. NBER working paper 24196. https://doi.org/10.3386/w24196.

Addo, E., & Yagci, K. (2014). *Automation, tourism, encyclopedia of tourism*. Cham: Springer.

American Psychiatric Association. (2013). *Diagnostic and statistical manual of mental disorders (DSM-5)*. Arlington: APA Publishing.

Benjamin, W. (1993). *Pasajlar, Çev*. Ahmet Cemal, İstanbul: Yapı Kredi Yayınları.

Bolonkin, A. (2011). *Universe, human immortality and future human evaluation*. United States: Elsevier.

Bostrom, N. (2014). *Superintelligence: Paths, dangers, strategies*. Oxford: Oxford University Press.

Boyd, R., & Holton, R. J. (2018). Technology, innovation, employment and power: Does robotics and artificial intelligence really mean social transformation? *Journal of Sociology*, *54*(3), 331–345.

Buhalis, D., Harwood, T., Bogicevic, V., Viglia, G., Beldona, S., & Hofacker, C. (2019). Technological disruptions in services: Lessons from tourism and hospitality. *Journal of Service Management*, *30*(4), 484–506.

Çağatay, H. (2019). Yapay Zekâ ve Tekillik: Teknolojik Tekillik Bize Ne Kadar Yakın ve Neden Önemli? *Metazihin yapay zeka ve zihin felsefesi dergisi*, *2*(2), 231–242.

Çerkez, M., & Kızıldemir, Ö. (2020). Yiyecek–İçecek İşletmelerinde Yapay Zekâ Kullanımı. *Türk Turizm Araştırmaları Dergisi*, *4*(2), 1264.

Chui, M., Manyika, J., & Miremadi, M. (2017). Where machines could replace humans—and where they can't (yet). *Digital McKinsey*. http://www.mckinsey.com/business-functions/digital-mckinsey/our-insights/where-machines-could-replace-humans-and-where-they-cant-yet.

Colvin, V. L. (2003). The potential environmental impact of engineered nanoparticles. *Nature Biotechnology*, *21*, 1166–11670.

Danaher, J. (2017). Will life be worth living in a world without work? Technological unemployment and the meaning of life. *Science and Engineering Ethics*, *23*(1), 41–64.

Dilek, S. E., Doğan, M., & Kozbe, G. (2019). The ınfluences of the ınteractive systems on museum visitors' experience: A comparative study from Türkiye. *Journal of Tourism Intelligence and Smartness*, *2*(1), 27–38.

Doborjeh, Z., Hemmington, N., Doborjeh, M., & Kasabov, N. (2022). Artificial intelligence: A systematic review of methods and applications in hospitality and tourism. *International Journal of Contemporary Hospitality Management*, *34*(3), 1154–1176. https://doi.org/10.1108/IJCHM-06-2021-0767.

Dobrev, D. (2012). A definition of artificial ıntelligence. *Institute of Mathematics and Informatics Bulgarian Academy of Sciences*, *1210*, 1–7.

Dutton, T. (2018). *An overview of national AI strategies*. https://medium.com/politics-ai/an-overview-of-national-ai-strategies-2a70ec6edfd. (accessed February 3, 2024).

Erebak, S., & Turgut, T. (2021). Anxiety about the speed of technological development: Effects on job insecurity, time estimation, and automation level preference. *Journal of High Technology Management Research*, *32*, 100–419.

Fomby, D. (2019). AI in the hospitality industry: Pros and cons. *HotelOnline*. https://www.hotel-online.com/press_releases/release/ai-in-the-hospitality-industry-pros-and-cons/ (accessed January 15, 2024).

Frey, C. B., & Osborne, M. A. (2013). *The future of employment: How susceptible are jobs to computerisation?* Oxford, United Kingdom: University Martin School.

García-Madurga, M. A., & Grilló-Méndez, A. J. (2023). Artificial ıntelligence in the tourism ındustry: An overview of reviews. *Administrative Sciences, 13*, 172.

Gürkaynak, G., Yilmaz, I., & Haksever, G. (2016). Stifling artificial intelligence: Human perils. *Computer Law and Security Review*, *32*(5), 749–758.

Hennna Hotel. (2024). https://group.hennnahotel.com/ (accessed February 2, 2024).

Huang, A., Chao, Y., de la Mora Velasco, E., Bilgihan, A., & Wei, W. (2022). When artificial intelligence meets the hospitality and tourism industry: An assessment framework to inform theory and management. *Journal of Hospitality and Tourism Insights*, *5*(5), 1080–1100. https://doi.org/10.1108/JHTI-01-2021-0021.

Huang, M. H., & Rust, R. T. (2018). Artificial intelligence in service. *Journal of Service Research*, *21*(2), 155–172.

Huang, M. H., Rust, R., & Maksimovic, V. (2019). The feeling economy: Managing in the next generation of artificial ıntelligence (AI). *California Management Review*, *61*(4), 43–65.

Ivanov, S., & Webster, C. (2019). Robots in tourism: A research agenda for tourism economics. *Tourism Economics*, *26*(7), 1065–1085.

Ivanov, S., & Webster, C. (2019a). Perceived appropriateness and intention to use service robots in tourism. In J. Pesonen & J. Neidhardt (Eds.*), Information and communication technologies in tourism 2019* (pp. 237–248). Cham: Springer.

Ivanov, S., & Webster, C. (2019b). What should robots do? A comparative analysis of industry professionals, educators and tourists. In J. Pesonen & J. Neidhardt (Eds.), *Information and communication technologies in tourism 2019* (pp. 249–262). Cham: Springer

Jabeen, F., Al Zaidi, S., & Al Dhaheri, M. H. (2022). Automation and artificial intelligence in hospitality and tourism. *Tourism Review*, *77*(4), 1043–1061.

Kong, H., Wang, K., Qiu, X., Cheung, C., & Bu, N. (2023). 30 years of artificial intelligence (AI) research relating to the hospitality and tourism industry. *International Journal of Contemporary Hospitality Management*, *35*(6), 2157–2177. https://doi.org/10.1108/IJCHM-03-2022-0354.

Kopacek, K. (2012). Roboethics. *IFAC Proceedings, 45*(10), 67–72.

Kurzweil, R. (2005). *The singularity is near: When humans transcend biology*. New York: The Viking Press.

Leontief, W. (1983). Technological advance, economic growth, and the distribution of ıncome. *Population and Development Review, 9*(3), 403–410. https://doi.org/10.2307/1973315.

Limna, P., Siripipatthanakul, S., & Phayaphrom, B. (2021). The role of big data analytics in influencing artificial intelligence (AI) adoption for coffee shops in Krabi, Thailand. *International Journal of Behavioral Analytics*, *1*(2), 1–18.

Lin, P., Abney, K., & Bekey, G. (2011). Robot ethics: Mapping the issues for a mechanized world. *Artificial Intelligence*, *175*, 942–949.

Liu, A., Ma, E., Wang, Y. C., Xu, S. T., & Grillo, T. (2024). AI and supportive technology experiences of customers with visual impairments in hotel, restaurant, and travel contexts. *International Journal of Contemporary Hospitality Management*, *36*(1), 274–291. https://doi.org/10.1108/IJCHM-10-2022-1243.

Loureiro, D., Barbieri, F., Neves, L., Anke, L. E., & Camacho-Collados J. (2022). TimeLMs: Diachronic language models from Twitter. *Proceedings of the 60th Annual Meeting of the Association for Computational Linguistics: System Demonstrations, Dublin, Ireland* (pp. 251–260). Association for Computational Linguistics.

Lukanova, G., & ve Ilieva, G. (2019). Robots, artificial ıntelligence and service automation. In S. Ivanov & C. Webster (Eds.), *Robots, artificial ıntelligence, and service automation in travel, tourism, and hospitality*. Bingley: Emerald.
Manzoor, S. R., Ullah, R., Khattak, A., Ullah, M., & Han, H. (2024). Exploring tourist perceptions of artificial intelligence devices in the hotel industry: Impact of industry 4.0. *Journal of Travel and Tourism Marketing*, *41*(2), 272–291.
Nedelkoska, L., & Quintini, G. (2018). *Automation, skills use and training. OECD social, employment and migration.* Working papers, No. 202. Paris: OECD Publishing.
Petropoulos, G. (2018). The impact of artificial intelligence on employment. In M. Neufeind, J. O'Reilly, & F. Ranft (Eds.), *Praise for work in the digital age* (pp. 119–132). Rowman and Littlefield International.
Pham, Q. C., Madhavan, R., Righetti, L., Smart, W., & Chatila, R. (2018). The impact of robotics and automation on working conditions and employment. *IEEE Robotics and Automation Magazine*, *25*(2), 126–128.
Prentice, C., Lopes, S. D., & Wang, X. (2020). The impact of artificial intelligence and employee service quality on customer satisfaction and loyalty. *Journal of Hospitality Marketing and Management*, *29*(7), 739–756.
Rahmadian, E., Daniel F., & Zwitter, A. (2022). A systematic literature review on the use of big data for sustainable tourism. *Current Issues in Tourism, 25*, 1711–1730.
Romano, A. (2022). *These 12 famous museums offer virtual tours you can take on your couch*. https://www.travelandleisure.com/attractions/museums-galleries/museumswith virtual tours. (accessed January 16, 2024).
Russell, S., & Norvig, P. (2010). *Artificial intelligence: A modern approach*. Prentice Hall.
Russell, S., Dewey, D., & Tegmark, M. (2015). Research priorities for robust and beneficial artificial intelligence. *AI Magazine*, *36*(4).
Say, C. (2021). *50 Soruda Yapay Zeka*. İstanbul: Bilim ve Gelecek Kitaplığı.
Schwab, K. (2016). *The fourth industrial revolution*. Geneva: World Economic Forum.
Soliman, M., Tarek, F., Islam E., & Figueiredo, R. (2023). Exploring the major trends and emerging themes of artificial ıntelligence in the scientific leading journals amidst the COVID-19 era. *Big data and cognitive computing* (pp. 7–12).
Tussyadiah, I. (2020). A review of research into automation in tourism: Launching the annals of tourism research curated collection on artificial ıntelligence and robotics in tourism. *Annals of Tourism Research*, *81*, 102883. https://doi.org/10.1016/j.annals.2020.102883.
Tussyadiah, I. P. (2017). Technology and behavioral design in tourism. In D. R. Fesenmaier & Z. Xiang (Eds.), *Design science in tourism*. Cham: Springer.
Urban T. (2015). *The AI revolution: The road to superintelligence*. http://waitbutwhy.com/2015/01/artificial-intelligence-revolution-1.html (accessed January 20, 2024).
Veruggio, G. (2010). Roboethics. *IEEE Roboethics Automotion Magazine*, *17*, 105–9.
Vinge, V. (2017). "The Coming Technological Singularity: How to Survive in a Post-Human Era." R. Latham (Der.), Science Fiction Criticism: An Anthology of Essential Writings içinde (s. 352-365). London: Bloomsbury Academic.
Walsh, T. (2018). *Machines that think: The future of artificial ıntelligence*. United States: Prometheus Books.
Walsh, T., Miller, K., Goldenfein, J., Chen, F., Zhou, J., Nock, R., ... & Jackson, M. (2019). *Closer to the machine: Technical, social and legal aspects of AI*. Swinburne.

Wang, W., & Siau, K. (2019). Artificial ıntelligence, machine learning, automation, robotics, future of work and future of humanity. *Journal of Database Management*, *30*(1), 61–79.
World Bank Annual Report. 2019. https://documents.worldbank.org/en/publication/documents-reports/documentdetail/156691570147766895/the-world-bank-annual-report-2019-ending-poverty-investing-in-opportunity. (accessed December 20, 2023).
Zhu, D. H. (2022). Effects of robot restaurants' food quality, service quality and high-tech atmosphere perception on customers' behavioral intentions. *Journal of Hospitality and Tourism Technology*, *13*(4), 699–714. https://doi.org/10.1108/JHTT-01-20210022.

CHAPTER 9

Innovation in Tourism and Hospitality Amidst Geopolitical Tensions: Digital Warfare

MAHMOUD IBRAHEAM SALEH

Tourism Studies Department, Faculty of Tourism and Hotel Management, Capital University, Cairo, Egypt

ABSTRACT

Many studies have examined the impacts of specific geopolitical tensions on tourism markets or have evaluated how destinations deployed specific digital innovations during crises. However, there is a lack of research into the connection between geopolitical tensions escalation, digital warfare emerging forms between states, and their influence on innovation in tourism. To address this gap, this study proposes a new conceptual framework that bridges political science, information warfare, and tourism literature together to contribute to the current theoretical understanding of the causal interactions between geopolitical disputes, digitalization, and their impacts on tourism risk and innovation. The model argues that digital warfare mediated the relationship between geopolitical tensions and travelers' risk perceptions and certainty. Also, digital innovation in hospitality and tourism weakened the relationship between geopolitical tension and perceptions of digital warfare. At the same time, digital innovation weakened the relationship between geopolitical tension and travelers' uncertainty about destinations, leading to enhanced experiences and rebuilding trust for tourists and guests.

Digitalization in Tourism. Hulya Akdemir Cengiz, Seza Zerman, Aysegul Acar, and Faizan Ali (Eds.)

DOI: 10.1201/9781779644770-12

9.1 INTRODUCTION

Geopolitical tensions occur from territorial disputes, differing ideologies, and conflicting foreign policies between nations (Hall, 2020) producing certain risks that discourage potential travelers and introduce uncertainty for tourism enterprises. As shown in historical examples like the Cold War (Ioannides and Timothy, 2010), the Yugoslav Wars (Hall, 2020), the Israeli–Palestinian conflict, ongoing South China Sea tensions over island claims (Doshi, 2020), and the Russia–Ukraine war (Nicolau et al., 2024), such strains have long-term negative impact on specific tourism markets. Economies reliant on tourism face financial challenges when geopolitical tensions result in declining revenue or travelers shifting to alternate destinations (Papagianni et al., 2023; Buchanan, 2016). However, some research has also investigated how conflicts can spur particular forms of war-related or solidarity tourism in some contexts (Josiassen et al., 2022; Higgins-Desbiolles, 2022; Buchanan, 2016; Bigley et al., 2010; Rolston, 1995; Ioannides and Apostolopoulos, 1999). Nations now use digital tools for information operations like propaganda, disseminating misinformation, and cyberattacks to attain strategic aims (Van den Heede et al., 2018; Lehto, 2018; Taddeo, 2020).

As conflicting states increasingly compete in the information space, these digital hostilities introduce added risk, uncertainty, and distrust that consumers must grapple with (Asmolov, 2022; Lu, 2022). Examples include disinformation campaigns related to COVID-19 (Korstanje and George, 2023; Brennen et al., 2020), or territorial disputes. For tourism, the proliferation of state-sponsored disinformation in social norms (Winter, 2009) and media and online environments compound existing geopolitical risks (Henry, 2021). At the same time, new forms of digital activism and protests have also emerged around issues impacting tourism, such as the Airbnb effect (Garay et al., 2020). However, digital innovations also offer opportunities to mitigate some tensions and impacts. Countries have leveraged digital tools to promote their tourism industries and destinations through virtual experiences during conflicts or health crises like the Covid-19 pandemic (Naeem et al., 2023; Korstanje and George, 2023; Ketter and Avraham, 2021; Melović et al., 2023). This allows them to keep their tourism offerings in mind for potential future visitors. Individuals can also stay connected to distant places through technology and engage in new forms of digital nomadism (Holleran and Notting, 2023). Digital tools enable rapid recovery campaigns post-crises to revive tourism demand (Sun et al., 2021). However, questions remain about the effectiveness of virtual experiences compared to actual in-person visits in appeasing geopolitical adversaries and achieving destinations' strategic goals (Nautiyal and Polus, 2022). The impact of digitization in mitigating tensions requires further examination.

While some studies have evaluated the impacts of specific geopolitical tensions on tourism markets (Papagianni et al., 2023; Henry, 2021; Winter, 2009) or examined how destinations utilized specific digital innovations during crises (Ketter and Avraham, 2021; Melović et al., 2023;), few investigate the interconnections and interactions between all three aspects of geopolitics, digital warfare, and innovation (Gretzel et al., 2020). Comprehending these interrelated relationships is essential as they form emergent tourism development and management obstacles. This study aims to fill the current gap to build resilience against geopolitical risks and maximize tourism opportunities in the digital era. This study aims to do so through a comprehensive conceptual model. Specifically, it seeks to understand:

1. RQ1: How might government-run online deception campaigns tie into tensions between nations, and what influence do they exert on tourist movement patterns and feelings of safety?
2. RQ2: What digital transformations have countries instituted to lessen the effects of geopolitical friction on their tourism sectors, and to what degree have these solutions proven effective?
3. RQ3: What factors influence the effectiveness of digital innovations in reconstructing trust and tourism demand amid geopolitical hostilities?

Answering these questions can provide valuable insights for tourism stakeholders and policymakers grappling with risks introduced by geopolitical tensions and digital transformations. It can also help identify opportunities to leverage technology for economic resilience and competitiveness.

9.2 LITERATURE REVIEW AND CONCEPTUAL MODEL

9.2.1 THE EVOLVING LANDSCAPE OF DIGITAL WARFARE IN GEOPOLITICAL CONFLICTS

Territorial disputes have long been a source of geopolitical conflict as states jealously defend sovereignty and territorial integrity (Butler and Suntikul, 2013). Digital technologies have provided new means for asserting claims, such as leveraging tourism development on disputed lands to strengthen positions under international law (Yang, 2020). In ongoing South China Sea disputes (Winter, 2009; Lisle, 2000), countries like Malaysia, Vietnam, and China have developed tourist facilities on controlled islands to bolster territorial assertions (Butler and Suntikul, 2013). However, as valuable resources are at stake, disputants have grown increasingly aggressive in recent decades through actions like China's seizure of additional islands by force (Butler and Suntikul, 2013). Everyday geopolitics are also shaped through platforms like social media, where national identities are constructed and circulated reciprocally between countries (Lee and Shahin, 2023; Henry, 2021). Digital narratives reproduced borders and differentiated mobilities during travel blogging (Henry, 2021). Modern conflicts exhibit "omnipresent participatory warfare" through extensive connective action networks (Asmolov, 2022). States developed nuanced information warfare practices like China's disinformation campaigns targeting global audiences rather than direct military threats (Lu, 2022).

Russia similarly employed feminizing rhetoric against foreign policy targets to legitimize further aggression (Gaufman, 2022). Across various contexts, nonstate actors are empowered to engage in hostilities directly through new cyber and social media battlespaces (Merrin and Hoskins, 2020). Future research should examine emerging issues such as the role of AI and challenges regulating digital conflict domains (Taddeo, 2020). Representation across developing states and consideration of factors like manager characteristics could also expand knowledge in this field (Papagianni et al., 2023; Henry, 2021). Thus, as presented, geopolitical conflicts are increasingly digitizing. From asserting territorial claims and shaping public opinion to sophisticated disinformation warfare (Asmolov, 2022; Lu, 2022), states extensively leverage diverse online platforms and technologies in pursuing strategic objectives (Martin et al., 2023; Ketter and Avraham, 2021). Therefore, we hypothesize that:

> **H1:**"*Increased geopolitical tensions utilize digital warfare for information operations (propaganda, disinformation campaigns, cyber-attacks, etc.) at higher levels.*"

9.2.2 IMPACT OF DIGITAL HOSTILITIES ON TRAVEL RISK PERCEPTION

The increasing digitization of society has enabled new forms of digital hostilities that mediate geopolitical tensions and conflicts (Gordon, 1998). Digital warfare and information operations utilize online platforms to manipulate public narratives, empowering state and nonstate actors to directly wage warfare beyond physical domains by strategically shaping global public opinion (Merrin and Hoskins, 2020; Lu, 2022). Stealthy disinformation campaigns exemplify this mediating role of digital warfare. Through techniques like suggestive half-lies diffused across borders on digital networks, such campaigns can consolidate state authority while transcending national boundaries to impact international politics covertly (Lu, 2022). By recruiting netizens and manufacturing consent, these hostilities obscure adversaries' realities and fuel geopolitical tensions in opaque ways that raise uncertainty (Lu, 2022). Similarly, digital mediation through gendered rhetoric delegitimizes adversaries' lived experiences. Feminizing portrayals depict threatened countries as helpless dependents to justify conflicts by manipulating securitization audiences (Gaufman, 2022). These manipulative framings distort geopolitical narratives in ways that obscure opponents' agency and intensify tensions (Gordon, 1998).

The rise of participatory yet ambiguous digital hostilities thus increases perceived dangers among potential visitors. As land disputes and political volatility amplify digitally, it grows more challenging to track intensifying online tensions due to widespread technologies and skewed information (Merrin and Hoskins, 2020). With adversaries' public narratives manipulated and hazards obscured online, digital mediation fuels geopolitical uncertainty, deterring travel related to escalating conflicts. Initial case studies provide tentative support (Martin et al., 2023), correlating extensive Sino-focused misinformation and Russo-focused delegitimization with travel risks in contested areas (Lu, 2022; Gaufman, 2022). The proliferation of disruptive digital warfare abilities has ushered in new unpredictability in modern conflicts. Offensive tactics like cyberattacks targeting critical infrastructure (Lehto, 2018; Guyonneau and Le Dez, 2019) and online disinformation campaigns (Lu, 2022; Asmolov, 2022) are being leveraged by state and nonstate actors to further geopolitical interests. This blending of digital and physical warfare spheres carries implications for social perspectives and economic risk tolerance (Khan et al., 2023).

As digital hostilities become more prevalent, general wariness grows due to awareness of new threats like critical infrastructure vulnerabilities (Lehto, 2018), rising inter-societal tensions fueled by propaganda (Lu, 2022; Asmolov, 2022), and invasive surveillance overstepping privacy (Taddeo, 2020; Guyonneau and Le Dez, 2019). These elements create uncertainty and negatively affect intentions in activities that depend on stability and goodwill between nations, such as international tourism during the war (Lisle, 2000). Therefore, we hypothesize that:

> **H2:**"*Higher levels of digital warfare result in increased uncertainty and risk perception among potential travelers*".

9.2.3 THE MEDIATING ROLE OF DIGITAL WARFARE

The increasing use of digital technologies in modern warfare has transformed conflicts into participatory digital battlefields that directly connect state and nonstate actors to global audiences (Merrin and Hoskins, 2020; Lu, 2022). This emerging form of digital warfare plays a crucial mediating role in contemporary geopolitical disputes and tensions. Through new digital tactics like information operations on social media and autonomous weapons systems, parties to conflicts can wage warfare beyond physical domains by manipulating public narratives and perceptions on a global scale (Merrin and Hoskins, 2020; Lu, 2022; Gaufman, 2022). China exemplifies this mediating role of digital warfare through its sophisticated disinformation campaigns that covertly "subdue enemies without fighting" by leveraging digital networks, recruiting netizens, and transcending borders (Lu, 2022). These stealthy information campaigns allow actors to impact public opinion both domestically and abroad in ways that raise tourism uncertainty (Naeem et al., 2023). Russia similarly employs digital mediation through gendered rhetoric that feminizes adversaries like Ukraine, casting them as helpless and dependent on delegitimizing their realities and justifying conflicts like its 2022 invasion (Gaufman, 2022). Such manipulative portrayals obscure adversaries' agency and fuel geopolitical tensions through altered public perceptions.

As territorial disputes and political instability intensify their digital dimensions, it becomes more difficult for audiences and potential travelers to track escalating tensions in the tourism industry reliably (Gordon, 1998) and conflicts due to their participatory yet opaque online mediation

(Merrin and Hoskins, 2020). While more research is still needed, recent case studies provide preliminary support. Examples like sustained Sino-centric disinformation and gendered Russo-centric delegitimization tactics correlate with perceived risks of traveling in regions like the South China Sea and Ukraine amid disputes (Lu, 2022; Gaufman, 2022). As digital warfare results from conflicts in participatory yet opaque ways online, uncertainty and risk perception faced by global audiences like potential travelers are likely to increase commensurate with escalating conflict cyber dimensions. Therefore, we hypothesize that:

> **H3:**"*Digital warfare mediates the relationship between geopolitical tensions and risk perception among potential travelers*".

9.2.4 THE MITIGATING ROLE OF DIGITAL INNOVATION

Geopolitical tensions have long driven tourism demand and development patterns, yet emerging digital technologies weaken this relationship (Lisle, 2000). Traditionally, regions facing political unrest or conflicts experienced declines in visitor arrivals due to inflamed risk perceptions and travel advisories discouraging travel (Ioannides and Apostolopoulos, 1999; Lee, 2006). However, virtual experiences enabled by new platforms allow individuals to safely engage with destinations facing tensions through interactive simulations and immersive content (Nautiyal and Polus, 2022). For instance, virtual tours of sensitive sites like the Gaza Strip or West Bank foster cultural learning without security concerns, while digital communities discussing travel to conflict-affected places like Ukraine promote grassroots diplomacy. Such digitally mediated interactions help satisfy travel-related interests that geopolitical turbulence may otherwise deter, thus dampening tensions' influence over comfort levels (Martin et al., 2023). Additionally, social networking blurs boundaries by connecting dispersed populations, enabling them to counter misleading media portrayals of contested regions by sharing firsthand accounts from outside official political narratives (Henry, 2021). As digital tools continue diversifying information streams and satisfying travel urges remotely, their dissemination of varied viewpoints challenges preconceptions shaped by territorial disputes (Cheesman, 2022).

Geopolitics also drives tourism through the strategic assertion of territorial claims, yet digital innovations are diminishing this link. Governments like Malaysia and disputing South China Sea claimants historically backed sovereignty assertions through tourism development on contested islands, aiming to establish jurisdiction under international law (Yang, 2020). However, virtual representations now offer alternatives to physical access for signaling control. Digital platforms providing virtual tours or simulations of disputed territories allow multiple claimants to attract audiences and legitimize claims through cyberspace without security escalations that maritime maneuvers risk (Butler and Suntikul, 2013). The link between territorial disputes and risk perceptions influencing travel diminishes as emerging technologies empower grassroots diplomacy. Where conflicts were traditionally amplified through restricted information flows dominated by competing government narratives, individuals can circumvent such barriers using social networking to connect directly and share localized perspectives (Bigley et al., 2010).

Regions facing international isolation or boycotts historically struggled to participate in international exchange and the growing tourism industry (Lee, 2006; Rolston, 1995). Yet platforms now offer alternatives. For example, e-commerce networks circumvent trade barriers by connecting businesses globally (Melović et al., 2023). Streaming services satisfy cultural interests that regional political tensions may discourage by providing online access to music, television, and film (Ketter and Avraham, 2021). Virtual exchanges satisfy related economic and social needs without physical proximity requirements. As digital innovations integrate divided societies and meet travel-related commercial interests that geopolitics previously deterred, their continued proliferation will likely weaken the historical relationship between political tensions and development obstacles Cheesman, 2022). In weakening these linkages, digital advancements decrease tensions' hold over economic mobility.

This study argues that emerging digital technologies are weakening the traditionally strong relationships between geopolitical tensions, travel risks, and economic development mobility constraints (Lisle, 2000). New communication platforms, online cultural access, and virtual representations open alternative avenues for satisfying travel urges, signaling control over territories, promoting grassroots diplomacy, and facilitating international exchange. By diversifying information flows and satisfying related needs without physical access barriers, digital innovations reshape risk perceptions and decrease the influence of tensions. Based on the previous argument, we hypothesize that:

H4:"*Digital innovation weakens the relationship between geopolitical tensions and digital warfare's impact on traveler perceptions*".

H5:"*Digital innovation weakens the relationship between geopolitical tensions and digital warfare's impact on traveler perceptions*".

9.2.5 DIGITAL INNOVATION AND TRAVELER EXPERIENCE DURING GEOPOLITICAL TENSIONS

Digital technologies are increasingly building customer trust during periods of geopolitical tensions through various mechanisms. For instance, online platforms allow for solidarity initiatives like virtual tours that can boost reputation and increase stock prices, according to recent research on tourism industry responses to the Ukraine crisis (Nicolau et al., 2024). These virtual experiences cultivate trust by sensitively representing conflict-affected destinations. For example, virtual tours of contested areas can promote cultural understanding without safety concerns, as found in a study of such tours (Nautiyal and Polus, 2022). Platforms also curate empathy-focused content, which has been shown to foster user goodwill toward companies (Josiassen et al., 2022). As crises amplify polarization, technologies decentralize official narratives and emphasize shared humanity, lowering tensions (Henry, 2021). By diversifying information sources, technologies challenge preconceptions and reshape risk perceptions historically harmful to trust (Henry, 2021). User-generated content provided civilian perspectives that countered disputed territory portrayals in mainstream media, reconceptualizing places as inhabited by interconnected rather than isolated communities (Henry, 2021).

Technologies help circumvent barriers to information dissemination that exacerbate tensions by bringing in diverse viewpoints (Naeem et al., 2023). Their spread of varied grassroots narratives challenges assumptions and reconnects segmented audiences (Lisle, 2000). Thus, the new mediums strengthen these grassroots networks, weakening territorial conflicts' psychological hold over residents (Cheesman, 2022). Such disputes have historically constrained the tourism industry's stability and recovery (Naeem et al., 2023). However, digital tools are mitigating impacts through various means.

Moreover, streaming satisfies cultural interests suppressed by unrest, while e-commerce aids marginalized businesses (Ketter and Avraham, 2021; Melović et al., 2023). Virtual representations project sovereignty and attract interest safely. Digitalization provides virtual experiences and market integration irrespective of geopolitics' severity (Khan et al., 2023). Technologies minimizing borders lessen reliance on stability and shift advantages to resilience (Cheesman, 2022). They stabilize markets and diversify participation, insulating sectors from fallouts of political turbulence. In summary, digital innovations enhance engagement and industry resilience amid disputes through these various channels. Based on the previous arguments, we hypothesize that:

H6:"*Digital innovation enhances customer trust reconstruction even during periods of geopolitical tensions.*"

H7:"*Digital innovation enhances customer experience and engagement even during periods of geopolitical tensions.*"

9.3 CRAFTING A COMPREHENSIVE MODEL AND MAPPING HYPOTHESES LINKAGES

The conceptual framework proposes several hypotheses regarding the relationships between geopolitical tensions, digital warfare, and digital innovations in tourism. These hypotheses can also help generate specific research questions to investigate the proposed linkages further (see Table 9.1). Table 9.1 maps this study's hypotheses, associated research questions, and relevant concepts that could help explain observed patterns. It serves to integrate the critical elements of the conceptual model and visually demonstrates the logic of the conceptual framework. Each hypothesis proposes a potential causal pathway the research questions aim to explore further through empirical examination. Hypothesis 1 contributes novel insights by focusing on how states leverage digital tools for information operations during geopolitical tensions. While information warfare has been studied, directly linking it to tourism contexts through quantitative and qualitative social media analyses, examinations of propaganda tactics, and investigations of disinformation campaigns targeting travel perceptions provides new understandings not found by isolated examinations.

Hypothesis 2 presents an innovative approach examining how digital hostilities like cyber threats and online misinformation shape uncertainty and risk perceptions influencing travel behavior. Empirically measuring changes in risk levels over time regarding various digital warfare activities could provide originally uncovered data on mediating impacts. Considering emerging technological dimensions like deep fakes offers perspectives not previously addressed. Hypothesis 3 conceptually breaks new ground by exploring digital spheres as mediums connecting geopolitical tensions to online audiences in participatory yet opaque ways. Investigating this mediation process through complex systems theories while contrasting online versus traditional disputes yields a holistic perspective absent from isolated studies. Considering grassroots counter-narratives, moderating roles offer novel, nuanced insights beyond top-down examinations.

Hypothesis 4 presents an original angle arguing that virtual experiences weaken ties between tensions and travel by satisfying related motivations through alternative participation avenues less contingent on stability. Quantifying virtual tourism promotions' effects on brand visibility and arrivals through country case studies could generate compelling evidence reconfiguring understandings of crisis impact relationships in innovative ways. Hypothesis 5 contributes innovatively by highlighting grassroots initiatives leveraging social media to challenge official narratives and decrease tensions' influence on travel. Exploring how networks theoretically decentralize propaganda and influence perceptions provides insights beyond conventional analyses. Examining influencers countering politicized narratives offers a user-focused perspective on trust rebuilding. Hypothesis 6 presents a practical novel approach to restoring trust after disputes by considering destinations' and businesses' digital communications. Analyzing crisis response tactics, functional communication elements, and impacts on virtual experiences/loyalty generates valuable, uncovered initial data.

The focus on strategies normalizing risks also offers practical crisis management implications not sufficiently addressed previously. Hypothesis 7 makes an original contribution by arguing emerging technologies broaden access pathways amid unrest through virtual interactions and enhance stakeholder engagement with restricted destinations. Exploring evidence that digital cooperation weakens disputes' mobility influences advances understanding of technology's dual capacities. Investigating program impacts on region perceptions, factors influencing virtual experiences as economic substitutes, and specific innovations provides novel empirical and theoretical insights. Overall, all hypotheses consider new angles like information operations, grassroots initiatives, digital mediation of risks, and virtual access avenues that have not been comprehensively examined before across disciplines. The potential investigations suggest creative empirical analyses and mixed-method approaches leveraging different data sources for innovative understanding.

TABLE 9.1 Conceptual Contribution Linking Hypotheses, Research Questions and Concepts.

Hypotheses Pathway	Questions	Potential Investigations
H1: Information warfare	How have states utilized specific digital tools like social media, websites, and apps for information operations related to territorial disputes and other sources of geopolitical tensions? What tactics, like coordinated inauthentic behavior or disinformation campaigns, have been most commonly used in digital warfare? How do online propaganda and misinformation levels correlate with the escalation of tensions in specific disputes? Which government agencies or military branches are primarily responsible for conducting digital information operations? What regulatory or technological challenges exist in monitoring and containing state-sponsored digital disinformation?	States' use of digital tools like social media, websites for propaganda campaigns, and cyberattacks relating to geopolitical tensions.
H2: Risk perception, information warfare	What evidence is there that state-sponsored digital disinformation campaigns and online propaganda have directly contributed to increased uncertainty and changed risk perceptions among potential travelers to certain destinations? How have emerging cyber threats to critical infrastructure or mass data breaches influenced general wariness levels about travel safety? What factors, like campaign virality and visual/narrative techniques, determine disinformation efficacy in altering traveler mindsets? How do risk perceptions evolve with continued exposure to online hostilities during protracted disputes? What indicators can be used to empirically measure changes in perceived travel risks resulting from digital warfare?	Evidence that digital disinformation/ hostilities directly contribute to increased uncertainty and changed travel risk perceptions.
H3: Mediation theory, risk perception	Through what mechanisms have digital hostilities like disinformation campaigns mediated and exacerbated the relationship between actual geopolitical tensions and perceived travel risks? How do specific case studies illustrate mediation of tensions through participatory online battlefields vs more traditional diplomatic/military disputes? What theoretical models from fields like international relations or complex systems best explain digital mediation of geopolitical risks? How do grassroots counter-narratives spread via user-generated content moderate linkages compared to top-down campaigns?	Mechanisms through which digital spheres mediate the relationship between tensions and perceived travel risks.

TABLE 9.1 *(Continued)*

Hypotheses Pathway	Questions	Potential Investigations
	What factors of a dispute (issue, actors, regional vs. global scale) influence the degree of digital mediation vs direct tensions?	
H4: Technological determinism, digital diplomacy	In what instances have virtual tourism promotions and simulations helped mitigate the negative impacts of tensions on demand by appealing to travel motivations during conflicts? How have platforms facilitating online cultural/economic participation weakened dependency on territorial access and stability? What quantitative analyses show the effectiveness of virtual experiences for maintaining brand visibility and revival of arrivals? Through what mechanisms do digital tools reshape links like dispersed information, strengthening everyday diplomacy? How do specific country/industry case studies highlight the weakened relationship between tensions and innovations?	Instances where virtual experiences/ platforms mitigate tensions' negative impacts by satisfying travel motives and opening participation channels less reliant on stability.
H5: Digital diplomacy, everyday geopolitics	What grassroots initiatives have leveraged social media to reconnect communities and challenge narratives escalating disputes? How have networks decentralizing official propaganda influenced destination perceptions and travel risk comfort? What role have travel influencers played in countering politicized media portrayals through on-the-ground storytelling? In what contexts did user activities online have observable impacts on de-escalating tensions or rebuilding trust? How do theoretical models explain the weakening relationship between tensions, digital hostilities, and perceptions?	Grassroots initiatives leveraging social media challenge official narratives and citizen activities online lessening tensions' influence over travel behaviors.
H6: Resilient development, risk perception	What strategies have destinations and businesses successfully adopted through websites and social media to rebuild customer trust after incidents exacerbated by political disputes?	Strategies through digital communications rebuild trust after incidents exacerbated by disputes by normalizing risks.
	How did firms' transparent and quick response tactics like solidarity appeals influence reputation/sales during uncertainty? What content/design elements of crisis communications were most effective for normalizing tensions and stabilizing demand?	

TABLE 9.1 *(Continued)*

Hypotheses Pathway	Questions	Potential Investigations
	How did customers' digital experiences and brand engagement correlate to loyalty during/after conflicts? In what industries/contexts did virtual interactions better satisfy the needs to support stakeholders vs. avoid risks?	
H7: Resilient development, digital diplomacy, technological determinism	How have emerging technologies enhanced engagement with destinations inaccessible due to unrest through virtual simulations and immersive experiences? What innovations in AR/VR, gamification, and user-generated content broadened participation pathways amid tensions? What evidence suggests digital interactions established grassroots will to cooperate that weakened disputes' influence over mobility? How did virtual cultural/educational programs shape perceptions of sensitive regions in ways appealing post-conflict? What factors influenced virtual experiences as economic substitutes facilitating recovery irrespective of political constraints?	Technologies enhancing engagement with inaccessible destinations through virtual interactions broadening access pathways amid unrest.

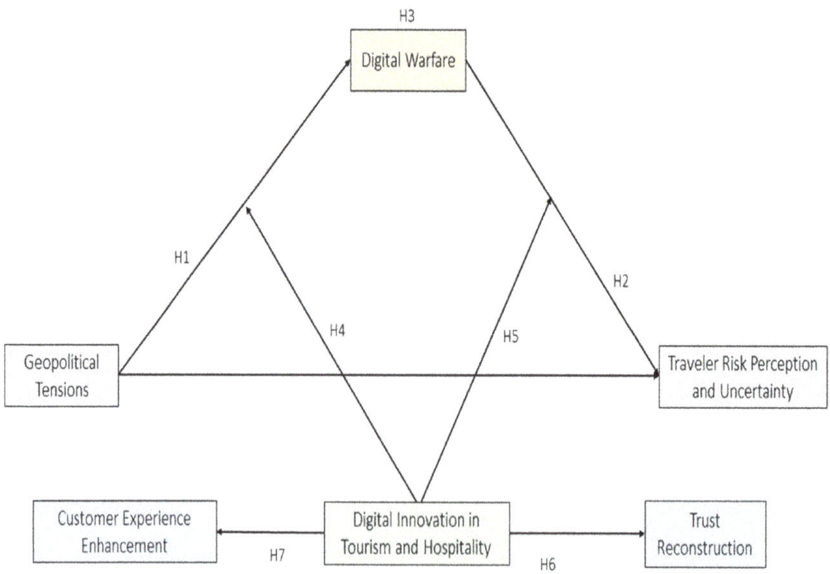

FIGURE 9.1 Conceptualizing the relationships between geopolitical tensions, digital hostilities, and emerging technologies in tourism.

9.4 CONCLUSION

This study conducted a comprehensive examination of the relationships between geopolitical tensions, digital warfare, and digital innovation in tourism. It was put forth that geopolitical conflicts are increasingly being propagated and mediated through digital platforms, with states leveraging emerging tools like disinformation campaigns and targeted rhetoric to wage informational hostilities online. This novel dimension of digital warfare introduces added layers of risk, uncertainty, and distrust that negatively impact travel behaviors. However, it was also postulated that digital innovations can mitigate some of these tensions and consequences. Technologies enable virtual experiences and grassroots exchanges and substitute satisfying tourism motivations amid disputes. Across four in-depth paragraphs, empirical evidence from the literature substantiated the conceptual framework of these interconnected dynamics. This study demonstrates the proliferation of digital warfare tactics accompanying escalating geopolitical disputes. Research also validated perceptions of heightened uncertainty bred by the opaqueness of online hostilities. Meanwhile, case examples established how countries promote tourism and sovereignty through virtual representations. Studies likewise corroborated technologies empowering decentralized discourses that reconceptualize destinations and challenge preconceptions. Based on the comprehensive analysis and logical progression of arguments built, it was hypothesized that digital innovation could weaken the influence of political tensions on risk perceptions and travel impacts. In conclusion, this chapter presented a holistic framework examining the interplay between geopolitics, digital warfare, and innovation in tourism. It argued digital technologies can amplify tensions through new mediums of conflict while also helping mitigate impacts. The formulated hypotheses can guide further empirical testing to help build industry resilience against geopolitical risks in the digital era.

9.4.1 THEORETICAL CONTRIBUTION

This study makes a theoretical contribution to understanding the linkages between geopolitical tensions, digital warfare, and digital innovation in tourism. It advances knowledge by proposing an integrated conceptual model that bridges existing gaps in the literature by examining these interconnected relationships through a holistic framework. The model hypothesizes that as more geopolitical conflicts occur in digital information domains, new challenges will emerge for tourism that emerging technologies can help address. In doing so, this study formulates hypotheses proposing novel theoretical propositions regarding the relationships between critical constructs that had not been tested together previously. Specifically, it hypothesizes that digital warfare mediates geopolitical tensions' impacts on risk perception and that digital innovations weaken these relationships. This conceptualization meaningfully advances theory by linking three previously under-explored phenomena into an integrated framework and identifying their causal interaction effects. It goes beyond existing knowledge by synthesizing gaps traditionally examined independently (Lisle, 2000; Van den Heede et al., 2018; Lehto, 2018). The model theorizes how geopolitical conflicts are increasingly propagated through digital information activities, introducing novel challenges for tourism mitigated by digital technologies (Merrin and Hoskins, 2020; Lu, 2022; Taddeo, 2020).

Empirical evidence from case studies provides preliminary validation of model relationships. For example, research substantiates conceptions regarding the increasingly using digital information operations amid disputes (Van den Heede et al., 2018; Lu, 2022; Gaufman, 2022). Studies also validate conceptions of technologies reshaping risk perceptions (Henry, 2021; Cheesman, 2022) and weakening geopolitical constraints on tourism (Martin et al., 2023; Naeem et al., 2023). This lends initial support to this study's theoretically innovative integration. The model also suggests avenues for future empirical testing. Beyond proposing a novel theoretical framework, this study contributes methodologically through its comprehensive interdisciplinary literature review and development of rigorous research questions to unpack the model's propositions, strengthening methodological robustness for knowledge advancement.

9.4.2 MANAGERIAL IMPLICATIONS

This study offers several practical implications for tourism destinations and business managers. First, they should develop robust digital strategies utilizing technologies like social media and virtual/augmented reality to showcase destinations and cultural assets during conflicts or health crises. Examples demonstrate promoting heritage trails on YouTube during COVID-19 or countering political divisions through online festivals. Platforms foster awareness and satisfy travel motivation remotely to facilitate quicker recoveries. Second, managers should facilitate virtual, grassroots exchanges between divided communities to rebuild trust amid hostilities. Partnerships between travel influencers/leaders from disputing sides to co-produce collaborative counter-misinformation content on social media counter fear through empathetic storytelling, reshaping risk perceptions.

Third, destinations in conflict zones should partner with supportive firms and digital art initiatives broadcasting emotional solidarity. Platforms enable patrons to support cause-based VR/AR financially, highlighting solidarity actions like healthcare worker statues worldwide. Medium-intensity digital solidarity marketing fosters stronger stock reactions, offsetting the economic impacts of geopolitical downturns. Fourth, user-generated content platform-based inclusion promotes reconciliation. Tourism boards cultivating diverse forum moderators/guidelines and user-generated itineraries depicting contested areas' lives counter official framing.

Finally, leveraging e-commerce and streaming to integrate international exchange circumvents geopolitical barriers. Virtual trade fairs nonpolitically showcase endangered handicrafts. Coordinated heritage site hashtags to publicize virtual accessibility. Digitalization satisfies related needs and builds competitive advantages, weathering political turbulence impacts through diversified, resilient participation pathways. These examples illustrate practical digital strategies organizations can adopt to strengthen geopolitical resilience through virtual experiences, dialogues, collaborations, and innovative e-markets. Harnessing opportunities while mitigating challenges maximizes potential amid conflicts through integrated, inclusive technological solutions.

9.4.3 LIMITATIONS AND FUTURE RESEARCH

This study advances theoretical understanding through a conceptual model examining the relationships between geopolitics, digital warfare, and innovation in tourism. However, as an initial conceptualization, some limitations must be acknowledged to guide future research efforts. A key limitation was that the model development relied on a literature review that may exhibit biases in the contexts, themes, regions, and technologies studied. For example, much of the existing research focused on analysis at the country level without considering subnational impact variations. Future studies employing mixed methods could evaluate its generalizability across more diverse case studies and spatial scales to test the model's applicability. Another limitation was this study's cross-sectional and conceptual nature, prohibiting empirical testing of relationships proposed in the model. To fully unpack the dynamic aspects and causal mechanisms involved, longitudinal research designs utilizing quantitative, qualitative, or mixed methods approaches over extended periods are needed. This could help establish whether relationships hold consistently or vary depending on intervening conditions. Relatedly, a predominantly theoretical review precluded incorporating diverse stakeholder voices that future research could consider through interviews. In addition, individual manager characteristics were not accounted for but may condition digital innovation adoption decisions, a factor future research should examine. Finally, examining linkages through a review of literature centered on a few major digital technologies and platforms poses a methodological limitation. Emerging technologies are rapidly expanding the digital environments, shaping conflicts and hostilities. A broader technological scope may reveal new risk mitigation strategies to strengthen model validity. Addressing such limitations through diverse multimethod research designs across contexts can augment the theoretical foundations of this initial conceptual framework.

KEYWORDS

- **digital warfare**
- **geopolitics**
- **information management**
- **risk perception**
- **tourism digitalization**
- **tourism innovation**

REFERENCES

Asmolov, G. (2022). The transformation of participatory warfare: The role of narratives in connective mobilization in the Russia–Ukraine war. *Digital War, 3*(1–3), 25–37. https://doi.org/10.1057/s42984–022–00030–5

Bigley, J. D., Lee, C. K., Chon, J., & Yoon, Y. (2010). Motivations for war-related tourism: A case of DMZ visitors in Korea. *Tourism Geographies, 12*(3), 371–394. https://doi.org/10.1080/14616688.2010.503700

Brennen, J. S., Simon, F. M., Howard, P. N., & Nielsen, R. K. (2020). *Types, sources, and claims of COVID-19 misinformation.*

Buchanan, A. (2016). "I felt like a tourist instead of a soldier": The occupying gaze—War and tourism in Italy, 1943–1945. *American Quarterly, 68*(3), 593–615. https://doi.org/10.1353/aq.2016.0055

Butler, R., & Suntikul, W. (Eds.). (2013). *Tourism and war* (Vol. 34). Routledge.

Cheesman, M. (2022). Self-sovereignty for refugees? The contested horizons of digital identity. *Geopolitics, 27*(1), 134–159. https://doi.org/10.1080/14650045.2021.1954650

Doshi, R. (2020). The United States, China, and the contest for the fourth industrial revolution. *US Senate Committee on Commerce, Science, and Transportation.*

Garay, L., Morales, S., & Wilson, J. (2020). Tweeting the right to the city: Digital protest and resistance surrounding the Airbnb effect. *Scandinavian Journal of Hospitality and Tourism, 20*(3), 246–267. https://doi.org/10.1080/15022250.2020.1776822

Gaufman, E. (2022). Damsels in distress: Fragile masculinity in digital war. *Media, War & Conflict*. https://doi.org/10.1177/17506352221130271

Gordon, B. M. (1998). Warfare and tourism: Paris in World War II. *Annals of Tourism Research, 25*(3), 616–638. https://doi.org/10.1016/S0160–7383(98)00016–6

Gretzel, U., Fuchs, M., Baggio, R., Hoepken, W., Law, R., Neidhardt, J., ... & Xiang, Z. (2020). e-Tourism beyond COVID-19: a call for transformative research. *Information Technology & Tourism*, *22*(2), 187–203.

Guyonneau, R., & Le Dez, A. (2019). Artificial intelligence in digital warfare. *The Cyber Defense Review, 4*(2), 103–116. https://cyberdefensereview.army.mil/Portals/6/Documents/2019_summer/11_Guyonneau_Le%20Dez.pdf

Hall, R. C. (2020). *The Balkan Reconquista and Türkiye's forgotten refugee crisis.* In William H. Holt (Ed.), Salt Lake City, University of Utah Press, 2019, ISBN 9781607816959.

Henry, J. (2021). The geopolitics of travel blogging. *Geopolitics, 26*(3), 817–837. https://doi.org/10.1080/14650045.2020.1806654

Higgins-Desbiolles, F. (2022). The question of solidarity in tourism. *Journal of Policy Research in Tourism, Leisure and Events,* 1–10. https://doi.org/10.1080/19407963.2022.2061780

Holleran, M., & Notting, M. (2023). Mobility guilt: Digital nomads and COVID-19. *Tourism Geographies,* 1–18. https://doi.org/10.1080/14616688.2023.2194535

Ioannides, D., & Apostolopoulos, Y. (1999). Political instability, war, and tourism in Cyprus: Effects, management, and prospects for recovery. *Journal of Travel Research, 38*(1), 51–56. https://doi.org/10.1177/004728759903800109

Ioannides, D., & Timothy, D. (2011). *Tourism in the USA: A spatial and social synthesis*. Routledge.

Josiassen, A., Kock, F., & Assaf, A. G. (2022). In times of war: Place solidarity. *Annals of Tourism Research, 96*, 102961. https://doi.org/10.1016/j.annals.2022.102961

Ketter, E., & Avraham, E. (2021). #StayHome today so we can #TravelTomorrow: Tourism destinations' digital marketing strategies during the Covid-19 pandemic. *Journal of Travel & Tourism Marketing, 38*(8), 819–832. https://doi.org/10.1080/10548408.2021.1984976

Khan, K., Khurshid, A., & Cifuentes-Faura, J. (2023). Investigating the relationship between geopolitical risks and economic security: Empirical evidence from Central and Eastern European countries. *Resources Policy, 85*, 103872. https://doi.org/10.1016/j.resourpol.2023.103872

Korstanje, M. E., & George, B. (2023). The ghost city: Chronicles of the apocalypse after COVID-19. *International Journal of Tourism Cities, 9*(1), 1–12. https://doi.org/10.1108/IJTC-01–2022–0003

Lee, K. K., & Shahin, S. (2023). Reciprocity and asymmetry in digital diplomacy: Geopolitics of national identity in South Korea–Japan and South Korea–US relations. *Policy & Internet, 15*(3), 415–430. https://doi.org/10.1002/poi3.322

Lee, Y. S. (2006). The Korean War and tourism: Legacy of the war on the development of the tourism industry in South Korea. *International Journal of Tourism Research, 8*(3), 157–170. https://doi.org/10.1002/jtr.572

Lehto, M. (2018). The modern strategies in the cyber warfare. In *Cyber security: Power and technology* (pp. 3–20). Routledge.

Lisle, D. (2000). Consuming danger: Reimagining the war/tourism divide. *Alternatives, 25*(1), 91–116. https://doi.org/10.1177/030437540002500104

Lu, I. F. (2022). To subdue the enemies without fighting: Chinese state-sponsored disinformation as digital warfare. *Digital War, 3*(1–3), 96–106. https://doi.org/10.1057/s42984–022–00041–2

Martin, A., Sharma, G., de Souza, S. P., Taylor, L., van Eerd, B., McDonald, S. M., & Dijstelbloem, H. (2023). Digitisation and sovereignty in humanitarian space: Technologies, territories and tensions. *Geopolitics, 28*(3), 1362–1397. https://doi.org/10.1080/14650045.2022.2078466

Melović, M., Baynazoğlu, M. E., & Šerić, N. (2023). Family businesses in tourism–The use of digital technologies in times of uncertainty and crisis. *Journal of Family Business Management, 13*(1), 185–209. https://doi.org/10.1108/JFBM-01–2022–0013

Merrin, W., & Hoskins, A. (2020). Tweet fast and kill things: Digital war. *Digital War, 1*, 184–193. https://doi.org/10.1057/s42984–020–00018–9

Naeem, M. A., Arfaoui, N., Karim, S., & Lim, W. M. (2023). Tourism market in turbulent times: Evidence of asymmetric connectedness. *Current Issues in Tourism*, 1–30. https://doi.org/10.1080/13683500.2023.2175046

Nautiyal, R., & Polus, R. (2022). Virtual tours as a solidarity tourism product? *Annals of Tourism Research Empirical Insights, 3*(2), 100066. https://doi.org/10.1016/j.annale.2022.100066

Nicolau, J. L., Poretti, C., & Heo, C. Y. (2024). Solidarity actions with Ukraine and hospitality firm value. *Tourism Management, 100*, 104813. https://doi.org/10.1016/j.tourman.2023.104813

Papagianni, E., Evgenidis, A., Tsagkanos, A., & Megalooikonomou, V. (2023). Tourism demand in the face of geopolitical risk: Insights from a cross-country analysis. *Journal of Travel Research*. https://doi.org/10.1177/00472875231206539

Rolston, B. (1995). Selling tourism in a country at war. *Race & Class, 37*(1), 23–40. https://doi.org/10.1177/030639689503700103

Sun, Y. Y., Sie, L., Faturay, F., Auwalin, I., & Wang, J. (2021). Who are vulnerable in a tourism crisis? A tourism employment vulnerability analysis for the COVID-19 management. *Journal of Hospitality and Tourism Management, 49*, 304–308. https://doi.org/10.1016/j.jhtm.2021.09.005

Taddeo, M. (2020). Information warfare: A philosophical perspective. In *The ethics of information technologies* (pp. 461–476). Routledge.

Van den Heede, P., Ribbens, K., & Jansz, J. (2018). Replaying today's wars? A study of the conceptualization of post-1989 conflict in digital "war" games. *International Journal of Politics, Culture, and Society, 31*, 229–250. https://doi.org/10.1007/s10767-018-9290-6

Winter, C. (2009). Tourism, social memory and the Great War. *Annals of Tourism Research, 36*(4), 607–626. https://doi.org/10.1016/j.annals.2009.03.005

Yang, C. (2020). Staging Israel/Palestine: The geopolitical imaginaries of international tourism. *Environment and Planning C: Politics and Space, 38*(6), 1075–1090. https://doi.org/10.1177/2399654420937314

CHAPTER 10

The Future of Travel Technology: Foundations and Conceptual Underpinnings

NAVIDREZA AHADI[1*], SAIMA KAREEM[2], and SARAH HUSSAIN[2]

[1]*College of Business, Law and Social Sciences University of Derby, Derby, UK*

[2]*Department of Tourism and Hospitality Management, Faculty of Management Studies, Jamia Millia Islamia, New Delhi, India*

*Corresponding author

ABSTRACT

The dawn of the technological revolution has the potential to significantly transform and reinvent the future possibilities for travel industry. This chapter attempts to unravel the intricacies of the facilitation and endorsement of the transformative journey ahead. Hence, poised at the intersection of innovation and exploration, this conceptual contribution delves into the cutting-edge technologies that are set to redefine the travel landscape. The study delves into the existing academic literature to explore advancements in the travel sector. It focuses on technologies such as virtual and augmented reality, robots, and automation to enhance future traveler experiences. The use of Big Data, AI, and Smart Tourism is a growing trend for personalized recommendations and itinerary planning. This study also examines the potential applications of chatbots, nonfungible tokens (NFTs), and metaverse for the future travel industry. Metaverse, in particular, presents a paradigm shift that disrupts the conventional boundaries between the physical and digital realms, hence offering opportunities for engaging in immersive experiences for future travels.

Digitalization in Tourism. Hulya Akdemir Cengiz, Seza Zerman, Aysegul Acar, and Faizan Ali (Eds.)

DOI: 10.1201/9781779644770-13

In addition, the potential impact of advanced forms of transportation in the future, such as autonomous pods, supersonic jets, hyperloop systems, and perhaps teleportation, will dramatically alter the progression of tourism infrastructure. This chapter additionally probes the cosmos, exploring the potential of space tourism as the final frontier in human quest, with a vision of preparing the stakeholders for "Navigating Tomorrow." Finally, this chapter presents implications for various stakeholders, including enthusiasts, industry professionals, researchers, and policymakers and proposes future research directions to further advance the knowledge in this field.

10.1 INTRODUCTION

The landscape of travel is undergoing a profound transformation, driven by the relentless march of technology. We find ourselves on the cusp of a new era, where innovation and exploration converge to redefine the very essence of the traveler's journey. In this era of extraordinary technological advancements, our chapter seeks to unravel the complexities and possibilities that path ahead, charting a course through the advanced technologies that will shape the future of travel. As we embark on this exploration, our gaze extends to the forefront of technological evolution, where artificial intelligence (AI) and augmented reality (AR) as well as robotic technologies promise to revolutionize the travel experience. The cooperation of these technologies seems to transcend the idea of convenience; it appears to be paving the way for a new mind-set of experiencing reality, or at least the near-reality of cyberspace. Sustainable solutions in travels are highlighted befitting the transformative plot that is required to depict sustainable practices in the sector. Big Data and AI involvement is not just limited to the personal experience but also paves the foundations of tourism. Society acquires a new feature with robots and automation as core substructures of the mechanisms as they make work become effective and useful. Smart Tourism appears as the beacon of light as it can use technology to suggest location-based services, as well as create personalized itineraries and the inclusion of tourism chatbots. The chapter also looks at the possibility of nonfungible tokens (NFTs) in the formation of the new tourism environment. The travelers are brought as virtual avatars into the metaverse that seems as the crossover between the physical and virtual worlds, thus being very good for exploration. This specifically frees the travelers to go on virtual tours and exploration beyond usual possibilities.

Looking forward to the future, our line of sight goes up to the stars—by encompassing the concept of space tourism as the final frontier of human expansion. In essence, the chapter provides a clear roadmap for the researchers, industry experts, and those interested in traveling this technology rich roadmap of the future of tourism and travel. Ultimately, "Navigating Tomorrow" is not just a tagline but a call to action, inviting all stakeholders to embark on this transformative journey into the future of travel. The triad of tourism, travel, and hospitality industries shares a unified objective: delivering both essential and personalized services to travelers (O'Grady et al., 2009; Zatori et al., 2018). Within these sectors, enterprises engage in multifaceted information processing to manage diverse operations, spanning accommodations (e.g., hotels, motels, casinos, and conference centers), transportation services (e.g., airplanes, cruises, ships, and buses), food and beverage operations (e.g., catering, bars, vending machines, and banquets), retail establishments (e.g., souvenirs, handicrafts, and gift shops), and a spectrum of activities from recreation to cultural festivals (Kim et al., 2016; Zhang et al., 2018a, b). The exploration of space tourism underscores our innate desire for discovery and challenges us to contemplate the limitless potential that lies beyond our atmosphere.

As we explore into the domain of Smart Tourism, the chapter not only emphasizes personalized experiences but also delves into the ethical considerations surrounding data privacy and the responsible use of emerging technologies. It prompts a reflection on the delicate balance between innovation and ethical stewardship, ensuring that the evolution of travel technology aligns with the values of inclusivity and sustainability. Addressing various challenges such as infrastructure, transparency, security, safety facial recognition tech using AI is seen as the solution and possibly for the other three as well. Another issue for SMEs with introductory outsourcing plans is how to sustain optimum service quality while labor relations are in constant fluctuation. Therefore, to the best of the authors' knowledge, it becomes paramount to undertake a scoping review, examining the shifting dynamics and opportunities of using facial recognition technology powered by AI in the travel and tourism industry.

New to the analysis is the idea of NFTs in the sphere of tourism, which focuses on opportunities for digital, exclusive assets to improve the experience and value of tourism. This application of the blockchain technology provides interesting questions about ownership and authenticity regarding digital travels souvenirs. When thinking about the metaverse, one is not only thinking about a new digital space but about a change in the culture where information is both digital and physical. The so-called metaverse rises to the rank of rewriting social interactions and relations, questioning linear formations of connectivity, and offering the prospect for new communities in the digital environment. Besides being a theoretical analysis, this chapter is also a guide for practitioners involved in constructing the future of travel technology. All the stakeholders—researchers working in the field, industry professionals, and enthusiasts—are welcome to go through the layers of innovation described here and obtain the information needed to make strategic decisions and coordinate joint activities in the sphere of travel technology. From short- and long-haul travels, to domestic and global tourism, the industry not only enables the "getting there" but the "going out" and "searching and finding" (Bromberg et al., 2020; González-Rodríguez et al., 2020). In other words, "Navigating Tomorrow" is more than just a slogan; it is a commitment to shape the future of travel technology in a positive way that will bring joy and meaning to everybody's lives while challenging the technological status quo to do it in a smart way while being moral, humane, and ecologically conscious. As pushing the world advancement and opening up new horizons in innovation, this chapter invites all the stakeholders to change for creating a new world, a new outlook in traveling as technology is seamlessly placed into different industries. Various constituents including healthcare (Nasseef et al., 2021) and security (Chiu et al., 2009) perform some significant roles, in the management of a large amount of information for operational improvement. Travel operators and regional tourist offices are indirect contributors to the industry since they assist tourists in choosing a variety of bundled products such as travel, accommodation, transport from the hotel to various attractions and back and business opportunities for incorporating distinct technologies (Gaur et al., 2021; Xu et al., 2021).

10.2 INFLUENCE OF AI AND TECHNOLOGY ON FUTURE TRAVEL AND TOURISM

The impact of technology on the future of travel does not only lie in a single aspect, but the integration of technology reaches every aspect of the travel experience, structuring experiences and processes and redefining the framework of travel. In this part, we cover the intricate unified structure created by the entwinement of Big Data, AI, and automation in the texture of the travel sector. The sector of travel and tourism understands the need for identity verification before allowing access to facilities in relation to travel and staying (González-Rodríguez et al., 2020; Samala et al., 2020). AI becomes a dominant key in the future of travel at that point—with dynamic recommendation as option worth considering. The assistant is embedded with these alphabets of AI and gets to actualize into a companion that evolves from the user responses. This learning process fine tunes the recommendations, as a result providing the traveler with suggestions that are in harmony with the travelers' gradual changing needs. However, due to the issues of authentication irregularities several opportunities offered by self-service kiosks, message-based platforms and remote which check-in has been exploited thus leaving guest dissatisfied and identifying service gaps to explore (Watts, 2019). Implementing AI-based recognition technology helps the travel and tourism organizations avail numerous social, economic, and environmental benefits (Arenas et al., 2019; Bednar and Welch, 2020; Xue et al., 2020).

For instance, the hotels can add an improvement to the booking process whereby the guest can provide a photograph that can be used in integrating with airline bookings and other services available after the arrival of the travelers (Buhalis et al., 2019). Nevertheless, other technologies, including NFTs, advance customer experience by offering memorable and personalized digital assets and travel experiences. Such tokens—the tokens that may symbolize a virtual tour or individual itinerary—represent one of the interesting new forms of travel souvenirs. With the current NFT marketplaces being decentralized, travel agencies get an opportunity to be innovative and monetize on the digital content directly. The changing nature of AI recommendations goes beyond the typical travel guide and can thus respond to the specific needs and wants of each traveler. It turns into a virtual guide and begins to present a series of highly individualized recommendations that will fit the sophisticated demands of contemporary tourists. Out of these applications solution like facial recognition stands out due to their fast response to information, high accuracy, and solving security issues and challenges (Thales, 2020). The use of AI-integrated biometric facial recognition has the possibilities of increasing personalization in relation to traveler (Collins et al., 2021, Thales, 2020). In this regard, the application of AI in the recognition of facial characteristics is useful in evaluating the demographic and the psychographic profiles of the guests allowing the communication of different sites while on their journey to make the providers powerful in delivering great services (Buhalis et al., 2019).

Given the dynamic nature of the travel industry, which operates on the principles of the experience economy, a comprehensive analysis of each aspect of a guest's experience is vital for designing effective processes and services (Zatori et al., 2018). While existing studies touch upon physical kiosks, document scanning, and self-check-in and check-out processes in the travel and tourism industry, they often miss key highlights that could usher in a paradigm shift. Building upon the exciting applications outlined above, our study delves into analyzing travelers' experiences to redefine current and future travel services. Facial recognition technology, supported by AI, assumes a pivotal role in facilitating seamless and rapid payment authorizations. Its applicability extends to various scenarios, including check-out procedures without staff interaction, front-office transactions, and automatic payments at restaurants (Ciftci et al., 2021; González-Rodríguez et al., 2020; Zhong et al., 2021). Through advanced AI-driven facial recognition, hotels can discern images, sounds, and services that align with traveler profiles, enabling the travel and tourism industry to construct psychological profiles and tailor offerings accordingly (Arenas et al., 2019; Samala et al., 2020). Unlike other documentation methods, airports using this technology encounter a 40% rise in travelers' processing rate (Del Rio et al., 2016). For instance, check-in time at one of the Marriott's hotels in China was cut from 3 to 1 min to demonstrate the increase in competence (Buhalis et al., 2019). Its usage goes as far as transport and service preordering and customized arrangements of lodges/accommodations, airports, and immigrations. The fact that normally, the process of customs clearance and other immigration documentation can be lengthy proves to be less inconvenient with the incorporation of facial recognition reduction of hassles faced by tourists. Beyond these conveniences, technology plays a crucial role in ensuring security and safety during information processing with different partners, such as insurers for specific visits (Bromberg et al., 2020). Furthermore, it aids in crime prevention and the identification of suspicious travelers (Culot et al., 2019; Del Rio et al., 2016), empowering hotel security staff to cover areas beyond the reach of CCTV systems and instantly identify suspects (Chan and Lam, 2013). Similarly, Royal Caribbean, in the cruise sector, significantly reduced processing times using facial recognition for customs clearance compared with conventional methods (Lu et al., 2019). Beyond tourist applications, enterprises, including those in travel and tourism, utilize AI-driven facial recognition for various stakeholder purposes, such as tracking the attendance of employees and contractors to maintain service levels (Zatori et al., 2018). This innovation facilitates real-time attendance monitoring, offering a significant improvement over traditional attendance systems and eliminating queuing in time offices (Andrejevic and Selwyn, 2020).

10.2.1 BIG DATA—INFORMATION SUPERHIGHWAY

The new phenomenon of Big Data introduced a world of constant information stream and generated a superhighway of insights that changes the perception and interaction with travel. In the same way, as travelers go about their trips, they engage with numerous touch points, and in the process, produce a lot of data. Coordinated well, this data is one of the most effective tools for changing the entire landscape of the travel industry and world as a whole. Furthermore, as with any field based on big data analysis, both academic and practical work on the subjects of Big Data in tourism and hospitality studies are expanding progressively, with constantly developing approaches, methods, and algorithms to investigate the themes under analysis in the present work (He et al., 2022; Ma et al, 2020). As one of the significant developments of the data technology revolution, big data is expected to provide a wide-ranging influence on the processes and approaches of knowledge construction involved in thinking styles and in the values and ethics that underpin modern tourism and hospitality research. For example, Big Data can be used by the travel companies to come up with in-depth understanding of the clients' behavior and decisions. By understanding these patterns, businesses can tailor their offerings to meet the evolving needs of travelers, providing a more personalized and enriching experience. From predictive analytics that anticipate travel trends to targeted marketing strategies, Big Data becomes a cornerstone in crafting a future where travel is not just a journey but a bespoke adventure. The tourism and hospitality industries, recognizing the potential value, have harnessed big data analytics to transform voluminous data into valuable insights. This capability proves instrumental in enhancing tourism and hospitality management, offering substantial competitive advantages (Liu et al., 2017).

In our present high-tech landscape, a vast and diverse array of data is generated and consumed regularly. The evolution of data science has given rise to the concept of big data, sparking innovative research that underscores the role of big data analytics in practical knowledge generation. On one hand, the sheer scale, comprehensiveness, and diversity of big data surpass the capabilities of traditional database tools for capture, storage, management, and analysis (Elragal and Klischewski, 2017). On the other hand, big data leans heavily toward a new inductive statistical approach, potentially ushering in a paradigm shift from theory-driven to data-driven perspectives in research (Ibili et al., 2019).

10.2.2 ROBOTS—AUTOMATING HOSPITALITY

The part of the robots in the hospitality sector can be regarded as a major step forward to the necessary levels of productivity and advancement. Automation of robots in the hotel setting is no longer something that is rolled out in the sci-fi; rather, these automatic programs depict a revolution in method through which services are rendered. From the check-in and checkout services to food delivery, a robot helps in the hotel business as an effort to make services better for guests. They can picture themselves in a hotel wherein during registration they are welcomed, given their key cards, and assisted by a welcoming robot should they have any questions to ask. In this way, the often conservative and repetitive nature of day-to-day processes no longer has to be managed by people, thus allowing them to concentrate on more differentiated and valuable tasks. Similarly, housekeeping can also be delegated to robots and this makes sure that the house is very clean always. Such developments include robots that are able to cook rather complex meals and serve customers.

In the United States, a California-based creator has unveiled a burger robot for making up to 120 burgers per hour (Troitino, 2018); the same as Café X has begun preparing robot baristas that prepare three beverages at a time in 40 s (Canales, 2018). At the same time, several hotels in Japan have substituted a great deal of frontline service workers with robotics (Osawa et al., 2017), the food technology landscapes, especially restaurant robots in the United Kingdom, is gradually opening up to investment and innovation (Dobberstein, 2019). This automated hospitality environment does not only enhance the working processes but also meets new trends of a smart generation of tourists. Robotics in hospitality can be seen as the industry that consistently applies the use of new technologies with the goal of improving the experience of customers. When it comes to hospitality service interactions, service robotics is considered to be one of the most revolutionary innovations in the recent years (Ivanov and Webster, 2019a). Ongoing trends in electrical and mechanical engineering at computer science, by enhanced raw computing capability, big data accumulation, and the introduction of techniques such as machine learning and deep neural networks, robots have gone beyond the manufacturing industry and are now present in dynamic human environments (Ivanov et al., 2019). In particular, the last few years have seen a very fast rate of innovation in the shipping and design of service robots for use in the hospitality sector (Murphy et al., 2019).

10.3 AI, ASSISTIVE TECHNOLOGIES, AND AUTOMATION IN TOURISM INFRASTRUCTURE

From chatting bots in tourism helping with the planning of the trip, to smart locks in accommodations improving security, automation emerges as the less visible but incredibly important element improving the efficiency of the travel system. They are proactive intelligence tour guides in resorts and destinations who provide real-time information and suggestions. Such chatbots could assist in itinerary planning, give recommendations on sights to visit, and even aid in problem solving in the course of the trip. The facility of reaching out that is brought by the chatbots reinvents the traveler's approach to information, and therefore, the process of travel is not only smooth but engaging. This form of authentication not only helps organizations to provide memorable and remarkable service experiences of courteous interaction to the patrons as a way of serving them (Zatori et al., 2018) but also plays a significant role in protecting the enterprises' staff as well as the whole society from the effects of the pandemics (Del Rio et al., 2016). This technology assists the identification of the previous clients by the hotel employees and added service delivery that would make their experience even better (Gaur et al., 2021; Lehrer et al., 2018). AI-supported facial recognition can also facilitate control of the climate preferences or automatically alter them with the help of established facial patterns as well as order meals in advance according to the guest's preference (Zhang et al., 2020). The idea is that the AI assistant integrated with the location data and the previous preferences of the given traveler can suggest what is worth to visit, eat, and even discover nearby. Such an approach not only adds great value to the overall picture of the traveling process but makes the traveler feel that this or that place is rather familiar. In the future, the application of AI facial recognition will diversify toward vehicles to cover all security aspects of driving, parking, and vehicle entry throughout all the available types of transportations (Lu et al., 2019). The technology's capability of recognizing blink rate, which is effective in avoiding an accident, is useful in monitoring signs of drowsiness through the period of travel (Yang et al., 2020). Automation, again, is seen when it comes to smart locks that change security mechanisms in the accommodations. Generally, smart locks improve the security of the guests since the traditional keys are replaced by the digital ones, not forgetting the benefits that accompany the keyless check-in and checkout. All these incorporations of technology into the details of the necessity of travels add up to the sensation of security and easiness. The technological impact that defines travel's future is not limited to these since it even redefines the very concept of the traveler. Big Data, AI, and robots and automation all mix together to make every inch of the trip unique, tailored, and efficient. As we move to the next level of this great transformation the utilization of these technologies is no longer a mere add on but a core ingredient in fashioning out a world where travel is synonymous to excellence, innovation, and efficiency.

10.3.1 ASSISTIVE TECHNOLOGIES FOR INCLUSIVE TOURISM

In the rapidly growing topic of travel technology the aspects go beyond convenient traveling to providing equal access to technology solutions regardless of disability status. The role of technology in the inclusive tourism experiences as it relates to the disabled and the elderly is the focus this section. Ivanov et al. (2017), as well as Ivanov and Webster (2019a, 2019b), characterized current growing interest in hospitality service robotics by various factors. These are increased cost-sensitivity, better resource utilization, better modeling of demand, better quality control, better management of processes, reduction of errors by man.

For physically challenged persons, the beginning of technology in this regard becomes a ray of hope and offers a new meaning to the word accessibility when it comes to tourism. Smart mobility apps, inclusive navigation, and so on: the use of technology provides an efficient and enriching experience for anyone who may need it. Many other developed countries are also reported to be experiencing the same trend as mentioned by Frey and Osborne (2017) and hence in the near future utilization of service robots will be instrumental in maintaining high productivity and economic growth in GDP (International Federation of Robotics, 2018). Real-time mobility applications including wheelchair navigation apps assist people with the appropriate routes that consider things like ramps, lifts, and accessible amenities. This not only helps persons with disability to be able to move around in the society on but also extends their traveling opportunities that had earlier been considered difficult. Also, AR apps that improve the tangible setting will be beneficial to the visually impaired persons. When AR gives descriptions of the current environment by providing a voice-over or vibrating regarding the environment, it becomes an enabler of access to traveling. This not only makes the travel safer but also makes the experience more fulfilling for individuals who depend on sense other than sight.

10.3.2 COGNITIVE TECHNOLOGIES FOR MENTAL WELLNESS

Thus, the assessment of the effect from the angle of inclusive tourism is realized not only in the context of physical disability of the tourists but their psychological condition also. In this aspect, the traveling seems to be a challenge to persons with cognitive impairments or persons with mental health disorders. But this is where cognitive technologies' progress opens the way to more friendly and perceptive travel setting. As such, there is a possibility of unfolding such ideas as AI-powered chatbots with the empathy sense. Such of these chatbots can identify nonverbal signals in the interactions with users and adjust their responses to be compassionate and encouraging. This becomes especially valuable for people who can experience anxiety or, for example, have communication difficulties during their trips. Another key component of making travel experiences accessible is virtual reality (VR) that provides those persons with simulations for them to become accustomed to the environment they will be in during their travel. Taking the example of Autism, for people with such condition, which emphasizes on structure and predictability, VR offer means of rehearsing to new environments that minimize stress resulting from the inability to forecast the situation. Research shows that tourism is an important determinant of satisfaction of social needs for the tourists mainly in areas of psychological capital, recreation, and family. The emotional benefits arising from a tourism experience make a considerable contribution toward a happiness quotient (Dolnicar et al., 2012; McCabe and Johnson, 2013). Thus, Su and Huang et al. (2015) studied service quality and fairness with reference to Xiamen tourists to examine the effects on the tourists' behavior and their self-reported well-being. Service fairness appeared to have a stronger effect on tourists' subjective well-being than service quality according to the studies. Saayman et al. (2018) examined the relationship between the tourism experience, perceived tourist satisfaction and well-being among the South African tourists. It was seen that satisfaction level of the participants with the destination services had a signification impact over their perceived self-actualization.

10.3.3 AGING POPULATION, AUTOMATION, AND ASSISTIVE TECHNOLOGIES

Since the number of elderly people is gradually increasing worldwide, the travel industry acknowledges the need to accommodate the elderly. Technology then comes out as a strong enabler that would help the aging population continue to stumble, discover, and enjoy the world with ease. Intelligent processors can recognize working preferences, suggest collaborations, and improve the skills of different stakeholders—patients, among others (Mele et al., 2021). Health-monitoring devices that are worn become virtually essential companions for older travelers. They can monitor pulse rates, administer dosage information, and even healthcare alerts in cases for example of a heart attack. The application of such technologies not only provides safety but also gives confidence both for the travel and the family of the elderly. Smart home automation expands its control over the sphere of travel providing homes that are uniquely suited for elderly people. Starting with the beds that can be adjusted, moving to the washrooms fitted with sensors, hi-tech transforms the conventional accommodation into comfortable and convenient lodgings. The effects of new technology especially the help/assistant robots on healthcare are becoming more apparent in service research as pointed by Berry (2019). Nevertheless, a cluster of studies recognizes the benefits of cognitive computing that refers to both hardware and software technologies mimicking human cognition abilities (Russo Spena et al., 2019). Therefore, assistant robots help create value to consumers in terms of task performance while at the same time creating efficiency value for healthcare providers (Kaartemo and Helkkula, 2018). Cognitive computing in the delivery of healthcare services entails a revolution, which if embraced could facilitate delivery of efficient healthcare services.

10.3.4 INCLUSIVE TOURISM: A COLLABORATIVE FUTURE

Hence, transformative, and innovative technological enhancement for the making of an inclusive tourism is a collaborative process of all the stakeholders from diverse sectors. Suppliers, architects, construction professionals, and tourist authorities coalesce in order to build an environment of architectural, cultural, physical, and perceptual accessibility for the traveler. Its elements tend to include the concerns of the accessible design, thereby pushing for the transformation of the physical world of travel alongside the digital counterpart. Modern web pages and applications can come equipped with voice controls, contrast options and in options such as specific font sizes making it easy for anyone with a disability to be able to access information.

Collaborative platforms emerge, connecting travelers with similar needs and experiences, fostering a sense of community and shared wisdom. These platforms not only provide valuable insights into accessible destinations but also create a support network where individuals can exchange tips, recommendations, and encouragement. The integration of technology-assisted experiences in inclusive tourism not only dismantles physical and cognitive barriers but also fosters a sense of empowerment and belonging for all travelers. As we navigate toward a future where travel is truly inclusive, the collaboration between technology and empathy becomes the cornerstone in crafting journeys that transcend limitations, celebrate diversity, and enrich the lives of every individual, regardless of their unique abilities or age.

10.4 FUTURISTIC TRANSPORTATION TECHNOLOGIES

Transportation technology has made great progress in terms of its scope and scale, covering nearly every facet of the transportation system.

This progress has been particularly notable after the 1990s, primarily to the emergence of intelligent transportation system (ITS) technology (Ran et al., 2012). Having a modern, well-built conveyance infrastructure that is both reliable and secure is a hallmark of industrialized nations in contemporary world. The whole transportation system relies on the synergy between humans and technological systems. The desire for increased speed and comfort are the significant factors propelling advancements in the transportation system in the decades to come.

Owing to revolutionary advancements in technology, a seamless communication across all components including humans, vehicles, and infrastructure in transit networks has recently been successfully attained. Aside from allowing transit systems to gather data in instantaneously, this kind of connectivity also makes it possible to actively coordinate automobiles in real time (Ran et al., 2012). People planning trips in the future have all sorts of transportation ideas, ranging from capsules to supersonic planes to teleportation (Feldtkeller et al., 2016). Many travelers demand improvements in travel convenience. They desire innovations in transportation infrastructures and facility designs such as seats that shape themselves to human bodies. Other methods to alleviate travel discomfort include being placed in a "stasis" mental state or "animation mode" for the whole trip (Feldtkeller et al., 2016).

Autonomous electric cars, often known as driverless automobiles, are becoming more popular. The roads of the United States and several other countries have been taken over by autonomous vehicles. They are initiating complications and challenges that the general population have never previously encountered or observed (Hancock et al., 2019). Given that they are already present in our society, present dilemmas regarding autonomous vehicles no longer center on the implementation or nonimplementation these advancements. They have already become a reality. In the future, there may be a possibility of using either fully electric automobiles or plug-in hybrid electric vehicles (Zhu et al., 2016). Potentially feasible completely automated and regulated transit systems might emerge in the future as a result of advancements in electronic communication and smart vehicle innovations within the motor vehicle sector (Ran et al., 2012).

Potential advancements in transport technology might include the use of hyperloop systems. A hyperloop is an advanced mode of transit that operates at elevated rates on the ground. It utilizes magnetic levitation and electromagnetic propulsion to move people or objects through a vacuum tube at rates comparable to that of a jet aircraft. This high-speed transportation system is capable of reaching speeds of up to 760 miles per hour and is designed to link large urban centers. The advancements being made will inevitably lead to a transformative shift in the movement of both goods and people in the future.

10.4.1 METAVERSE TECHNOLOGY FOR TRAVEL

When Facebook updated its name to "Meta"—a metaverse company—the concept of the metaverse gained immense popularity (Kim, 2021; Gursoy et al., 2022). In essence, the metaverse is a unified, enduring, and engaging alternate universe that is formed by merging all digital realms into a single space, allowing humans to effortlessly navigate across it. The real and virtual worlds merge in the metaverse, enabling people to move freely through realms. The hyper-connected metaverse not solely fulfils users' innate need for socialization and brings physical reality into sharp focus, but it also offers a transcendental place for individuals to express freely using avatars (Smart et al., 2007). Through the use of online immersion, humans are able to digitally visit bygone eras, explore space, or even brave potentially catastrophic natural disasters like volcanic eruptions (Buhalis et al., 2023).

While the metaverse cannot fully substitute physical travel, advancements in technological innovation and the enhanced functionality of VR headsets are motivating digitally native individuals and technologically adept users to participate in simulated exploration of the world (Gursoy et al., 2022). It enables travelers to tap into online worlds and digital assets even while they are not physically there. In this way, they may evaluate the attractiveness and appropriateness of destinations and amenities before they ever set foot in them (Buhalis et al., 2023). While digitally present at the geographical locations, metaverse enables utilization of digital assets to improve the user interaction and understanding of the location.

Take the Korean tourism app ZEPETO World as a perfect instance. It facilitates users build their own avatars and explore the country. The journey features an intricately designed engaging graphic of Han River Park (Constantin *et al.,* 2023). The ancient city of Hegra, located in Saudi Arabia, is yet another instance. It is the first UNESCO World Heritage Site to be featured in the metaverse. It enables virtual travelers discover the vicinity, including Hegra's Tomb of Lihyan, the son of Kuza (Duziak, 2023). The idea of Metaverse is to make traveling more immersive. The Metaverse is designed to augment the authentic experiences of travelers. Having already experienced the destination in the metaverse, travelers are expected to have an easier time interacting with their intended location (Dwivedi et al., 2022). Hence, the metaverse displays great promise as a game-changer for the travel and tourism industry in the future.

10.4.2 SPACE TOURISM FOR FUTURE TRAVEL

The realm of space is a promising new frontier for luxurious consumer offerings. Duval and Hall (2015) define space tourism as the willful departure of humans from Earth's atmosphere on a temporary basis for recreational and leisurely intentions. It offers travelers of a renewed sense of interconnectedness with the planet and fellow beings (Kim et al., 2024). After Virgin Galactic, Blue Origin, and SpaceX successfully launched space tourism between 2021 and 2023, there is a lot of interest from consumers, businesses, and governments in suborbital and orbital space tourism (Kim et al., 2023a, 2023b). A record number of people are considering going space tourism as a result of the development of reusable launch vehicles (RLVs), especially after Virgin Galactic's first commercial flights in June and August 2023 (Kim et al., 2024).

Space tourism is an emerging sector that is quickly expanding and will likely become accessible to the general public in the near future. individuals go to space for a variety of reasons, including exploring new places, having fun, and expanding their horizons (Chang and Chern, 2013). While for the most of us, it has long been an elusive aspiration, it is now beginning to materialize as a tangible possibility. At present, there are three main categories of space tourism missions: suborbital space tourism, orbital space tourism, and space tourism around the moon. Private enterprises must learn more about space tourism requirements to tailor their offerings (Mesa-Arango et al., 2023). Moreover, travel and transport authorities need direction to assist with the administration of funds associated with commercial space adventure.

Space travelers have a significant preoccupation with safety and security. Spector (2020) lists a number of health hazards associated with space tourism as an exploration activity. They include cosmic radiation exposure, microgravity, intense G-forces, bone loss, muscular atrophy, and the existential dangers of launching and returning to Earth (Spector, 2020). Other hazards that people believe encompass privacy, security, and budgetary concerns (Mehran et al., 2023; Kim et al., 2023a). In order for space tourism to be lucrative, it is crucial to prioritize the careful consideration of how consumers evaluate potential dangers. Moreover, cost has a crucial role in influencing the desire for travel. Space flight is characterized by exorbitant expenses (Mesa-Arango et al., 2023). Despite this, the implementation of cost-cutting measures may ultimately make space travel pricing accessible to the broader population.

10.5 DISCUSSIONS AND IMPLICATIONS

The current research investigates the potential of technology for traveling in the near future. In this age of phenomenal technical developments, curiosity and technological breakthroughs are coming together to reimagine the very foundation of the adventure that a traveler takes. Notwithstanding the discoveries and contributions, there is an insufficient comprehension about the use of technology for traveling. This chapter undertakes an extensive endeavor to identify and forecast the future of the transit system, including its anticipated evolution in the decades to come.

The use of AI-based detection technology offers significant benefits to organizations operating in the travel and tourism industry (Arenas et al., 2019). By permitting guests to upload their picture, which can be linked to airline tickets and assistance upon arrival, hotels may be able to streamline their reservation processes (Buhalis et al., 2019). Facial recognition technology, supported by AI, assumes a pivotal role in facilitating seamless and rapid payment authorizations. It may also be used for self-checkout, front-office operations, and dining self-payment (Ciftci et al., 2021).

When travelers begin their trips, their encounters with different points of contact provide a large amount of information. When used efficiently, this information has the potential to completely transform the whole transport industry. When algorithms are correctly used, this data continuously analyzes the rising subjects in travel and hospitality. This has completely transformed the whole transport environment. Through comprehending these trends, companies may customize their offers to align with the changing requirements of travelers, therefore delivering a more individualized and immersive encounter.

Furthermore, the hotel sector has additionally employed robotic assistance to improve customer services. This presence of robots in hotels symbolizes an operational transformation in the hospitality business, rather than being a mere speculative idea. This intelligent hotel environment enhances both operational efficiency and meets the ever-evolving demands of technologically proficient travelers. Travel chatbots, driven by AI, function as digital instructors, providing immediate support and suggestions.

Location-based data and the traveler's prior inclinations allow the AI assistant to propose neighborhood sites, eateries, and undiscovered treasures in the present moment. This personalization enriches the traveling encounter and connects the traveler to the geographic area. AI-driven identification of faces will soon improve vehicular security, including driving, parking, and gaining entry (Lu et al., 2019). Smart locks, another automation innovation, transform the safety and security along with hassle-free check-in and checkout experiences in the hotel while traveling. Given the perpetual evolution of these technologies, it is incumbent upon management to adapt and employ such technologies strategically.

In the ever-changing world of travel technology, accessibility for persons of all ages and abilities has been revolutionized by technology-enhanced experiences. This enhances the inclusivity of travel especially for those with the disabilities and the elderly. In addition to smart mobility solutions, which utilize real-time data to offer wheelchair-friendly navigation apps, VR and AR serve as transformative tools for enhancing inclusivity in travel experiences. This not only enables persons with impairments to traverse public settings autonomously but also expands the range of travel possibilities that were previously seen as impossible. Hence, these emerging technologies serve as a symbol of optimism, dismantling obstacles and reinventing the notion of travel accessibility. This guides the travel industry administrators to meet the expectations and requirements of users for future travel by developing unique and customized offerings.

Smart devices not only simply improve safety but also provide a feeling of confidence for both older travelers and relatives. Wearable gadgets with health-monitoring functions monitor critical indicators, lend reminders for medications, and deliver immediate medical notifications during crises. As a result, intelligent assistants facilitate the improvement of medical professionals' efficiency in operations while simultaneously augmenting the task performance of patients (Kaartemo and Helkkula, 2018). Voice navigation, high contrast interfaces, and customizable font sizes make websites and applications accessible to people with different abilities. Collective platforms bring travelers with identical requirements and interests together, forming networks and expertise. As we strive for a future that is marked by inclusiveness, these websites give information about locations that are accessible and offer a support network for sharing advice, suggestions, and motivation.

Zhu et al. (2016) suggested that plug-in hybrid electric vehicles or entirely electric cars might be the way of the future when it comes to transportation. Electric vehicles that are capable of driving themselves, sometimes referred to as driverless cars, are gaining popularity. The fact that autonomous cars are now in operation in our modern world indicates that they have already reached the point of becoming a reality. The future of travel may be shaped by revolutionary mobility technologies such as automated transit systems, connected and self-driving vehicles (CAVs), and mobility-as-a-service (MaaS). The introduction of the metaverse is yet another aspect of future travel technology. It allows users to be virtually present in physical locations while also making use of technological resources to enhance their engagement with and comprehension of those places. According to Smart et al. (2007), the hyper-connected metaverse provides a space for people to explore themselves creatively via avatars, in addition to satisfying their inherent desire to socialize and bringing the actual world into full view.

Likewise, the invention of RLVs has a significant impact on space travel, particularly after Virgin Galactic's first commercial flights in June and August 2023 (Kim et al., 2024). People go into space for several purposes, such as the exploration of uncharted territories, seeking enjoyment, and broadening their perspectives (Chang and Chern, 2013). The area of space tourism is rapidly growing and is expected to become widely available to the general population in the coming years. The chapter as a whole offers comprehension of the fundamental concepts for future travelers to comprehend the application of travel technology. According to the findings, through the use of various travel technology, travelers will be able to more effectively manage their traveling experiences. Hence, these emerging travel technologies are anticipated to profoundly influence the future of the travel industry.

The insights provided in this chapter have strengthened our comprehension of how different forms of travel innovation influence consumer attitude and their desire for future travel. Thus, it is imperative that the travel industry meets the larger demands for services of its customers while simultaneously contributing to the society as a whole. Professionals and practitioners may develop and execute effective strategies to include a broad spectrum of users in employing different devices and applications for futuristic travel. The level of preparedness of tourists to utilize new technologies should be the top priority for travel technology suppliers and managers. To improve their ability to employ technology, they should provide a wealth of pertinent information on novel approaches and a variety of programs and instructional materials.

The most important factors that influence the desire to employ novel travel technology are its simplicity in use and satisfaction. Experts and planners may develop and implement successful methods to encourage the use of different technologies and apps for futuristic transportation. Producers of software and other hedonic systems should prioritize the production of esthetically pleasing designs, user-friendly functionality, and a variety of customization possibilities when making gadgets and apps.

10.5.1 FUTURE RESEARCH DIRECTIONS

Although there have been conclusions and contributions, there is still a lack of full comprehension of the widespread usage of innovative technology. There are several opportunities to further explore the relationship between travel innovation and consumer adoption. Therefore, future investigations need to address several concerns, particularly in the context of automated travel, metaverse, and the societal embrace of AI-based technological innovations. Conducting research in various cultural contexts is particularly important due to potential variations in attitudes toward travel innovation among different regions. This will enable an assessment of the degree to which the generalizability may be extended to a wider range of travel settings.

Demographics might additionally play a significant role. Further study should explore if certain demographics of customers exhibit varying levels of satisfaction for a technological advance in travel and tourism market.

There are variations among segments when it comes to other aspects of the offering or customer traits, such as how sensitive consumers are to pricing. Hence, it is important to include demographic factors in future research since they play a pivotal role in adopting cutting-edge travel methods and influencing people' decision-making process. Curiosity is the gratifying impetus to investigate and gain understanding of unique, intriguing, and unaccustomed encounters. Further research may be warranted to examine the impact of individual curiosity, among other variables, on the inclination and inspiration to utilize innovative technologies for traveling.

In conclusion, this chapter has uncovered an array of cutting-edge technologies that an individual may in the future be inclined to embrace while traveling. Compatibility between people and technologies is vital for the well-functioning of transportation system as an entire phenomenon. These technologies gratify the inherent human desire for enhanced mobility and convenience, which will drive future developments in the transit system. Developed countries in the future will be distinguished by their sophisticated, reliable, and safe transportation networks.

KEYWORDS

- **future travel demand**
- **innovative technology**
- **transport**
- **travel**
- **travel technology**

REFERENCES

Andrejevic, M., & Selwyn, N. (2020). Facial recognition technology in schools: Critical questions and concerns. *Learning, Media and Technology, 45*(2), 115–128.

Arenas, A. E., Goh, J. M., & Urueña, A. (2019). How does IT affect design centricity approaches: Evidence from Spain's smart tourism ecosystem. *International Journal of Information Management, 45*, 149–162.

Bednar, P. M., & Welch, C. (2020). Socio-technical perspectives on smart working: Creating meaningful and sustainable systems. *Information Systems Frontiers, 22*(2), 281–298.

Berry, L. L. (2019). Service innovation is urgent in healthcare. *AMS Review, 9*(1), 78–92.

Bromberg, D. E., Charbonneau, É., & Smith, A. (2020). Public support for facial recognition via police body-worn cameras: Findings from a list experiment. *Government Information Quarterly*. https://doi.org/10.1016/j.giq.2019.101415.

Buhalis, D., Harwood, T., Bogicevic, V., Viglia, G., Beldona, S., & Hofacker, C. (2019). Technological disruptions in services: lessons from tourism and hospitality. *Journal of Service Management, 30*(4), 484–506.

Buhalis, D., Leung, D., & Lin, M. (2023). Metaverse as a disruptive technology revolutionising tourism management and marketing. *Tourism Management, 97*, https://doi.org/10.1016/j.tourman.2023.104724

Canales, K. (2018). This futuristic café relies on robots to take your order and make your coffee—No human interaction required. https://www.businessinsider.com/cafe-x-robotic-coffee-bar-automation-2018-6.

Chan, E. S., & Lam, D. (2013). Hotel safety and security systems: Bridging the gap between managers and guests. *International Journal of Hospitality Management*, *32*, 202–216.

Chang, Y. W., & Chern, J. S. (2013). From spirit of St. Louis to SpaceShipTwo: A study on the challenge of future space tourism development. *Journal of Aeronautics, Astronautics and Aviation. Series A, 45*(2), 135-154.

Chiu, D. K., Yueh, Y. T., Leung, H. F., & Hung, P. C. (2009). Towards ubiquitous tourist service coordination and process integration: A collaborative travel agent system architecture with semantic web services. *Information Systems Frontiers, 11*(3), 241–256.

Ciftci, O., Choi, E. K. C., & Berezina, K. (2021). Let's face it: Are customers ready for facial recognition technology at quick-service restaurants? *International Journal of Hospitality Management*. https://doi.org/10.1016/j.ijhm.2021.102941.

Collins, C., Dennehy, D., Conboy, K., & Mikalef, P. (2021). Artificial intelligence in information systems research: A systematic literature review and research agenda. *International Journal of Information Management*. https://doi.org/10.1016/j.ijinfomgt.2021.102383.

Constantin, M., Genovese, G., Munawar, K., & Stone, R. (2023). Tourism in the metaverse: Can travel go virtual? McKinsey & Company. https://www.mckinsey.com/industries/travel-logistics-and-infrastructure/our-insights/tourism-in-the-metaverse-can-travel-go-virtual (accessed 27 Jan 2024).

Culot, G., Fattori, F., Podrecca, M., & Sartor, M. (2019). Addressing Industry 4.0 cybersecurity challenges. *IEEE Engineering Management Review, 47*(3), 79–86.

Del Rio, J. S., Moctezuma, D., Conde, C., de Diego, I. M., & Cabello, E. (2016). Automated border control e-gates and facial recognition systems. *Computers & Security, 62*, 49–72.

Dobberstein, A. (2019). Report: The growing and dominating UK FoodTech ecosystem. https://medium.com/forwardfooding/report-the-growing-and-dominating-uk-foodtech-ecosystem-10917deb212e

Dolnicar, S., Yanamandram, V., & Cliff, K. (2012). The contribution of vacations to quality of life. *Annals of Tourism Research, 39*(1), 59–83.

Duval, D. T., & Hall, C. M. (2015). New destinations, new challenges. In *The Routledge handbook of tourism and sustainability*.

Duziak, D. (2023). The metaverse. In *Blockchain for hospitality and tourism: A guide to the future* (pp. 87–113). Apress.

Dwivedi, Y., Hughes, L., Baabdullah, A., Ribeiro-Navarrete, S., Giannakis, M., AlDebei, M., Dennehy, D., Metri, B., Buhalis, D., Cheung, C., Conboy, K., Doyle, R., Goyal, D. P., Gustafsson, A., Jebabli, I., Kim, Y.-G., Kim, J., Koos, S., Kreps, D. et al. (2022). Metaverse beyond the hype: Multidisciplinary perspectives on emerging challenges, opportunities, and agenda for research, practice and policy. *International Journal of Information Management, 66,* 102542.

Elragal, A., & Klischewski, R. (2017). Theory-driven or process-driven prediction? Epistemological challenges of big data analytics. *Journal of Big Data, 4,* 1–20.

Feldtkeller, S., Anderson, C., Daily, K., & Stefani, E. (2016). Compliant air skates, an experiment.

Frey, C., & Osborne, M. (2017). The future of employment: How susceptible are jobs to computerization? *Technological Forecasting & Social Change, 114,* 254–280.

Gaur, L., Afaq, A., Singh, G., & Dwivedi, Y. K. (2021). Role of artificial intelligence and robotics to foster the touchless travel during a pandemic: A review and research agenda. *International Journal of Contemporary Hospitality Management.* https://doi.org/10.1108/IJCHM-11-2020-1246.

González-Rodríguez, M. R., Díaz-Fernández, M. C., & Gómez, C. P. (2020). Facial-expression recognition: An emergent approach to the measurement of tourist satisfaction through emotions. *Telematics and Informatics.* https://doi.org/10.1016/j.tele.2020.101404.

Gursoy, D., Malodia, S., & Dhir, A. (2022) The metaverse in the hospitality and tourism industry: An overview of current trends and future research directions. *Journal of Hospitality Marketing & Management, 31*(5), 527–534. https://doi.org/10.1080/19368623.2022.2072504

Hancock, P. A., Nourbakhsh, I., & Stewart, J. (2019). On the future of transportation in an era of automated and autonomous vehicles. *Proceedings of the National Academy of Sciences, 116*(16), 7684–7691.

He, Z., Deng, N., Li, X., & Gu, H. (2022). How to "read" a destination from images? Machine learning and network methods for DMOs' image projection and photo evaluation. *Journal of Travel Research, 61*(3), 597–619.

Ibili, E., Resnyansky, D., & Billinghurst, M. (2019). Applying the technology acceptance model to understand maths teachers' perceptions towards an augmented reality tutoring system. *Education and Information Technologies, 24,* 2653–2675.

International Federation of Robotics. (2018). Robots and the workplace of the future [Positioning Paper]. https://ifr.org/downloads/papers/IFR_Robots_and_the_Workplace_of_the_Future_Positioning_Paper.pdf

Ivanov, S. H., Webster, C., & Berezina, K. (2017). Adoption of robots and service automation by tourism and hospitality companies. *Revista Turismo & Desenvolvimento, 27*(28), 1501–1517.

Ivanov, S., Gretzel, U., Berezina, K., Sigala, M., & Webster, C. (2019). Progress on robotics in hospitality and tourism: A review of the literature. *Journal of Hospitality and Tourism Technology, 10*(4), 481–521.

Ivanov, S., & Webster, C. (2019a). *Robots, artificial intelligence, and service automation in travel, tourism and hospitality.* Emerald Publishing.

Ivanov, S., & Webster, C. (2019b). Robots in tourism: A research agenda for tourism economics. *Tourism Economics,* 1–21. https://doi.org/10.1177/1354816619879583

Kaartemo, V., & Helkkula, A. (2018). A systematic review of artificial intelligence and robots in value co-creation: Current status and future research avenues. *Journal of Creating Value, 4*(2), 211–228.

Kim, J. (2021). Advertising in the metaverse: Research agenda. *Journal of Interactive Advertising, 21*(3), 141–144. https://doi:10.1080/15252019.2021.2001273.

Kim, J. Y., Hlee, S., & Joun, Y. (2016). Green practices of the hotel industry: Analysis through the windows of smart tourism system. *International Journal of Information Management, 36*(6), 1340–1349.

Kim, M. J., Hall, C. M., & Kwon, O. (2023a). Space tourism: Do age and gender make a difference in risk perception? *Journal of Hospitality and Tourism Management, 57*, 13–17.

Kim, M. J., Hall, C. M., Kwon, O., Hwang, K., & Kim, J. S. (2023b). Orbital and sub-orbital space tourism: Motivation, constraint and artificial intelligence. *Tourism Review*. https://doi.org/10.1108/TR-01-2023-0017

Kim, M. J., Hall, C. M., Kwon, O., & Sohn, K. (2024). Space tourism: Value-attitude-behavior theory, artificial intelligence, and sustainability. *Journal of Retailing and Consumer Services, 77*, 103654. https://doi.org/10.1016/j.jretconser.2023.103654

Lehrer, C., Wieneke, A., Vom Brocke, J., Jung, R., & Seidel, S. (2018). How big data analytics enables service innovation: Materiality, affordance, and the individualization of service. *Journal of Management Information Systems, 35*(2), 424–460.

Liu, Y., Teichert, T., Rossi, M., Li, H., & Hu, F. (2017). Big data for big insights: Investigating language-specific drivers of hotel satisfaction with 412,784 user-generated reviews. *Tourism Management, 59*, 554–563.

Lu, L., Cai, R., & Gursoy, D. (2019). Developing and validating a service robot integration willingness scale. *International Journal of Hospitality Management, 80*, 36–51.

Ma, S. D., Kirilenko, A. P., & Stepchenkova, S. (2020). Special interest tourism is not so special after all: Big data evidence from the 2017 Great American Solar Eclipse. *Tourism Management, 77*, 104021.

McCabe, S., & Johnson, S. (2013). The happiness factor in tourism: Subjective well-being and social tourism. *Annals of Tourism Research, 41*, 42–65.

Mehran, J., Olya, H., & Han, H. (2023). Psychology of space tourism marketing, technology, and sustainable development: From a literature review to an integrative framework. *Psychology & Marketing, 40*(6), 1130–1151.

Mele, C., Russo Spena, T., Kaartemo, V., & Marzullo, M. L. (2021). Smart nudging: How cognitive technologies enable choice architectures for value co-creation. *Journal of Business Research, 129*, 949–960.

Mesa-Arango, R., Pineda-Jaramillo, J., Araujo, D. S., Bi, J., Basva, M., & Viti, F. (2023). Missions and factors determining the demand for affordable mass space tourism in the United States: A machine learning approach. *Acta Astronautica, 204*, 307–320.

Murphy, J., Gretzel, U., & Pesonen, J. (2019). Marketing robot services in hospitality and tourism: The role of anthropomorphism. *Journal of Travel & Tourism Marketing, 36*, 784–795.

Nasseef, O. A., Baabdullah, A. M., Alalwan, A. A., Lal, B., & Dwivedi, Y. K. (2021). Artificial intelligence-based public healthcare systems: G2G knowledge-based exchange to enhance the decision-making process. *Government Information Quarterly*. https://doi.org/10.1016/j.giq.2021.101618.

O'Grady, M. J., O'Hare, G. M., Chen, J., & Phelan, D. (2009). Distributed network intelligence: A prerequisite for adaptive and personalised service delivery. *Information Systems Frontiers, 11*(1), 61–73.

Osawa, H., Ema, A., Hattori, H., Akiya, N., Kanzaki, N., Kubo, A., Koyama, T., & Ichise, R. (2017, Aug 28–Sept 1). Analysis of robot hotel: Reconstruction of works with robots. In *The 26th IEEE International Symposium on Robot and Human Interactive Communication (RO-MAN)*, Lisbon, Portugal.

Ran, B., Jin, P. J., Boyce, D., Qiu, T. Z., & Cheng, Y. (2012). Perspectives on future transportation research: Impact of intelligent transportation system technologies on next-generation transportation modeling. *Journal of Intelligent Transportation Systems, 16*(4), 226–242.

Russo Spena, T., Mele, C., & Marzullo, M. (2019). Practising value innovation through artificial intelligence: The IBM Watson case. *Journal of Creating Value, 1*, 11–24.

Saayman, M., Li, G., Uysal, M., & Song, H. (2018). Tourist satisfaction and subjective well-being: An index approach. *International Journal of Tourism Research, 20*(3), 388–399.

Samala, N., Katkam, B. S., Bellamkonda, R. S., & Rodriguez, R. V. (2020). Impact of AI and robotics in the tourism sector: A critical insight. *Journal of Tourism Futures*. https://doi.org/10.1108/JTF-07-2019-0065.

Smart, J. M., Cascio, J., & Paffendorf, J (2007) Metaverse roadmap overview. *Accelerated studies foundation.* http://metaverseroadmap.org. (accessed 29 Aug 2021).

Spector, S. (2020). Delineating acceptable risk in the space tourism industry. *Tourism Recreation Research, 45*(4), 500–510.

Su, L., Huang, S., & Chen, X. (2015). Effects of service fairness and service quality on tourists' behavioral intentions and subjective well-being. *Journal of Travel & Tourism Marketing, 32*(3), 290–307.

Thales. (2020). Facial recognition top 7 trends. https://www.thalesgroup.com/en/markets/digital-identity-and-security/government/biometrics/facial-recognition (accessed 6 Aug 2020).

Troitino, C. (2018, June 21). Meet the world's first fully automated burger robot: Creator debuts the Big Mac killer. *Forbes*. https://www.forbes.com/sites/christinatroitino/2018/06/21/meet-the-worlds-first-fully-automated-burger-robot-creator-debuts-the-big-mac-killer/#7959e2926a89

Watts, R. (2019). Facial recognition as a force for good. *Biometric Technology Today, 2019*(3), 5–8.

Xu, F. Z., Zhang, Y., Zhang, T., & Wang, J. (2021). Facial recognition check-in services at hotels. *Journal of Hospitality Marketing & Management, 30*(3), 373–393.

Xue, J., Liang, X., Xie, T., & Wang, H. (2020). See now, act now: How to interact with customers to enhance social commerce engagement? *Information & Management*. https://doi.org/10.1016/j.im.2020.103324.

Yang, T., Zhao, X., Wang, X., & Lv, H. (2020). Evaluating facial recognition web services with adversarial and synthetic samples. *Neurocomputing, 406*, 378–385.

Zatori, A., Smith, M. K., & Puczko, L. (2018). Experience-involvement, memorability and authenticity: The service provider's effect on tourist experience. *Tourism Management, 67*, 111–126.

Zhang, L., Yan, Q., & Zhang, L. (2018a). A computational framework for understanding antecedents of guests' perceived trust towards hosts on Airbnb. *Decision Support Systems, 115*, 105–116.
Zhang, M., Zhang, G. Y., Gursoy, D., & Fu, X. R. (2018b). Message framing and regulatory focus effects on destination image formation. *Tourism Management, 69*, 397–407.
Zhang, D., Li, J., & Shan, Z. (2020, November). Implementation of Dlib deep learning face recognition technology. In *2020 international Conference on Robots & İntelligent System (ICRIS)* (pp. 88-91). IEEE.
Zhong, Y., Oh, S., & Moon, H. C. (2021). Service transformation under industry 4.0: Investigating acceptance of facial recognition payment through an extended technology acceptance model. *Technology in Society*. https://doi.org/10.1016/j.techsoc.2020.101515.
Zhu, M., Liu, X. Y., Tang, F., Qiu, M., Shen, R., Shu, W., & Wu, M. Y. (2016). Public vehicles for future urban transportation. *IEEE Transactions on Intelligent Transportation Systems, 17*(12), 3344–3353.

CHAPTER 11

The Future of Travel Technology: Applications and Future Directions

LAIBA ALI

Post Doctoral Researcher, IRC for Finance and Digital Economy, KFUPM Business School, King Fahd University of Petroleum and Minerals, Dhahran, Saudi Arabia.

ABSTRACT

This chapter explores the transformative impact of technological advancements on tourism, with a focus on cyborg tourism and its potential implications for tourists, particularly those with disabilities. It delves into the intersection of tourism and technology, highlighting how wearable devices, augmented reality, and technological implants are shaping the future of travel. The rise of cyborg tourism, which involves enhancing human capabilities through technology, aligns with the Fourth Industrial Revolution and the shift toward Tourism 4.0. This chapter also examines the expectations of potential cyborg tourists and explores how transhumanism and technological innovations can create more accessible tourism experiences. Additionally, this chapter addresses the societal and ethical considerations of these advancements, emphasizing the need for an inclusive approach to ensure that all tourists, regardless of their abilities, can benefit from the ongoing digital revolution. By understanding the expectations of future cyborg tourists and addressing their concerns, tourism stakeholders can design more immersive and personalized travel experiences.

Digitalization in Tourism. Hulya Akdemir Cengiz, Seza Zerman, Aysegul Acar, and Faizan Ali (Eds.)

DOI: 10.1201/9781779644770-14

11.1 INTRODUCTION

In today's world, technology is changing how we travel. From planning a trip to coming back home, technology plays an ever-expanding role. The intersection of technology and tourism has given rise to a novel phenomenon known as cyborg tourism, where ideas that once seemed like they belonged in science fiction stories and movies are now influencing every aspect of the journey (Gupta et al., 2023). This emerging trend involves the integration of technological enhancements with travelers' bodies, promising to revolutionize the way individuals experience and engage with destinations. This surge aligns with the Fourth Industrial Revolution, which integrates advanced technologies, digitalization, artificial intelligence (AI), and wearable technology, leading to the emergence of Tourism 4.0 (Pencarelli, 2020). While technological advancements hold the potential to enhance efficiency and improve experiences, they also raise questions about their societal impact and ethical considerations.

As technology advances, discussions about what the future might be like, including living longer or even achieving immortality are becoming more prevalent. The tourists who augment their capabilities and sensory experiences through wearable devices or technological implants under the realm of cyborg tourism prompt the ideas of how this type of tourism might stimulate societal values during traveling (Cohen, 2019). However, tourism researchers in their empirical studies despite these discussions have yet to explore posthumanist perspectives. These shifts call for a comprehensive examination of current practices and future implications. Notably, the increasing representation of persons with disabilities (PWDs) in the tourism industry requires significant solutions and an inclusive approach for fulfilling their diverse needs, a segment often overlooked in existing studies (Ali et al., 2023). Moreover, despite the rise of cyborg technologies, including wearable devices, augmented reality (AR) glasses, and implantable microchips, little research has been conducted on how these technologies influence tourist behavior, perceptions, and overall travel experiences for both disabled and non-disabled tourists (Ali et al., 2023). Therefore, studies adopting a future approach should shed light to understand how these current technologies can shape the experiences of tourists in general and more precisely tourists with disabilities and their health conditions.

Existing studies primarily focus on the benefits and challenges of cyborg technologies in other contexts, such as healthcare and communication

(Almahameed et al., 2021; Oliva and Borondo, 2020; Orive et al., 2020), rather than their application within the tourism domain. Consequently, there is a notable research gap in understanding the implications of cyborg enhancements on tourist interactions with destinations, attractions, and local cultures. Thus, this chapter aims to explore the future of tourism, considering technological advancements, demographic shifts, and societal aspirations. It also aims to expand our understanding of cyborg tourism beyond traditional explanations and explore new opportunities presented by cyborg technologies for tourists in general and more specifically for tourists with disabilities. In this chapter, we present various aspects of technological advancements in tourism and transhumanism. These topics include transformative tourism, transhumanism and cosmic travel, transhumanism and accessible tourism, cyborg, the expectations of potential cyborg tourists, and implantable technological implants. Together, these contributions aim to provide more meaningful and comprehensive cyborg tourist experiences.

11.2 TRANSFORMATIVE TOURISM

Digitalization has changed travel and tourism a lot. It has opened new opportunities for businesses in the tourism industry (Kumar and Shekhar, 2020). The blending of information and communication technology (ICT) with the tourism industry is crucial for its growth. Numerous studies have examined the impact of ICT on the tourism sector, highlighting its benefits (Shanker, 2008). These benefits include the rapid spread of information, shrinking geographical distances, and greater transparency. However, the advantages of ICT extend beyond these fundamental benefits and led to the idea of "smart tourism." As we move toward advancements in tourism, we wonder what smart tourism really means. Gretzel et al. (2015) and Femenia-Serra et al. (2019) defined "smart" as advances in technology, economy, and society. New advancements including big data, sensors, AI, autonomous transportation, AR, near field communication (NFC), Internet of Things (IoT), and the use of cyborg technologies have now been encompassed (Pencarelli, 2020).

Studies have discussed the significant effect of digital technologies on tourism by highlighting various trends (Gelter, 2017). Firstly, transformation in technological devices has greatly influenced the behaviors and lifestyles of people, which offer customizable experiences through increasingly powerful tablets and smartphones, the emergence of "smart" wearables, like watches, bracelets, glasses, and lenses. These wearables can blend real-life experiences with virtual alternatives and create AR environments. Besides, technological advancements have allowed the production of personalized souvenirs for tourists and made 3D printing widely accessible. Furthermore, tourists are sharing their travel experiences and documenting them on social media platforms by increasingly utilizing action cameras and 180° double lens cameras. Lastly, robotics is now being integrated into the tourism sector despite of being traditionally confined to industrial settings (Karabegovic and Husak, 2018). This includes its use in hospitality settings like hotels, where robots can perform routine tasks, such as room booking and management, and transportation, such as self-driving cars and planes.

Previous studies in the literature have suggested that transformation in many cases incidentally occurs on gaining new opinions or perspectives from other people on innovation, or culture before, during, or after a trip (Saunders et al., 2014). Advancements in internet-based innovation with both hardware and software over the past 2 years have signaled the evolution of the Internet. In early 1990s, the passive use of internet for basic communication has emerged into user generated content, e-interactive behavior, and the emergence of Youtube, Whatsapp, Facebook, and other social media platforms during 2000–2010. The emergence of this digital era has promoted consumer online reviews and booking platforms particularly for the tourism industry. In my opinion, transformative tourism occurs when tourists get frustrated from their current situation and search or experiment for something new. Thus, this leads to two main features of transformative tourism, including the deliberate intentions of tourists to transform and the lifelong impact of transformation to the behavior and thinking of tourists. In comparison with other types of tourism, both these features indicate that the services of transformative tourism attribute to transformative services which aim to influence individuals and their well-being (Ostrom et al., 2015). These transformative services specifically after the emergence of Web 3.0 can enhance AI, machine learning, enhanced connectivity, and semantic web technologies to provide a more intuitive user experience. Karabegovic and Husak (2018) have emphasized on the usage of transformative technology and mentioned that nowadays companies utilize AI technology and data mining to provide consumers with personalized services, and tourists can post reviews and engage with virtual reality (VR) experiences. Likewise, the CEO of Wildland Adventures, Kurt Kutay and the cofounder of Transformational Travel Collaborative and founding president have said that the world needs a higher consciousness which can be achieved through transformational tourism (Trimblet, 2017). If we apply the paradigm of Industry 4.0 to the tourism sector, recent innovations could profoundly affect it. For instance, the emergence of autonomous travel advisors and electronic agents enables tourists to compare prices, plan, and book travels more conveniently. These agents also serve as personalized "digital travel friends," accompanying travelers throughout their journey and handling all related matters. Designed as screen-less smartphones or wearable devices, like jewelry, watches, or goggles, these e-agents allow users to interact conversationally, providing information and connecting them to Web 4.0 (Pencarelli, 2020).

Likewise, the crucial role of technology and digitalization in aiding countries, industries, and organizations to tackle significant challenges cannot be overstated (Soluk et al., 2021). Particularly noteworthy is the shift toward digitalization, which has transformed how companies analyze market information, manage delivery processes, and engage with customers (Youssef et al., 2021; Kohtamaki et al., 2020). However, digitalization has recently taken on a broader meaning, encompassing its integration with other advanced technologies, such as intelligent digital robots (Karabegovic and Husak, 2018). However, it will not stop here, the three-dimensional technologies will see widespread applications, and brain-computer interfaces (BCI) or brain-machine interfaces (BMI), neurostimulations, underskin-chips, and technological implants will be seen to further enhance human capabilities (Ali et al., 2023). These technologies will directly connect individuals to VR, AR, and digital companions, blurring the lines between humans and technology and introducing the era of transhumanism. However, the full impact of transhumanism remains uncertain, though it is likely to lead to even greater integration between smart systems and people's everyday lives.

11.3 TRANSHUMANISM AND COSMIC TRAVEL

Social scientists have become increasingly interested in space travel and tourism in recent years (Cohen and Spector, 2019). Much of this research focuses on the near-future possibility of suborbital and orbital flights around Earth, as well as the potential for tourist flights to the Moon and Mars in the first half of this century (Benjamin, 2018). Lately, Cohen and Spector (2019) took a longer-term perspective, exploring the possibilities and forms of deep cosmic travel beyond the solar system, into the galaxy, and even further. They had discussed the complex sociological, philosophical, and ethical issues raised by potential future developments in space travel. It's important to note that we don't make a clear distinction between travel and tourism in this context. Instead, we view tourism as a "fuzzy cluster of 'discretionary mobilities'" (Cohen and Cohen, 2015). This approach is fitting for spaceflight, where advancements in tourist travel are likely to impact scientific and technical missions, and vice versa. As Cohen and Spector (2019) have mentioned that space tourism is increasingly intertwined with broader efforts to explore and colonize the cosmos.

The modern concept of space and human exploration has evolved over time, influenced by various factors (Dickens and Ormrod, 2007; Ormrod and Dickens, 2017). Initially, the focus was on manned spacecraft, but it shifted toward sending machines controlled by humans from Earth (Launius and McCurdy, 2007). Eventually, the idea of combined human and robotic (cyborg) flights emerged, supported by the transhumanist movement. This chapter is highlighting the idea of humans traveling through space in the future. In the near future, we can see that for most people the necessary changes to our bodies and the long travel times involved will make space tourism difficult. Instead, tourism in space will likely be limited to nearby parts of our solar system. We question the optimistic portrayals of space travel presented by space agencies and industries. They talk about making spaceflight accessible to everyone, but the reality of long-distance travel in space, along with advancements in modifying human bodies, makes it unlikely that space will be open to everyone. As of now, the idea of regular people traveling through the galaxy, as described by Adams in 1979, remains a fantasy (Adams, 1979).

11.4 TRANSHUMANISM AND ACCESSIBLE TOURISM

Accessible tourism is often referred to by various terms, such as inclusive tourism, barrier-free tourism, or universal tourism (Agovino et al., 2017; Biddulph and Scheyvens, 2018). These terms all share the goal of removing barriers for travelers with disabilities. Accessibility encompasses different aspects, including information availability, affordability, and physical infrastructure (Darcy and Dickson, 2009). For example, planning a trip involves various stages, such as destination choice, transportation, accommodation, and local amenities, all of which must be accessible to individuals with different needs (Cassia et al., 2021). However, ensuring accessibility throughout the entire travel journey can be challenging. For instance, are websites designed to accommodate individuals with vision or hearing impairments? Is the check-in process at hotels accessible to guests with disabilities? Are there adequate facilities for tourists with limited mobility in restaurants? If any of these services lack accessibility, it can affect the overall experience of travelers with disabilities. As a result, it can be difficult for destinations to meet the criteria of inclusive and accessible tourism.

Simultaneously, technological implants, such as cyborgs, have been proposed to restore functions for PWDs (Ali et al., 2023). These implants, once considered science fiction, are now widely available, particularly for those with mobility impairments. This advancement in technology presents new opportunities for individuals with distinct disabilities to achieve greater independence in traveling. The International Classification of Function (ICF) framework illustrates that advanced technology holds the potential to eliminate mobility disabilities, especially for individuals with spinal cord injuries (Boninger et al., 2012). Rupal et al. (2017) have highlighted the benefits of cyborg products for disabled tourists as they require minimal adjustments and facilitate travel more freely. Based on that, Ali et al. (2023) have also concluded in their study that the technological implants (cyborgs) have further emphasized the potential of technological implants, or cyborgs, to make previously inaccessible destinations accessible for disabled tourists. Consequently, it can be inferred that impaired cyborg tourists may travel independently to otherwise inaccessible destinations in the future.

11.5 CYBORG

The term "cyborg" has blurred the traditional boundaries of identity (Haraway, 1985). Scholars in literature have defined cyborgs in many ways. Some have defined a cyborg as an individual with technological implants inside his or her body (Christie and Bloustien, 2014; Oudshoorn, 2015; Schermer, 2009). Others defined cyborgs as a person who implants technological devices in the body to improve innate capabilities (Buchanan-Oliver and Cruz, 2011; Jarrett, 2013; Pelegrin-Borondo et al., 2020). Clark and Erickson (2004) projected that human beings in the more reflecting sense of human-technology symbionts would soon become cyborgs. Du Toit (2019) further suggests that in the 21st century, humans will likely make significant efforts to achieve immortality. With advancements in science, we have the ability to modify our bodies both internally and externally. This has led some to argue that society is already transitioning into a post-human era, with transhumanism gaining traction as an active movement. Moreover, technological developments enable us to alter our physical appearance, further blurring the lines between human and machine. Extending human lifespan has been a longstanding focus of scientific research, raising questions about the limits of human longevity and their ethical implications. Ultimately, the extent to which we pursue these advancements remains uncertain.

Gray (1995) in his book, "Cyborg Handbook" suggested four kinds of human-machine cyborgs that are normalizing, restoring, enhancing, and reconfiguring. Normalizing cyborgs involve the use of those technological products into the human body that are indistinguishable or not visible in the biological human body. An example can be a dispensation of lithium daily to keep the moods of an individual pleasant or a pacemaker implanted in someone's chest. The restorative cyborgs are comparatively the most visible kind of cyborg that involve the addition of synthetic elements to a human biological body to repair its functions, or one or more of their lost body parts, such as a person with prosthetic limbs, technological implants used by PWDs, or even an elderly person wearing glasses. Both normalizing and restorative kinds of cyborgs are used out of necessity. Enhancing cyborgs involves those products that make the biological human body smarter, stronger, faster, and longer lived. Such cyborgs usually have no abnormality or missing body parts. Some appropriate examples can be mind-controlled exoskeletons designed by military engineers, state-of-the-art shoes, glasses, poles, or suits worn by Olympic athletes, and human plus AI stock traders. Lastly, reconfiguring cyborgs, as the most powerful cyborgs, wish to overcome evolutionary and environmental barriers that are beyond human possibilities by reinventing humans as proto-biological creatures. They do not hold the recognized notion that humans can be enhanced, normalized, or restored. Examples can be bioengineering humans that can preserve selfhoods or can feed on an inorganic matter that is outside the limits of biological humans, as in projects of mind uploading. Both enhancing and reconfiguring cyborgs are called "by choice cyborgs" (Kath et al., 2019). By comparing cyborgs by necessity with cyborgs by choice, it can be found that cyborgs are the products and the means for both dependence and independence. However, necessity-based cyborgs are significant for the need to be normalized or restored to a specific degree of selfhood and/or autonomy.

11.6 THE EXPECTATIONS OF POTENTIAL CYBORG TOURISTS

The generation Z and millennials, born in the 1990s and onward, grew up with technology and are very comfortable using digital devices. These generations are quick to learn and adapt, and they are always connected to technology. They use smartphones and apps for almost everything they do, making them an important group for the tourism industry. In tourism industry, the focus is on providing memorable experiences. With the rise of smart devices and wearable and technological implants, these experiences are changing and improving for the generation Z, who are expected to make extensive use of these technologies when they travel (Ozdemir-Guzel and Bas, 2021). Simultaneously, the concept of cyborg tourism, wherein individuals enhance their travel experiences through technological integration with their bodies, has sparked considerable interest among researchers and practitioners. For shaping the future of this emerging trend, it is paramount to understand the expectations of potential cyborg tourists. According to Suhud et al. (2023), cyborg tourism offers tourists opportunities to augment their sensory experiences and capabilities, and represents a convergence of technology and travel. As such, investigating the expectations of potential cyborg tourists becomes crucial in designing tailored experiences that resonate with their desires and preferences.

Studies suggest that potential cyborg tourists often express a keen interest in leveraging technological enhancements to enrich their travel experiences. For instance, research by Chuah (2018) found that travelers are intrigued by the prospect of utilizing wearable devices or implants to access real-time information about their surroundings, enhance navigation, and engage in immersive cultural interactions. Moreover, the expectation of seamless integration between technology and travel is a recurring theme among potential cyborg tourists. As highlighted by Ozdemir-Guzel and Bas (2021), travelers anticipate a frictionless experience where wearable devices or implants seamlessly facilitate activities, such as language translation, currency conversion, and personalized recommendations based on individual preferences. Furthermore, the desire for personalized and adaptive technologies is evident among potential cyborg tourists. Fan et al. (2022) emphasize the importance of customizable features that cater to the unique needs and preferences of travelers, allowing for a more personalized and immersive journey experience. However, it is essential to acknowledge the concerns and apprehensions surrounding cyborg tourism among potential travelers. Privacy, security, and ethical considerations associated with the use of technological implants or wearable devices remain significant factors influencing tourists' expectations and decision-making processes (Istin et al., 2022).

11.7 IMPLANTABLE TECHNOLOGICAL IMPLANTS

According to the principles of disruptive justice, disabled people often face barriers that prevent them from fully participating in society as they should (DePauw and Gavron, 2005). Therefore, there is a call to redesign the world to make it more accessible for everyone (Van Hilvoorde and Landeweerd, 2010). This raises the question: "what barriers need to be removed to include PWDs in all aspects of life?" Likwise, for inaccessible destinations, it is impossible to make all the buildings, transportation systems, and businesses accessible for tourists with different disabilities. So, the only option left is to make tourists with disabilities accessible during traveling by making them into normal or restorative cyborgs. Thus, this led us to discuss the role of digitalization in the healthcare sector.

Medical technology within the last decades is one of the growing technology branches. Catherwood et al. (2015) defined medical implants as implants that medical practitioners prescribe to alleviate the symptoms of chronic diseases, sustain life, and/or replace missing biological body parts. The efficiency of technology facilitates new implants with an extensive application field, for instance, technological stents that can be placed precisely and deeper into the sensitive areas of the body, including small blood vessels, eyes, ears, brain, and spinal cord (Schaar and Ziefle, 2011). Other than medical stents, there are other technological devices for medical purposes, including implantable cardioverter defibrillators (ICD) and pacemakers for controlling and pacing the heart, a cochlear implant for partially restoring hearing, functional electrical stimulation helps arm and hand function for object manipulation, and prosthetic limbs make it possible for an individual with mobility impairment to walk or travel (Reinares-Lara et al., 2016; Schaar and Ziefle, 2011; Udlis, 2013). These implantable devices act as life-saving devices for disabled people. For a few years, these technological implants are used in the medical sector, and therefore are rather known to the public.

In general, medical technologies specifically implantable devices provide a variety of device types and application fields, starting from chips for storing electronic records of patients, to placing directly under the skin, up to implantable devices into the body parts. These implantable technologies, along with their medical purposes, are also used for non-medical reasons, for example, cosmetic surgeries and enhancement of innate capabilities. For instance, many people around the world mainly adults go for cosmetic surgeries to match their bodies based on socially accepted beauty standards as well as to increase their seductive capacities (Adams, 2010; Lawton, 2004). In the United States, in 2007, 11.8 million cosmetic surgeries were performed, among which, breast augmentation appeared to be the most prominent one (Chauhan et al., 2010; Siclovan and Jomah, 2008). Pelegrin-Borondo et al. (2016) and Pelegrin-Borondo et al. (2017) conducted their studies on the acceptance of technological implants to increase innate capacities. The ethical consideration toward the use of technological implants for non-medical purposes has also been investigated (Reinares-Lara et al., 2018). In addition, technological implants to compensate for visual impairment, such as brain implants and prostheses, and hearing disabilities (Pray and Jordan, 2014), such as cochlear implants, are widely accepted and their application is extensive.

Currently, wheelchairs are the most common and significant technology used for mobility and are more likely to remain in the next 10 years. The improvements in the design of wheelchairs, customization, increased ease of mobility, and low weight allow autonomous navigation. Herr (2009) has found that in the next decades, wheelchairs may be replaced by exoskeletons. The term exoskeleton describes a device, such as a brace that is external to the body. The exoskeleton systems help to augment functions but the application is not much widespread. The reasons can be mainly due to the weight and size of the systems which makes the performance difficult in the natural environment. Some of the exoskeletons, such as robotic treadmills have gained acceptance. It is expected that the new developments in exoskeletons through sensory circuitry materials, battery powers, and hydraulic actuators will make the future of exoskeletons a Second Skin Space Suit to spin off people with disabilities. Boninger et al. (2012) in their study predicted that people in 2024 will bear exoskeletons while walking down homes, streets, and malls, yet in reality we still need to see it. Likewise, rehabilitative robotics can help individuals with mobility disability through devices like robotic upper limb retraining devices and robotic treadmill ambulation devices (Hesse et al., 2003). Last but not least, direct brain interfaces and VR simulation can achieve mobility in different activities, including driving and walking (Chowdhury, 2019). The brain-computer interface implantable helps people who are paralyzed to control wheelchairs, TV, and other tools (Reinares-Lara et al., 2018). Despite the growing prevalence of these cyborg technologies, little research has been conducted on how these technologies will influence tourists with disability-related behavior, perceptions, and overall travel experiences.

11.8 CONCLUSION

This chapter explores how technology is changing the world, people, and travel. The rise of digitalization started at the beginning of the 21st century and is expected to continue for the next few years. Utilizing technology to simplify the lives of people is the key for future success. This digitalization revolution began with the invention of the Internet, which allowed online tour planning and booking. Gradually, digital technologies with the help of AI will further promote the tourism and travel industry by making sure to provide a seamless experience to the visitors during traveling. Technologies including AI, biometric immigration systems, passenger drones, AR, and cyborg technology have the highest capacity of delivering streamline operations and personalized experiences to the travelers and have made the travel experiences more exciting and sophisticated. However, despite the increasing importance of these advancements, there are emerging niches in tourism that focus on providing unique experiences. Travelers are seeking more than just digital interactions; they desire authentic experiences that connect them with others and enhance their lives through automation.

Gradually, we might find ourselves flying passenger drones over Singapore or taking trips to space to see our planet from a whole new perspective. Now, with advancements like AI, AR, autonomous taxis, passenger drones, biometric immigration systems, futuristic hotels, and cyborg tourists, our travel experiences are becoming more sophisticated and looks incredibly exciting. It also has the great potential to promote each and every aspect of the experiences of visitors. Challenges including security, data privacy, and AI algorithms-based biasness needs to be addressed by technology. Travel-based companies can navigate these challenges by improving and adopting this technology to ensure visitors' smooth operations, and seamless and better travel experiences while making a memorable and enjoyable trip for the tourists.

The influence of digital media and networking offers new opportunities for traveling and connection, but it also brings greater responsibility in managing data and information. Digitization presents both enormous potential and challenges for the tourism industry. Booking platforms allow tourists to quickly and easily gather information about destinations and accommodations. Companies must stay vigilant in monitoring market trends and offering products and services that meet the needs of their clients. However, it is not just about making travel easier for us; it is also about protecting the culture and environment of the places we visit. We are working toward safer, healthier, and more sustainable travel options, while also making sure everyone's privacy and rights are respected in our connected world.

The increasing advancements in the innovative technologies have achieved radical changes across different fields including the human body. Since many years, scientists are trying to extend the abilities of the human body. After extensive experiments, the notion of cybernetic organism or in other words cyborg came into picture. Cyborgs with half human body organs and half machine is not a science fiction anymore. Robotic progression, including nanotechnology, genetic engineering, molecular biology, medicine, and AI are still in the phase of testing, and is gradually becoming a part and parcel of everyday experiences. The idea of cyborg is forcing the future to be more evolving upon us as the innovations are creating and changing at more prominent pace than before. This chapter presents a comprehensive discussion and overview of technological advancements and human transformation to cyborgs, which ultimately leads to cyborg tourists. It gives the idea of cyborg tourists whether as a science fiction or the nearest future.

The emergence of the Fourth Industrial Revolution, advancements in technological devices, and the evolution of the Internet are significantly reshaping tourism. This transformation characterizes the current era as "Tourism 4.0," where the digital revolution is fundamentally altering the behaviors of tourists, including tourists with disabilities, businesses, and tourist destinations, propelling them toward a smart perspective. Therefore, understanding the expectations of potential cyborg tourists is crucial for shaping the future tourism landscape. By addressing their desires for enhanced experiences, seamless integration of technology, and personalized solutions while also addressing concerns, tourism stakeholders can tackle the potential of cyborg tourism to offer innovative and engaging travel experiences. The expectations of potential cyborg tourists play a pivotal role in shaping the path of this rapidly growing field. Understanding these expectations is essential for tourism stakeholders to design effective experiences that strongly match with travelers' desires and preferences. Consequently, there is a need for a comprehensive exploration of the expectations of potential cyborg tourists, providing insights into their motivations, preferences, and concerns regarding the integration of technology into their travel experiences.

Moreover, the integration of technology and tourism offers great opportunities. However, it is significant to ensure that tourists, despite of their abilities, can enjoy tourism equally. Exploring technological advancements in tourism is exciting because it means that technology can be used to make travel better for everyone. This shift is about making sure that technological advancements benefit tourists with disabilities. Cyborg tourism, which sits at the crossroads of technology and travel, offers an exciting chance to dig into how humans interact with technology in the tourism sector. While we have seen a lot of focus on technology in tourism, like online booking sites, VR tours, and even metaverse, we have not really looked closely at how cyborg technologies affect tourists with disability experiences. Thus, this chapter is also a call for a thoughtful and inclusive approach toward the usage of cyborg technology in tourism. We want to ensure that the well-being and needs of all individuals, especially those who might face challenges, are prioritized.

KEYWORDS

- **accessibility**
- **cyborg tourism**
- **digitalization**
- **Tourism 4.0**
- **technological implants**
- **transhumanism**
- **wearable technology**

REFERENCES

Adams, D. (1979). *The hitchhiker's guide to the Galaxy*. Pan Books.

Adams, J. (2010). Motivational narratives and assessments of the body after cosmetic surgery. *Qualitative Health Research, 20*(6), 755–767.

Agovino, M., Casaccia, M., Garofalo, A., & Marchesano, K. (2017). Tourism and disability in Italy. Limits and opportunities. *Tourism Management Perspectives, 23*, 58–67.

Ali, L., Kilic, H., & Öztüren, A. (2023). From disabled tourists to impaired cyborg tourists: What would it take to transform? *Universal Access in the Information Society,* 1–18.

Almahameed, A., Oliva, M. A., & Borondo, J. P. (2021). Cyborg acceptance in healthcare services: The use of cyborg as a surgeon. In *Moving technology ethics at the forefront of society, organisations and governments* (pp. 127–144). Universidad de La Rioja.

Benjamin, S. (2018). Exploration to exploitation: An industry analysis of suborbital space tourism. *New Space, 6*(1), 87–98.

Biddulph, R., & Scheyvens, R. (2018). From ethical consumption to transformative tourism: Creating the change we seek. *Journal of Sustainable Tourism, 26*(7), 1055–1070.

Boninger, M. L., Cooper, R. A., Fitzgerald, S. G., Lin, J., & Cooper, R. (2012). Advancing measurement and analysis of mobility technology outcomes: A state- of-the-science workshop report. American *Journal of Physical Medicine & Rehabilitation, 91*(9), S191–S204.

Buchanan-Oliver, M., & Cruz, A. (2011). Discourses of technology consumption: Ambivalence, fear, and liminality. *Advances in Consumer Research, 39*(5), 287–291.

Cassia, F., Castellani, P., Rossato, C., & Baccarani, C. (2021). Finding a way towards high-quality, accessible tourism: the role of digital ecosystems. *TQM Journal, 33*(1), 205–221.

Catherwood, P. A., Finlay, D. D., & McLaughlin, J. A. D. (2015, Nov). Subcutaneous body area networks: A SWOT analysis. In *2015 IEEE International Symposium on Technology and Society (ISTAS)* (pp. 1–8). IEEE.

Chauhan, N., Warner, J., & Adamson, P. A. (2010). Adolescent rhinoplasty: Challenges and psychosocial and clinical outcomes. *Aesthetic Plastic Surgery, 34*, 510–516.

Chowdhury, T. I. (2019). Virtual reality disability simulation: A tool to reduce implicit bias towards persons with disabilities and a motivation to create a virtual ability simulation (Doctoral dissertation, The University of Texas at San Antonio).

Christie, E., & Bloustien, G. (2014). I-cyborg: Disability, affect and public pedagogy. In *Disability matters* (pp. 80–95). Routledge.

Chuah, S. H. W. (2018, Dec 13). Why and who will adopt extended reality technology? Literature review, synthesis, and future research agenda. Literature Review, Synthesis, and Future Research Agenda.

Clark, A., & Erickson, M. (2004). Natural-born cyborgs: Minds, technologies, and the future of human intelligence. *Canadian Journal of Sociology, 29*(3), 471.

Cohen, E. (2019). Posthumanism and tourism. *Tourism Review, 74*(3), 416–427.

Cohen, E., & Cohen, S. A. (2015). A mobilities approach to tourism for emerging world regions. *Current Issues in Tourism, 18*(1), 11–43.

Cohen, E., & Spector, S. (Eds.). (2019). *Space tourism: The elusive dream*. Elsevier.

Darcy, S. & Dickson, T. J. (2009). A whole-of-life approach to tourism: The case for accessible tourism experiences. *Journal of Hospitality and Tourism Management, 16*, 32–44.

DePauw, K. P., & Gavron, S. J. (2005). *Disability sport*. Human Kinetics.

Dickens, P., & Ormrod, J. S. (2007). *Cosmic society: Towards a sociology of the universe*. Routledge.

Du Toit, C. W. (2019). Artificial intelligence and the question of being. *HTS: Theological Studies, 75*(1), 1–10.

Fan, X., Jiang, X., & Deng, N. (2022). Immersive technology: A meta-analysis of augmented/virtual reality applications and their impact on tourism experience. *Tourism Management, 91*, 104534.

Femenia-Serra, F., Neuhofer, B., & Ivars-Baidal, J. A. (2019). Towards a conceptualisation of smart tourists and their role within the smart destination scenario. *The Service Industries Journal*, *39*(2), 109–133.

Gelter, H. (2017). Digital tourism. *An analysis of digital trends in tourism and customer digital mobile behaviour,* Interreg Nord.

Gray, C. H. (1995). *The cyborg handbook*. Ed. with the assistance of Heidi J. Figueroa-Sarriera and Steven Mentor, 1996, *45*(B43), 103–110.

Gretzel, U., Sigala, M., Xiang, Z., & Koo, C. (2015). Smart tourism: Foundations and developments. *Electronic Markets, 25*, 179–188.

Gupta, S., Modgil, S., Lee, C. K., & Sivarajah, U. (2023). The future is yesterday: Use of AI-driven facial recognition to enhance value in the travel and tourism industry. *Information Systems Frontiers, 25*(3), 1179–1195.

Haraway, D. (1985). A manifesto for cyborgs, 65–107.

Herr, H. (2009). Exoskeletons and orthoses: Classification, design challenges and future directions. *Journal of NeuroEngineering and Rehabilitation, 6*, 21.

Hesse, S., Schulte-Tigges, G., Konrad, M., Bardeleben, A., & Werner, C. (2003). Robot-assisted arm trainer for the passive and active practice of bilateral forearm and wrist movements in hemiparetic subjects. *Archives of Physical Medicine and Rehabilitation, 84*(6), 915–920.

İştin, A. E., Eryılmaz, G., & Üzülmez, M. (2022). Technology applications in the Asian tourism industry in future. In *Technology application in tourism in Asia: Innovations, theories and practices* (pp. 441–469). Springer Nature Singapore.

Jarrett, H. (2013). *Environmental quality in a growing economy: Essays from the sixth RFF forum*. RFF Press.

Karabegović, I., & Husak, E. (2018). Industry 4.0 based on industrial and service robots with application in China. *Journal Mobility and Vehicle, 44*(4), 59–71.

Kath, E., Guimarães, O. C., & Buzato, M. E. K. (2019). Posthumanism and assistive technologies: On the social inclusion/exclusion of low-tech cyborgs. *Trabalhos em linguística aplicada, 58*, 679–703.

Kohtamäki, M., Parida, V., Patel, P. C., & Gebauer, H. (2020). The relationship between digitalization and servitization: The role of servitization in capturing the financial potential of digitalization. *Technological Forecasting and Social Change*, *151*, 119804.

Kumar, S., & Shekhar. (2020). Digitalization: A strategic approach for development of tourism industry in India. *Paradigm, 24*(1), 93–108.

Launius, R. D., & McCurdy, H. E. (2007). Robots and humans in space flight: Technology, evolution, and interplanetary travel. *Technology in Society, 29*(3), 271–282.

Lawton, L. (2004). The joy of thinking: the beauty and power of classical mathematical ıdeas. *Library Journal, 129*(18), 127–128.

Oliva, M. A., & Borondo, J. P. (2020). Cyborg as a surgeon: A theoretical framework for cyborg acceptance in healthcare service. In *Societal challenges in the smart society* (pp. 57–70). Universidad de La Rioja.

Orive, G., Taebnia, N., & Dolatshahi-Pirouz, A. (2020). A new era for cyborg science is emerging: The promise of cyborganic beings. *Advanced Healthcare Materials, 9*(1), 1901023.

Ormrod, J. S., & Dickens, P. (2017). *The Palgrave handbook of society, culture and outer space*. Springer.

Ostrom, A., Parasuraman, A., Bowne, D., Patricio, L. & Voss, C. (2015). Service research priorities in a rapidly changing context. *Journal of Service Research, 18*(2), 127–159.

Oudshoorn, N. (2015). Sustaining cyborgs: Sensing and tuning agencies of pacemakers and implantable cardioverter defibrillators. *Social Studies of Science, 45*(1), 56–76.

Ozdemir-Guzel, S., & Bas, Y. N. (2021). Gen Z tourists and smart devices. In *Generation Z marketing and management in tourism and hospitality: The future of the industry* (pp. 141–165). Springer International Publishing.

Pelegrín-Borondo, J., Arias-Oliva, M., Murata, K., & Souto-Romero, M. (2020). Does ethical judgment determine the decision to become a cyborg? Influence of ethical judgment on the cyborg market. *Journal of Business Ethics, 161*(1), 5–17.

Pelegrin-Borondo, J., Reinares-Lara, E., & Olarte-Pascual, C. (2017). Assessing the acceptance of technological implants (the cyborg): Evidences and challenges. *Computers in Human Behavior, 70*, 104–112.

Pelegrín-Borondo, J., Reinares-Lara, E., Olarte-Pascual, C., & Garcia-Sierra, M. (2016). Assessing the moderating effect of the end user in consumer behavior: The acceptance of technological implants to increase innate human capacities. *Frontiers in Psychology, 7*, 182818.

Pencarelli, T. (2020). The digital revolution in the travel and tourism industry. *Information Technology & Tourism, 22*(3), 455–476.

Pray, J. L., & Jordan, I. K. (2014). The deaf community and culture at a crossroads: Issues and challenges. *Controversies and Disputes in Disability and Rehabilitation,* 100–125.

Reinares-Lara, E., Olarte-Pascual, C., & Pelegrín-Borondo, J. (2018). Do you want to be a cyborg? The moderating effect of ethics on neural implant acceptance. *Computers in Human Behavior, 85*, 43–53.

Reinares-Lara, E., Olarte-Pascual, C., Pelegrín-Borondo, J., & Pino, G. (2016). Nanoimplants that enhance human capabilities: A cognitive-affective approach to assess individuals' acceptance of this controversial technology. *Psychology & Marketing, 33*(9), 704–712.

Rupal, B. S., Rafique, S., Singla, A., Singla, E., Isaksson, M., & Virk, G. S. (2017). Lower-limb exoskeletons: Research trends and regulatory guidelines in medical and non-medical applications. *International Journal of Advanced Robotic Systems, 14*(6), 1729881417743554.

Saunders, R. E., Laing, J. H. & Weiler, B. (2014). Personal transformation through long-distance walking. In S. Felip & P. L. Pearce (Eds.), *Tourist experience and fulfilment: Insights from positive psychology* (pp. 127–146). Routledge.

Schaar, A. K., & Ziefle, M. (2011, May). Smart clothing: Perceived benefits vs. perceived fears. In *2011 5th International Conference on Pervasive Computing Technologies for Healthcare (PervasiveHealth) and Workshops* (pp. 601–608). IEEE.

Schermer, M. (2009). The mind and the machine: On the conceptual and moral implications of brain-machine interaction. *Nanoethics, 3*, 217–230.

Shanker, D. (2008). ICT and Tourism: Challenges and opportunities.

Siclovan, H. R., & Jomah, J. A. (2008). Advantages and outcomes in subfascial breast augmentation: a two-year review of experience. *Aesthetic plastic surgery, 32*(3), 426–431.

Soluk, J., Kammerlander, N., & Darwin, S. (2021). Digital entrepreneurship in developing countries: The role of institutional voids. *Technological Forecasting and Social Change, 170*, 120876.

Suhud, U., Allan, M., Prihandono, D., & Monoarfa, T. (2023). We are cyborgs: The role of narcissism and self-esteem to become social media and tourism addicts. *International Journal of Data and Network Science, 7*(1), 73–82.

Trimblet, M. (2017). Why "Transformative travel" will be the travel trend of 2017, Vogue, January 3. Retrieved 7 Jan 2020, from https://www.vogue.com/article/transformative-travel-trend-2017.

Udlis, K. A. (2013). The impact of technology dependency on device acceptance and quality of life in persons with implantable cardioverter defibrillators. *Journal of Cardiovascular Nursing, 28*(6), E65–E73.

Van Hilvoorde, I., & Landeweerd, L. (2010). Enhancing disabilities: Transhumanism under the veil of inclusion? *Disability and Rehabilitation, 32*(26), 2222–2227.

Youssef, A. B., Boubaker, S., Dedaj, B., & Carabregu-Vokshi, M. (2021). Digitalization of the economy and entrepreneurship intention. *Technological Forecasting and Social Change, 164*, 120043.

PART IV

New Business Models, Strategic Management, and Crisis Management in the Digital Age

CHAPTER 12

The Network Hospitality and Tourism

SONIA LIM ERN YI[1*] and GERALDINE ANNE TAN WERN-YI[2]

[1]*Independent Researcher*

[2]*School of Hospitality, Tourism & Culinary Arts, University of Wollongong (UOW), Shah Alam, Selangor, Malaysia*

*Corresponding author

ABSTRACT

The network hospitality (NH) fueled and facilitated by digitalization has quickly gained popularity in this modern society. A shift in tourist behavior is apparent in this era of always being "on the move" and the pursuit of exploring off-the-beaten paths in tourism practices. The global phenomenon of NH promotes collaborative or peer-to-peer consumption. It enables society to explore new experiences or to pivot from conventional practices. There are multiple definitions of this evolution. However, based on the traditions of hospitality, NH can be defined as online social networking and the exchange of accommodation fueled by technology. Dubbed a "cosmopolitan utopia," NH is driven by digital social interactions. Consequently, digitalization in tourism benefits consumers and service providers by enhancing the overall user experience through convenience and the ability to provide big data. This chapter conceptually explores NH's evolution, definitions, and types. Additionally, the impacts of digitalizing tourism through the NH lens are examined to illustrate how travel and tourism businesses may optimize their functionalities.

Digitalization in Tourism. Hulya Akdemir Cengiz, Seza Zerman, Aysegul Acar, and Faizan Ali (Eds.)

DOI: 10.1201/9781779644770-16

12.1 INTRODUCTION

The travel trend has shifted as society has advanced. Society today is well-informed and has an enormous amount of information. People will travel more than ever before because of the setback of the COVID-19 pandemic; "revenge travel" is on the rise. They want more than the traditional mass tourism product. Today it is common to see travelers from developed and developing countries participating in different types of tourism to gain satisfaction and pleasant experiences compared to the previous generations (Tiah, 2019). The more technology advances, the more alternative ways to travel emerge. Tourists today are searching for authenticity and unique themes with personalized service and the opportunity to be socially responsible (Gamil, 2022).

With all the demands of tourists, businesses are encouraged to design different and new types of tourism that enhance the travel experience. Tourists' demand, rise of business and entrepreneurship opportunities, and the advancement of technology encouraged network hospitality (NH) to be introduced to society. The advancement of technology enables the relationship between the host and the guest to be the focus, and it also allows various forms of sociality to be developed through tourism and service exchanges (Marques and Matos, 2020). This is known as the network society (Castells, 2000). Wittel (2001) uses the term "network sociality" to explain these social changes linked to the advancement of technologies. Based on this concept, Molz (2011) develops it within the hospitality industry and suggests the concept of "NH."

12.2 DEFINITIONS OF NETWORK HOSPITALITY

The term "NH" is defined as online social networking and the exchange of accommodation through hospitality-exchange services (Ikkala and Lampinen, 2015). NH is based on the traditions of hospitality, featuring the relationship of host and guest. Accommodation sharing is a major part of NH, but it could also be based on sharing meals, rides, and travel, where locals show the travelers around their town (Molz, 2014). NH represents the accommodation sector of the overall "sharing economy." PricewaterhouseCoopers (2015) identified seven major industries of the sharing economy: accommodation, transportation, finance, retail and consumer goods, services, media and entertainment, and machinery. The sharing economy is based on the idea of "access to" instead of "ownership of" possessions (Botsman and Rogers, 2010).

Botsman (2013) defines the sharing economy as "an economic model based on sharing underutilized assets from spaces to skills to stuff for monetary or non-monetary benefits." In 2015, the term "sharing economy" was listed in the Oxford English Dictionary and it is defined as "an economic system in which assets or services are shared between private individuals, either free or for a fee, typically by means of the Internet." The sharing economy is not necessarily only limited to the accommodation sector as NH does; it can be extended to catering, transportation, and activities. In 2010, Rachel Botsman published "What's Mine is Yours, the Rise of Collaborative Economy," which captured the gist of the "sharing economy" today and presented it as a travel trend fueled by technology. The term "sharing economy" is the most recognized term to describe the sharing concept in all industries (Botsman, 2019; Chua et al., 2019) because it is popularized by the public sector, especially businesses and companies (Gorog, 2018). To reach a bigger market, companies promote themselves as having a "sharing economy business model" (Fallon-O'Leary, 2023; Gorog, 2018). During this process, the term emerged as a new buzzword and became so popular that eventually most businesses, companies, and entrepreneurs brand themselves as a sharing economy business (Gorog, 2018).

Initially, Botsman and Rogers (2010) coined the term "collaborative consumption," but the term has since developed into various terms, such as access-based consumption (Bardhi and Eckhardt, 2012), "peer-to-peer exchange" (Bellotti et al., 2015), connected consumption (Schor and Fitzmaurice, 2015), hybrid economy (Rifkin, 2015), including sharing economy. The term "peer-to-peer exchange" arises from the open-source software movement, and it explains the open connection within the communities of collaborating individuals (Benkler, 2006). It is then further replaced with the term "peer economy" which refers to a multi-range of peer services for both profit and non-profits that is aided by technology and the economic usage of assets (Bellotti et al., 2015). Similarly, collaborative consumption is described as a mechanism that balances the needs of an individual with the needs of the community (Botsman and Rogers, 2010). It is also based on the traditional concept of sharing, lending, gifting, bartering, trading, and swapping, but these exchanges are redefined through technology (Botsman, 2013).

John (2013) suggests that there are three ways that collaborative consumption is built as a technological phenomenon. Technology performs as an "enabler" and as a "driver," while "terminology" and "metaphors" from the technological world also support collaborative consumption by writing. Molz (2011) adopts a similar definition and uses the term "NH" to describe this phenomenon but within the boundaries of hospitality. While many debatable arguments exist about the right terminologies to explain this phenomenon, the concept remains the same. Sharing is the key concept that connects technology and collaborative consumption (John, 2013). While the settings are both online and offline, sharing here refers to an interpersonal relationship that is based on trust, equality, considerateness, mutuality, and other comparable values (John, 2013). In other ways, sharing also implies a type of emotional communication that refers to the intimacy between people (Carbaugh, 1988) and the belief that it is good to talk (Illouz, 2008).

12.3 THE EVOLUTION OF NETWORK HOSPITALITY

NH exchange has existed since after the Second World War (Molz, 2014). In 1949, Bob Luitweiler founded Servas International as a non-profit NH platform. It encourages tolerance and promotes world peace through cultural exchange. Members of Servas International call themselves "peacebuilders." The organization heavily emphasizes peace and social justice. The network works as a system to reach out to people with similar goals and those who will offer free hospitality to like-minded people. Previously, members of Servas International used letters, postcards, and telephones to communicate with each other. In the 1990s, when the Internet took over, printed lists were no longer used and some of the hospitality exchange organizations emerged online (Ikkala and Lampinen, 2015). These hospitality exchange organizations are known as NH platforms.

The concept of NH in today's modern society is based on Wittel's (2001) concept of network sociality. The term "network sociality" was coined based on Castells's (2000) concept of the network society. Network sociality refers to the multiple networks formed in societal terms and explains the construction of social relationships. Network sociality has five characteristics:

1. Individualization—the merging and demerging of individuals in a community;
2. Short-lived and intense connections—social connections are categorized by their duration of interactions and intensity;
3. From narration to information—a shift in forming one firm narrative to searching for bits of information can be seen;
4. Blurred boundaries—boundaries between work and leisure are blurred;
5. Technology—the blending of various types of daily used technology including face-to-face touch.

Social interactions from the days when Servas International existed have developed in many ways. The intricacies of interactions and relationships between individuals have increased with various networks and types of communications intersecting with space and time (Marques and Matos, 2020). These changes are then explained within the hospitality context, and the term NH was created (Molz, 2011). All the NH practices maximize online platforms to assist social interactions in person and encourage users to exchange their materials and sociable resources (Molz, 2014). In brief, the advanced networked technology today has created a new mixed space of social interaction, comprising "complex interplay of mobility and immobility, online and offline interaction, brief but intense encounters, and local articulations of a global project" (Molz, 2014: p. 216-217).

Society is heading to a very mobile era; strangers meet and interact more than ever. These meetings can be by chance encounters, such as at public places or by using new online technologies to arrange pre-planned meetings with strangers (Bialski, 2011). Online technologies can be social networks, websites, and devices. This allows people to be always "on the move" (Pellegrino, 2011, p. 6). Bialski (2011) suggests the term "technologies of hospitality" which refers to the tools that enable planned encounters between strangers. These tools can create new norms of meeting and new relationships that sometimes cannot define the borderline between friend, acquaintance, stranger, and enemy.

One trend of evolution of the rental-like model suggested by Cesarani and Nechita (2017) is the advancement of technology that complements the business model of NH to expand rapidly to more markets, making it flexible and convenient. It is undeniable that technology has become a part of modern society's daily lives. Technology fuels the growth of NH. NH platforms are available on mobile phones, and users can download the application and use the platform wherever and whenever they want. This convenience of NH technology has shaped the behavior of modern society (Quinones and Augustine, 2015) where Molz (2014) describes it as "mobile sociality" in NH.

The smartphone adoption, in this case with the support of digital payment, also built a fertile ecosystem for new businesses to form and grow. Digital payment is not new in numerous industries, but traditionally, transaction occurs between consumers and firms. Now, transactions and interactions between individuals are based on experiences and observations (Botsman, 2016). Another key point is the shift of accessibility to a peer-to-peer-based business model (Cesarani and Nechita, 2017). NH allows companies to utilize the marketplace to connect individuals who own certain assets and skills with individuals who need these assets and skills temporarily (Goudin, 2016). Moreover, the peer-to-peer NH model is suggested to revolutionize the way digital payment is used (Cesarani and Nechita, 2017).

NH enables the digital transfer of funds between two individuals across the platform after the completion of a service or exchange of goods. This component is critical because it provides a faster and safer environment for users to transfer funds among themselves (Olson and Kemp, 2015). By using digital payment, the physical presence of cash and credit cards is no longer prevalent. Hence, the risk of robbery and fraud is minimized (Olson and Kemp, 2015). In short, technology and the sharing economy have made it more convenient and reliable for users. The accessibility of NH is what attracts modern society to it.

12.4 THE NETWORK HOSPITALITY EXPERIENCE

The NH experience is like a homestay. Homestay means staying in someone else's home. Homestays are commercial homes offered by local people to let tourists or visitors stay at their places to learn more about the host's culture (Lynch et al., 2009) and to interact with the local host community (Ministry of Tourism, Government of India, 2022). The objectives of the homestay are to produce income for the community and to support the government's agenda to lower the poverty rate by increasing job opportunities (Zamzuki et al., 2023; Ministry of Tourism, Government of India, 2022).

The characteristics of homestay and NH are similar, but the objectives are different. The scale of NH's community is more global than the scale of homestay, which mainly involves a certain ethnic or a local group of people. In Malaysia, the homestay program has been proven to offer different accommodation choices to tourists searching for a different type of holiday experience than traditional tourism packages (Zamzuki et al., 2023). Also, the Ministry of Tourism, Government of India (2023) has launched the National Strategy to promote rural homestays in India. It aims to develop tourism in rural areas in India, fostering entrepreneurship and job creation. Furthermore, a competition for the best rural homestay is held to further boost the growth of rural homestays. The Government of India recognized homestays as an alternative accommodation for developing tourism and prioritized this initiative as a driver in their economy. In the same fashion, NH also provides alternative accommodation options for its users.

However, in this modern world, the concept of homestay might be irrelevant and outdated. It is important to highlight that it is about the technicality, promotion, and process aspects of homestay rather than its aim or purpose. Perhaps it is how homestay has been promoted, where it is often through the traditional way of tourism and hospitality. To acquire information about homestay, tourists must search either on the Internet or go through a channel, such as a travel agency to communicate with the homestay host. Minimal computerization and low connectivity are some challenges that homestay owners face (Ministry of Tourism, Government of India, 2022). The community in NH is more independent than the community in a homestay because it is built upon individuals and strangers who can be connected easily via technology through dedicated NH platforms.

The community of NH is a globalized community. Molz (2007) refers to Couchsurfing as a cosmopolitan utopia, where interactions between hosts and guests promote an exchange of culture and mutual learning (Chen, 2017). It can be more relevant and attractive to the advanced society today, as it is fueled by technology. It can also be considered a traditional concept that has been revitalized by technology. NH is a product of globalization, and it offers a global experience where the concentration or scope of homestay is relatively small. In this globalized world, it is borderless for most that wish and seek a new tourism experience. The Government of India recognized the challenges that homestays faced. One key point in implementing the National Strategy is to utilize digital platforms to reach a global audience (Ministry of Tourism, Government of India, 2022).

The homestay experience requires a host or host family that welcomes their guests and shares spaces with them. In return, guests are immersed in the local culture and traditions (Zamzuki et al., 2023). Like the homestay experience, there is a host and guest in NH. A guest is a user who seeks accommodation, and a host is a user who has space to offer to the guest. On NH platforms like Couchsurfing, usually a non-profit organization, there are options available for users to just meet up without the need to host. On NH platforms, if a user wants to be a host, there are different guidelines to follow. A host needs to sign up as a host and follow all the procedures. Hosts usually need to pay hosting fees depending on which service fee options they choose, and tax, depending on which cities they live in.

NH platforms rely on reputation systems to create trust among strangers. This reputation mechanism works by collecting feedback (reviews, ratings, and references), and displays the average feedback ratings made by prior members who have exchanged on the platform (Cheng et al., 2021). For example, on Airbnb, after a guest has experienced a stay in the host's place, the guest will review the stay based on six factors (cleanliness, check-in, communication, accuracy, location, and value). It works the same for the guests, except the review is general, subjective, and not necessarily based on the six factors. Another example is Couchsurfing, where the concept works the same but includes a personal reference. A personal reference is a testimony from friends or family, and it is not based on post-stay experience.

Since experiences are different for every person in NH, it solely depends on the host and the guests themselves to develop the experiences. However, most of the time, the guest will get to know the local culture better because the guest will be introduced to the local way of doing things during the stay. It challenges the traditional method of tourism because it is a mobility phenomenon that is built and maintained across borders (Steylaerts and Dubhghaill, 2011). It brings people with diverse cultural backgrounds closer to each other, and it provides the perception of a more authentic tourism experience.

12.5 TYPES OF NETWORK HOSPITALITY PLATFORMS

A person could be from China wishing to travel to Alaska but with a limited budget. This person could communicate online with any available hosts in Alaska and then be hosted in Alaska for free or for a certain amount of money. With these NH platforms, it does not matter where a person is from. If they are connected to the Internet and engage with the NH community, it is a step to get to know the world. There are three types of NH platforms: rental, free, and reciprocal:

Rental

1. Managed by individual host: Airbnb, Vrbo, 9flats, Homestay, Booking.com, Agoda Homes, Tripadvisor Vacation Rentals, HolidayLettings, Flipkey, Niumba, Plum Guide, TravelStaytion, Only-Apartments, Landfolk, Novasol, Human-Hotel, Kid & Coe, Xiaozhu, and Atraveo
2. Managed by an organization: Homes & Villas by Marriott Bonvoy, Blueground, Sonder, Getaway, Vacasa, Tujia, Casamundo, Onefinestay, and Interhome

Free

Couchsurfing, TrustRoots, Servas International, Hospitality Club, BeWelcome, Couchers.org, Warm Showers, Hostwriter, Host A Sister, LGHEI, and Welcome to My Garden

Reciprocal

1. Home exchange: HomeExchange, Home Link, Love Home Swap, Intervac Home Exchange, Green Theme Home Exchange, Guardian Home Exchange, and My Twin Place
2. Home sitting: House Sitting, Nomador TrustedHouseSitters, House Carers, House Sit Match, and MindMyHouse
3. Stay in exchange for a service: Staydu, Worldpackers, Working Traveller, TeachSurfing, WWOOF, HelpX, Workaway, and HippoHelp

There are two types of rental NH platforms: managed by individual hosts or by an organization. Rental platforms for individual hosts are marketplaces that match individuals who want to rent out space with individuals who are seeking a place to stay. It is a peer-to-peer exchange governed by the platform, adopting a consumer-to-consumer model. Individual hosts can decide how much they would like to charge for their accommodation and the area offered. In return, the platforms would charge a commission from the income earned by the host. Rental platforms managed by organizations are marketplaces that match individuals who want to rent out their space through short/long-term leasing with tourists. It is a business-to-consumer model. Individual hosts do not host in this case, and the organization will manage their properties ranging from hosting, pricing, and guest handling. In return, individual hosts will receive a fixed monthly income. In most cases, property management agencies are involved, and a local property manager is employed to manage the spaces. The traditional housing leasing/rental models are blurred in this case, but these platforms are marketed toward travelers and tourists, focusing on short-term stays.

Airbnb is the most established and popular NH platform (Laker, 2023). With the growth of NH, Airbnb and other similar platforms have become a major development in the tourism industry that expands boundaries, crosses borders, and encourages intercultural relationships with like-minded people. In 2008, Brian Chesky, Joe Gebbia, and Nate Blecharczyk founded Airbnb. Chesky and Gebbia, both unemployed, struggled to pay their rent and were searching for ways to make additional money. A conference was held in the city, and it attracted numerous visitors. They started noticing that all the hotel rooms were fully booked because of this. It gave them the idea to rent out their home to accommodate the visitors. They bought a few airbeds and established a site called “Air Bed and Breakfast.”

This small idea inspired them to start an organization called Airbnb. As of December 2023, Airbnb has over 7.7 million active listings in over 100,000 cities in 220 countries and regions (Airbnb, 2024). Airbnb’s goals are to build a world where everyone fits in and to provide a travel experience that is local, inclusive, diverse, sustainable, and genuine. Airbnb has further launched Airbnb Luxe and Airbnb Experiences. Airbnb Luxe features high-end homes with a travel specialist who helps book any services on the trip, such as childcare, car rental, butler, chef, spa, and equipment rental. Airbnb Experiences are local activities offered by the locals. Each experience offered is unique to the area where locals share it with the guests. In brief, the concept is like activities offered on a tour.

In recent years, large corporations like Agoda have started extending their business models from business-to-consumer to consumer-to-consumer. Agoda is an online travel agency that offers lodging (primarily hotels), flights, ground transportation, and activities. The launch of Agoda

Homes enables individuals to list their homes on Agoda; although it might not be as personalized as Airbnb, the functionality is the same. Similarly, Tripadvisor has been offering "Vacation Rentals," which works the same way. Tripadvisor is an online travel platform that provides travel guidance based on a large amount of reviews and rating data. Flipkey, Holiday-Lettings, and Niumba are owned by Tripadvisor. These three platforms are more focused on homestays, although the listings are shared among Tripadvisor platforms.

In 2021, Landfolk was founded by seven former colleagues from Airbnb (Landfolk, 2024). The functionality of the platform is the same as Airbnb, with a focus on summer holiday homes. While all these NH platforms are online marketplaces to match individuals for accommodation, other NH platforms offer accommodation for a different purpose. Human-Hotel is a NH platform that connects traveling creatives, artists, change-makers, and activists to share their homes. Kid & Coe is a NH platform that connects families with children with child-friendly homeowners. All the listings on this platform are equipped with family-friendly amenities, such as cribs, toys, and highchairs for children.

The other type of NH platform is free. Arguably, Couchsurfing is the most established for this type of NH platform, having been under the spotlight pre-pandemic (Iyer, 2020). Couchsurfing is a social network and online-based hospitality exchange platform where anyone can join as a member and enjoy free accommodation or host other members from all around the world if they are connected to the Internet. Besides the accommodation exchange, it is also an online community. Members can meet and/or interact with other members. Members can set up meetings, seek and/or provide travel advice and organize events and gatherings. In 2004, Couchsurfing was founded by Casey Fenton, Daniel Hoffer, Sebastian Le Tuan, and Leonardo Bassani da Silveira.

In 1999, Fenton flew to Iceland, and he was searching for a place to stay. He emailed over 1500 students in Reykjavik to ask if anyone would be interested in sharing their home with him—a stranger. A new network of friends was made, and he experienced a stay that he categorized as a more genuine tourist experience. Following that, it inspired him to start a new non-profit organization, which is Couchsurfing. Couchsurfing strongly believes in the connection between people through cultural exchange and respect. Today, Couchsurfing might not be as active as it used to be (Fedorov, 2021), but the ethos for the free type of NH platform remains largely among other free NH platforms. The revolution of Couchsurfing just before COVID-19, and that accelerated with COVID-19, showed its transformation from a community of travelers on an online platform to a commercial enterprise. The introduction of a paywall in May 2020 created a massive exodus of members who were interested in the community and free hospitality mindset, not the commercial environment.

A reciprocal type of NH platform is a marketplace that matches individuals who host or let out their spaces for something in exchange with individuals who are seeking a place to stay but are willing to provide something in return. A fee (annual subscription or pay per night) is required to access the community of home exchange hosts. The home exchange under the reciprocal type of NH is like the traditional form of bartering, but in today's society, it has been revitalized (Forno and Garibaldi, 2014). It is a mutual exchange of one's home for a certain period for work, holiday, or other reasons. The practice of home exchange can be dated back to the Middle Ages, and the modern practice today can be traced back to the 1950s between the United States and Great Britain (Forno and Garibaldi, 2014). In 1953, Jan Ryder from Great Britain and David Ostroff from New York, both strangers to each other, decided to exchange their homes among friends for summer vacations. They spent some time getting to know each other and then realized that their ideas could spread globally. They created HomeLink, which is still active today.

Members can opt for reciprocal or non-reciprocal exchanges. For reciprocal exchanges, both members agree to travel at the same time to swap their houses, whereas in non-reciprocal exchanges, both members can travel at different times, or only one of them is traveling. Home sitting type of reciprocal NH platform is where the house sitter takes care of the homeowner's property while they are away. This includes pet sitting if the homeowner has a pet. In the same manner, NH users can stay at one's home in exchange for a service. Volunteering is usually part of the experience. For instance, Worldpackers has multiple volunteering opportunities, such as participating in an eco-village, teaching in a non-profit school, working in a non-governmental organization, working on a farm, or any permaculture project. WWOOF stands for Worldwide Opportunities on Organic Farms. As stated in the organization's name, members get to stay for free by volunteering to work on farms.

12.6 IMPACTS OF NETWORK HOSPITALITY

12.6.1 SOCIAL IMPACTS OF NETWORK HOSPITALITY

Technology has affected not only the way individuals travel but also every aspect of tourism and the hospitality industry (Kaira, 2023). As society advances, technology offers a convenient solution to everything. NH relies heavily on technology because without technology, not all the strangers in the world have the chance to meet (Bialski, 2011). Technology connects them personally. NH is unique in the sense that two contradicting aspects are combined and yet they work well together. To be specific, the modern aspect of hospitality, which is the technology, and the traditional aspect of hospitality, which is the personal touch are combined to enhance the overall users' experience.

However, hospitality technologies create different rules for strangers to interact (Bialski, 2011). Indeed, using technologies of hospitality facilitates people to interact, but when people depend heavily on technology, the element of personal touch will slowly fade. Using the same example, with just one click away to book everything, the tourist does not need to interact with anyone. This type of scene is a typical example of what everyday life is like with technology. Ironically, tourism experience, including hospitality experience, is all about human interaction (Chen et al., 2020). From a service perspective, Sullivan (2011) remarks that self-service in the hospitality industry reduces the number of complaints, but the importance of customer service and customer relationships in the hospitality industry is often missed. Although self-services have their advantages (time and cost-saving), they cannot offer a personal touch or build a relationship with people (Chen, 2011).

Correspondingly, Adler and Gordon (2013) researched the role of hotel concierges regarding technology and uncovered that the human touch is still the key advantage of hotel concierges, which any sort of technology cannot provide. It was understood that computers cannot provide the skills required to connect and provide a personal touch to the guests (Chen, 2011). People use the Internet to find information about places, but they want to connect with an actual person who has been to the exact place in order to gain feedback about the place (Adler and Gordon, 2013). One respondent in their research also specifically mentioned that the information provided on the Internet can be misrepresented and guests go to his hotel because of the personal touch provided by him and his employees.

Stors and Kagermeier (2015) discovered that both host and guest of NH share similarities and the fundamental similarity is that they are motivated to join and use the NH platform because of the personal interaction between the two. Other major factors of motivation are to save money, meet new people, have direct contact with the locals, gain insider tips from the host, explore new things, and gain the perspective of the inhabitants. Existing literature shares similar findings. For instance, meeting new people when staying with Airbnb Malaysian guests (Razli et al., 2018), interacting with Airbnb North American guests (Guttentag et al., 2017), and having direct contact with locals through Couchsurfing in Yugoslavia (Miljkovic et al., 2021).

By comparing this set of motivations to the statement from the respondent about concierge, the role of a hotel concierge is to advice and provide a personal touch that technology cannot replace. Users of NH demand a higher and more personal level of engagement, like the hotel concierge. NH is a platform for strangers to meet. With this technology, the process of encounters varies, as it is an online setting which gets transferred to an offline setting. The interactions between strangers are not clearly defined, and the different meetings stimulated through such settings will challenge and renegotiate some parts of the interaction process (Bialski, 2011). For example, strangers become closer to each other quickly; it is most often for a noticeably short amount of time. This is also the way for them to gain trust and make judgments about each other based on the different signs, not obtainable in other contexts.

Referring to Elliott and Urry (2010, p. 54) "obligations to family and friends involve very strong normative expectations of presence and attention." Bialski (2011) agrees, that the technologies of hospitality work similarly, generating relationships between strangers, not family or friend, but bear certain obligations. The interaction among strangers who meet using NH platforms can experience moments of "real warmth and affection," closeness, trust, and generosity, but it can also be difficult, further stimulating moments of awkwardness, misunderstanding, distrust, and abuse of power. Loneliness might be a factor that drives these interactions to occur. Loneliness has been recognized as an illness in this modern society (Alberti, 2018). It could be emotional or social isolation (Weiss, 1973). When a person experiences emotional loneliness, it is because of the absence of close relationships and this is related to the quality of social interactions, whereas when a person is experiencing social loneliness; it is the lack of social networks (DiTommaso and Spinner, 1993).

Studies acknowledge that this is an epidemic in modern society and unintentionally, NH has become a place to fill the void. Loneliness is a leading factor that drives NH users to actively seek social interactions (Farmaki and Stergiou, 2019). Based on Airbnb users, Farmaki and Stergiou (2019) suggest that the loneliness interaction depends on the durability and intensity of the interaction. For instance, when the intensity and the durability of the interaction are high, the user is seeking long-term meaningful interaction. This is a result of emotional loneliness. When both the intensity and durability of interaction are low, the user is driven by the need for frequent interactions, and this is a result of social loneliness. Many researchers have also discussed social interactions between guests and hosts (Ozanne and Prayag, 2022; Moon et al., 2019; Putova, 2018).

Lin et al. (2019) identify three types of social contact that occur during Airbnb guests' stay: guest-host, guest-community, and guest-guest. Under these social contacts, various activities generate different interactions, with each having an impact on the depth of the social connection, as suggested by Farmaki and Stergiou (2019). However, it is reported that most of the contacts generated a positive attitude, which signifies that social contact in NH is important. This, in return, has created a new type of tourist, tourists who actively seek social interactions through technology. NH bridges this gap by offering users a platform to socialize, and each experience differs. It is the local cultural experience and social interactions with hosts that separate NH activities from traditional hospitality services. Not only has NH facilitated social interactions, but it has also created opportunities for entrepreneurs and consumers and empowered individuals, especially women, to be entrepreneurs (Lim and Bouchon, 2021).

12.6.2 ECONOMIC IMPACTS OF NETWORK HOSPITALITY

The multifaceted nature of modern society today might have been a contributory factor to the growth of NH. Modern society today faces complex issues, such as slow economic growth, increase in aging population, increasing single-person households, and reducing personal income (Bloom and Zucker, 2023; Ortiz-Ospina, 2019). The Great Recession is suggested to be one of the key drivers of the development of the overall sharing economy (Cesarani and Nechita, 2017). It is almost impossible for households to escape the financial crisis and economic recession, especially with the COVID-19 outbreak in December 2019. Full or partial lockdown was implemented globally to curb the outbreak. Because of the lockdown, global economic activity dropped significantly, various businesses shut down, and people lost their jobs (Naseer et al., 2023). Tourism and hospitality are one industry that received the hardest hit (Madden, 2021).

As a result, households are compelled to figure out ways to maximize the utilization of their existing physical assets and control personal consumption. Consumers are more mindful of their expenses and search for cheaper alternatives. NH enables individuals with resources to share their goods and services with other individuals. It created markets from things that were not considered monetizable before (Geron, 2013). To participate in the overall sharing economy, the barrier is low, as users do not need to physically own assets and if they do, the capital to start is also low (Washington State University, 2023). Hence, NH users benefit from utilizing necessary resources at a lower cost, and they can earn income from their physical assets (Kang et al., 2019).

NH enables property owners to diversify the potential streams of income they generate from owning homes (Bivens, 2019). Property owners who want to rent out their units can opt for a long-term rental or short-term rental. Short-term rentals often come with transaction costs, which NH platforms can reduce and make this option more feasible (Bivens, 2019). In 2019, Malaysian Airbnb hosts invested in properties during the upturn to sell the properties at a higher price (Mahalingam and Toh, 2019). The property market slumped, and many of these Malaysian investors found selling or renting out their properties challenging. They needed income to pay their loans. These investors turned to Airbnb to settle their mortgages. The extra income earned from Airbnb is used to manage their finances or to pay off their loans (Chia, 2019). This was further supported by Airbnb through a commissioned study which found 84% of Malaysians agreed that Airbnb creates opportunities for local business owners and over 82% agreed that Airbnb drives the economy and allows them to generate more income (Airbnb, 2023).

Additionally, investors are investing in the real estate market to build portfolios of homes to rent out on Airbnb (Clark, 2021). reAlpha, an Ohio-based real estate company is spending 1.5 billion USD, including debt, to purchase short-term rentals, approximately 5000 homes (Clark, 2021). The company uses artificial intelligence software to evaluate home listings and make fast decisions on how much it will pay. The same software will be used to evaluate 100 to 500 homes in Austin, Miami, and Dallas as part of the house purchase plan. reAlpha's strategy is to deploy the capital as soon as possible because the Airbnb business model has been proven, and the opportunity is presented—the post-pandemic travel boom.

Big investors such as reAlpha might benefit from Airbnb and the NH community, along with other blooming NH platforms managed by the organization. However, the key in NH is personalization with a local touch, where investment and growth such as reAlpha could contradict because of the possibility of uniformity or a hotel-like experience. Overall, undoubtedly, NH offers opportunities for individuals to be entrepreneurs, a platform to empower individuals financially, professionally, and socially through hosting (Lim and Bouchon, 2021).

12.7 CONCLUSION

In addressing the research objectives of this chapter, it is definite that technology and the rise in digital natives have disrupted the hospitality industry, resulting in contradictory implications for the industry. From the extensive review of the concept of NH, it is apparent that NH is not a new phenomenon, but it has been gaining popularity in recent years due to the modernized society—a technology-dependent society. Due to the continuous demand for easy accessibility, convenience, affordable alternatives, and the search for unique experiences, hospitality providers are forced out of their comfort zones regarding how businesses are usually conducted. Instead of moving away from digitalization, businesses are leveraging its benefits. Changes in travelers' demands and how travel decisions are made have revitalized the concept of NH. Today, different types of NH have diversified the accommodation sector within the hospitality sector, providing ample choices for travelers. On the other hand, its existence is a threat and competition for other forms of lodging properties as people tend to choose NH for its advantages.

The implications of NH may be conflicting like a "double-edged sword." For example, the global society is seen to be leaning toward sharing their personal spaces and converting properties into business forms as it becomes a new stream of income. Moreover, despite different motivational factors in either being a host or guest within the NH network, its epitome of sharing, converged with technology (John, 2013), has managed to market itself as a form of solace for individuals who experience solitude or sentiments related to loneliness (Alberti, 2018). In light of the increasing usage of digitalization in the service industry, hospitality-related providers such as NH are implementing varied systems and online marketplaces. However, it is imperative to note that overreliance on technology may hinder service providers from honing their interpersonal skills, which is the essence of all service-related operations.

Although the NH society attempts to minimize the negative implications, it is not as straightforward as it seems because the globalized world depends on technology to move forward and have a competitive advantage over its competitors. On that note, despite it is apparent that NH is expanding and is diversified; further studies should explore the different types of NH operators as it may serve as a guideline in developing relevant policies to support the hospitality industry in addressing negative implications while optimizing its benefits. In addition, a comparative study between NH in Western and Asian settings would provide a comprehensive outlook of NH. This chapter on NH is an attempt to continue and widen the discourse on NH among scholars in academia and to collaborate with players in the hospitality industry.

KEYWORDS

- **collaborative consumption**
- **digitalization in hospitality**
- **digitalization in tourism**
- **network hospitality**
- **network sociality**
- **peer-to-peer consumption**
- **sharing economy**

REFERENCES

Adler, H., & Gordon, S. (2013). An analysis of the changing roles of hotel concierges. *Journal of Tourism and Hospitality Management, 1*(2), 53–66.

Airbnb. (2024). *About us.* Retrieved from https://news.airbnb.com/about-us/

Airbnb. (2023). *Malaysians say short-term rentals drive local economic activity.* Retrieved from https://news.airbnb.com/ms/malaysians-say-short-term-rentals-drive-local-economic-activity/

Alberti, F. B. (2018, Nov 1). Loneliness is a modern illness of the body, not just the mind. *The Guardian.* Retrieved from https://www.theguardian.com/commentisfree/2018/nov/01/loneliness-illness-body-mind-epidemic

Bardhi, F., & Eckhardt, G. M. (2012). Access-based consumption: The case of car sharing. *Journal of Consumer Research, 39*, 881–898. https://doi.org/10.1086/66

Bellotti, V., Ambard, A., Turner, D., Gossmann, C., Demková, K., & Carroll, J. M. (2015). A muddle of models of motivation for using peer-to-peer economy systems. In *Conference on Human Factors in Computing Systems* (pp. 1085–1094). Association for Computing Machinery. https://doi.org/10.1145/2702123.2702272

Benkler, Y. (2006). *The wealth of networks: How social production transform markets and freedom.* Yale University Press.

Bialski, P. (2011). Technologies of hospitality: How planned encounters develop between strangers. *Hospitality and Society, 1*(3), 245–260. https://doi.org/10.1386/hosp.1.3.245_1

Bivens, J. (2019). *The economic costs and benefits of Airbnb.* Economic Policy Institute.

Bloom, D. E., & Zucker, L. M. (2023). *Aging is the real population bomb.* Retrieved from https://www.imf.org/en/Publications/fandd/issues/Series/Analytical-Series/aging-is-the-real-population-bomb-bloom-zucker

Botsman, R. (2013, Nov). *The sharing economy lacks a shared definition.* Retrieved from https://www.fastcompany.com/3022028/the-sharing-economy-lacks-a-shared-definition

Botsman, R. (2016). *The sharing economy with Rachel Botsman.* Retrieved from https://www.youtube.com/watch?v=0MHrkeG5HiQ&t=183s

Botsman, R. (2019). *Trust leaps.* Retrieved from https://medium.com/@rachelbotsman/trust-leaps-bae279d841a

Botsman, R., & Rogers, R. (2010). *What's mine is yours: The rise of collaborative consumption.* HarperCollins Publishers.

Carbaugh, D. A. (1988). *Talking American: Cultural discourses on Donahue.* Ablex Pub. Corp.

Castells, M. (2000). *The rise of the network society. Volume I: The information age: Economy, society and culture* (2nd ed.). Blackwell Publishers Ltd.

Cesarani, M., & Nechita, F. (2017). Tourism and the sharing sconomy. An evidence from Airbnb usage in Italy and Romania. *Symphonya: Emerging Issues in Management,* 3, 32. https://doi.org/10.4468/2017.3.04cesarani.nechita

Chen, D. J. (2011). Global concept, local practice: Taiwanese experience of CouchSurfing. *Hospitality and Society, 1*(3), 279–297. https://doi.org/10.1386/hosp.1.3.279_1

Chen, D. J. (2017). Gendered couchsurfing: Women from Western Europe and East-Asia contesting de-sexualised cosmopolitanism. *Gender, Place & Culture, 24*(8), 1090–1106. https://doi.org/10.1080/0966369X.2017.1372375

Chen, Y., Chen, J., Liu, W., & Sharma, T. (2020). Expected benefits of people interactions and guest experiences. *International Hospitality Review, 34*(2), 187-202. https://doi.org/10.1108/IHR-04-2020-0010

Cheng, X., Mou, J., & Yan, X. (2021). Sharing economy enabled digital platforms for development. *Information Technology for Development, 27*(4), 635-644. https://doi.org/10.1080/02681102.2021.1971831

Chia, R. G. (2019). 3 million tourists used Airbnb in Malaysia last year—and demand in local towns shot up because people want "experiences." *Business Insider*. Retrieved from https://www.businessinsider.my/3-million-tourists-used-airbnb-in-malaysia-last-year-and-demand-in-local-towns-shot-up-because-people-want-experiences/

Chua, E. L., Chiu, J. L., & Bool, N. C. (2019). Sharing economy: An analysis of Airbnb business model and the factors that influence consumer adoption. *Review of Integrative Business and Economics Research, 8*(2), 19–37.

Clark, P. (2021, June 25). Investors chasing housing target massive pools of Airbnb rentals. *Bloomberg*. Retrieved from https://www.bloomberg.com/news/articles/2021-06-25/investors-chasing-housing-target-massive-pools-of-airbnb-rentals

DiTommaso, E., & Spinner, B. (1993). The development and initial validation of the social and emotional loneliness scale for adults (SELSA). *Personality and Individual Differences, 14*(1), 127–134. https://doi.org/10.1016/0191-8869(93)90182-3

Elliott, A., & Urry, J. (2010). *Mobile lives: Self, excess and nature*. Routledge.

Fallon-O'Leary, D. (2023). *The state of the B2B sharing economy*. Retrieved from https://www.business.com/articles/b2b-sharing-economy/

Farmaki, A., & Stergiou, D. P. (2019). Escaping loneliness through Airbnb host-guest interactions. *Tourism Management, 74*, 331–333. https://doi.org/10.1016/j.tourman.2019.04.006

Fedorov, A. (2021). *Paradise lost: The rise and ruin of Couchsurfing.com*. Retrieved from https://www.inverse.com/input/features/rise-and-ruin-of-couchsurfing

Forno, F., & Garibaldi, R. (2014). Not only low-cost: Home swapping as an alternative tourism strategy. In A. P. Russo & G. Richards (Eds.), *Alternative and creative tourism* (pp. 114–124). ATLAS.

Gamil, R. E. (2022). Exploring travel belaviour post-COVID-19: Towards a more responsible tourism. *Academica Turistica, 12*(2), 203–216. https://doi.org/10.26493/2335-4194.15.203-216

Geron, T. (2013, Jan 23). Airbnb and the unstoppable rise fo the share economy. *Forbes*. Retrieved from https://www.forbes.com/sites/tomiogeron/2013/01/23/airbnb-and-the-unstoppable-rise-of-the-share-economy/#166c45e8aae3

Görög, G. (2018). The Definitions of Sharing Economy: A Systematic Literature Review. *Management*, 175–189. https://doi.org/10.26493/1854-4231.13.175-189

Goudin, P. (2016). *The cost of non-Europe in the sharing economy*. Brussels.

Guttentag, D., Smith, S., Potwarka, L., & Havitz, M. (2017). Why tourists choose Airbnb: A motivation-based segmentation study. *Journal of Travel Research, 57*(3), 342–359. https://doi.org/10.1177/0047287517696980

Kang, S., Kim, W. G., & Song, H. J. (2019). Exploring the role of travel and tourism in sharing economy activities: A case study of South Korea. *Journal of Quality Assurance in Hospitality and Tourism, 20*(5), 599–616. https://doi.org/10.1080/1528008X.2019.1579079

Lim, S. E. Y., & Bouchon, F. (2021). The effects of network hospitality on women empowerment. *International Journal of Tourism Cities, 7*(10), 32–45. https://doi.org/10.1108/IJTC-07-2019-0112

Ikkala, T., & Lampinen, A. (2015). Monetizing network hospitality: Hospitality and sociability in the context of Airbnb. In *CSCW 2015—Proceedings of the 2015 ACM International Conference on Computer-Supported Cooperative Work and Social Computing* (pp. 1033–1044). Association for Computing Machinery, Inc. https://doi.org/10.1145/2675133.2675274

Illouz, E. (2008). *Saving the modern soul: Therapy, emotions, and the culture of self-help*. University of California Press.

Iyer, S. (2020). *Ditch the hotels stay in someone's home on your next vacay.* Retrieved from https://www.outlooktraveller.com/travelnews/people/5-couchsurfing-apps-and-websites-for-your-solo-travels

John, N. A. (2013). Sharing, collaborative consumption and Web 2.0. In B. Cammaerts & N. Anstead (Eds.), *Media@LSE Electronic Working Paper*. Media@LSE.

Kaira, D. (2023, Feb 19). Road to India@100: The future of tourism is tech. *Business Today*. Retrieved from https://www.businesstoday.in/magazine/columns/story/road-to-india100-the-future-of-tourism-is-tech-368989-2023-02-05

Lin, P. M. C., Fan, D. X. F., Zhang, H. Q., & Lau, C. (2019). Spend less and experience more: Understanding tourists' social contact in the Airbnb context. *International Journal of Hospitality Management, 83*, 65–73. https://doi.org/10.1016/j.ijhm.2019.04.007

Laker, B. (2023, July 6). Redefining leadership: The rise and evolution of the sharing economy. *Forbes*. Retrieved from https://www.forbes.com/sites/benjaminlaker/2023/07/06/redefining-leadership-the-rise-and-evolution-of-the-sharing-economy/?sh=733cd82d1b3f

Landfolk. (2024). *What is landfolk?*. Retrieved from https://landfolk.com/en/s/about

Lynch, P. A., McIntosh, A. J., & Tucker, H. (2009). *Commercial homes in tourism: An international perspective*. Routledge.

Madden, D. (2021, Jan 24). The covid-19 pandemic has cost the global tourism industry $935 billion. *Forbes*. Retrieved from https://www.forbes.com/sites/duncanmadden/2021/01/14/the-covid-19-pandemic-has-cost-the-global-tourism-industry-935-billion/?sh=66d90b3b7d40

Mahalingam, E., & Toh, K. I. (2019). More Malaysians using Airbnb to settle mortgages. *The Star*. Retrieved from https://www.thestar.com.my/business/business-news/2019/07/03/md-the-cost-and-security-issue-of-airbnb

Marques, L., & Matos, B. G. (2020). Network relationality in the tourism experience: Staging sociality in homestays. *Current Issues in Tourism, 23*(9), 1153–1165. https://doi.org/10.1080/13683500.2019.1594722

Miljković, J., Božović, T., & Čapeta, I. (2021). Couchsurfing as a modern waay of destination exploring. *ToSEE, 6*, 455–466. https://doi.org/10.20867/tosee.06.30

Ministry of Tourism Government of India. (2022). *National strategy for promotion of rural homestays: An initiative towards Aatmanirbhar Bharat*. Retrieved from https://tourism.gov.in/sites/default/files/2022-09/National%20Strategy%20for%20Promotion%20of%20Rural%20Homestays%202022.pdf

Ministry of Tourism Government of India. (2023). *Best rural homestay competition.* Retrieved from https://nidhi.nic.in/BTA/View/AboutUsHomestay.aspx#:~:text=The%20

Ministry%20of%20Tourism%2C%20Government,form%20of%20accommodation%20for%20tourists

Molz, J. G. (2007). Cosmopolitans on the Couch: Mobile hospitality and the internet. In J. G. Molz & S. Fibsin (Eds.), *Mobilizing hospitality: The ethics of social relations in a mobile world* (pp. 65–80). Ashgate.

Molz, J. G. (2011). CouchSurfing and network hospitality: "It's not just about the furniture." *Hospitality and Society, 1*(3), 215–225. https://doi.org/10.1386/hosp.1.3.215_2

Molz, J. G. (2014). Toward a network hospitality. *First Monday, 19*(3). https://doi.org/10.5210/fm.v19i3.4824

Moon, H., Miao, L., Hanks, L., & Line, N. D. (2019). Peer-to-peer interactions: Perspectives of Airbnb guests and hosts. *International Journal of Hospitality Management, 77*, 405–414. https://doi.org/10.1016/j.ijhm.2018.08.004

Naseer, S., Khalid, S., Parveen, S., Abbass, K., Song, H., & Achim, M. V. (2023). COVID-19 outbreak: Impact on global economy. *Frontiers in Public Health, 10.* https://doi.org/10.3389/fpubh.2022.1009393

Olson, M. J., & Kemp, S. J. (2015). Sharing economy: An in-depth look at its evolution & trajectory across industries. *PiperJaffray.*

Ortiz-Ospina, E. (2019). *The rise of living alone: How one-person households are becoming increasingly common around the world.* Retrieved from https://ourworldindata.org/living-alone

Ozanne, L. K., & Prayag, G. (2022). Exploring Airbnb host wellbeing and host-guest conflicts in network hospitality. An analysis of the changing roles of hotel concierges. *Frontiers in Psychology, 13.* https://doi.org/10.3389/fpsyg.2022.805761

Pellegrino, G. (2011). *The politics of proximity: Mobility and immobility in practice.* Ashgate.

PricewaterhouseCoopers. (2015). *Sharing or paring? Growth of the sharing economy.* Budapest. Retrieved from https://www.pwc.com/hu/en/kiadvanyok/assets/pdf/sharing-economy-en.pdf

Půtová, B. (2018). Anthropology of tourism: Researching interactions between hosts and guests. *Czech Journal of Tourism, 7*(1), 71–92. https://doi.org/10.1515/cjot-2018-0004

Quinones, A., & Augustine, A. (2015). *Technology and trust: How the sharing economy is changing consumer behavior.* Retrieved from https://www.bbvaresearch.com/wp-content/uploads/2015/11/151119_US_SharingEconomy.pdf

Razli, I. A., Jamal, S. A., & Zahari, M. S. M. (2017). Airbnb: An overview of a new platform for peer to peer accommodation in Malaysia. *Advanced Science Letters*, *23*(8), 7829–7832. https://doi.org/10.1166/asl.2017.9587

Rifkin, J. (2015). *The zero marginal cost society: The internet of things, the collaborative commons, and the eclipse of capitalism*. Palgrave Macmillan.

Schor, J. B., & Fitzmaurice, C. J. (2015). Collaborating and connecting: The emergence of the sharing economy. In L. Reisch & J. Thogersen (Eds.), *Handbook of research on sustainable consumption* (pp. 410–425). Edward Elgar.

Steylaerts, V., & O'Dubhghaill, S. (2011). Couchsurfing and authenticity: Notes towards an understanding of an emerging phenomenon. *Hospitality and Society*, *1*(3), 261–278. https://doi.org/10.1386/hosp.1.3.261_1

Stors, N., & Kagermeier, A. (2015). Motives for using Airbnb in metropolitan tourism—Why do people sleep in the bed of a stranger? *Regions Magazine, 299*(1), 17–19. https://doi.org/10.1080/13673882.2015.11500081

Sullivan, J. (2011). The forgotten art of service. *Nation's Restaurant News, 45*(5).

Tiah, C. (2019, Sept 30). How travel is changing: "It's all about personalisation." *Channel News Asia.* Retrieved from https://www.channelnewsasia.com/news/asia/travel-industry-changing-personalisation-tourism-singaporeans-11887322

Washington State University. (2023). *How the sharing ecoomy is transforming business.* Retrieved from https://onlinemba.wsu.edu/blog/how-the-sharing-economy-is-transforming-business

Weiss, R. S. (1973). *Loneliness: The experience of emotional and social isolation.* The MIT Press.

Wittel, A. (2001). Toward a network sociality. *Theory, Culture & Society, 18*(6), 51–76. https://doi.org/10.1177/026327601018006003

Zamzuki, F. A., Lola, M. S., Aruchunan, E., Muthuvulu, M. S., Jubilee, R. V. W., Zainuddin, N. H., et al. (2023). Assessing the sustainability of the homestay industry for the East Coast of Malaysia using the Delphi approach. *Heliyon, 9*(11). https://doi.org/10.1016/j.heliyon.2023.e21433

CHAPTER 13

Digital Marketing Strategies for Tourism Businesses: An Overview of Digital Marketing Strategies for Tourism Industry Members

ESRA TOPCUOGLU SCHOEN

Department of Hospitality and Tourism Management, Indiana University Kokomo, Kokomo, Indiana, USA

ABSTRACT

Digital marketing creates a win–win situation for both sellers and buyers by offering many advantages to customers. Customers can have easy and fast access to different types of information that help them to make travel-related decisions. As a result of this process, customers can buy more, become buzz marketers, generate more revenue for specific travel brands, and become loyal. Therefore, the butterfly effect of digital marketing cannot be denied. The wide usage of digitalization in marketing has brought the need of tech savvy human resources and patrons, after sales service support, and new jobs such as digital marketing specialist and e-commerce manager. Accordingly, this chapter provides an overview of digital marketing strategies in tourism field from different perspectives. It emphasizes the importance of digital marketing for both tourism organizations and for customers and explains the way digital marketing works for tourism, the considerable change in customer behavior in the digital age, best practices in digital marketing, common digital marketing tools used by tourism organizations, digitalization in

Digitalization in Tourism. Hulya Akdemir Cengiz, Seza Zerman, Aysegul Acar, and Faizan Ali (Eds.)

DOI: 10.1201/9781779644770-17

marketing research, opportunities and challenges in digital marketing, and digital marketing careers.

13.1 INTRODUCTION

13.1.1 JUST A CLICK AWAY!

The emergent technological landscape has changed the tourism ecosystem followed by the evolution of tourism marketing strategies. Incorporating digitalization in the tourism marketing strategies has become indispensable for surviving the competition in the customer-centric industry (Labanauskaite et al., 2020). Currently, digital marketing practices are needed for the global tourism industry whose products have an experiential and intangible nature (Evans, 2016). Due to this experiential aspect, customers do not have a chance to try the product before the consumption time (Yin et al., 2020). Then, they may perceive purchasing a tourism service risky for having potential negative consequences such as poor service and overpromised service (Hu and Yang, 2021). By utilizing e-marketing tools, tourism businesses can make tourism products less intangible by allowing customers to experience products visually (e.g., visual tours of destinations). For tourism businesses, the benefits of digital marketing include, but are not limited to, acquiring customer information segmenting and targeting customers, smartly communicating with the targeted audience, improving customer loyalty, promoting products and brands, and boosting sales (Singh et al., 2024). Both profit and nonprofit tourism institutions have seen the need and advantage to merge digitalization into their marketing strategies. Travel companies, lodging businesses, food and beverage companies, theme parks, and meetings-events facilities are some profit tourism organizations that grow their business by digital marketing methods (De Palsmacker et al., 2018). Marriott Hotels and Resorts sell their guest rooms, promote meetings and event facilities, provide information about their properties around the world, and offer promotions through the company brand website www.marriott.com. Busch Gardens, an amusement park located in Williamsburg, VA, allows ticket sales and provide park-related information on its brand website (Figure 13.1).

FIGURE 13.1 The Website of Busch Gardens Amusement Park

Busch Gardens is an amusement park in Williamsburg, VA. The park takes advantage of digital marketing tools to maximize the traffic to the property and improve the experience of its target audience. In its brand website, the park allows customers to buy tickets, provides information about the park, and directs customers to its brand app. Destination marketing organizations (DMOs), also called Convention and Visitor Bureaus and tourism associations are some nonprofit organizations that promote tourism destinations and engage visitors (Confetto et al., 2023). Choose Chicago, the official DMO for Chicago, Illinois, provides information and links to purchase tickets for citywide events and attractions on its own website. To improve the international visitor experience, the DMO offers a multilanguage website with a dropdown language-switching menu (Choose Chicago, 2024). Most benefits of digital marketing can be attributed to its two-way communication aspect that allows tourism brands to learn more about their existing and potential customers. Then, these brands can gather relevant customer data, understand target customer behavior, and keep up with the industry trends faster and efficiently. A tourism company can design a digital marketing tool (e.g., a product-ordering app) in a fashion that customizes the products and asks for customer information relevant to the product of interest. Then the customer can provide data about their product preferences to the tourism company by customizing the purchase.

Global food and beverage companies including Pizza Hut, Burger King, and Starbucks take advantage of ordering apps to increase their sales and offer promotions (Wang et al., 2019). Some significant features of these catering apps are ordering product, distributing coupons, offering deals, managing loyalty program, and creating an order history for each customer who uses the app (Okumus and Bilgihan, 2014; Wang et al., 2019).

In the case of ordering food through the company's brand app, customers provide information about their purchasing patterns to the brand, such as food preferences, special diets, amount of food ordered, beverage choice, and the time of the order. So, every food purchase on the brand app allows the company collect and store data about that customer as shown in Figure 13.2. The company can use this data for reminding the previous order to speed up their decision-making or sending the customers similar products-related promotions and advertising.

Burger King is one of the fast-food chains that implements digital marketing strategies efficiently.

The well-known brand uses its brand food-ordering app to offer customized food and beverages, communicate promotions, and learn about their customers. Each order is customized with different preferences for the fast food offerings, delivery, and payment.

Moreover, digital marketing creates a win–win situation for both sellers and buyers by offering many advantages to customers. Customers, on the other hand, can have easy and fast access to different types of information that help them to make travel-related decisions. As a result of this process, customers can buy more, become buzz marketers, generate more revenue for specific travel brands, and become loyal. Therefore, the butterfly effect of digital marketing cannot be denied. The wide usage of digitalization in marketing has brought the need of tech savvy human resources and patrons, after sales service support, and new jobs such as digital marketing specialist and e-commerce manager. Educational institutions that offer tourism and hospitality programs have started to include digital technology courses in their curriculum. This chapter provides an overview of digital marketing strategies in tourism from different perspectives. It emphasizes the importance of digital marketing for both tourism organizations and customers. As digital marketing is an interactive practice and allows customers to be involved in the marketing process, it is crucial to understand the perspectives of both seller and buyer parties in tourism. Within tourism industry, this chapter explains how digital marketing works, changing customer behavior in the digital age, best practices in digital marketing, common digital marketing tools used by tourism organizations, digitalization in marketing research, opportunities and challenges in digital marketing, and digital marketing careers.

13.1.2 HOW DIGITAL MARKETING WORKS IN TOURISM

Tourism is a service industry with offerings that have an experiential nature. Some significant aspects of this experiential nature are the intangibility and inseparability of tourism products (Evans, 2016). An example would explain these two characteristics of tourism products. A leisure traveler cannot experience in advance a booked trip to Athens, Greece. This traveler must take the flight, go through the airport procedures at Athens International Airport, check in to his/her hotel, interact with the locals of Athens, and explore the city attractions to experience the destination. In similar scenarios, the travelers would like to have an idea about their potential trip to the destination. This planned trip cannot be produced without the traveler being present at the airport, at the airplane, and arriving at the destination. Therefore, the traveler and the provider/s of the purchased services must co-produce the service. This is the inseparability aspect of the tourism products.

In terms of intangibility, the traveler cannot experience the trip before arriving at the final destination because the products of flight, hotel stay, and the destination cannot be shown to the traveler before the time of consumption at the service encounters (e.g., airport, hotel, and the destination). The service quality of the flight, the cleanliness of the hotel room, and the attractions at the destination are some examples of intangible tourism products. Therefore, these businesses reduce the risk of purchasing intangible products by using digital marketing strategies. The 3E's Model explains in a simple and clear way how digital marketing works in tourism as shown in Figure 13.2. The model was developed by the chapter author based on insights and findings from the tourism and hospitality literature (Confetto et al., 2023; De Palsmacker et al., 2018, Jayawardena et al., 2023; Kotler et al., 2021; Labanauskaite et al., 2020, Wong et al., 2020).

FIGURE 13.2 The 3E's model of how digital marketing functions

1. **Expose:** The three-step process starts with exposing the target audience to the specific marketing campaign or product of a tourism brand. At this stage, the purpose is to create awareness of potential customers and increase awareness of existing customers for the company products and brand. At exposing stage, matching the customized content with the target audience needs is the key to success. Digital marketing offers two different paths to increasing brand visibility in the fastest way. One way is through the tourism businesses' own brand platforms (e.g., Hyatt.com, @pizzahut). Digital marketing boosts customer traffic to the brand platforms with search engine optimization (SEO), pay-per-click, and display advertising tools (Angeloni and Rossi, 2021). The other path is increasing visibility through third-party travel platforms. In the competitive tourism industry, it is essential to engage in partnerships with online intermediaries that already have an established and large customer base globally (Damnjanovic et al., 2020). These are third-party platforms that promote and sell different tourism products including hotel rooms, travel bundles, food, and rental cars (Talwar et al., 2020). They create different packages and offer promotions to attract customers and increase sales. Furthermore, these intermediaries allow peer-to-peer interaction and thus leads to electronic word-of-mouth (E-WOM) with the customer-generated content features (Kim et al., 2021a). DoorDash, for example, is a well-known online food-ordering platform, whereas TripAdvisor and Skyscanner are among the travel meta-search platforms. As a result, tourism products must first inform the customer about their presence and remind the customers to encourage product sales.

2. **Engage:** After the expose stage, now it is time to engage the customer who has become more familiar with the specific tourism brand. Engaging is important to seek customers to spend time and

money for the tourism brand (Lei et al., 2020). Engaged customers start to enjoy the brand offerings and become more positively receptive to the brand's digital content. In digital marketing, customer engagement can be explained as increasing the time customers spend on digital platforms, encouraging the customers to share more information about themselves, and sharing favorable evaluations about a specific tourism brand. In this stage, the tourism marketer focuses on engaging the target audience with the brand and products by entertaining them with customized marketing content or platform. Understanding customers' needs is essential to design relevant content that will appeal to the expectations and lifestyles of each target market and entertain them. Customers differ based on their demographics (age, income, education, nationality, etc.) and lifestyles. Accordingly, their perception of entertainment differs from one to another. A fun vacation, an all-inclusive cruise trip, a weekend at a wellness resort, a national park visit, or a cultural tour could be among the entertainment options for engaging different customer segments. Millennials who represent the largest customer group today, are a good example to understand the influence demographics' influence on customer behaviors.

Millennials have distinct characteristics such as being tech savvy, looking for unique experiences during their travel, and enjoying different cultures (Kim and Park, 2020). A way of engaging millennials is providing testimonials (such as customer reviews and videos of local experiences, etc.) of unique experiences at social media pages of a specific tourism business. A local DMO can engage millennial visitors with the destination by posting videos about local events, street food, and the architecture of the destination on the brand website or social media account. Las Vegas Convention and Visitor Authority (LVCVA), the official DMO of Las Vegas, Nevada, tends to engage potential visitors with its brand website. Las Vegas has a diverse visitor profile with different entertainment expectations such as gambling, Las Vegas shows, meetings and conventions, nightlife, sporting events, hiking, dining at Michelin starred restaurants, and many more (TripAdvisor, 2024). To meet the expectations, LVCVA provides information about all these aspects of the destination to engage each visitor profile in its official website (LVCVA, 2024).

3. **Enhance:** In this context, enhance refers to encouraging favorable customer intentions and behaviors including higher intention to purchase tourism products, recommending the tourism products to the others, and becoming loyal to the brand. Customers who are engaged with the brand and the products of a tourism business, will become the brand ambassadors of that business. Customers who become brand ambassadors, would spread favorable WOM about that brand and promote the brand for free (Serra-Scallops et al., 2020). They will prefer the travel products of that brand over the others and will become less price sensitive. The tourism businesses must continue to design engaging and relevant content for the travelers who are at the "enhance" stage of digital marketing. In this technology age, well-crafted digital marketing strategies play a significant role in maintaining long-term relationships with the customers and continuing to enhance customer loyalty.

The following scenario demonstrates how 3E's Model of digital tourism marketing works for promoting intangible tourism and travel products. The scenario is about a leisure trip of U.S. traveler from Chicago to Istanbul, Türkiye. The traveler needs information about flights to Istanbul (preferably a direct flight), hotel options close to tourist attractions, and things to do at the destination. The customer starts searching for information on the internet for reaching different travel websites, finding better deals, and discovering the attractions at the destination (Kim et al., 2021b). Accordingly, this potential customer is ready to become an actual customer for the travel companies by starting to look for travel options. This is the best time for travel companies to attract this traveler and promote their products, who is ready to purchase. The strategy for attracting the customer to the airline's brand website could be the keyword of "direct flight." After the web search, the traveler books their direct flight with Turkish Airlines. Turkish Airlines uses its website and brand app to provide an effective communication of a future flight experience. The airline provides flight-related information and online check-in features, and allows the traveler to manage in-flight experience in these digital marketing platforms. Then, travelers can select a seat, request a special menu for their dietary needs, learn about baggage rules, and purchase extra baggage for a specific flight (Turkish Airlines, 2024). Next thing to do is finding a hotel close to attractions or at the city center and represents the Turkish culture. The hotels that are listed on the web as close to attractions and as local chains will attract the customer. The individual reserves a room at The Marmara Taksim Hotel that is a branch of a local hotel corporation and located at the heart of Istanbul. Through the brand website or the OTA website, the hotel allows the customer to modify the booking, take a visual tour at the property, learn destination- and location-related information, and review visuals of the hotel products (The Marmara Hotels, 2024). Thus, digital marketing creates a win–win situation for both the travel companies and the customers. It helps the companies sell their products to their target customer, and the customer find the solutions to their needs.

In addition to the above-mentioned scenario, the role of collaboration between the tourism industry and the customers is critical for the functioning of digital marketing in tourism. Digital marketing platforms and tools enhance collaboration and co-creation between tourism organizations and the customers (Buhalis and Foerste, 2015). They create digital service encounters where the company and customer interact and co-create customer experiences. Consider the following scenario: A leisure traveler will fly to a vacation destination. The customer needs to go through some steps before boarding the plane, such as purchasing a flight ticket, checking in, verifying luggage information, providing identification, and so forth. The airline company requires each traveler to complete these steps to provide a safe and positive flight experience. For this reason, the airline develops its own brand website where one can complete all these mandatory steps and find flight-related information. The website has a user-friendly design where the traveler can do one-stop shopping, find all flight-related information, and allow customers to share their flight experience. As a result, the traveler is satisfied with the pre-flight experience by completing the required steps at the smartly designed airline website. Then, the airline is satisfied with gaining the traveler information to deliver the flight experience. After reaching the destination, the traveler satisfied with the experience, shares a positive review on the airline's website. The outcome is a co-creation of the flight experience by the happy airline company and the happy leisure traveler. This example demonstrates the role of digitalization in reaching marketing goals of a travel company (e.g., selling products, delivering customer experience, and increasing customer word-of-mouth).

13.2 DIGITAL MARKETING TOOLS

Tourism organizations select and utilize different digital strategies to reach their marketing goals and respond to the target audience's needs. When doing this, they should align the digital marketing practices with the overall marketing strategy of a tourism business. In other words, digital marketing activities should provide a consistent and a unified message as the Integrated Marketing Communications (IMC) of the organization (Porcu et al., 2019). A tourism business that utilizes multiple digital marketing tools (social media advertising and website), must convey a transparent and consistent marketing message to their target audience. It is important for differentiating the brand from that of competitors and avoid overwhelming customers with conflicting marketing information. The smart design of the marketing content is the key for a successful campaign and promotion. Here are common digital marketing tools implemented by tourism organizations:

1. **Mobile Advertising:** Today, an average customer spends a quarter of his/her day using mobile devices (Law et al., 2018). Therefore, mobile advertising is a smart tool to reach most of the customers who are engaged with their mobile devices such as smartphones and tablets. For this reason, tourism marketers advertise their brand and product through different digital methods and channels. Mobile advertising allows the marketer knowing where a customer is physically located at any given time, narrowly segmenting the market for delivering timely and relevant information (Cannon et al., 2024). This leads to sending customized marketing messages to the customers which provide immediate solutions to the customer needs such as finding an Italian restaurant nearby (Lei et al., 2020).

2. **Social Media Marketing:** This chapter does not discuss social media tools in detail. Because, it merits to have more coverage with all aspects of social media platforms and their functionality within tourism marketing. Therefore, this textbook dedicated a whole chapter to social media within tourism. Social media has brought a whole different perspective to tourism marketing. It has changed how tourism brands communicate with customers and promote and sell their products (Garrido-Moreno et al., 2018).

It allows two-way communication between tourism organizations and customers, and between customers through knowledge sharing and creation. Facebook, Instagram, LinkedIn, Twitter, TikTok, and YouTube are some popular social media platforms with millions of users. They have become a playground for tourism marketers to expose, engage and enhance customers with the brand social media accounts. On the other hand, customers have become marketers through social media platforms. They post experiences with the tourism products and recommend tourism brands on social media platforms.

3. **E-mail Marketing:** E-mail marketing is a cost-effective digital marketing tool (Leung and Tsou, 2019). A marketing email must be targeted, have an interesting title and content to attract the receiver. E-mail marketing can be used with different marketing purposes including offering a new promotion, sharing brand updates, sending greetings, and learning customer opinions. A marketing e-mail can also include links to the sender's brand website. When the receiver clicks the link, they land on the website where they can find product information, sign up for the company newsletter, or purchase a travel product. It is an effective way to increase brand awareness of customers and increase traffic to the brand platforms.

4. **Websites:** A strong website helps tourism companies define their brands, match their products with the target audience, and allow their target customers to explore the products. With a carefully designed brand website, tourism brands will simplify information processing and information overload for their target audience. A brand website of a tourism company is considered the first encounter between the brand and the target customer (Law, 2019). It is an all-in-one information hub for the customers for making purchase decisions for travel products. A brand website (e.g. www.southwest.com) helps to reduce the risk of purchasing experiential tourism products. It provides product-related information, visuals, customer reviews, purchasing points, and so on.

5. **Apps:** Today, mobile software applications are a smart way to communicate with tech savvy customers (Kim et al., 2021b).

These apps also collect and store valuable customer data. Brand apps are easy to download and have various functionality such as booking, purchasing, saving products for future purchases, and reading customer reviews. Tourism brands send notifications about product updates and sales promotions to their customers with the brand apps. Furthermore, they can send reminders to the customers for purchasing the saved items at the customer' e-cart with their brand apps.

13.3 BEST PRACTICES IN DIGITAL MARKETING FOR TOURISM BUSINESSES

Serving different target markets requires to develop customized digital marketing strategies and use appropriate digital platforms. Besides, there are some practices that have led to successful digital marketing campaigns for most customer segments.

TABLE 13.1 Best Practice in Digital Marketing

- Knowing your audience
- A clear and simple message
- Up-to-date content
- High-quality content
- Adaptability to different electronic devices: smartphone, tablet, laptop, etc.
- User-friendly design
- Measurable content and objectives
- Engaging features

Table 13.1 lists some best practices in digital marketing for tourism industry members. These stakeholders must know their customer group in terms demographics, purchasing patterns (e.g., frequency of purchase, time of purchase, etc.). They must develop a clear and simple message about their product and/or brand for its existing or potential target audience so that the audience understands the message. They must deliver content anytime to increase the accessibility of product and brand information for customers. In addition, this way customers do not need to follow the schedule of the platform or adapt their schedule to that of the platform to be exposed to the content. The digital marketing content must be up to date (price, availability, the validity of a deal, etc.) and high quality (visual, correctness of the information, relevance of the information, etc.). The content must be synchronized on multiple devices. Customers may prefer to use different electronic devices to access digital platforms (e.g., mobile phones, computers, laptops, and tablets) across a variety of formats (e.g., the brand website, social media, e-mail, etc.). As smartphone usage is growing significantly (Taylor, 2023; Wang et al., 2019), hospitality companies develop marketing communication tools compatible with smart phones. Hotels develop mobile versions of their brand websites to reach customers anytime and increase customer responsiveness to their marketing messages. A mobile website has a lot of advantages for a hotel such as understanding booking intentions, learning favorite feature of the website, and customer opinions about the products (Wong et al., 2020). Another good practice is designing user-friendly digital marketing tools for serving customers with different tech-savviness levels and demands. Any feature of the marketing tool that helps them reach information easily provides advantages for both customers and tourism businesses. Customers have access to the product information they need, then they familiarize themselves with the product features and benefits. In turn, they have a higher probability of purchasing the product which is the desired outcome by the tourism companies. Also, tourism marketers must develop measurable digital marketing strategies to evaluate the success of the campaign or tool. Engaging features are crucial to attracting more and more customers to the brand and products and increase sales.

13.4 CHANGING CUSTOMER BEHAVIOR AND NEEDS IN DIGITAL AGE

Today, the tourism industry cannot think marketing strategy development isolated from understanding their target customers' expectations and needs. In other words, contemporary marketing is customer centric. Digital transformation and changing demographics (Jayawardena et al., 2023) have contributed to this service-oriented approach. Today, most of the customers belong to Millennial (born between 1980s and 1990s) and Gen Z (also known as Zoomers: born between 1990s and 2010s) generations. These individuals have different behaviors than Baby Boomers (born between 1940s and 1960s). They are tech savvy, engaged with their smart phones, like to share their travel experiences with others, and do research before making a product purchase decision (Fan et al., 2023). These patrons are powerful as they have fast access to different tourism products and product-related information on digital marketing platforms. Moreover, they share their product-related experiences with the tourism companies and the other customers on these platforms. They like to give feedback to their favorite brands and to those they are not satisfied with. They also expect to interact with their favorite tourism brands via digital platforms such as apps, websites, or corporate social media accounts.

A significant change in customer behavior has also been observed due to the global pandemic of COVID-19 (Ketter and Avraham, 2021). Individuals' food ordering and dining behaviors changed during COVID-19. Ordering food from online channels (e.g., brand websites and apps, third party websites), downloading food ordering apps, ordering fast food through restaurants' drive through system, or picking up the pre-ordered food at the restaurant curbside are some examples. A major characteristic of today's customers is information search. Customer purchasing behavior is mostly driven by information search (Angeloni and Rossi, 2021). Common information sources are online review websites (e.g., TripAdvisor, Expedia), online stores of tourism companies, brand websites of tourism brands (e.g., www.marriott.com), apps, social media platforms (e.g., Instagram, Facebook), and so forth. So, information search has become an essential step for making a travel product-related decision. Customers are searching for product-related information on different platforms. A common platform is online review websites that allow customers to learn more about travel products and share their experience and opinions with others. Customers search for information for different purposes such as product price, product quality, experience, product availability, product performance, and product benefits.

User-generated content (UGC) has become an important external factor that influences purchasing decisions for tourism products whose nature is experiential. Some customers produce their own content on online review websites (e.g., Expedia, TripAdvisor) are also the marketers of their favorite brand and act as brand ambassadors. Some examples are buzz marketing and influencer marketing. In the case of buzz marketing, customers who like or are loyal to a brand, act as the marketer of that brand by spreading positive word-of-mouth (WOM), sharing their positive experiences about the brand, and encourage others to try the products of that brand. When it comes to influencer marketing, tourism companies pay individuals who have built a reputation on social media for expertise or knowledge about a topic (e.g., travel, gastronomy, etc.) for promoting their products and driving sales (HSMAI, 2024). These influencers could be regular customers who have become product experts or opinion leaders over time or celebrities who are a good fit with the brand offerings.

13.5 DIGITALIZATION IN GAINING CUSTOMER AND INDUSTRY INSIGHTS

How does a tourism business decide the best digital marketing strategy to adopt? What do the target customers expect from a specific product or brand? There are many questions that tourism industry members want to answer and develop strategies to fulfill the customer needs. Developing customer-oriented digital marketing strategies and surviving the competition have brought the need to learn more about customers and industry trends. Accordingly, conducting marketing research and collecting market data have become common practices among tourism industry members (Line et al., 2020). Moreover, digital marketing's ability to gain market insights has increased appetite of tourism industry for data-driven marketing. Big data analytics has become a sophisticated way of conducting marketing research. Big data helps to understand the target audience behaviors, their needs, and industry trends. Furthermore, big data allows tourism companies to find customer complaints and identify patrons who are unsatisfied with the service delivered (Cannon et al., 2024). Digital transformation in big data analytics has led to the collection of fast, smart, and various data. The tourism industry can organize the collected data from different sources and make sense of it with the technology incorporation. This data collection process helps them develop their own organizational database about the customers and the tourism industry.

Tourism organizations can learn more about their customers and the market in two ways. The first one is collecting their own data for a specific purpose or research question. A tourism brand has many sources of information such as the brand website, social media platforms, UGC in the online review websites (e.g., TripAdvisor), and mobile apps (Line et al., 2020). Some common digital tools for collecting customer data are online reservation forms, online customer surveys, customer reviews posted on brand websites or online review websites, loyalty program, and so on. A hotel can learn the main reason for low reservation numbers from leisure customers by reading customer reviews in an online travel agency where the hotel sells its guest rooms, or the number of reservations received from the own brand website. The second way is hiring a marketing research agency or research company as an expert in data collection and analysis. This way might be more costly, but it allows the tourism company to work with an expert that uses sophisticated data collection and analysis techniques. These agencies also have access to different and large number of customer segments. Distributing online questionnaires, conducting text analysis of customer reviews, and assessing ratings and testimonials for the effectiveness of a specific advertising campaign are some methods used by marketing research agencies.

BOX 13.1 Tourism marketers need to answer some questions before developing and launching a digital marketing campaign.

- What is our mission?
- What is our company size?
- What do we want to accomplish with this promotional campaign?
- What is our marketing mix? (product, price, place, and promotion)
- Who is our target audience?
- What is the best way to reach our target audience?
- What are the digital marketing strategies in the competition?
- What are our digital strengths/capabilities?
- What are our digital weaknesses/limitations?

13.6 OPPORTUNITIES AND CHALLENGES OF DIGITAL MARKETING IN TOURISM

Digitalization in marketing provides various benefits to the tourism industry. It allows access to new target markets, identify potential target markets, appeal to specific target markets, increase brand awareness, and enhance continuous communication with the customers. Furthermore, digital marketing is an efficient way to build and maintain long-term relationships with the customers. On the other hand, it has brought a lot of opportunities and challenges to the tourism industry.

13.6.1 OPPORTUNITIES FOR MARKETING RESEARCH IN TOURISM

- Reaching a broader audience
- Increased visibility
- Cost effective communication
- Enhanced customer engagement
- Improved analytics
- Tech savvy millennials and zillennials (Gen Z)

13.6.2 CHALLENGES OF DIGITAL MARKETING

- Legal and privacy issues in digital marketing
- Digital marketing requires continuous update
- Digital marketing is initially costly to install a system
- IMC: All promotional tools must be aligned with each other and carefully crafted
- Tech savviness level differs from one customer to another.
- Online reviews can make or break your business
- Working with a third party or managing your digital marketing by your own

13.7 DIGITAL MARKETING CAREERS IN TOURISM

The rise of digitalization in tourism has brought the need for qualified digital marketing professionals to survive the intense competition. The demand for these tech savvy and skilled professionals comes both from the tourism businesses and the customers. Tourism companies are willing to hire professionals who could develop, use, monitor, and improve digital marketing strategies. They are looking for digitally skilled individuals to improve the competitive advantage of their brand and maintain effective communication with their target market. Certificate programs with a digital marketing focus are developed to meet the needs of the tourism industry. Hospitality Sales and Marketing Association International (HSMAI) Academy offers "Certified Hospitality Digital Marketer" certification program for professionals who want to improve their digital marketing skills. The certification program includes owned media, earned media, paid, medial, digital intermediaries, trends in digital marketing, and measuring digital performance (HSMAI, 2024).

On the other side, tech savvy customers want to have two-way and fast communication with their favorite tourism service providers. Accordingly, these patrons demand a marketing specialist who could create relevant, innovative, and engaging content for making travel product-related purchase decisions. Today, customers tend to prefer purchasing the products of travel companies that have a solid digital presence. Specifically, a user-friendly brand website is an indispensable digital marketing tool to inform and engage customers as an all-in-one communication platform. As a result of all these factors, new careers have emerged in the tourism industry:

- Social media specialist
- Digital advertising agent
- Digital marketing specialist
- E-commerce manager
- Website builder
- Digital marketing content creator
- Influencer
- Influencer public relations agent
- SEO (search engine optimization) specialist
- Director of engagement
- Content manager
- Content strategist

13.8 CONCLUSION

In the competitive tourism industry, digital marketing is no longer a luxury but an essential strategy that paves the way to sustainable success. Tourism marketers must provide useful and relevant content to their existing and potential target audience. Experiential tourism products can only be communicated more effectively with smart digital marketing strategies to customers. Moreover, customers have access to multiple tourism brands and products in digital platforms and they are likely to switch to another brand's site if they do not find the platform interesting and relevant to their needs.

Undoubtedly, digitalization has improved the marketing efficiency of tourism businesses with the interactive, engaging, and fast communication aspects. Shortly, by utilizing digital marketing strategies, tourism organizations respond to the expectations of 21st-century customers who exhibit dynamic behaviors and represent different generations. Digital marketing helps tourism organizations transform their customers from passive receivers of marketing messages to active marketers and brand ambassadors.

Then, a question comes to mind about digital marketing future. Will digitalization in marketing replace human touch within the human-centric tourism industry? Not really. Some standardized tasks can be accomplished by automated digital marketing tools. However, there are situations where problem solving and coordination among different tourism businesses are needed. A visitor of Vienna, Austria can book a table at a Figlműller Restaurant to eat world-famous Wiener schnitzel on the restaurant's brand website. Imagine this visitor has not been to Vienna before or does not have an idea about signature Vienna tastes. In this case, this visitor can ask the concierge of the hotel they stay at for a restaurant recommendation in town. The concierge can filter the options based on the vicinity of the restaurant to the hotel, price, waiting time, and menu. Beyond doubt, the future of tourism marketing is digital. However, let us not forget that there are several tasks to be completed and marketing decisions to be made that can be made by humans. The marketing strategies need to be developed, the marketing messages must be designed, the platforms to communicate those messages need to be selected, and so on.

KEYWORDS

- **digital age**
- **digital marketing**
- **digital marketing careers**
- **the 3Es model**

REFERENCES

Angeloni, S., & Rossi, C. (2020). Online search engines and online travel agencies: A comparative approach. *Journal of Hospitality and Tourism Research, 45*(4), 720–749. https://doi.org/10.1177/1096348020913289.

Buhalis, D., & Foerste, M. (2015). SoCoMo marketing for travel and tourism: Empowering co-creation of value. *Journal of Destination Marketing and Management, 4*(3), 151–161. https://doi.org/10.1016/j.jdmm.2015.04.001.

Cannon, J. P., Perreault, W. D., & McCarthy, E. J. (2024). Chapter 13. Promotion-introduction to integrated marketing communications. In *Essential of Marketing: A Marketing Strategy Planning Approach* (18th ed.). McGraw-Hill.

Choose Chicago. (2024). Choose Chicago.com. https://www.choosechicago.com/.

Confetto, M. G., Conte, F., Palazzo, M., & Siano, A. (2023). Digital destination branding: A framework to define and assess European DMOs practices. *Journal of Destination Marketing and Management, 30*, 100804. https://doi.org/10.1016/j.jdmm.2023.100804.

Damnjanovic, V., Loncaric, D., & Dlacic, J. (2020). Digital marketing strategy of Accor Hotels: Shaping the future of hospitality. *Tourism and Hospitality Management, 26*(1), 233–244. https://doi.org/10.20867/thm.26.1.12.

De Palsmacker, P., van Tilburg, S., & Holthof, C. (2018). Digital marketing strategies, online reviews and hotel performance. *International Journal of Hospitality Management, 72*, 47–55. https://doi.org/10.1016/j.ijhm.2018.01.003.

Evans, N. G. (2016). Sustainable competitive advantage in tourism organizations: A strategic model applying service dominant logic and tourism's defining characteristics. *Tourism Management Perspectives, 18*, 14–25. https://doi.org/10.1016/j.tmp.2015.12.015.

Fan, A., Shin, H. W., Shi, J., & Wu, L. (2023). Young people share, but do so differently: An empirical comparison of peer-to-peer accommodation consumption between millennials and Generation Z. *Cornell Hospitality Quarterly, 64*(3), 322–337. https://doi.org/10.1177/19389655231171819.

Garrido-Moreno, A., Garcia-Morales, V. J., Lockett, N., & King, S. (2018). The missing link: Creating value with social media use in hotels. *International Journal of Hospitality Management, 75*, 94–104. https://doi.org/10.1016/j.ijhm.2018.03.009.

HSMAI Academy. (2024, March 23). Glossary Index. HSMAI. https://hsmaiacademy.org/glossary/paid-influencer/.

Hu, X. S., & Yang, Y. (2021). What makes online reviews helpful in tourism and hospitality? A bare-bones meta-analysis. *Journal of Hospitality Marketing and Management, 30*(2), 139–158. https://doi.org/10.1080/19368623.2020.1847175.

Jayawardena, C., Ahmad, A., Valeri, M., & Jahadarak, A. A. (2023). Technology acceptance antecedents in digital transformation in the hospitality industry. *International Journal of Hospitality Management, 108*, 103350. https://doi.org/10.1016/j.ijhm.2023.103350.

Ketter, E., & Avraham, E. (2021). #StayHome today so we can #TravelTomorrow: Tourism destinations' digital marketing strategies during the Covid-19 pandemic. *Journal of Travel and Tourism Marketing, 38*(8), 819–832. https://doi.org/10.1080/10548408.2021.1984976.

Kim, D. Y., & Park, S. (2020). Rethinking millennials: How are they shaping the tourism industry? *Asia Pacific Journal of Tourism Research, 25*(1), 1–2. https://doi.org/10.1080/10941665.2020.1709953.

Kim, H., Huh, C., Song, C., & Lee, M. J. (2021a). How can hotel smartphone apps enhance hotel guest experiences? An integrated model of experiential value. *Journal of Hospitality and Tourism Technology, 12*(4), 791–815. https://doi.org/10.1108/JHTT-08-2020-0197.

Kim, M., Lee, S. M., Choi, S., & Kim, S. Y. (2021b). Impact of visual information on online consumer review behavior: Evidence from a hotel booking website. *Journal of Retailing and Consumer Services, 60*, 102494. https://doi.org/10.1016/j.jretconser.2021.102494.

Kotler, P., Bowen, J. T., & Baloglu, S. (2021). *Marketing for hospitality and tourism* (8th ed.). Pearson Education.

Labanauskaite, D., Fiore, M., & Stasys, R. (2020). Use of E-marketing tools as communication management in the tourism industry. *Tourism Management Perspectives, 34*, 100652. https://doi.org/10.1016/j.tmp.2020.100652.

Law, R. (2019). Evaluation of hotel websites: Progress and future developments. *International Journal of Hospitality Management, 76*, 2–9. https://doi.org/10.1016/j.ijhm.2018.07.003.

Law, R., Chan, I. C. C., & Wang, L. (2018). A comprehensive review of mobile technology use in hospitality and tourism. *Journal of Hospitality Marketing and Management, 27*(6), 626–648. https://doi.org/10.1080/19368623.2018.1423251.

Lei, S. I., Ye, S., Wang, D., & Law, R. (2020). Engaging customers in value co-creation through mobile instant messaging in the tourism and hospitality industry. *Journal of Hospitality and Tourism Research, 44*(2), 229–251. https://doi.org/10.1177/1096348019895559.

Leung, D., & Tsou, M. (2019). The impact of incentive framing format and language congruency on readers' post-reading responses to email advertisements. *International Journal of Contemporary Hospitality Management, 31*(8), 3037–3057. https://doi.org/10.1108/IJCHM-09-2018-0744.

Line, N. D., Dogru, T., El-Manstrly, D., Buoye, A., & Malthouse, E. (2020). Control, use and ownership of big data: A reciprocal view of customer big data value in the hospitality and tourism industry. *Tourism Management, 80*, 104106. https://doi.org/10.1016/j.tourman.2020.104106.

LVCVA. (2024). Destination marketing. Las Vegas Convention and Visitor Authority. https://www.lvcva.com/destination-marketing/. (accessed April 12, 2024).

Okumus, B., & Bilgihan, A. (2014). Proposing a model to test smartphone users' intention to use smart applications when ordering food in restaurants. *Journal of Hospitality and Tourism Technology, 5*(1), 31–49. https://doi.org/10.1108/JHTT-12-2012-0034.

Porcu, L., del Barrio-Garcia, S., Alcantara-Pilar, J. M., & Crespo-Almendros, E. (2019). Analyzing the influence of firm-wide integrated marketing communication on market performance in the hospitality industry. *International Journal of Hospitality Management, 80*, 13–24. https://doi.org/10.1016/j.ijhm.2018.12.001.

Serra-Scallops, A., Cardona, J. R., & Salvi, F. (2020). Antecedents of positive WOM in hotels: Exploring the relative role of satisfaction, quality and positive emotional experiences. *International Journal of Contemporary Hospitality Management, 32*(11), 3457–3477. https://doi.org/10.1108/IJCHM-02-2020-0151.

Singh, S., Singh, G., & Dhir, S. (2024). Impact of digital marketing on the competitiveness of the restaurant industry. *Journal of Food service Business Research, 27*(2), 109–137. https://doi.org/10.1080/15378020.2023.2255774.

Talwar, S., Dhir, A., Kaur, P., & Maentymaeki, M. (2020). Why do people purchase from online travel agencies (OTAs)? A consumption values perspective. *International Journal of Hospitality Management, 87*, 102486. https://doi.org/10.1016/j.ijhm.2020.102486.

Taylor, P. (2023, July 19). Number of smartphone mobile network subscriptions worldwide from 2016 to 2022, with forecasts from 2023 to 2028. *Statista.com*. https://www.statista.com/statistics/330695/number-of-smartphone-users-worldwide/. (accessed April 6, 2024).

The Marmara Hotels. (2024, April 10). The Marmara Hotels. https://www.themarmarahotels.com/taksim.

TripAdvisor. (2024). Plan your trip: Las Vegas. https://www.tripadvisor.com/Tourism-g45963-Las_Vegas_Nevada-Vacations.html. (accessed April 12, 2024).

Turkish Airlines. (2024, April 10). Turkish Airlines. https://www.turkishairlines.com/.

Wang, Y. S., Tseng, T. H., Wang, W. T., Shih, Y. W., & Chan, P. Y. (2019). Developing and validating a mobile catering app success model. *International Journal of Hospitality Management, 77*, 19–30. https://doi.org/10.1016/j.ijhm.2018.06.013.

Wong, E., Leung, R., & Law, R. (2020). Significance of the dimensions and attributes of hotel mobile website from the perceptions of users. *International Journal of Hospitality and Tourism Administration, 21*(1), 15–37. https://doi.org/10.1080/15256480.2019.1598911.

Yin, J., Cheng, Y., Bi, Y., & Ni, Y. (2020). Tourists perceived crowding and destination attractiveness: The moderating effects of perceived risk and experience quality. *Journal of Destination Marketing and Management, 18*, 100489. https://doi.org/10.1016/j.jdmm.2020.100489.

CHAPTER 14

Customer-Centric Digitalization: The Key to Shaping the Future of Medical Tourism

MIRAY URKMEZER[1*] and HAKAN CENGIZ[2*]

[1]*Beykoz Vocational School of Logistics, Beykoz University, İstanbul, Türkiye*

[2]*Faculty of Business Administration, Karabuk University, Karabuk, Türkiye*

*Corresponding authors

ABSTRACT

Collection, storage, and analysis of patient data have brought massive changes to the healthcare industry. As data-driven business models have become increasingly prevalent in health care, they have intensified competition, pushing providers to adopt more customer-centric approaches. The landscape of such competition made the medical tourists more empowered, demanding, and choosy than ever. These limitless expectations of this new category of customers require proper management of the process of digitalization. This chapter discusses how digital transformation is taking shape in medical tourism, considering which trends are likely to dominate in the near future. While nobody clearly foresaw the pace and bounds of digitalization within this area, it is beyond doubt that a customer-centric approach using digital means will characterize the future. Therefore, any businesses operating in this field will find it relevant to configure their strategies with these two dynamics intermingled: digitalization and customer-centricity.

Digitalization in Tourism. Hulya Akdemir Cengiz, Seza Zerman, Aysegul Acar, and Faizan Ali (Eds.)

DOI: 10.1201/9781779644770-18

14.1 INTRODUCTION

Today, rapid changes in diet and lifestyle, prolonged hours at work, shrinking living spaces, and technological advancement together are profoundly changing the way we live our lives. Inevitably, therefore, people can now afford to travel more than ever before, and this gradually turns them into discerning consumers of cross-border healthcare services. Moreover, medical tourism is not only a search for health improvement but also an opportunity for people to ask for more personalized, safe, and accessible care using advanced technologies. Medical tourism has transformed from the simple need for physical well-being into an informed consumer behavior driven by pressures and challenges in contemporary life. All these dynamics underline the critical role of digitalization and the grave paradigm changes happening now in the realm of medical tourism.

Given the rapid pace of digital advancements in medical tourism, it's clear that academic insights and predictions in this field are becoming outdated almost as soon as they are made. What was once considered distant future possibilities are now materializing faster than anticipated. While previous studies and discussions remain valuable, the industry has evolved at an unprecedented rate. For example, the market value, estimated to reach a value of US$47 billion by 2024, is anticipated to increase two-fold in just four years. Such rapid growth, driven by evolving consumer trends and continuous technological development, suggests that real growth may significantly exceed these projections.

The rapid changes in technology and digitalization have reduced costs in medical tourism dramatically, shifting demand toward the providers of services at low prices. These, together with reduced transport and accommodation costs, increase access to medical tourism, hence making it a diversified industry. This is an industry allied with global technologies to bring into being a dynamic, growing economy, providing opportunities for new enterprises, practices of trade, management, and methods of marketing. This growth, in such record time, rooted itself first in advanced economies and then spread to the emerging markets, linking with their natural resources of health and manpower. What is more, with the accelerating digitalization and an overall decrease in the cost of those technologies, they became more accessible and easier to implement, which fuels further growth both individually and across the sector (Bookman and Bookman, 2007, p. 94).

As a result, medical tourism services have begun to reach a much wider audience. Initially considered a luxury, affordable only to the upper social classes, medical tourism later became accessible to the middle-income group (Gray and Poland, 2008; Woo and Schwartz, 2014). However, the recent transformation has blurred these distinctions, with cost-conscious lower-middle-income consumers increasingly seeking medical tourism services. This digitally driven shift is now influencing every aspect of life, making medical tourism a viable option for a broader range of people. The primary objective of this chapter is to examine the developments occurring in the rapidly transforming field of medical tourism. In doing so, it also aims to highlight the increasingly powerful position of medical tourists as consumers in the market.

14.2 A PARADIGM SHIFT IN THE INDUSTRY: TRANSITION TO CUSTOMER-CENTRICITY IN HEALTH AND MEDICAL TOURISM

The World Health Organization (WHO) defines health not just as the absence of disease or infirmity, but as a state of complete physical, mental, and social well-being (World Health Organization, 2006). People undertake various efforts to achieve and maintain their health, including the long-established practice of traveling in search of medical care. Health tourism and medical tourism are two prominent examples of such movements. Although these terms are sometimes used interchangeably, medical tourism differs from health tourism—in that it specifically involves medical interventions, whereas health tourism may not include such procedures (Adirasari, 2014). In this context, medical tourism can be considered a subset of health tourism (Budakkiran and Mercan, 2021). Connell (2006, p. 1094) describes medical tourism as the phenomenon where people travel long distances to foreign countries to receive medical, dental, and surgical care while also enjoying the experience as tourists. On the other hand, health tourism generally involves traveling to other countries in pursuit of wellness and well-being. While this chapter provides an overall assessment within the broader framework of health tourism, it focuses specifically on the concept of medical tourism.

14.2.1 REDEFINING PATIENT EXPERIENCE: FROM CARE RECIPIENTS TO EMPOWERED CONSUMERS

Traveling for medical care and wellness has been a longstanding practice (Connell, 2013). Today, health and medical tourism are rapidly becoming thriving industries, driven by the increasing number of patients seeking planned medical treatments abroad. People travel to access care not available locally or to spend less than they would in their home countries (Bookman and Bookman, 2007). While health has long been considered a consumer good (Hofer et al., 2012), individuals seeking healthcare services today are acting more like consumers than ever before. This demanding attitude has taken on a new dimension with the rise of health tourism. In recent years, healthcare providers have increasingly focused on meeting patient needs, making the healthcare industry more customer centric (Bhuiana, Menguc and Bell, 2003). Patients are no longer passive recipients of care but active consumers with specific needs and preferences. This shift has contributed to the growth of health and medical tourism and the emergence of new consumer groups. Today, these new consumers are referred to as medical consumers, and their behaviors are described as medical consumerism (Sulik and Eich-Krohm, 2008).

14.2.2 CONSUMER DYNAMICS AND REGIONAL VARIATIONS IN MEDICAL TOURISM

Medical tourism regions across the globe are typically categorized by the patient traffic originating from different continents (Tham, 2018). The main factors in seeking health care by medical tourists are time, cost, quality of service, and other after-treatment services. The health tourists who can afford to buy these services show varied demographic, behavioral, and characteristic differences in various aspects (Gan and Frederick, 2013; Guy et al., 2015).

The drivers of medical consumerism are not limited to the demographic and personal attributes of the consumers. The demand for such services is further influenced by the insurance and health status of the consumers (Fetscherin and Stephano, 2016). It is, therefore, significant to understand the diverse attitudes and consumptions of both users and non-users of health and medical tourism across different contexts. Hospitals are mainly non-profit institutions that strike a reasonable balance in responding to social concerns without the profit drive of the private sector or the bureaucracy of the public sector (Kotler, 1979). However, the growing need for hospital services and technological costs has elevated healthcare expenditures (Borg and Ljungbo, 2018). Among those patients who do not wish to incur these costs combine treatment with tourism. Further, such dynamics relating to the healthcare sector force people to seek treatment in foreign countries. Nowadays many people travel to foreign countries as they are unhappy with the healthcare systems of their respective countries. Some people seek to travel for minor operations, and some travel for more complex operations (Noree et al., 2014). This mobility has been an important contributor to medical tourism and in turn, has encouraged organizations in this field to enrich their services with customer-centric solutions.

14.3 DIGITALIZATION IN MEDICAL TOURISM: BRIDGING THE GAP BETWEEN EXPECTATION AND DELIVERY

Digital technologies continue to bear greater importance in health and medical tourism, as they have totally revolutionized the way healthcare access and delivery have been conducted across borders. Among the most striking developments is perhaps the increasing integration of new technological tools that are capable of tracking and storing, in real-time, a variety of health indicators (Baran and Karaca, 2023). This has led to two important deliverables: better health awareness by the consumer and easier access to health information by health professionals. For this reason, digital access to health records has cut down on diagnosis and treatment times, especially for foreign patients. With these guarantees of speed, convenience, and efficiency, consumers are more ready than ever to share their personal health information with healthcare providers. In turn, this ensures a much quicker and smoother medical tourism experience. The digitization of medical tourism has also pushed changes to consumer behavior, especially in the way they adapt to technology use. One example is moving away from the traditional way of paying to mobile payments for healthcare services. Digital tools, in this respect, enhance convenience and prepare patients more for healthcare services (Hsieh, 2021).

This increased digital readiness helps bridge the gap between patient expectations and the quality of care they receive, thus improving the overall customer journey in medical tourism. Moreover, digitalization offers unique opportunities for accessing global markets, enabling even small and medium-sized enterprises to compete internationally and discover new growth avenues. The future success of businesses in this sector will depend on their ability to integrate smart health technologies—such as mobile health, telehealth, blockchain, cloud technology, the Internet of Medical Things (IoMT), virtual reality (VR), and artificial intelligence (AI)—into their operations (Dar and Kashyap, 2023). Those who can adapt quickly to these digital trends will be the ones driving the future of medical tourism.

In orthopedics, for example, digital advancements have created new opportunities and provided more efficient, accurate, and objective methods for understanding diseases and planning surgical procedures (Chen et al., 2012). Initially, it was predicted that the rise of the Internet would fuel the growth of medical tourism (Connell, 2006), and later, the use of advanced technologies would enhance the quality of medical services (Sanderson and Kirwan, 2009). Today, these predictions have been far exceeded, particularly with the advancements in AI and machine learning (ML). The digital transformation in medical tourism has significantly contributed to the development of consumer-centric services, making the healthcare experience more personalized and accessible than ever before.

14.3.1 DIGITAL HEALTH SERVICES IN CONSUMER-CENTRIC MEDICAL TOURISM

The rapid advancement of technology in healthcare is changing how medical services are delivered, especially in medical tourism. One of the earliest examples of digital transformation in healthcare is Professor Taylor's development of the ROBODOC system in the United States. This robotic system, first used in total hip arthroplasty in 1992, allowed surgeons to receive real-time feedback through clinical visualization, marking the beginning of a journey that has led to the use of robots in surgeries, 3D printing for orthopedic models, and even organ and limb transplants (Paul et al., 1992; Starosolski et al., 2014). Just as it's impossible to assess the evolution of medical services without considering digitalization and technological advances, today's customer-centric approach has become inseparable from digital transformation. Digitalization has proven to be a significant force in enhancing the efficiency and reach of healthcare services, including medical tourism. The increased accessibility of e-health facilities and services is a boon for medical tourists, providing them with a seamless experience from diagnosis to treatment.

Smart health systems, like mobile health, telehealth, and blockchain technology are becoming integral to the global expansion of medical services, offering new market opportunities and promoting international growth (Dar and Kashyap, 2023).

The development of digital health platforms and the establishment of electronic health records (EHRs) marked the first significant step in the rapid growth of medical tourism. This was followed by the advancement of various e-health solutions and the enhancement of personalized customer experiences within the industry. The future of customer-centricity in medical tourism will be shaped by elevating these interconnected relationships to the next level through AI and ML. The recent developments in consumer-centric digital health services in medical tourism and future projections are illustrated in Figure 14.1.

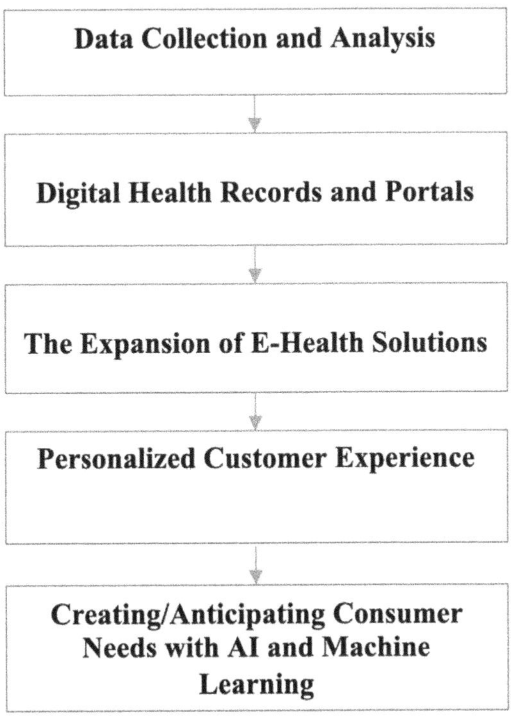

FIGURE 14.1 Core components of customer-centric digitalization process in medical tourism.

Source: Authors' own work.

14.3.1.1 DATA COLLECTION AND ANALYSIS

Data forms the foundation of contemporary digital healthcare services. Beyond just the health data reflecting patients' medical conditions, demographics, characteristics, and behavioral information also provide significant advantages to healthcare providers in developing strategic approaches. Businesses can anticipate customer/patient behavior and deliver higher-quality services through this data. However, achieving this requires high-quality and actionable data. Today, organizations that can obtain valid and reliable data and transform it into actionable and processable information are shaping the future of medical tourism.

While digitalization has made data access easier, it has also led to the accumulation of vast datasets. Thus, the challenge is not merely acquiring data but strategically analyzing it to serve specific objectives. In other words, converting big data into actionable insights is crucial in medical tourism. Big data in medical tourism is typically derived from patient records, travel histories, and customer feedback. In most cases, this is unstructured or semi-structured data. Only after cleaning, structuring, and analyzing this data will it be possible. The scientific filtering of big data and the processing through AI and ML will be discussed in the following sections, where it is important to outline that this processing of data stands at the core upon which the subsequent insights are based. This process dramatically impacts the course and quality of various phases, including diagnosis, treatment, planning of travels, and personalization in digital health services of medical tourism.

14.3.1.2 THE ROLE OF DIGITAL HEALTH RECORDS AND PORTALS

The role of digitalization in recording and availing information when required has thus become highly significant. An EHR is a digitally stored systematic collection of health information in electronic form for patients and populations. EHRs would contain the list of a patient's demographic profile, medical history, medication, allergies, immunizations, laboratory and radiology test results, vital signs, personal statistics, such as height and weight, and billing information.

Medical tourism destinations that aim to attract international patients tend to focus on meeting the growing needs of these patients. These destinations are positioned as places where patients receive high-quality care and have access to interpreters and all necessary support services. This positioning is often achieved through the branding of the destination (Borg and Ljungbo, 2018). Besides these touristic factors that create enabling environments for branding a destination, technological dynamics also play a major role. Digital health records have contributed in various ways to transforming a number of tourist destinations worldwide into medical tourism hubs. This is because such records can correlate various health-related data with the demographic and characteristic features for beneficial health outcomes.

The digital health record created in the process has become an intrinsic part of this transformation by offering a host of conveniences to the consumer. These records shall not only be available to the patients but also to the various stakeholders, like academic institutions, regulatory bodies, policy framers, and clinical researchers. EHRs will form the backbone for consumer-centric healthcare in diagnostics, treatment, follow-up, and overall patient satisfaction (Cowie et al., 2017). E-health portals and virtual care coordination make medical tourism much easier; thus, they offer access to health and efficiency for the patients. With the increased adoption of EHRs, the transmission of patient information across borders for continuity of care can become easier. Multilingual hospital websites and virtual care platforms enhance the engagement of patients through information provided in the patient's mother tongue and remote coordination of care. Digital tools ease the logistics of medical travel—from consultations before arrival to follow-up after treatment—causing less stress for the patients in the process (Borg and Ljungbo, 2018). By integrating these technologies, health service providers increase the level of patient satisfaction and expand their services on the global front to meet the various needs of international patients.

14.3.1.3 THE EXPANSION OF E-HEALTH SOLUTIONS

E-health solutions have rapidly expanded in recent years, driven by the increasing demand for accessible, consumer-centric healthcare services. The integration of EHRs has been pivotal in this expansion, providing a digital foundation for storing and sharing patient information securely across different healthcare systems. This has been particularly beneficial in medical tourism, where seamlessly transferring health records between countries can significantly improve the quality and continuity of care (Cowie et al., 2017).

E-health solutions, such as telemedicine, mobile health applications, wearable devices, and VR offer unique conveniences to medical tourists. For instance, these technologies allow patients to plan both their tourist activities and medical treatments without needing to relocate physically. This not only provides them with a sense of psychological well-being but also makes them more likely to choose destinations that offer these services professionally. This can be seen as another advantage of customer-centric approaches. In the past, institutions that stood out due to their medical equipment now find success only if they invest in patient communication and a patient-centered perspective.

While all age groups require health medical services, yet the increasing rate of adoption in these e-health solutions by the aging populations is observed to be quite remarkable. With more numbers of old people are getting associated with medical tourism, their requirement for digital supporting tools for independent living and quality life has been felt more than ever (Kampmeijer et al., 2016). Digital solutions allow elderly individuals to remain independent in their homes longer, improving their quality of life while reducing the burden on caregivers (Watson et al., 2021). E-health solutions, such as telehealth platforms and mobile health applications, empower patients to manage their health actively. By doing so, these technologies improve patient outcomes and reduce the burden on healthcare systems by promoting preventive care and early intervention. As digital health technologies continue to evolve, their role in enhancing consumer-centric medical tourism is set to expand, making health care more efficient, accessible, and personalized.

14.3.1.3.1 Remote Diagnosis and Treatment

Previous sections have discussed the critical role digital health records and platforms play in the digitalization process. In addition, it is critical to highlight the role of wearable devices in this digital transformation. Today, many health metrics are tracked by individuals via wearable devices.

Yet, some users are unwilling to share these data with healthcare providers, while others are having difficulties accepting these technological innovations. The advancement and widespread adoption of such technologies could facilitate their integration with existing health records. This integration would enable the easier sharing of a broader range of health indicators with medical service providers, thereby enhancing the variety and quality of customer-centric solutions.

The integration of digital tools into health care extends to remote diagnosis and treatment, and this is becoming increasingly significant in consumer-centric healthcare. As patients seek out medical care across borders, the ability to diagnose and initiate treatment remotely has become increasingly important. Technologies such as telehealth, mobile health, and remote monitoring systems allow healthcare providers to assess patients' conditions before they even step foot in a foreign hospital. This not only enhances the efficiency of the healthcare process but also ensures that patients receive timely and accurate care tailored to their specific needs (Neufeld et al., 2023). For example, patients can regularly complete digital surveys and record symptoms, leading to earlier detection of health issues and timely professional intervention (Potluka et al., 2023).

The adoption of 5G technology has further revolutionized this by making real-time communication and data sharing between the patient and the health professional possible, even across different parts of the world. For example, with the help of advanced imaging and communication tools, robotic surgeries can be performed. This opened up possibilities for much safer and more precise medical procedures (Zhang et al., 2018). The shift toward health e-solutions allows not only access to health care but also places patients at the very center of health care, full of confidence that, indeed, their health is managed and monitored to the letter, regardless of any geographical barriers.

14.3.1.4 PERSONALIZED CUSTOMER EXPERIENCE

Personalization within medical tourism is turning out to be an important foundation in the improvement of patient satisfaction and treatment outcomes. There is an increasing inclination toward receiving personalized approaches to healthcare service provision due to the diverse needs and expectations which different medical tourists seek across borders.

This, therefore, calls for personalization that addresses individual patients based on their preferences and health condition, while considering cultural nuances and giving care that relates to an individual's own journey. With the latest technologies, like AI, big data, and ML at disposal, it now lies within the capability of healthcare providers to deliver personalized treatment programs, after-treatment support, and even travel support based on the real preferences of a patient.

Moreover, in a world where data flows instantly and continuously, the ability to analyze large datasets helps medical tourism providers gain deeper insights into patient behaviors and preferences. These insights allow providers to offer personalized services, from selecting the best hospitals and doctors to tailoring recovery and wellness experiences. Personalization enhances the patient's overall experience and builds trust and loyalty, positioning destinations that invest in these technologies as leaders in the competitive medical tourism industry. In this regard, destinations that have kept up with this type of transformation are called smart tourism destinations in the literature (Buhalis and Amaranggana, 2015). Personalization is a crucial aspect of the customer experience and is referred to as person-centered practice in health care (Sanderson and Lewis, 2012). Believing that future trends in medical tourism will be shaped by personalization, we have focused our approach primarily on AI and ML.

14.3.1.5 FUTURE DIRECTIONS AND TRENDS IN MEDICAL TOURISM

As digital health technologies continue to evolve, their role in medical tourism will only become more pronounced. Hospitals and healthcare providers are developing advanced websites and mobile applications to interact more effectively with current and potential patients, offering real-time updates and facilitating remote consultations. These advancements enhance patient satisfaction and enable businesses to operate more efficiently, making medical tourism more accessible and affordable for a global audience (Borg and Ljungbo, 2018; Budakkiran and Mercan, 2021). By embracing these digital transformations, medical tourism providers can ensure they meet the growing demand for consumer-centric healthcare, ultimately leading to better patient outcomes and a stronger global presence in the medical tourism industry. The previous section addressed why digitalization is one of the critical factors that will drive the future of medical tourism. However, it did not explore how and in what ways personalization will be achieved in the future. At this point, we focus on the crucial role that AI, autonomous systems, and ML will play in shaping the future of personalization as described in the following section.

14.3.1.5.1 Artificial Intelligence, Autonomous Systems, and Machine Learning

The rapid rise of the Internet, with its advantages of fast dissemination, widespread access, strong interactivity, low cost, and freedom from time and place constraints, has opened new opportunities for the dissemination and use of health information. Today, both the provision and acquisition of health information are inextricably linked to the Internet (Yuan et al., 2024). The swift advancement of mobile technologies has provided healthcare institutions with significant opportunities to create new payment solutions and offer value-added services to their customers (Hsieh, 2021). The new digital techniques, easily accessible around the clock, now encourage users to manage their health processes at the most convenient time and place for them (Barbosa et al., 2021).

One of the most important features that stand out for patients in medical tourism is the provision of a well-prepared, personalized treatment plan before their visit. This requires an effective communication process. In treatment planning, communication and planning errors caused by humans are significant factors. To minimize human errors, virtual assistants known as chatbots are used, allowing individuals to input their data online (Yener and Kose, 2023). Chatbots can be considered the simplest form of autonomous systems widely used in consumer-centric medical tourism. These technologies provide responses from company personnel through text or voice dialogues with customers (Amato et al., 2017, p. 3). By using this technology effectively, healthcare institutions can make decisions about accurate diagnosis and treatment before the patient even begins their journey, which significantly impacts the patient's satisfaction with the service provided (Yavuz, 2018). It is inevitable that in the future, many new technologies like this one will continue to develop, creating new opportunities for both patients and businesses.

ML, a subfield of computer science and an offshoot of AI, is a multidisciplinary domain that combines statistical and computer science algorithms commonly used for predictive analysis and classification tasks. In recent years, the field of AI has evolved into a broad and exciting area within computer science, focusing on preparing machines to perform tasks that typically require human intelligence (Singh, Kumar and Nagar, 2019). ML and AI have made significant advancements, leading to the emergence of AI-generated content as a prominent phenomenon (Tuomi, 2023). ML and data mining algorithms are utilized in various sectors, including computer networks, the travel and tourism industry, financial forecasting, telecommunications, and electricity load prediction (Xiuyi and Yuxia, 2018). As AI continues to improve and reshape traditional business and management practices, it is crucial for researchers to understand how these changes are being addressed, what topics are being explored, and what key research outcomes are emerging. A deeper understanding of the opportunities and challenges presented by AI will enable organizations and policymakers to make more informed decisions (Ahani et al., 2021).

The increasing demand and economic factors have made innovation indispensable in the rapidly evolving medical tourism sector. Numerous companies have invested in AI and ML and announced that they will continue to engage in such activities in the future. This area has become so influential that even the largest technology firms are now investing in it. Companies such as Apple, Samsung, Google, Amazon, Philips, Nike, and Meta are among the first that come to mind when thinking of those investing in this sector. There are many reasons for their involvement, including economic gains, societal benefits, the desire to be industry leaders, and the need to keep pace with rapidly advancing technological developments. The rise of AI technologies has created new opportunities for many businesses connected to health care, particularly those serving international markets, offering them the chance to establish a presence in this emerging field.

Digital health records have contributed to the creation of large datasets, or "big data." When combined with big data, AI has the potential to surpass human decision-making processes and capabilities across industries (Liu and Zeng, 2021). In medical tourism, AI and ML are undoubtedly at the forefront of advancements that exceed previous expectations. When it comes to consumer-centric digitalization, AI and ML offer the ability to anticipate consumer behavior even before they are aware of it. Today, these technologies are used not only in diagnostic and treatment processes in medical tourism but also in enhancing the tourist experience. These experiences range from offering personalized recommendations during travel and treatment planning to providing predictive insights about patients' health and nutrition statuses. Many healthcare organizations are now collaborating with different technology and software brands in this area.

Google Health AI is one of the most prominent examples of such initiatives. Google Health aims to help everyone stay healthier everywhere by developing products and services that connect and make sense of health information, empowering people with the knowledge they need to take action regarding their health. This technological solution is designed to make it easier for the healthcare sector to deliver more coordinated care. Google Health has announced that it is exploring the use of AI to help with cancer diagnosis, prevent blindness, and much more. As this research advances, expected developments, include AI-powered imaging and diagnostics, the realization of tasks previously thought impossible, improved access to and understanding of skin disease information, and initiatives to help prevent blindness (GoogleHealth.com, 2024). One of the applications in the field of AI-supported patient services and counseling is Google Fit, an app developed to determine how much or what type of activity is needed for health, based on the importance of being active. Google has also collaborated with the WHO to develop "Heart Points," an activity goal proven to impact health, based on WHO's global recommendations (GooglePlay.com, 2024).

These initiatives aim to be accessible and beneficial to all individuals with health concerns, particularly those who have access to technology and are at a certain economic and educational level. One such initiative is Visualise. Founded in 2012 by Henry Stuart, Visualise is a London-based VR and AR (augmented reality) agency with partners and clients worldwide. The company describes its services as creating immersive content, offering a broad range of solutions from VR, AR, and MR production to 360° video, live streaming, post-production, binaural audio, and immersive applications. They also have technological partnerships, such as with "Meta Camera," which produces high-end 360 video cameras and other immersive technology hardware and software. Visualise believes that immersive technologies are key to transforming the healthcare sector and that it is essential for health care and technology professionals to use these tools for clinical examinations and teaching purposes (Visualise.com, 2024).

As human lifespans increase, there is potential to delay or even reduce the incidence of metabolic diseases, yet there remain areas where no effective treatment exists, and even the smallest advancements are crucial. One such area is the frequent occurrence of memory loss and dementia in our time. AI programs, which are being utilized across various fields, are also applied in scientific research. One of these research areas is Alzheimer's and dementia. Scientists are using AI to combine and delve into multiomic datasets. AI helps researchers uncover disease mechanisms and drug targets, identify hidden features among thousands of MRI scans, and understand what shapes amyloids in fibril twists. AI is also proving useful in biomarker discovery and in detecting early signs of dementia in speech, even before individuals notice anything is amiss (Alzforum.org, 2024).

14.4 CONCLUSION

The foundation of the digital transformation in health and medical tourism lies in the systematic recording of patient data. This pivotal shift has not only streamlined the collection and storage of vast amounts of health-related information but has also paved the way for more advanced data analysis. By analyzing these datasets, healthcare providers can gain a nuanced understanding of patient needs and preferences, allowing them to tailor their services more effectively. Institutions that harness digital technologies and excel in data management are now at the forefront of medical tourism, offering competitive, customer-centric digital solutions that enhance every aspect of the patient journey, from treatment planning to post-care follow-up.

The digitalization of the patient journey itself has become a central theme in modern medical tourism. What initially focused on digital tools to make simplifications of certain treatment and planning processes has now transformed into a holistic approach wherein the entire patient experience is digitized. This chapter highlights two aspects of such evolution: the shifting of medical tourism to a more consumer-oriented approach and the greater use of digital technologies that enable such a transformation. These two dynamics are intertwined, but both are significant for the sustained growth of the sector. To try and control them individually could result in a number of major issues that would disrupt the seamless experience which modern medical tourists have become accustomed to.

The rapid development of medical tourism has exceeded the expectations of practitioners, decision-makers, and researchers alike. The pace of change is so swift that predicting future trends in this field is increasingly difficult. However, one thing is clear—the competition within this sector will be fierce, and those who can deliver customer-centric digital solutions will lead the way. The role of AI and ML in shaping these solutions cannot be overstated. These technologies will drive the personalization of services, enabling healthcare providers to anticipate patient needs with unprecedented accuracy. At the core of this capability is the ability to collect, process, and analyze vast amounts of data—a skill that will define the future leaders in medical tourism.

As this chapter discussed, any prediction of the future for medical tourism has to take into account an understanding that digitalization cannot be separated from consumer-centric approach as well as data security and patient privacy. Such factors will be interlinked and play a determining role in further digital transformation within the sector. While this chapter tried to provide an overall picture of the current state and future directions of medical tourism, it has to be stated that this research could not consider specific issues of digitalization, in particular, with regard to data security and privacy. Notwithstanding that, tackling this challenge constitutes a firm starting point for assuring those benefits from digital transformation. These are, therefore, the recommendations that should be made: mitigation of risks and increasing overall security concerning patient data in the modern, digital world.

KEYWORDS

- **artificial intelligence**
- **big data**
- **customer-centricity**
- **digital transformation**
- **electronic health records**
- **medical tourism**
- **machine learning**

REFERENCES

Adirasari V. (2014). *Analysis implementasi medical tourism: Studi Kasus di Wing Amerta Rumah Sakit Umum Pusat Sanglah Denpasar Bali*. Universitas Indonesia.

Ahani, A., Nilashi, M., Zogaan, W. A., Samad, S., Aljehane, N. O., Alhargan, A., ... & Sanzogni, L. (2021). Evaluating medical travelers' satisfaction through online review analysis. *Journal of Hospitality and Tourism Management*, *48*, 519–537.

Alzforum.org. (2024). Artificial intelligence everywhere you look: Dementia research. *Alzheimer's forum*. Retrieved August 15, 2024, from https://www.alzforum.org/news/research-news/artificial-intelligence-everywhere-you-look-dementia-research

Amato, F., Marrone, S., Moscato, V., Piantadosi, G., Picariello, A., & Sansone, C. (2017, November). Chatbots meet eHealth: Automatizing healthcare. In *WAIAH@ AI* IA* (pp. 40–49).

Baran, Z., & Karaca, Ş. (2023). Next-Generation technologies in health tourism. In *Global perspectives on the opportunities and future directions of health tourism* (pp. 138–164). IGI Global.

Barbosa, S. D. F. F., Abbott, P., & Dal Sasso, G. T. M. (2021). Nursing in the digital health era. *Journal of Nursing Scholarship*, *53*(1), 5–6. https://doi.org/10.1111/jnu.12620

Bhuiana, S. N., Menguc, B., Bell, S. J. (2003). Just entrepreneurial enough: The moderating effect of entrepreneurship on the relationship between market orientation and performance. *Journal of Business Research*, *58*(2005) 9–17.

Bookman, M. Z., & Bookman, K. R. (2007). Introduction to medical tourism. In M*edical tourism in developing countries* (pp. 1–19). Palgrave Macmillan US.

Borg, E. A., & Ljungbo, K. (2018). International market-oriented strategies for medical tourism destinations. *International Journal of Market Research*, *60*(6), 621–634.

Budakkiran, M., & Mercan, Ş. O. (2021). The evaluation of health tourism in the context of digitalization and digital marketing. *Tourism Studies and Social Sciences*, *327*.

Buhalis, D., & Amaranggana, A. (2015). Smart tourism destinations enhancing tourism experience through personalisation of services. In *Information and Communication Technologies in Tourism 2015: Proceedings of the International Conference in Lugano*, Switzerland, February 3–6 (pp. 377–389). Springer International Publishing.

Chen, Y. X., Zhang, K., Hao, Y. N., & Hu, Y. C. (2012). Research status and application prospects of digital technology in orthopaedics. *Orthopaedic Surgery*, *4*(3), 131–138.

Connell, J. (2006). Medical tourism: Sea, sun, sand and… surgery. *Tourism Management*, *27*(6), 1093–1100.

Connell, J. (2013). Contemporary medical tourism: Conceptualisation, culture and commodification. *Tourism Management*, *34*, 1–13.

Cowie, M. R., Blomster, J. I., Curtis, L. H., Duclaux, S., Ford, I., Fritz, F., ... & Zalewski, A. (2017). Electronic health records to facilitate clinical research. *Clinical Research in Cardiology*, *106*, 1–9.

Dar, H., & Kashyap, K. (2023). Smart healthcare system (SHS): Medical tourism delivering, consumption, and elevating tool in the ages of smart technologies. *Tourism Planning & Development*, *20*(3), 397–415.

Fetscherin, M., & Stephano, R. M. (2016). The medical tourism index: Scale development and validation. *Tourism Management*, 52, 539–556.

Gan, L. L., & Frederick, J. R. (2013). Medical tourists: who goes and what motivates them? *Health Marketing Quarterly*, *30*(2), 177–194.
GoogleHealth.com. (2024). Imaging and diagnostics. *Google Health Research*. Retrieved August 15, 2024, from https://health.google/health-research/imaging-and-diagnostics/
GooglePlay.com. (2024). Google Fit: Activity tracker. *Google Play Store*. Retrieved August 15, 2024, from https://play.google.com/store/apps/details?id=com.google.android.apps.fitness&hl=tr&pli=1
Gray, H. H., & Poland, S. C. (2008). Medical tourism: crossing borders to access health care. *Kennedy Institute of Ethics Journal*, *18*(2), 193–201.
Guy, B. S., Henson, J. L. N., & Dotson, M. J. (2015). Characteristics of consumers likely and unlikely to participate in medical tourism. *International Journal of Healthcare Management*, *8*(2), 68–76.
Hofer, S., Honegger, F., & Hubeli, J. (2012). Health tourism: Definition focused on the Swiss market and conceptualisation of health(i)ness. *Journal of Health Organization and Management*, *26*(1), 60–80.
Hsieh, P. J. (2021). Understanding medical consumers' intentions to switch from cash payment to medical mobile payment: A perspective of technology migration. *Technological Forecasting and Social Change*, *173*, 121074.
Kampmeijer, R., Pavlova, M., Tambor, M., Golinowska, S., & Groot, W. (2016). The use of e-health and m-health tools in health promotion and primary prevention among older adults: A systematic literature review. *BMC Health Services Research*, *16*, 467–479.
Kotler, P. (1979). Strategies for introducing marketing into nonprofit organizations. *Journal of Marketing*, *43*(1), 37–44.
Liu, Z., & Zeng, X. (2021). Hybrid intelligence in big data environment: concepts, architectures, andapplications of intelligent service. *Data and Information Management*, *5*(2), 262–276.
Neufeld, A., Babenko, O., & Bhella, V. (2023). Family physician motivation and well-being in the digital era. *The Annals of Family Medicine*, *21*(6), 496–501.
Noree, T., Hanefeld, J., & Smith, R. (2014). UK medical tourists in Thailand: They are not who you think they are. *Globalization and Health*, *10*, 1–7.
Paul, H. A., Bargar, W. L., Mittlestadt, B., Musits, B., Taylor, R. H., Kazanzides, P., ... & Hanson, W. (1992). Development of a surgical robot for cementless total hip arthroplasty. *Clinical Orthopaedics and Related Research®*, *285*, 57–66.
Potluka, O., Švecová, L., Kubát, V., Liskova-Nedbalova, V., Nečas, T., Lhotská, L., & Hejdová, K. (2023). Evaluation of eHealth assistance in-hospital care for improved quality of life in patients. *Evaluation and Program Planning*, *97*, 102261.
Sanderson, H., & Lewis, J. (2012). *A practical guide to delivering personalisation: Person-centred practice in health and social care*. Jessica Kingsley Publishers.
Sanderson, T., & Kirwan, J. (2009). Patient-reported outcomes for arthritis: Time to focus on personal life impact measures? *Arthritis Care & Research*, *61*(1), 1–3.
Singh, M. A., Yadav, K. P., Kumar, S., & Nagar, H. (2019). *Performance comparison of machine learning algorithms for crop seed detection*. An Efficiency Analysis.
Starosolski, Z. A., Kan, J. H., Rosenfeld, S. D., Krishnamurthy, R., & Annapragada, A. (2014). Application of 3-D printing (rapid prototyping) for creating physical models of pediatric orthopedic disorders. *Pediatric Radiology*, *44*, 216–221.

Sulik, G. A., & Eich-Krohm, A. (2008). No longer a patient: The social construction of the medical consumer. In *Patients, consumers and civil society* (Vol. 10, pp. 3–28). Emerald Group Publishing Limited.

Tham, A. (2018). Sand, surgery and stakeholders: A multi-stakeholder involvement model of domestic medical tourism for Australia's Sunshine Coast. *Tourism Management Perspectives*, *25*, 29–40.

Tuomi, A. (2023, January). AI-generated content, creative freelance work and hospitality and tourism marketing. In *ENTER22 e-Tourism Conference* (pp. 323–328). Cham: Springer Nature Switzerland.

Visualise.com. (2024). Virtual reality healthcare. *Visualise*. Retrieved August 15, 2024, from https://visualise.com/virtual-reality/virtual-reality-healthcare

Watson, P., Bearpark, T., & Ling, J. (2021). The impact of rapid response and telecare services on elderly and vulnerable residents. *Health & Social Care in the Community*, *29*(4), 897–904.

Woo, E., & Schwartz, Z. (2014). Towards assessing the knowledge gap in medical tourism. *Journal of Quality Assurance in Hospitality & Tourism*, *15*(2), 213–226.

World Health Organization. (2006). A state of complete physical mental and social well-being and not merely the absence of disease or infirmity. *Constitution of the World Health Organization Basic Documents*, *45*, 1–20.

Xiuyi T, Yuxia G (2018) Research on application of machine learning in data mining. In *IOP Conference Series, Materials Science and Engineering* (vol. 392, p. 5). *Intelligent Manufacturing and Information Technology*.

Yavuz, M. C. (2018). *Türkiye'de sağlık turizmi hizmetleri algısının hasta ve müşteri memnuniyeti üzerine etkisi: İç Anadolu bölgesi örneği* (Master's thesis, İstanbul Gelişim Üniversitesi Sosyal Bilimler Enstitüsü).

Yener, S., & Köse, İ. (2023). Treatment prediction using artificial intelligence-integrated chatbots in call centers in medical tourism. *Turkish Studies-Economics, Finance, Politics*, *18*(2).

Yuan, C., Wei, X., Wu, X., Liu, H., & Jiang, Z. (2024). Correlation between habits of using online health information and e-health literacy in middle-aged and older Chinese adults. *Chinese General Practice Journal*, *1*(1), 42–47.

Zhang, Q., Liu, J., & Zhao, G. (2018). Towards 5G enabled tactile robotic telesurgery. *arXiv preprint* arXiv:1803.03586.

CHAPTER 15

Crisis Management in the Digital Age

GULSEL CIFTCI

Associate Professor, Faculty of Applied Sciences, Trakya University, Edirne, Türkiye

ABSTRACT

The ability of the tourism sector to keep up with the development of technology has brought with it many advantages that positively affect businesses; however, there are also challenges that come with it. It is possible to express the advantages of increasing efficiency and improved customer relationship management and expanding market. At the same time, other advantages can be expressed as making accurate predictions thanks to data analytics technology; advanced networking capabilities and being able to manage costs effectively, as well as advances in service delivery and environmental sustainability practices. Considering the vulnerability of the tourism sector to various crisis situations, it becomes imperative to adopt an adaptable approach to using digital tools to quickly disseminate real-time information that reaches stakeholders effectively and to manage reputation efficiently. This chapter emphasizes the importance of digital techniques, as well as social media usage and online evaluations, in effectively managing crises for destinations and businesses in today's digital environment. It discusses the necessity of having crisis management strategies while emphasizing the integration of technology and the commitment to continuous learning in order to adapt while coping with unexpected obstacles. In addition, this chapter discusses the basic elements of crisis management that tourism businesses should take into account in order to protect themselves from adverse conditions and ensure their sustainable

Digitalization in Tourism. Hulya Akdemir Cengiz, Seza Zerman, Aysegul Acar, and Faizan Ali (Eds.)

DOI: 10.1201/9781779644770-19

prosperity. It examines why this importance is sought and the advantages of crisis management for such companies in detail, in order to help readers, and to understand why crisis management is so important in the tourism sector in today's digital age.

15.1 INTRODUCTION

In recent years, digitalization has been a major development in crisis communication and crisis management (Schwarz et al., 2016). The rapid increase in social media and similar digital platforms has made crisis communication and management more challenging. The rapid spread of information shared by users on digital platforms can positively and/or negatively affect the effects of the crisis (Cetin Gurkan and Ciftci, 2020). Therefore, it is of utmost importance to communicate with stakeholders at the right time and in the right way for accurate and effective crisis communication. Social media platforms, chatbots, and other digital tools enable businesses to manage crises faster and more effectively (Agarwal et al., 2022). Instant information sharing on digital platforms brings with it inherent risks, such as sharing incorrect or incomplete information during a crisis, inaccurate reporting, and cyber-attacks. Therefore, it is very important for businesses to have a well-planned crisis management and communication plan considering these effects (Ciftci et al., 2017).

It is crucial for tourism businesses to have a good crisis management plan in this rapidly evolving digitalization process (Rogers, 2016). This chapter explores the importance of crisis management for tourism businesses in the context of digitalization. It aims to comprehensively examine the positive and negative effects of proper and effective crisis management on tourism businesses in a rapidly digitalizing world. The ability of tourism businesses to anticipate the dangers of crises and manage these crises in the most effective and fastest way can reduce the negative effects of crises (Ritchie, 2004). Proactive crisis management strategies play a crucial role in enabling tourism businesses to respond quickly to crises, communicate effectively with stakeholders, and ensure business continuity. Identifying proactive strategies is crucial to mitigate the negative impacts of crises on tourism businesses and the tourism industry (Gkoumas, 2022). In the rapid digitalization process brought on by COVID-19, it is extremely important for businesses to be prepared for possible crises (Lee and Trimi, 2021).

The communication strategies employed by Caribbean medical tourism businesses are the main thrust of Mason et al.'s (2019) study during the 2017 hurricane season, including how disaster communication messages will be sent through digital media. New technologies are explored by AlHinai (2020), who looks for ways they can change national disaster management systems. They intend to propose new models and paradigms that will allow these systems to adapt to them and reap the benefits from changing digitally while dealing with challenges at hand. In recent years, Hassankhani et al. (2021) have examined the role of technology in crisis management. They provide policy recommendations for combating COVID-19. Their study shows that crisis management, community well-being, and urban resilience policies and actions driven by technology have had an enormous impact on society over the past twenty years. During crises, technology increased participation and social ties; it made people healthier both mentally and physically, and helped keep education alive as well as businesses afloat. According to Fenwick et al. (2021), the current reset provides a unique historical opportunity to re-evaluate regulatory methods across numerous domains and build regulatory models that are more consistent with a more decentralized society. COVID-19, albeit a worldwide tragedy, can be exploited as a learning opportunity to envisage a more socially and environmentally responsible future. This article by Arora et al. (2023) explores the shock moments as well as the ability to recover in the digital era; it provides an epitome of the tourism industry from its inception to its future trajectory. The purpose of the research by Rehman et al. (2023) is to examine the determination of social media on customer value analysis and crisis management. Abbas et al. (2023) examine recruitment managers' reactions to social media recruiting technology and its impact on the financial crisis. Aziz et al.'s (2023) study analyzes the complicated links among maladaptive perception, protection motive (intention), and health-protective action in the context of COVID-19 and the tourism business within the digital revolution. Abraham and Thazhathethil (2023) plan to investigate existing chatbots in the tourist and disaster management sectors. This chapter examines the crisis management process in the tourism sector within the context of digitalization. It examines the threats and opportunities of digitalization and highlights the critical role of effective communication in mitigating the negative effects of crises.

15.2 DIGITAL TRANSFORMATION IN TOURISM

Tourism is among the sectors that have embraced digitalization by using various platforms. This has enhanced the travel experience through improved business adaptability and the use of online tools. Other technologies include big data analytics, Internet of Things (IoT), blockchain technology, virtual reality (VR), augmented reality (AR), social media, artificial intelligence (AI), and contactless technology for online bookings and ratings. Thus, the tourism industry has been influenced by these digital advancements in various ways (Opute et al., 2020). In this regard, users' lives have become more convenient while businesses and employees have performed better, thanks to digitization in the tourism industry. Tourism has received various advantages from digitalization, transforming it positively. However, it also comes with some setbacks. Some of the benefits, include increased efficacy, enhanced customer experience, a worldwide market, data-based insights, better communication systems and reduced costs, innovative services provision, and environmental sustainability (Buhalis and Leung, 2018). Certainly, digitization has changed the way we live and do business. However, this has led to several challenges as well. One of them is the digital divide that exists between those who have access to information technology and those who lack it. In addition, there are cyber security concerns that threaten our online safety and privacy. Another challenge that needs to be dealt with is overreliance on technology as it leads to reduced human interaction and social skills development. Issues related to privacy and regulation are also major concerns that have to be addressed. The increasing use of automation and AI is another issue resulting in job displacement. Other obstacles are infrastructure limitations and fake reviews. Lastly, misinformation coupled with fake news has become a major challenge in this age of digital revolution (Williams, 2018). It is important for the tourism industry to balance these challenges with witnessing all the benefits of digitalization—as this will be necessary for sustainable development. In order for digitalization to foster a positive impact for the sector, these issues—currently portrayed as security concerns and control zone status problems—must be addressed.

15.3 DIGITAL AGE AND CRISIS MANAGEMENT

The rise of the digital age has dramatically changed crisis management and added new obstacles for organizations to work through crises (Schwarz et al., 2016). Over time, how information is disseminated, how crises evolve, and how stakeholders can communicate with one another have been transformed by digital technologies as well as online communication platforms. In the digital age, the rapid spread of information makes it challenging for entities to control and ensure the correctness of narratives during a crises (Kozyreva et al., 2020).

Real-time communication using social media, websites, and other digital channels allows organizations to deliver immediate updates, rectify any misinformation, and regulate public opinion. The sentiments of a society, positive or negative, tend to get amplified on media platforms that are social in nature (Stieglitz and Dang-Xuan, 2013). In times of crisis, it is crucial to reach out to stakeholders, manage worries, and tap into internet communities. In the age of digitalization, two-way communication has increased its significance (Falkheimer and Heide, 2014). Plenty of access is available through digital channels where stakeholders are freely able to voice opinions and concerns, expecting an instant response right down to a personalized level. These are real people, and organizations need to be ready not only for a flood of communications but also for automated processes that will find the right human responses. Another matter that has emerged is digital cooperation.

Crisis response efforts will also necessitate digital collaboration between stakeholders. With the widespread adoption of digital tools and collaborative platforms, crisis response teams, government agencies, and other stakeholders now interact and coordinate more effectively (Cherbib et al., 2021). Advanced analytics tools are necessary for monitoring the digital landscape for incipient issues and sentiment analysis (Batrinca and Treleaven, 2015). Digital monitoring solutions deliver the ability to monitor online conversations, sentiment, and emerging trends that offer organizations rich fodder for decision-making. Emergency preparedness is also crucial, and it necessitates well-considered realistic training exercises (Reddin et al., 2021). Through digital platforms, organizations can practice crisis simulations under realistic circumstances to prepare and train teams in a simulated environment before the actual occurrence of a real-life crisis. At the same time, crises have global importance and reach (Hickman and Silva, 2018); meaning organizations must learn to communicate globally in times of crisis. Digital communications targeting the world: consistent messaging and updating everywhere for global stakeholders' reputation management is also a big issue. The dangers to the brand image from an online dimension can remain for a longer term (Oncioiu et al., 2020). By engaging on social media, addressing the negative feedback, and responding with how you are handling it, an organization can organically manage their online reputation. The rapid nature of digital communication makes it imperative that organizations get out in front of their crisis communications. A crisis communication plan and other proactive digital strategies (Ciftci et al., 2017) can help organizations expect crises coming their way, enabling them to manage the effects of these events by also increasing resilience. Bad happenings on digital platforms can turn into a crisis in no time. Fast response, transparency, and communications on digital media will maybe turn the tide or even prevent a crisis from taking disastrous proportions. Technological innovations, such as the use of AI chatbots, automated communication, and data analytics can help to improve efficiency in crisis response (Hansen et al., 2018). To conclude this post, the digital age has brought about new dimensions and communication channels rendering crisis management different than what it was decades ago. Leykin et al. (2016) argue that organizations that are more digitally orientated, transparently facilitated, and digitally interactive with stakeholders, experience relatively less negative impact in terms of the ability to cope with crises.

15.3.1 THE ROLE OF SOCIAL MEDIA IN CRISIS MANAGEMENT

Social media platforms play an important role in crisis management and mitigation. During disasters and emergencies, social media networks, such as Twitter, Facebook, and Instagram play an instrumental role in broadcasting information, and mobilizing relief workers en masse to disaster zones for effective response operations while providing real-time situation updates. These platforms have been used to communicate information in a timely and effective way, since they are so well-utilized and allow them to reach large audiences quickly (Mason et al., 2019). During a crisis, social media platforms enable organizations to get the word out on critical updates and information that is relatively contemporaneous with what is taking place. They provide stakeholders with awareness of the ever-changing situation and rapidly disseminate information to a broad audience regarding emergency alerts, warnings, and relevant instructions (White, 2011).

It is possible to use social media platforms to talk directly with the stakeholders, answer their questions and doubt, reply in case of any related query, or communicate. This ensures transparency and open communication, maintaining a certain level of cordiality in the relationship between them. Social media monitoring tools provide insights into public sentiment and running a crisis command center offers myriad benefits—to assist with internal communication, quickly identifying upcoming issues by often sharing your perspective, and seeing how crises are experienced from outside of your organization. This clearly shows that in visual communication, social media tools are very important. Since visual material (e.g., photos and videos) can capture the effects of a crisis, along with response activities, these kinds of tools enable organizations to distribute visuals too in ways that convey the impact or the undertaken efforts (Stahl and Kaihovirta, 2019).

With infographics and various types of aids, it becomes possible to share information as soon as possible and give a quick understanding. Deliberately, it can be quite helpful to get information from the public, as social networks can turn into a compilation of materials and data that would be useful in managing the crisis. In addition, social media enables organizations to reply and respond to complaints, clear the air on misconceptions, and control their public image during and after the occurrence of the disaster. Indeed, organizations can leverage these platforms to portray a positive angle of their operations, including philanthropic causes, disaster response, and support to society (Simon et al., 2015). Social media listening or monitoring tools may be used to track trends or emerging issues to do with the crisis. To work around these trends, organizations can then prioritize their communication handling in a precise way. Besides, it is relevant to continue communication on social media platforms after a crisis. For organizations, it acts as a way to construct and narrate key messages on matters to ensure that the public gets accurate messages and information (Ruggiero and Vos, 2014). Moreover, social media provides the organization with an opportunity to convey a message to an international audience, especially during a crisis to gain an international audience. Hence, to harness social media during a crisis, there is a need to have a clear crisis communication strategy, protocols, and a good crisis team. It is therefore important that organizations engage their audiences with utmost clarity, and genuinely communicate to them when they are down as much as when they are up.

15.4 CHALLENGES AND OPPORTUNITIES OF MANAGING CRISIS IN THE DIGITAL AGE

It is worth noting that crisis management in today's IT-supported environment is not as easy as it used to be. There are numerous threats and opportunities for organizations to manage crises in the era of digital disruption. Whether it is about cyber-crime and hacking instances or missed opportunities along with social media mishaps and ORM, a lot is at stake and people can lose big. Crisis communication management must rely on an adequate appreciation of the digital media environment, and timely, appropriate, and adequate actions must be taken to address the effects of the crisis and its general damage to the reputation of the organization (Nisar and Javed, 2022). Dealing with crises in the context of information and social media remains a mixed blessing for most organizations. In the present day, due to the existence of technology and social networks, information can easily be passed and reach a bigger group of people. This implies that companies react to a crisis, as it happens in real-time, reducing the consequences of this virtually unforeseen disaster. While this is positive for brands that are doing the right thing, it also means bad news can travel at an unprecedented pace. As a result, every organization needs to be prepared with a well-laid crisis management plan taking into account the landscape of the digital age (Millar and Heath, 2003). Enterprises should constantly be prepared for crises to weather the storm and/or navigate them successfully. These businesses should also learn from previous experiences and use them as learning tools. Effective crisis management allows for the transformation of crises into opportunities (Ciftci et al., 2017). In today's digital age, crises will have a completely different dimension, and in the meantime, it will also provide some unique opportunities. The speed at which digital technology can spread information can either exacerbate or diminish crises. Managing a crisis in the digital age has both its pros and cons, which is why it is essential to understand what those challenges are and what opportunities exist. When facing a crisis, it is vitally important to overcome those challenges and use the opportunities that a digital crisis offers as an advantage. The first step in managing a crisis begins with understanding those challenges and utilizing the potential benefits of a digital crisis. Up to this point, we have discussed some of the challenges and issues that crisis managers have to face in the era of digital communications. One of these challenges is that information travels at an alarming speed during a crisis, and with the aid of digital platform users and sometimes intentionally, a crisis can escalate quickly. The next challenge is controlling the speed and virality of messages, and one of the important aspects is the speed of managing these potentially harmful messages. The third, and possibly most significant, is the issue of damage control that organizations may face during a crisis. Mastering the crisis plan involves maintaining your damage control strategy, messaging, and engaging in crisis communication techniques. All internal and external communications strategies must align. The last challenge is sorting fact from fiction in a time when lies can spread faster than the truth, and this is a common factor in any crisis. Several challenges will necessitate some quick and concise measures, and this will require some practice and following the principles of crisis management.

Excessive crisis news saturates digital channels, creating audience fatigue. People may become desensitized, disinterested, or unresponsive, making it difficult for organizations to capture and retain the audience's attention and communicate the message that needs to be conveyed (Liu et al., 2016). However, as much as crisis holds constraints, it also holds opportunities. Digital communication ensures real-time messaging which is crucial in ensuring that organizations share updates and respond quickly to emerging issues. Organizations can leverage this quick speed to communicate accurate information, manage perceptions effectively, and mobilize public opinion. Social media platforms enable information-sharing during a crisis, as the organization needs to be able to "crowd-source" data, see the conditions, and make developments (Liu et al., 2020). Digital communication allows organizations to engage directly with the audience. Transparent lines of communication are critical to building trust and transparency. Digital listening tools allow organizations to monitor conversations observe sentiment, both favorable and unfavorable, and respond. This data gathered from the digital conversations should influence decision-making and communication strategy. Digital channels enable organizations to work among teams within the organization and from state entities to glean a more effective and comprehensive response (Chen et al., 2011). Digital media can serve to help organizations build a contingency plan and/or identify preventative aspects of crisis, such as cyber security and crisis communication plans (Safitra et al., 2023). The digital age offers a variety of communication channels, including video conferencing, webinars, and podcasts, allowing organizations to choose platforms that suit their crisis communication strategies. Digital platforms provide organizations with tools for reputation management, including the ability to monitor online sentiment, respond to feedback, and rebuild trust after a crisis. Effectively navigating the challenges and leveraging the opportunities presented by the digital age requires a proactive and adaptable approach to crisis management (Thanitbenjasith and Kamkankaew, 2023). Organizations must develop comprehensive digital communication strategies and be prepared to address the unique dynamics of crises in the online environment.

15.5 CRISIS RESPONSE IN THE DIGITAL AGE

What counts is to act fast and appropriately in crisis management. Perhaps, the worst time to make an emergency response is during a crisis. The longer the organization waits to respond—there is an increasing chance for a risk to occur. Responding in a timely manner would minimize the size and seriousness of an incident, reducing human casualties (potentially saving lives), economic costs (less long-term damage), or causing further harm to the natural environment. A swift and coordinated response can also signal a commitment to the public's welfare (Ansell et al., 2010). It is also essential to gain and sustain trust with the public, affected population, and stakeholders. One of the key pillars in crisis management is trust, and a response to an emergency should come promptly toward building or retaining that factor. It also contributes to preventing crises from unfolding into problems of greater magnitude and complexity (Hardt, 2014). Early intervention can stop the spread of negative consequences and help contain the situation before it worsens. Rapid responses allow for better allocation and optimization of resources.

When a crisis is addressed promptly, resources can be directed more efficiently to areas most needed, preventing unnecessary waste or duplication. Delayed responses can have legal and reputational consequences. A quick and well-managed response can demonstrate accountability and responsibility, potentially minimizing legal liabilities and preserving the organization's reputation. Timely responses require effective coordination and communication among all involved parties, including emergency responders, government agencies, non-profit organizations, and the public (Shittu et al., 2018). Proper communication helps disseminate accurate information, reduces confusion, and facilitates a more organized crisis management effort. Rapid responses can help address the psychological impact of a crisis on individuals and communities. Knowing that action is being taken can provide security and stability, whereas delays may exacerbate anxiety and fear. They also provide opportunities for real-time learning and improvement. A post-crisis analysis helps organizations to recognize the strengths, weaknesses, and opportunities that arise within their crisis management strategies after an experience (Heath, 1998). In conclusion, it is key to value a quick and efficient response in crisis management. The crisis is not just mitigated with immediate repercussions; it also has broader effects on how the public sees you, your organizational reputation, and in recovering from and learning from such an experience.

15.5.1 STRATEGIES FOR EFFECTIVE CRISIS RESPONSE IN THE DIGITAL AGE

In the digital age, crisis response strategies must adapt to the rapid pace of information dissemination, increased connectivity, and the prevalence of social media. Harnessing digital tools for the immediate monitoring of social media, news outlets, and online platforms is crucial for swiftly recognizing and evaluating evolving crises. Additionally, integrating social listening approaches aids in comprehending public sentiment, pinpointing potential concerns, and evaluating the efficacy of crisis responses (Haddow and Haddow, 2013). Equally vital is the execution of digital crisis response training for essential personnel, guaranteeing their proficiency in utilizing digital communication tools, navigating social media platforms, and applying online crisis management strategies.

Furthermore, the development of a robust crisis communication plan is essential. This plan should encompass strategies specifically tailored for digital channels. Precise delineation of roles and responsibilities for overseeing digital communication during a crisis is imperative. The plan should also establish pre-approved messaging templates for diverse scenarios, guaranteeing a consistent communication approach across various digital platforms. Secondly, social media management: social media is social because it involves people working together on the same technology and problems (Ozanne et al., 2020). Developing a dedicated social media department that can immediately and accurately respond in crises is very important. Using social media to communicate, address questions, and dispel rumors during a crisis issue are some of the most fundamental strategies for effective crisis management. Community involvement is key. Creating and maintaining digital tribes who can help you in times of crisis is critical. Having a digital touchpoint regularly with stakeholders handles for your positive online presence. Everyone is worried about the product launch and answer their inquiries openly and demonstrate that you have a spirit of transparency, which helps develop trust among colleagues during hard times (Vohra and Bhardwaj, 2019).

Emphasizing on prioritizing data security and privacy protection is crucial during a crisis. One can conduct real-time data analysis, track sentiments, and recognize patterns by utilizing adaptive technologies, like AI and machine learning. The implementation of tools that automate specific facets of crisis response enables faster and more efficient actions. Acknowledging the ubiquity of mobile devices in crisis scenarios is crucial. Ensuring that communication strategies are mobile-friendly and take into account the distinctive challenges and opportunities linked to mobile platforms is important (Gwebu et al., 2018; Haddow and Haddow, 2013). Post-crisis analysis and learning play a crucial role in effective crisis management. It involves conducting a comprehensive digital post-crisis analysis to assess the efficacy of digital communication strategies. Utilizing insights derived from the analysis is essential for enhancing digital crisis response plans and adaptation to emerging technologies. By integrating these strategies, organizations can enhance their ability to respond effectively to crises in the digital age, maintaining trust and minimizing the impact of challenging situations.

15.5.2 DEVELOPING A DIGITAL CRISIS MANAGEMENT PLAN

In the present world, especially in the interconnected world where companies have a global outreach, crisis management has become imperative not a luxury. In today's world where information can be disseminated throughout the social networks and the Web in a few clicks, a failure can go viral, or, in other words, it can take a disastrous toll on a company's reputation. This is the reason why having a significant and efficient crisis management plan is so vital—it has to be instantly prepared and put into practice in case of necessity. Communication plans should be communicated through feasible communication channels, the strategies of handling the crisis, and measures being taken to secure the employees and customers. Crisis management is a strategic approach that if pursued by organizations can shield them from possible negative consequences of various adversities, and precisely strengthen them in the process of resolving complicities that confront them (Obrenovic et al., 2020).

Figure 15.1 illustrates the "crisis management plan" with specific measures and protocols designed for the tourism industry of the digital era. In the present, global environment with information dissemination going viral in social media, having a good crisis management plan is the key to protecting and rebuilding the reputation and stability of the businesses and destinations related to tourism.

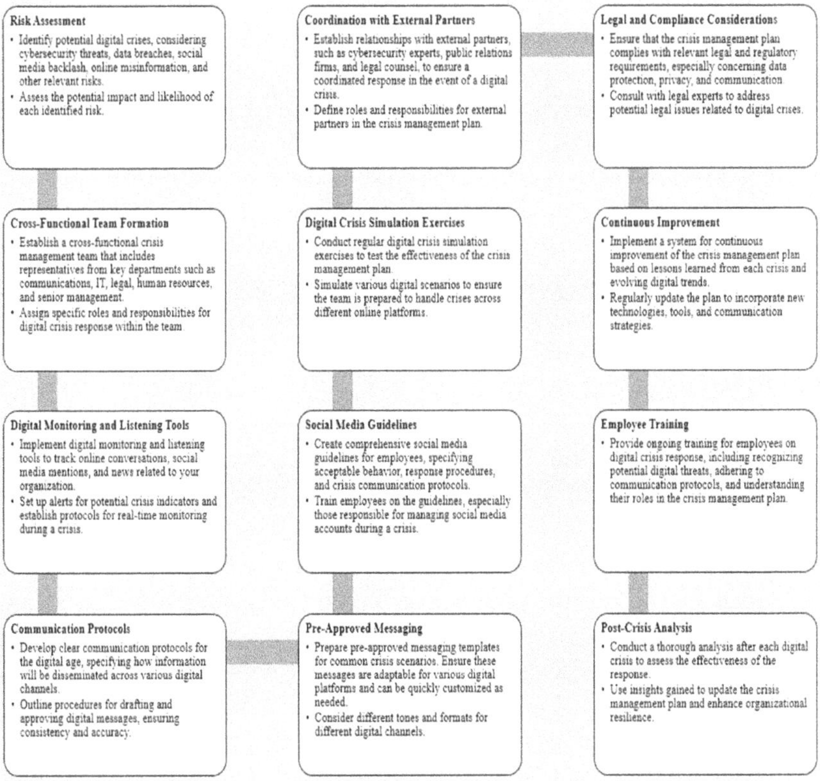

FIGURE 15.1 Crisis management plan.

Source: Created by author.

The procedure of creating a crisis management plan in the modern world presupposes the incorporation of measures, which are to reflect the peculiarities of working in the context of digital networks, social networks, and opportunities for the spread of information through the Internet. Given below is a sample case that provides a step-by-step guide for the development of a sound crisis management plan for the new age (Thanitbenjasith and Kamkankaew, 2023). In this way, organizations can work out detailed plans and strategies of how to effectively deal with crises that might be unique to the digital age and protect trust and reputation.

15.5.3 CRISIS COMMUNICATION STRATEGIES FOR THE DIGITAL AGE

How the target audience is informed in the digital context should be appropriate in terms of practicability and entanglement of internet sites and palatability. The multichannel kind of communication has more and more become one of the most significant aspects of crisis communication in today's world and is technologically advanced. Business organization must therefore exploit these various forms of new media for their benefit, such as social networking sites, e-mails, mobile applications, and instant messaging to pass information to the general public and a cross section of people. We ought to mention here that people of different age groups have different preferences and employ several modes guaranteeing that the message will reach the target population and they will interact with it (Khalifa and Ali, 2023). It is also necessary for the company to accord real-time communication significance to the response to queries, concerns, and trends immediately. The viewers of the digital platform are always expecting an instant reply and real-time engagement reinforces the authenticity of the brand. With this in mind, it indicates that the use of infographics and polls is effective in achieving attention (Jae-Seong, 2023). Visuals are easier to share and retain, thus generating more traffic due to the shorter time people take to share visual content. Another important issue is social media listening which is the process of tracking social media conversations that are relevant to the industry or the trends. It is most effectively utilized in social media listening; the application empowers brands to respond and get involved in the proper conversational streams. Another way is the application of personalization methods, which can offer content management based on user preferences, activity, and age (Perakakis et al., 2019). Perhaps, the most important reason is that specific targeting enhances relevance, interest, and thus, perceived satisfaction. It can be quite useful to apply storytelling in the brand's communication with the audience because it helps to develop emotions. Stories are memorable and make brands more relatable in the digital space. In today's digital age, it is important to use new technologies like user-generated content (UGC) as they serve as authentic endorsements and testimonials, fostering a sense of belonging among digital audiences. Data-driven decision-making helps to utilize data analytics in order to understand user behavior, preferences, and trends. These insights enable targeted communication, improving the effectiveness of digital campaigns (Roma and Aloini, 2019). Lastly, chatbots and AI communication processes provide quick and efficient responses. Having a crisis communication plan is crucial to managing digital crises effectively. Such plans must be developed and updated regularly to ensure swift and strategic communication that can help manage reputational damage. Mobile optimization is important to ensure that users have a seamless experience. Additionally, feedback loops through surveys, polls, and comments can help businesses understand audience sentiment and preferences. Continuous feedback allows for adaptability and improvement based on user preferences (Sankaranarayanan et al., 2011). By incorporating these strategies, businesses and organizations can create a dynamic communication approach that aligns with the preferences of the digital audience. This, in turn, can foster engagement, build trust, and enhance brand visibility.

15.6 CONCLUSION

Therefore, this chapter seeks to present fresh ideas, information, and recommendations to the known literature by offering ways that various businesses and organizations can interact and communicate with their customers in the digital space, gain their confidence, and improve their brand image. There are both positive aspects and negative aspects for the tourism industry with the advancement of digital technology. It is crucial to be prepared for future shocks, and only innovative approaches to the management of crises and the inclusion of digital resilience approaches will help the industry resolve uncertainty, protect tourist health, and ensure the sector's future viability. All the players in the industry should jointly ensure that the tourism sector is well protected against the vagaries of crises. There is a significant role of digital platforms in the management of the crisis, which is due to the effectiveness of the dissemination of the information during the crisis. Keeping the public informed means communicating with them at the right time to save lives, control the flow of the disaster, and counter fake news. Real-time data analysis and various systems and tools give a broad and encompassing perspective of the crisis. Cues to the environment provoke intelligence and allow decision-makers to make efficient decisions at the right time. They also aid in the right utilization of resources through the effects and the extent of crises that the digital tools reveal. This makes it possible for authorities to focus and allocate resources where they are vital, and hence enhance the response efforts. The social media application integrates different stakeholders in the crisis management regime, such as the government, emergency services, non-profit organizations, and enterprises. Coordinate control means real-time communication and data sharing, thus facilitating coordinated effort and greater efficiency.

The approach to the use of data analytics and predictive modeling allows the authorities to be prepared for crises. Social media platforms enhance the practical and manageable mimetic real-life crises. These simulations enable the organization and the responders to develop their plans, understand areas of the course, and have improved overall response for a multitude of potential crises. Technological advancement also enhances distant working, which encourages key professionals to interact in a single platform, no matter the distance they are from one another. This is especially so in circumstances which may hinder movement or physical access to the site. Social media can help with the dissemination of information to the public, the situation updates, safety measures, and escape procedures. All means of social networks, websites, and applications for mobile devices remain the key instruments for raising awareness and engaging the audience. It is thus possible to use information technologies on a digital resilience to counter new emerging threats. Crises are never static; they happen dynamically, and therefore call for flexibility and interventions that can allow for shifts of course during their surge. The evolution that is required in the current digital age concerning crisis management is in response to issues of security and privacy of data. Adopting stringent measures of security addresses information security and confidence that is needed by the members of the public. Therefore, the imperative for crisis management in the digital age is about strategically managing its shift and evolution to better meet the needs of organizations and society at large.

KEYWORDS

- **crisis management**
- **digital crisis**
- **data analytics**
- **digital age**
- **digital transformation**
- **social media platforms**
- **tourism**

REFERENCES

Abbas, J., Rehman, S., Aldereai, O., Al-Sulaiti, K. I., & Shah, S. A. R. (2023). Tourism management in financial crisis and industry 4.0 effects: Managers traits for technology adoption in reshaping, and reinventing human management systems. *Human Systems Management*, (Preprint), 1–18.

Abraham, S. T., & Thazhathethil, B. V. (2023). Tourism disaster management through chatbots as an alternative tool of communication. *Revista Turismo & Desenvolvimento (RT&D)/Journal of Tourism & Development*, (41).

Agarwal, P., Swami, S., & Malhotra, S. K. (2022). Artificial intelligence adoption in the post COVID-19 new-normal and role of smart technologies in transforming business: A review. *Journal of Science and Technology Policy Management.*

AlHinai, Y. S. (2020). Disaster management digitally transformed: Exploring the impact and key determinants from the UK national disaster management experience. *International Journal of Disaster Risk Reduction*, *51*, 101851.

Ansell, C., Boin, A., & Keller, A. (2010). Managing transboundary crises: Identifying the building blocks of an effective response system. *Journal of Contingencies and Crisis Management*, *18*(4), 195–207.

Arora, M., Kumar, J., & Valeri, M. (2023). Crises and resilience in the age of digitalization: Perspectivations of past, present and future for tourism industry. In *Tourism innovation in the digital era* (pp. 57–74). Emerald Publishing Limited.

Aziz, A., Umer, K., & Zaidi, S. N. B. (2023). Maladaptive perception, protection motivation and health protective behavior: The application of protection motivation theory in tourism industry amidst the digital revolution. *Business Review of Digital Revolution*, *3*(2), 11–22.

Batrinca, B., & Treleaven, P. C. (2015). Social media analytics: A survey of techniques, tools and platforms. *AI & Society*, *30*, 89–116.

Buhalis, D., & Leung, R. (2018). Smart hospitality-Interconnectivity and interoperability towards an ecosystem. *International Journal of Hospitality Management*, *71*, 41–50.

Chen, A. Y., Peña-Mora, F., & Ouyang, Y. (2011). A collaborative GIS framework to support equipment distribution for civil engineering disaster response operations. *Automation in Construction*, *20*(5), 637–648.

Cherbib, J., Chebbi, H., Yahiaoui, D., Thrassou, A., & Sakka, G. (2021). Digital technologies and learning within asymmetric alliances: The role of collaborative context. *Journal of Business Research*, *125*, 214–226.

Çetin Gürkan, G., & Çiftci, G. (2020). Developing a supportive culture in digital transformation. *Digital Business Strategies in Blockchain Ecosystems: Transformational Design and Future of Global Business*, 83–102.

Çiftçi, G., Küçükaltan, D., & Menteş, S. A. (2017). Empirical analysis of crisis management practices in tourism enterprises in terms of organizational learning. *Business and Management Studies: An International Journal*.

Falkheimer, J., & Heide, M. (2014). Strategic communication in participatory culture: From one-and two-way communication to participatory communication through social media. In *The Routledge handbook of strategic communication* (pp. 337–350). Routledge.

Fenwick, M., McCahery, J. A., & Vermeulen, E. P. (2021). Will the world ever be the same after COVID-19? Two lessons from the first global crisis of a digital age. *European Business Organization Law Review*, *22*, 125–145.

Gkoumas, A. (2022). Developing an indicative model for preserving restaurant viability during the COVID-19 crisis. *Tourism and Hospitality Research*, *22*(1), 18–31.

Gwebu, K. L., Wang, J., & Wang, L. (2018). The role of corporate reputation and crisis response strategies in data breach management. *Journal of Management Information Systems*, *35*(2), 683–714.

Haddow, G., & Haddow, K. S. (2013). *Disaster communications in a changing media world*. Butterworth-Heinemann.

Hansen, N., Kupfer, A. K., & Hennig-Thurau, T. (2018). Brand crises in the digital age: The short-and long-term effects of social media firestorms on consumers and brands. *International Journal of Research in Marketing*, *35*(4), 557–574.

Hardt, H. (2014). *Time to react: The efficiency of international organizations in crisis response*. Oxford University Press.

Hassankhani, M., Alidadi, M., Sharifi, A., & Azhdari, A. (2021). Smart city and crisis management: Lessons for the COVID-19 pandemic. *International Journal of Environmental Research and Public Health*, *18*(15), 7736.

Heath, R. (1998). Looking for answers: Suggestions for improving how we evaluate crisis management. *Safety Science*, *30*(1–2), 151–163.

Hickman, C. R., & Silva, M. A. (2018). *Creating excellence: Managing corporate culture, strategy, and change in the new age*. Routledge.

Jae-Seong, S. (2023). Qualitative research design: How visual design marketing strategy can increase product brand value. *The Journal of Industrial Distribution & Business*, *14*(5), 1–9.

Khalifa, A., & Ali, O. B. (2023). Consumer behavior in the digital age: A multifaceted study on social media, Pet Product Marketing, and EdTech adoption. *Journal of Sustainable Technologies and Infrastructure Planning*, *7*(5), 1–21.

Kozyreva, A., Lewandowsky, S., & Hertwig, R. (2020). Citizens versus the internet: Confronting digital challenges with cognitive tools. *Psychological Science in the Public Interest*, *21*(3), 103–156.

Lee, S. M., & Trimi, S. (2021). Convergence innovation in the digital age and in the COVID-19 pandemic crisis. *Journal of Business Research*, *123*, 14–22.

Leykin, D., Aharonson-Daniel, L., & Lahad, M. (2016). Leveraging social computing for personalized crisis communication using social media. *PLoS Currents*, *8*.

Liu, B. F., Fraustino, J. D., & Jin, Y. (2016). Social media use during disasters: How information form and source influence intended behavioral responses. *Communication Research*, *43*(5), 626–646.

Liu, Y., Lee, J. M., & Lee, C. (2020). The challenges and opportunities of a global health crisis: the management and business implications of COVID-19 from an Asian perspective. *Asian Business & Management*, *19*, 277–297.

Mason, A., Flores, L., Liu, P., Tims, K., Spencer, E., & Gire, T. G. (2019). Disaster communication: An analysis of the digital communication strategies used by the medical tourism industry during the 2017 Caribbean hurricane season. *Journal of Hospitality and Tourism Insights*, *2*(3), 241–259.

Millar, D. P., & Heath, R. L. (Eds.) (2003). *Responding to crisis: A rhetorical approach to crisis communication*. Routledge.

Nisar, A., & Javed, H. (2022). Crisis communication in the digital era: Strategies and best practices. *Journal of Media And Business Studies Research*, *1*(2), 43–57.

Obrenovic, B., Du, J., Godinic, D., Tsoy, D., Khan, M. A. S., & Jakhongirov, I. (2020). Sustaining enterprise operations and productivity during the COVID-19 pandemic: "Enterprise effectiveness and sustainability model". *Sustainability*, *12*(15), 5981.

Oncioiu, I., Popescu, D. M., Anghel, E., Petrescu, A. G., Bîlcan, F. R., & Petrescu, M. (2020). Online company reputation—A thorny problem for optimizing corporate sustainability. *Sustainability*, *12*(14), 5547.

Opute, A., Irene, B., & Iwu, G. (2020). Tourism service and digital technologies: A value creation perspective. *African Journal of Hospitality, Tourism and Leisure*, *9*(2), 1–18.

Ozanne, L. K., Ballantine, P. W., & Mitchell, T. (2020). Investigating the methods and effectiveness of crisis communication. *Journal of Nonprofit & Public Sector Marketing*, *32*(4), 379–405.

Perakakis, E., Mastorakis, G., & Kopanakis, I. (2019). Social media monitoring: An innovative intelligent approach. *Designs*, *3*(2), 24.

Reddin, K., Bang, H., & Miles, L. (2021). Evaluating simulations as preparation for health crises like CoVID-19: Insights on incorporating simulation exercises for effective response. *International Journal of Disaster Risk Reduction*, *59*, 102245.

Rehman, H. M., Amin, A., Rehman, M., Nematova, G., Shamim, A., & Hossain, M. B. (2023). Transforming strategies in the digital era: The role of social media in customer value analysis and crisis management for tourism firms. *International Journal of Management Studies*, *30*(2), 373–396.

Ritchie, B. W. (2004). Chaos, crises and disasters: a strategic approach to crisis management in the tourism industry. *Tourism Management*, *25*(6), 669–683.

Rogers, D. L. (2016). *The digital transformation playbook: Rethink your business for the digital age*. Columbia University Press.

Roma, P., & Aloini, D. (2019). How does brand-related user-generated content differ across social media? Evidence reloaded. *Journal of Business Research*, *96*, 322–339.

Ruggiero, A., & Vos, M. (2014). Social media monitoring for crisis communication: Process, methods and trends in the scientific literature. *Online Journal of Communication and Media Technologies*, *4*(1).

Safitra, M. F., Lubis, M., & Fakhrurroja, H. (2023). Counterattacking cyber threats: A framework for the future of cybersecurity. *Sustainability*, *15*(18), 13369.

Sankaranarayanan, J., Hacigumus, H., & Tatemura, J. (2011). COSMOS: A platform for seamless mobile services in the cloud. In *2011 IEEE 12th International Conference on Mobile Data Management* (Vol. 1, pp. 303–312). IEEE.

Schwarz, A., Seeger, M. W., & Auer, C. (Eds.). (2016). *The handbook of international crisis communication research*. John Wiley & Sons.

Shittu, E., Parker, G., & Mock, N. (2018). Improving communication resilience for effective disaster relief operations. *Environment Systems and Decisions*, *38*, 379–397.

Simon, T., Goldberg, A., & Adini, B. (2015). Socializing in emergencies—A review of the use of social media in emergency situations. *International Journal of Information Management*, *35*(5), 609–619.

Ståhl, M., & Kaihovirta, H. (2019). Exploring visual communication and competencies through interaction with images in social media. *Learning, Culture and Social Interaction*, *21*, 250–266.

Stieglitz, S., & Dang-Xuan, L. (2013). Emotions and information diffusion in social media—sentiment of microblogs and sharing behavior. *Journal of Management Information Systems*, *29*(4), 217–248.

Thanitbenjasith, P., & Kamkankaew, P. (2023). Preparing for tomorrow's challenges: Integrating future thinking into crisis management in Thai higher education. *Online Submission*, *3*(5), 215–230.

Vohra, A., & Bhardwaj, N. (2019). From active participation to engagement in online communities: Analysing the mediating role of trust and commitment. *Journal of Marketing Communications*, *25*(1), 89–114.

White, C. M. (2011). *Social media, crisis communication, and emergency management: Leveraging Web 2.0 technologies*. CRC Press.

Williams, R. (2018). Fighting "fake news" in an age of digital disorientation: Towards "real news," critical media literacy education, and independent journalism for 21st century citizens. In *Critical media literacy and fake news in post-truth America* (pp. 53–65). Brill.

PART V

Ethics, Responsibility, and Future Perspectives in the Digital World

CHAPTER 16

Ethics and Responsibility in Digital Tourism

EDMIRA CAKRANI[1], RINA CAKRANI[2*], and ENRIKO CEKO[3]

[1]*Western Balkans University, Tirana, Albania*

[2]*Simon Fraser University, Vancouver, Canada*

[3]*Head of Business Administration & IT Department, Canadian Institute of Technology, Tirana, Albania*

*Corresponding author

ABSTRACT

Big data is crucial in the tourism industry, as it enables the identification and prediction of future behaviors and trends. As new information and communication technologies (ICTs) develop, a wider variety of technology-enabled experiences will emerge, posing new challenges for tourism knowledge and the need for caution. Privacy concerns have developed as a result of the vast gathering and processing of personal data in smart tourism locations, notably with regard to electronic surveillance, profiling, and disclosure of private data. Travelers are becoming more aware of how tourism and hospitality organizations (THOs) use their data to personalize services, making them more sensitive to data security and privacy concerns. This chapter presents a paradigm for ethical data management and governance that considers the need of building trust with stakeholders and customers, as well as legal and regulatory considerations.

Digitalization in Tourism. Hulya Akdemir Cengiz, Seza Zerman, Aysegul Acar, and Faizan Ali (Eds.)

DOI: 10.1201/9781779644770-21

16.1 INTRODUCTION: TOURISM IN THE ERA OF THE DIGITAL WORLD

According to Kraus et al. (2019), one major megatrend and force behind business is the rapid development and adoption of technology. This is because new technologies improve customer service and allow businesses to better research their customers, competitors, and the broader market environment. The tourist and hospitality sector, which offers the greatest number of goods and services supplied online in the majority of countries, is one area where the enormous impact of technology on business is becoming increasingly apparent. The travel sector may encounter opportunities and difficulties from smart tourism. According to Mehraliyev et al. (2019), smart technologies have an impact on several stakeholders in the tourism business. It is essential to comprehend the responsibilities and relationships of the many stakeholders in order to develop sustainable tourism. However, the majority of the stakeholders with significant links to this industry, mainly travelers and tourist companies, have been the focus of contemporary smart tourism research. The effects of smart tourism extend beyond these stakeholders, even if the industry is required to look at it based on consumer behavior, technological adoption, and destination management.

The surrounding community, the environment, and any future generations who might be impacted by the tourism destinations' presence are additional stakeholders in the tourism industry. The majority of current debates and studies on smart tourism take a positivist stance toward the advancement of information technology, constantly viewing cutting-edge innovations as beneficial to travel destinations and society at large. But there are still unanswered social, moral, and ethical concerns about who will profit or lose from the growth of smart tourism in certain locations. As new technologies proliferate, their detrimental effects might not be immediately apparent because of the delayed effects that result from adopting novel technologies. Therefore, it's possible that the detrimental effects on tourist attractions won't be ready for analysis until the harm is done. Regulating smart tourism practices and evaluating their effects on different stakeholders may take longer due to delay in establishing new rules than the evolution of new firms and practices. As a result, it is imperative that practitioners and researchers carefully consider any possible dangers related to smart tourism and make appropriate plans.

This chapter investigates the largely ignored subject of data ethics and governance in the tourist and hospitality industries, focusing on the consequences for consumer and traveler data privacy. It seeks to create a complete conceptual framework for ethical data management and governance that considers the interests of all stakeholders, including travelers, employees, government authorities, industry groups, complementary sectors, and the general public. This chapter aims to elucidate the relationship between data governance and digital tourism, while also addressing the ethical challenges posed by the integration of big data into digital tourism initiatives. This framework aims to protect the rights and privacy of both individuals and entities by carefully considering ethical and security issues in the gathering, storage, and analysis of tourist and hospitality data.

16.2 THE CONCEPTS OF DATA ETHICS AND DATA GOVERNANCE

Data ethics refers to the value decisions that organizations make when collecting, analyzing, and sharing data. It entails having a thorough understanding of data protection regulations and the sensible application of emerging technology (UK Government, 2018b). These characteristics demand organizations to have a complete awareness of the compliance standards pertaining to the use and management of data. In the processes of gathering, sharing, storing, and utilizing big data, prioritizing data ethics, security, and privacy is crucial (Yang et al., 2019). The line separating the public and private good (data), privacy and confidentiality, openness, equity of access, and informed use of information are some of the major ethical issues in using big data for organizational goals (Tam and Kim, 2018). Data ethics improves on the technology that has previously been supported in this research field by shifting the level of abstraction of ethical questions to data-centric, while also building on the foundation laid by information and computer ethics. This change highlights the various moral elements of all data, including information that is never directly translated into acts or behaviors but might be utilized, for example, to justify or inspire actions. It emphasizes how ethical evaluations must focus on the nature and content of computational operations—the relationships between data, software, and hardware—instead of the range of digital technologies that make them possible.

Data governance, which refers to the "exercise of authority and responsibility," is a collection of guidelines and practices that organizations use to manage data (Yallop and Seraphin, 2020). Frameworks for managing data as a significant strategic asset are known as data governance frameworks

(Abraham et al., 2019). According to Bracket and Earley (2009), data governance is the conceptual exercise of power and control over data management. According to established models that specify who can do what with what information, when, under what conditions, and with what tools, is a system of decision rights and accountabilities for information-related processes (Plotkin, 2013). Thus, assuring the accuracy and appropriate use of data, fulfilling legal obligations, and assisting in the use of data to generate value for the public are the objectives of data governance. This framework provides the appropriate datasets and useful insights for business decision-making (Riggins and Klamm, 2017). Creating a competitive advantage by taking a comprehensive approach to important organizational data is the main objective of data governance frameworks (Abraham et al., 2019). According to Yang et al. (2019), there is not a great number of big data governance models in the literature, and the ones that do exist are limited because they do not investigate big data ecosystems, which raise considerable ethical challenges in terms of big data privacy, transparency, and other ethical elements of organizational data processing.

The introduction of big data analytics has led to an increased emphasis on the transparency of automated decision-making. Although the majority of government agencies already understand the importance of data, it can be difficult to foster an environment where data is valued and used to support public employees in making data-driven decisions (Benfeldt et al., 2020). Although data governance has the potential to reduce data management expenses and generate value from data, data is frequently dispersed across numerous businesses with disparate data policies in place. Regardless of how the information was gathered—by volunteers, observations, inferences, or available sources, people have the right to know the source of information, where the controllers got the information from, and how automated judgments were made. Big data algorithms, which are also utilized in STD scenarios, are difficult to document because they learn and adapt in a (semi)autonomous manner. In addition, organizations frequently assert confidentiality over "how" data is processed due to concerns about copyright and commercial confidentiality, which protect the software and trade secrets.

One of the most important aspects of this new, networked data environment is how much of the information we voluntarily and unintentionally give up, is gathered by organizations that we don't clearly or directly interact with and utilize in methods that remain unseen to us. This is where the concept of data ethics comes into play. In this new world of networked data, information is gathered by unreliable parties whose goals may not coincide with our own. As a result, businesses you deal with have a stake in gathering as much information as they can about the consumers, and selling it to them for maximizing their gains. Disparate data pieces can be gathered and analyzed by machines to uncover characteristics about people that they themselves were unaware of or did not wish to divulge. For instance, the examination of a person's Facebook "likes," can potentially disclose information about their race, sexual orientation, immigration status, and other characteristics that they might want to keep hidden. Similarly, when it comes to digital tourism, the data gathered through personalized information determines what kind of services the individual gets, which puts into question the extent to which big data operates on an ethical basis.

16.3 THE EVOLVING CONCEPTUALIZATION OF CONSUMER VULNERABILITY

Customers are becoming more and more reliant on online platforms and accepting virtual interactions as their strategies for dealing with the pandemic and adapt to the "new normal." The complex network of smart speakers, smart home appliances, in-store surveillance, and apps and trackers that contribute to the data stream is combined with data-driven commercial initiatives. This data will eventually provide virtual representations of consumers and perhaps more crucially, consumer "commercialization potential." The ultimate purpose of these strategies is to make consumers more vulnerable to digital marketing tactics, which use digital technologies to streamline business processes in order to conduct sales with customers and offer goods and services. By doing this, the consumer can identify the products and services they want more easily, have a more positive shopping experience, and develop a more intimate and tailored relationship with the trader. Consumer policymakers and agencies have always prioritized protecting consumers when they are most vulnerable. The concept of consumer vulnerability is intricate and multifaceted. It simply means being vulnerable to injury. However, there isn't a single, widely agreed definition for it, and there is a lack of coherence in the scholarly literature (Rotzmeier-Keuper, 2020; Kaprou, 2020; Hill and

Sharma, 2020). In the literature, researchers have distinguished between two general categories of conceptualization (Kaprou, 2020; Rotzmeier-Keuper, 2020):

1. The first, known as the "class-based approach," looks at consumer vulnerability in terms of particular consumer groups that are prone to vulnerability due to personal traits like age or education level (see, e.g., Commuri and Ekici (2008)).
2. The second, dubbed the "state-based approach" and introduced more recently in the literature, holds that consumer vulnerability is the outcome of the interplay of internal and external factors that affect the consumer; these factors may be short-term or long-term in nature (Hill and Sharma, 2020; Helberger et al., 2021a). Class-based approaches have been criticized for a number of reasons, such as stigmatizing specific consumer groups; failing to characterize entire consumer groups as inherently vulnerable (Hill and Sharma, 2020); failing to identify the underlying causes of vulnerability (e.g., cognitive impairment or limited impulse control); and failing to consider other factors that could also increase vulnerability (Commuri and Ekici, 2008). On the other hand, it has been contended that the state-based strategy offers the benefit of permitting various factors to contribute to vulnerability, meaning that every customer may be at risk, contingent on their unique circumstances and the environment.

Personalized "persuasion profiles" combined with adaptive targeting techniques are the foundation of new targeted advertising strategies that seem to be taking over online advertising. These strategies would allow the right message to reach the right customer at the right time and location. (Strycharz et al., 2019). Examples of these tactics include contextual advertising and advertising methods based on generally specified demographics, such as gender or age. Matching observed behavior with demographic traits and extremely specific types of psychographic targeting—which rely on psychological insights into a customer's behavior, beliefs, opinions, and interests—are examples of more accurate targeting strategies. (Burkell and Regan, 2019). The 2010 OECD Consumer Policy Toolkit ("the Toolkit") notes: "All consumers can be vulnerable to detriment. They are, however, likely to be more susceptible at some times than others.

Vulnerability may be due to a consumer's psychological or financial state or the nature of a transaction. Service providers might, for example, be in a good position to prey upon a grieving person's sense of remorse and guilt to sell a higher-priced or overpriced product that the consumer would normally pass up. Moreover, research indicates that consumers may also be vulnerable by reasons of the place or context in which purchases take place" (OECD, 2010). The Toolkit makes a distinction between disadvantaged and vulnerable customers, with the latter being defined as those who may consistently be at risk of harm. The Toolkit lists disadvantaged consumer groups, such as targets of discrimination (e.g., racial, ethnic, or gender); low levels of literacy or (formal) education; language barriers (e.g., non-native speakers); immigrants and other outsiders who lack local knowledge; impaired vision, hearing, or mobility; learning disabilities or cognitive impairment, such as dementia; limited mobility; limited means of communication; geographic remoteness; unemployment; or low income (OECD, 2010).

Policy research has shown a shift in the conceptualization of consumer vulnerability in recent years, toward a state-based approach (Kaprou, 2020). Vulnerability is a dynamic term, according to a 2016 European Commission (EC) study known as "the 2016 EC vulnerability study" (EC, 2016) (Helberger et al., 2021b; Kaprou, 2020). A consumer who, due to sociodemographic traits, behavioral traits, personal circumstances, or the market environment: (1) is more likely to encounter unfavorable outcomes in the market; (2) has limited ability to maximize their well-being; (3) has trouble obtaining or assimilation of information; and (4) is less likely to buy, choose, or access suitable products; or (5) is more susceptible to certain marketing practices, is considered vulnerable, according to the study. (EC, 2016a, b). A strategy that goes beyond internal issues is also reflected in recent policy research and guidelines in various countries. For example, the UK Competition and Markets Authority (CMA) makes a distinction between two general types of consumer vulnerability: "vulnerability associated with personal characteristics," which includes physical disability or poor mental health and which the CMA notes may lead to these individuals experiencing particularly severe and persistent problems across markets; and "market-specific vulnerability," originating from the unique context of specific markets and impacts a wide range of consumers within those markets.

16.4 THE CURRENT STATE OF DIGITAL TOURISM AND THE ETHICAL IMPLICATIONS

16.4.1 THE RISE OF DIGITAL TOURISM

According to reports from the travel and tourism sector, technological advancements are expected to have a major impact over the next five years. The most significant technology expected to have an impact on the business is big data and analytics (The World Tourism Organization (UNWTO), 2020a, b). Unquestionably, companies in the tourist and hospitality industries depend on traveler data and information; these companies are increasingly using data and data analytics to provide insights and drive critical business decisions. (Yang et al., 2019). Recent reports indicate that the extraordinary challenge presented by the pandemic is projected to result in significant alterations for the travel, tourism, and hospitality sectors. These transformations are expected to be concentrated in two areas: touchless travel and digital health passports. These technologies will likely shape the future of these sectors and usher in the era of the "digital traveler," who may be required to provide more personal information and even medical or health data. Digital systems like the World Economic Forum's "Known Traveller Digital Identity" program are supporting these new digital technologies.

The worldwide big data analytics market and tourism sector are expected to reach $486.6 billion by 2033, at a compound annual growth rate (CAGR) of 8% between 2023 and 2033, according to recently released statistics by Future Market Insights (FMI). The market is forecast to be worth $225.4 billion in 2023. Tourism organizations can now collect and analyze enormous volumes of customer data, including demographics, behaviors, and preferences, thanks to big data analytics. Businesses are able to provide customized trip packages, individualized recommendations, and focused marketing campaigns thanks to this priceless information. Increased client loyalty and happiness are the outcomes. Through the analysis of previous booking data, seasonal patterns, events, and other pertinent aspects, big data analytics enables accurate demand forecasting. Because of this foresight, tourism businesses may maximize earnings during peak seasons and minimize the danger of under booking during low demand by optimizing pricing methods. For customer interaction, the tourism business mostly depends on social media channels and online review sites. Businesses can monitor these channels, assess customer mood, spot new patterns, and quickly handle customer concerns thanks to big data analytics. By using sentiment analysis, businesses may gain a deeper understanding of client feedback and modify their marketing and customer care tactics accordingly. Over the past ten years, the majority of industries have grown more digitally dependent. Particularly in the travel industry, there has been significant effort put into building an online presence. Artificial intelligence (AI) in travel and tourism is just one example of how quickly this industry is changing. In general, review and e-commerce websites about travel, make up the majority of the internet travel sector. Travel-related e-commerce websites focus on selling travel-related goods, such as tickets, lodging, and rental cars. These can be bought straight from an online travel agency (OTA) or via the website of a travel firm. Travelers can also share their thoughts on restaurants, lodging, and other tourist attractions online via travel review websites like Tripadvisor.

16.4.2 GROWING POTENTIAL FOR EXPLOITATIVE DATA-DRIVEN PERSONALIZATION PRACTICES

Technology can have both positive and negative impacts on consumers, potentially endangering their autonomy and rights. Data-driven technologies promise improved services, but ethical behavior is questioned. Technology's security and privacy implications are significant, impacting data governance frameworks and organizations' ethical practices in data governance. While privacy and security concerns affect many different industries, the hospitality and tourism sectors are particularly sensitive to them. This is because, in most countries, these services have surpassed all other categories of goods and services sold online in recent years. Furthermore, hospitality and tourism are highly information-based industries, and as such, they involve a disproportionate amount of consumer personal data in corporate transactions and activities when compared to other sectors. Thus, in addition to processing a large quantity of information (during pre-trip preparation, during travel, post-trip assessment, and data sharing), and use services that make travel easier and better, travelers must frequently divulge personal information. The data and information gathered may comprise, among other things, specifics about the interests of the travelers and identity attributes, such as their date of birth, place of residence, and physical traits, as well as dependent family information. Such additional data include location data, browsing habits, and lifestyle information (such as travel history and preferences) in an increasingly online and digital environment.

Furthermore, technological advancements have broadened the array of opportunities available to THOs for collecting traveler data. The deployment of real-time surveillance systems for increased safety and security, the collection of biometric data via automated check-in kiosks at airports, and the latest advancements in AI are some of the most notable examples. These AI advancements have facilitated the development of intelligent personal assistants capable of recognizing and responding to travelers' interests and behaviors (Yallop and Seraphin, 2020). Because microtargeting technology mostly depends on a consumer's digital footprints, privacy is an ethical conundrum that will ultimately arise. According to a number of studies (e.g., Buhalis and Amaranggana, 2013), privacy is a crucial issue of smart tourism that requires prompt attention. Travelers' mobile devices are frequently used to collect data without their knowledge. Consequently, travelers can experience a sense of being watched, which could cause anxiety. There are serious worries about the safety and privacy of tourists in light of potential data leaks from companies that own a lot of customer information. Lawsuits are pending against well-known online travel booking companies, like Hotels.com, L.P., and its parent business Expedia Group for a potential data breach that occurred in November 2020 and may have exposed customers' personal information. A data breach that compromised the personal and guest reservation information of up to 500 million consumers was confirmed by Marriott International in 2018. Studies have indicated that data security lapses can have a direct or indirect impact on customers' perceptions of an organization's trustworthiness, degree of satisfaction, propensity to recommend the company, and intention to revisit (Berezina et al., 2012; Chen and Jai, 2019; Zhang et al., 2019). Therefore, significant data breaches may result in irreversible harm to a destination's brand and a loss of customers.

Frauds and phony reviews are common ways that digital developments make it easier to trick customers online (CMA, 2019). AI-based generators can produce phony reviews and testimonials that appear extremely real, and they can also be used to create fraudulent advertisements that will elude internet platforms' monitoring. Scammers who prey on online shoppers frequently employ cutting-edge technology to create sophisticated, realistic-looking spoof websites for retailers. These websites may contain stolen company names, logos, or business identification numbers. In 2020, the most often reported fraud category in the United States that caused financial loss to individuals of all ages was online shopping fraud. For the past few years, privacy in the travel and hospitality industry has been the primary data issue and worry for organizations as well as scholars (Ioannou et al., 2020; Hall and Ram, 2019; Pizam, 2013). The security of consumer data is being impacted by an increase in data breaches (Ameen et al., 2021). Recent high-profile data breaches have made this concern worse (Armerding, 2018; PwC, 2016, 2017). Marriott International is a prime example of a major data breach that has affected both the company and its clientele. Around 500 million consumers globally were impacted by this data breach; around 100 million customers' credit card details were compromised (Armerding, 2018; Yallop and Seraphin, 2020).

Travelers' health and safety may benefit from smart technologies: in an emergency, they can utilize their smartphones to get real-time notifications, connect with authorities, or find an exit using the Global Positioning System (GPS). But when there's a security breach, the same technologies could become dangerous. For instance, technologies like cloud computing and Internet of Things (IoT) may make travelers more susceptible to damage, identity theft, and computer virus attacks. Furthermore, adopting smart technologies may lead to a dependence on them, making it impossible to go back to the way things were before the adaptation—a phenomenon known as socioeconomic irreversibility.

16.5 A SUGGESTED FRAMEWORK FOR DATA GOVERNANCE AND ETHICAL DATA MANAGEMENT IN THE TRAVEL AND HOSPITALITY INDUSTRIES

In many jurisdictions, policymakers and regulators have recognized the need for new measures to address a range of emerging consumer risks in the digital realm. This occasionally calls for modifications to consumer laws. The European Commission, for instance, started an assessment of a set of related policy interventions in 2022 on digital fairness. It specifically examined how well the UCPD, the Consumer Rights Directive, and the Unfair Contract Terms Directive addressed topics, such as dark patterns, influencer marketing, personalization practices, contract cancellations, subscription service contracts, virtual goods marketing, and compulsive digital product use. To further combat internet frauds, dangerous apps, phony reviews, and dark patterns, the Australian Competition and Consumer Commission

(ACCC) pushed for legislation prohibiting unfair commercial practices across the Australian economy in 2022. In several jurisdictions, there has been a specific attention on subscription traps, and phony and incentive reviews. For instance, regulations requiring companies to notedly display a cancellation option to enable the termination of online subscriptions were enacted in Germany and Argentina in 2020 and 2021, respectively, and the German government promised additional steps. The American Data Privacy and Protection Act (ADPPA) in the United States and the CCPPA in Canada, for instance, would establish a comprehensive federal framework for consumer privacy and data protection that is comparable in scope and principles to the GDPR. At the time of writing, privacy and data protection laws in Australia were also undergoing review and updating. The US Federal Trade Commission (FTC) hosted a public meeting and provided advance notice of proposed rulemaking in 2022. The FTC also indicated that it was exploring measures to address abusive commercial surveillance and inadequate data protection. At both the international and national levels, voluntary product safety pledges have been formed in the field of product safety, whereby online marketplaces agree to go above and beyond their current legal requirements in order to better protect customers.

Consumer protection issues can be handled by all branches and levels of government, as stated in the 2014 OECD Recommendation on Consumer Policy Decision-making. In this sense, authorities are tackling digital consumer and other challenges across several policy domains and industries in a more comprehensive manner. For example, particularly large online platforms of systemic importance to the EU internal market are subject to a number of regulations under the EU Digital Markets Act (DMA), which went into effect in 2022. In addition, several requirements on online platforms would be introduced under the proposed Online Safety Bill in the United Kingdom, including steps to combat fraudulent advertising and online scams. Several countries are now putting in place economy-wide data portability and sharing programs, such as the UK's Smart Data initiative and Australia's Consumer Data Right, to allow consumers to use their data and pertinent technology to bargain for lower prices in key sectors (such as communications, energy, or finance), particularly for those who may be more prone to disengagement. Following the CMA's inquiry into the "loyalty penalty" in the United Kingdom, the UK government and industry regulators either enacted or explored new steps to address consumer disengagement in critical consumer markets (including financial services and communications). These measures included price caps, opt-in subscription renewal, and automated switching mechanisms (CMA, 2020a, b, c). In an effort to combat exploitative personalization methods, notably targeted advertising, more regulations have been put forth or put into place. This may be a sign that the current regulatory frameworks are insufficient. Some have to do with educating the public and customers about personalization tactics. For example, in order for authorities, researchers, and civil society to analyze how advertisements were targeted, the EU DSA will require extremely large online platforms to retain and provide access to ad repositories. Additionally, these platforms must provide relevant details regarding the main criteria that are used to determine who the advertisement is intended for. Researchers have also proposed requiring online businesses to disclose to their customers—when a practice is personalized, along with the criteria that underpins the personalization. They should also publicly disclose their targeting strategy and guarantee that improper targeting of vulnerabilities does not arise. They also suggest the need for very large online platforms (Fletcher et al., 2021; Helberger et al., 2021b; Jablonowska et al., 2018) to provide pertinent consumer testing data.

Data protection and privacy laws might provide an additional means of combating algorithmic prejudice. For instance, processing personal data by algorithms would require compliance with transparency and permission requirements under data protection law. Additionally, the EU GDPR prohibits the processing of personal data related to several protected characteristics in some circumstances and offers several protections against decisions made using automated processing. However, there are situations when the protections provided by data protection laws may not be adequate, for example, when certain algorithms do not handle personal data. Proposed legislation pertaining to AI in multiple jurisdictions would mandate companies to carry out impact analyses to guarantee algorithms' impartiality. For instance, in order to reduce discriminatory outcomes, the EU AIA would require suppliers of "high-risk" AI systems—those used in certain commercial services that are deemed necessary, such as credit scoring—to perform ex ante conformity assessments, post-market monitoring plans, and ensure high-quality datasets. The proposed AI and Data Act in Canada would require those in charge of highly influential AI systems to recognize, evaluate, and reduce the likelihood of harm or biased results. In the United States, companies and large data holders would be required, among other things, to perform impact assessments of their automated decision systems or algorithms to check for bias under the proposed Algorithmic Accountability Act (AAA) and the American Data Privacy and Protection Act (ADPPA). Similar support has been shown by 86 researchers for requiring companies to create "bias impact statements" (Lee et al., 2019). The funding and investigative capabilities of regulatory bodies, such as equality bodies, human rights monitoring bodies, and consumer protection and data protection authorities have been improved; non-discrimination laws have been updated for the digital age, for example, by clarifying how they apply to algorithms (Lee et al., 2019); more sector-specific laws have been proposed, taking into account the various risks and principles that apply in various industries; and greater procedural "due process" protections have been established, among other things (Hirsch, 2020).

THOs should also be able to give feedback and/or explain to travelers the specific benefits they could expect from sharing their data when using THO services regarding their services on the internet (Yallop and Seraphin, 2020). Furthermore, it is anticipated that the COVID-19 pandemic will speed up the change in consumer attitudes and views. Specifically, consumers will now need to strike a compromise between their demands for greater control and transparency from government agencies and institutions and their expectations of privacy and autonomy. Therefore, it is reasonable to anticipate that consumer concern over the data kept on them and its utilization will likely grow (Manton, 2020). Travelers will therefore have control over the information they choose to provide, and THOs will need to make data decisions and develop data plans that will explain how this information may be used to others' advantage (Manton, 2020). Similarly, there is a clear connection between these problems and travelers' expectations regarding a just and equal exchange of their personal information.

16.6 CONCLUSION

Big data plays a critical role in commercial decision-making in the tourist and hospitality industries in an increasingly digital environment. The ubiquitous, always-on data collection about consumer visitors is increasingly being used by smart tourism to fuel travel experiences and create competitive markets. With the use of this data, future behaviors and trends can be identified and predicted; enabling the analysis of the processes involved in creating and improving goods and services, keeping clients, and in the end, is helpful for making decisions in the future. It is undeniable that as new ICTs develop in the years to come, a wider variety of technology-enabled experiences will flourish and provide new difficulties for the body of knowledge and caution surrounding tourism.

The extensive collection and processing of personal data using algorithm-driven methods in the context of smart tourism destinations has raised serious privacy issues. These concerns are particularly related to the widespread electronic surveillance, profiling, and disclosure of private data. In recent years, travelers have become increasingly conscious of the ways THOs use their personal data to personalize services, making them more sensitive to concerns regarding data security and privacy (Panetta, 2018; Chen and Jai, 2019). This study offers a paradigm for ethical data management and governance that considers the necessity of building reliable connections with stakeholders and customers in addition to legal and regulatory issues. Thus, travelers must be given discretion over the data and information they choose to provide, and THOs must guarantee their privacy and data security. Furthermore, because the nature of tourism activities may force them to share travelers' data with other stakeholders, THOs must ensure an ethical and equitable interchange of data and information that prioritizes tourists' rights to privacy and data security in big data decisions. In order to establish confidence with travelers and other stakeholders, THOs must uphold strong ethical corporate standards and principles. To guarantee equitable and transparent processing, automated decisions must account for all pertinent data-related circumstances. De-contextualized data or the results of data processing alone cannot serve as their foundation.

KEYWORDS

- **big data**
- **data privacy**
- **data governance**
- **data protection**
- **data breach**
- **ethical data management**
- **online shopping fraud**

REFERENCES

Abraham, S., Dodd, C., & Manca, S. (2019). Data ethics in tourism: Managing trust and transparency in the age of digitalization. *Tourism Review*, *74*(3), 495–509. https://doi.org/10.1108/TR-01-2019-0017.

Ameen, N., Tarhini, A., Reppel, A., & Anand, A. (2021). Customer experiences in the age of artificial intelligence. *Computers in Human Behavior*, *114*, 106548. https://doi.org/10.1016/j.chb.2020.106548.

Armerding, T. (2018). The 18 biggest data breaches of the 21st century. *CSO Online*. https://www.csoonline.com/article/2130877/the-biggest-data-breaches.html.

Benfeldt, O., Persson, J. S., & Madsen, S. (2020). Data ethics for responsible innovation in digital services. *Journal of Information, Communication and Ethics in Society*, *18*(4), 570–586. https://doi.org/10.1108/JICES-11-2019-0131.

Berezina, K., Bilgihan, A., Cobanoglu, C., & Okumus, F. (2012). Understanding satisfied and dissatisfied hotel customers: Text mining of online hotel reviews. *Journal of Hospitality Marketing and Management*, *21*(7), 791–812. https://doi.org/10.1080/19368623.2012.624293.

Burkell, J., & Regan, P. M. (2019). Gender, online privacy, and consent: Why social media privacy is a feminist issue. *Information, Communication and Society*, *22*(8), 1102–1116. https://doi.org/10.1080/1369118X.2017.1418404.

Chen, Y., & Jai, T. M. C. (2019). The impact of data breaches on hotel firms' performance: Event study approach. *Tourism Management*, *74*, 50–58. https://doi.org/10.1016/j.tourman.2019.02.013.

CMA. (2019). *Consumer vulnerability: Challenges and potential solutions*. https://www.gov.uk/government/publications/consumer-vulnerability-challenges-and-potential-solutions.

CMA. (2020a). *Loyalty penalty update: Progress two years on from the CMA's super-complaint investigation*.

CMA. (2020b). *Online platforms and digital advertising: Market study final report*.

CMA. (2020c). *Protecting consumers during the coronavirus (COVID-19) pandemic: Update on the work of the CMA's Taskforce*.

Commuri, S., & Ekici, A. (2008). An enlargement of the notion of consumer vulnerability. *Journal of Macromarketing*, *28*(2), 183–186. https://doi.org/10.1177/0276146708316049.

European Commission (EC). (2016a). *Consumer vulnerability across key markets in the European Union: Final report*. https://ec.europa.eu/info/sites/info/files/consumers-approved-report_en.pdf.

European Commission (EC). (2016b). *Study on the impact of marketing through social media, online games and mobile applications on children's behavior*.

Fletcher, A., Karatzas, A., & Kretschmer, T. (2021). *Consumer protection for online markets and large digital platforms: Policy discussion paper No. 1*.

Hall, C. M., & Ram, Y. (2019). Measuring the impacts of geopolitical conflicts on tourism: Israel as a case study. *Current Issues in Tourism*, *22*(3), 273–288. https://doi.org/10.1080/13683500.2017.1334761.

Helberger, N., Borgesius, F., & Reyna, A. (2021a). *EU consumer protection 2.0: Structural asymmetries in digital consumer markets*. https://www.beuc.eu/publications/beuc-x-2021-018_eu_consumer_protection.0_0.pdf.

Helberger, N., Borgesius, F., & Reyna, A. (2021b). Choice architectures in the digital economy: Towards a new understanding of digital vulnerability. *Journal of Consumer Policy, 44*(3), 387–416. https://doi.org/10.1007/S10603-021-09500-5.

Hill, R. P., & Sharma, E. (2020). Consumer vulnerability: A literature review. *Journal of Consumer Affairs, 54*(2), 391–419. https://doi.org/10.1111/joca.12309.

Hirsch, D. D. (2020). Privacy by design and the new EU general data protection regulation. *Information Law Journal, 45*(2), 87–98.

Ioannou, S., Kehagias, J., & Kyriakou, A. (2020). Tourism, security, and crisis communication: Lessons from conflict zones. *Tourism Management Perspectives, 35*, 100713. https://doi.org/10.1016/j.tmp.2020.100713.

Jabłonowska, A., Kuziemski, M., Micklitz, H. W., Palka, P., & Sartor, G. (2018). *Consumer law and artificial intelligence: Challenges to the EU consumer law and policy stemming from the business' use of artificial intelligence*. EUI Working Papers, 11.

Jerath, K., Ma, L., & Park, Y. H. (2014). Consumer click behavior at a search engine: The role of keyword popularity. *Journal of Marketing Research, 51*(4), 480–486. https://doi.org/10.1509/jmr.13.0099.

Kaprou, E. (2020). Protecting digital consumers in the EU: Vulnerability and empowerment in a data-driven world. *European Journal of Risk Regulation, 11*(2), 388–401. https://doi.org/10.1017/err.2020.23.

Lee, N., Resnick, P., & Barton, G. (2019). *Algorithmic bias detection and mitigation: Best practices and policies to reduce consumer harms*. https://www.brookings.edu/research/algorithmic-bias-detection-and-mitigation-best-practices-and-policies-to-reduce-consumer-harms/.

Manton, K. G. (2020). AI regulation and ethical implications for digital tourism. *Journal of Tourism Futures, 6*(4), 317–328. https://doi.org/10.1108/JTF-09-2019-0104.

OECD. (2010). Consumer policy toolkit. *OECD Publishing*. https://doi.org/10.1787/9789264079663-en.

Panetta, K. (2018, October 2). 5 trends appear on the Gartner hype cycle for emerging technologies, 2018. *Gartner Insights*. https://www.gartner.com/en/articles/5-trends-appear-on-the-gartner-hype-cycle-for-emerging-technologies-2018.

Pizam, A. (2013). Effects of terrorism on tourism: What do we know? *Tourism Review, 68*(1), 4–8. https://doi.org/10.1108/16605371311310084.

Plotkin, G. (2013). Big data and ethics: Balancing innovation and privacy. *Harvard Data Science Review, 5*(2), 17–28.

PwC. (2016). Global State of Information Security Survey 2016. PricewaterhouseCoopers. https://www.pwc.com/gx/en/issues/cyber-security/information-security-survey.html.

PwC. (2017). Consumer Intelligence Series: Protect.me. PricewaterhouseCoopers. https://www.pwc.com/us/en/services/consulting/library/consumer-intelligence-series-protect-me.html.

Riggins, F. J., & Klamm, B. K. (2017). Data governance and ethics in the era of analytics. *Information Systems Management, 34*(3), 234–245. https://doi.org/10.1080/10580530.2017.1330008.

Rotzmeier-Keuper, J. (2020). Conceptualizing consumer vulnerability in digital markets. *Journal of Consumer Policy, 43*(3), 543–566. https://doi.org/10.1007/s10603-019-09442-9.

Strycharz, J., van Noort, G., Helberger, N., & de Vreese, C. H. (2019). Understanding online advertising exposure: The role of ad relevance and privacy. *Computers in Human Behavior*, *93*, 53–62. https://doi.org/10.1016/j.chb.2018.12.007.

Tam, S., & Kim, J. (2018). Big data ethics: Privacy and transparency in the tourism industry. *International Journal of Contemporary Hospitality Management*, *30*(4), 1836–1854. https://doi.org/10.1108/IJCHM-03-2017-0135.

UK Government. (2018b). Data ethics framework. *Department for Digital, Culture, Media and Sport*. https://www.gov.uk/government/publications/data-ethics-framework.

Yallop, A., & Seraphin, H. (2020). Corporate social responsibility and data ethics in tourism: Reconciling technology and humanity. *Journal of Tourism Futures*, *6*(2), 123–136. https://doi.org/10.1108/JTF-09-2019-0098.

Yang, Y., Park, S., & Hu, X. (2019). Electronic word of mouth and hotel performance: A big data approach. *International Journal of Hospitality Management*, *84*, 102329. https://doi.org/10.1016/j.ijhm.2019.102329.

Zhang, T., Omran, B. A., & Cobanoglu, C. (2019). Generation Y's positive and negative eWOM: Use of social media and mobile technology. *International Journal of Contemporary Hospitality Management*, *31*(11), 4377–4396. https://doi.org/10.1108/IJCHM-10-2018-0852.

CHAPTER 17

Digital Adoption in Tourism: Challenges and Solutions

SADIA AFRIN ANANYA[1] and PETER O'CONNOR[2*]

[1]*PhD Candidate, Adelaide University, Adelaide, Australia*

[2]*College of Business and Law, Adelaide University, Adelaide, Australia*

*Corresponding author

ABSTARACT

The rapid evolution of technology, particularly information and communication technology (ICT), has significantly transformed the tourism industry. However, small and medium-sized tourism enterprises (SMTEs) have been slow to adopt these advancements, primarily due to financial, technical, and organizational constraints. This chapter explores the barriers and facilitators to ICT adoption in the tourism sector, focusing on SMTEs. Drawing on established adoption models, like Technology Acceptance Model (TAM), Unified Theory of Acceptance and Use of Technology (UTAUT) for contextual understanding, this study employs Technology-Organization-Environment (TOE) framework to analyze the organizational adoption of ICT in SMTEs. It emphasizes the importance of technological competence, organizational readiness, and external support in overcoming adoption challenges. This chapter concludes with recommendations for tourism stakeholders to foster innovation, enhance digital literacy, and support sustainable growth in an increasingly competitive and digitalized marketplace.

Digitalization in Tourism. Hulya Akdemir Cengiz, Seza Zerman, Aysegul Acar, and Faizan Ali (Eds.)

DOI: 10.1201/9781779644770-22

17.1 INTRODUCTION

In today's dynamic tourism sector, making efficient and effective use of technology-based systems has emerged as a critical determinant of success (O'Connor, 2024a, b). As destinations, suppliers, and intermediaries compete to attract travelers in an increasingly competitive digital marketplace, the role of ICT-based systems in driving innovation, improving competitiveness, boosting efficiency, enhancing customer experience, and enriching strategic decision-making cannot be overstated (Huang et al., 2022; Januszewska et al., 2015). Many tourism businesses are engaging in digital transformation processes because of technology's significant metamorphic effects on consumer preferences and industry market dynamics (Sigala, 2018). However, despite the acknowledged transformative effect of ICT, numerous studies have shown that some tourism organizations, particularly the multitude of small and medium-sized enterprises (SMEs) that typify the tourism sector, have been slow to embrace and effectively leverage Information Technology (IT)-based systems, leaving them at a competitive disadvantage (Ayinla and Adamu, 2018; Baabdullah et al., 2021).

Historically, tourism businesses have faced unique barriers to IT adoption, stemming from an interlinked combination of organizational and environmental characteristics. Firstly, financial constraints often limit the investment capacity of these typically smaller enterprises, making the upfront costs associated with ICT implementation prohibitive (AlBar and Hoque, 2019). Moreover, the perceived complexity of IT systems, coupled with a lack of technical expertise among managers/owners of SMEs, further exacerbates this adoption inertia. Unlike larger corporations with dedicated IT departments, SMEs typically lack the resources or knowledge to navigate the intricacies of IT integration effectively. Cultural and organizational factors also contribute to the reluctance toward IT adoption (Leong et al., 2023). Resistance to change, ingrained traditional practices, and a risk-averse mindset prevail within SMTEs, impeding the willingness to embrace technological innovation (de Mattos et al., 2023; Pappas et al., 2021). Additionally, the fragmented nature of the tourism sector, characterized by a myriad of small businesses operating independently, poses challenges for standardization and collaboration in ICT implementation efforts.

Despite these hurdles, the imperative for tourism SMEs to embrace ICTs cannot be overstated (O'Connor, 2024a). In an era where digitalization has become synonymous with competitiveness and resilience, SMEs in particular risk falling behind their peers, facing competitive disadvantage compared to larger counterparts who can capitalize on technology's advantages more effectively (Abed, 2020). ICT adoption holds the promise of streamlining operations, enhancing marketing effectiveness, improving customer engagement, and enabling data-driven decision-making—all critical components for sustainable growth and survival in the tourism sector. As a result, understanding the process by which new technologies are adopted and integrated into the daily operations of tourism businesses has become essential for attaining long-term success and remaining competitive (Chan et al., 2012).

This chapter aims to delve into the multifaceted reasons underlying the sluggish adoption of ICT among SMTEs, shedding light on the challenges encountered and exploring potential avenues for improvement. By understanding the nuances of this phenomenon, tourism stakeholders can devise informed strategies to bridge this digital divide and unlock the untapped benefits of ICT integration. The remainder of this chapter is organized as follows. Initially, the specific challenges faced by tourism businesses, and in particular tourism SMEs, in adopting IT-based systems will be explored. Subsequently, analyzing the extant research on technology adoption, and actionable recommendations for stakeholders across the tourism value chain to improve adoption are proposed. Throughout this discussion, we endeavor to equip tourism businesses with the knowledge and insights needed to successfully navigate IT adoption, empower them to take better advantage of technological advancements, compete more successfully, and support the industry's long-term growth and expansion.

17.2 TECHNOLOGY IN TOURISM

Technology plays a key role within the tourism industry. Advances in technology have brought profound changes in how tourism businesses and destinations function and engage with consumers (Januszewska et al., 2015). At a strategic level, technology-based systems have helped redefine the nature of competition within the sector, in particular by enabling the development of online intermediaries who engage in coopetition, simultaneously competing with and cooperating with tourism suppliers to secure the customer, thus reshaping the industry's competitive dynamics (O'Connor, 2023b). At an operational level, technology-based systems help enhance operational efficiency in SMTEs; for example, by automating repetitive tasks, reducing errors, and rationalizing processes, as well as by facilitating personalized experiences, thus enhancing digital communication, marketing, and guest-host interactions (Ashari et al., 2014). Technology-based systems also offer valuable insights through the provision of powerful data analysis, empowering managers to make informed, data-driven decisions (Buhalis et al., 2019). Overall, the successful adoption of technology-based systems has been shown to positively impact the success and growth trajectory of tourism businesses (Huang et al., 2022).

However, a key challenge in relation to technology use by tourism businesses stems from the predominance of SMEs within the sector (Ashari et al., 2014). Such enterprises, including primarily hotels, restaurants, travel agencies, entertainment, and attraction providers that service tourists, face challenges in leveraging technology effectively. Financial Constraints, limited staff training, specialized expertise, and limited management capacity collectively impede the adoption of technologies (Ashari et al., 2014; Masood and Sonntag, 2020). As a result, failing to effectively exploit appropriate technologies puts them at a competitive disadvantage with their larger peers (Gazzoli et al., 2008). For example, SMTEs have traditionally been grossly underrepresented in critical systems, like computer reservation systems (CRSs) and Global Distribution Systems (GDSs), vital for visibility in the fiercely competitive tourism marketplace (Januszewska et al., 2015), leaving them open to exploitation by emerging online travel agencies, which quickly asserted dominant control over the online distribution of such suppliers (O'Connor, 2023a). Considering these challenges, an understanding of how tourism businesses, and in particular SMTEs, adopt new technologies would be useful and potentially offer a pathway toward improved performance at both the organizational and the macro levels. Thus, the technology adoption process is explored in the following section.

17.3 UNDERSTANDING TECHNOLOGY ADOPTION

Adoption is the process by which individuals and organizations integrate a new technology into their daily workflows (Straub, 2009). This process is complex, involving being aware of a technology, carefully considering its potential advantages, and deciding whether to incorporate it into current processes. For organizations, understanding technology adoption is essential for remaining competitive, facilitating dynamic capabilities and allowing the timely integration of innovative tools and processes, ultimately enhancing productivity, cost-effectiveness, and overall business success (Rogers, 2003). Multiple theories of technology adoption have been postulated in the literature. For example, there are numerous well-established models of technology adoption, including the Technology Acceptance Model (TAM), Unified Theory of Acceptance and Use of Technology (UTAUT), Theory of Reasoned Action (TRA), and Theory of Planned Behavior (TPB), each of which provides valuable insights into the factors that drive technology adoption (Leung et al., 2015; Omrani et al., 2022). TAM, introduced in 1989 by Davis, emphasizes perceived usefulness and perceived ease of use as the key determinants of technology adoption. In contrast, UTAUT (Venkatesh et al., 2003) takes a more comprehensive approach, identifying three determinants of intention to use (namely, performance expectancy, effort expectancy, and social influence), as well as two determinants of usage behavior (behavioral intention and facilitating conditions). Despite their widespread use across academic disciplines and industries, both TAM and UTAUT are widely criticized, in particular for oversimplification; lacking context specificity by neglecting to consider crucial organizational, social, and financial factors; as well as primarily concentrating on the initial adoption decision to the detriment of post-adoption stages (Blut et al., 2022; Chatterjee et al., 2021; Venkatesh and Bala, 2008). Furthermore, although attempts have been made to utilize these models when considering technology adoption by businesses (Abou-Shouk et al., 2016; Chatterjee et al., 2021), their applicability has been limited as they essentially focus on the attitudes and beliefs of individuals, and are thus difficult to validly adapt to an organizational context.

In contrast, Diffusion of Innovation (DOI) theory focuses on the attributes of the innovation and the adopting entity from both individual and organizational perspectives (Alsetoohy et al., 2019). DOI maintains that the key attributes influencing adoption are relative advantage, compatibility, complexity, trialability, observability, and communicability, with adopters categorized into innovators, early adopters, early majority, late majority, and laggards based on their pace and style of adoption. Communication channels play a crucial role in spreading knowledge about innovations, and the adoption process involves stages, like knowledge, persuasion, decision, implementation, and confirmation. However, while widely used in technology adoption research, DOI is also felt to be limited, in particular by ignoring environmental aspects that need to be taken into consideration as organizations operate within specific environments with specific characteristics that undoubtedly affect adoption (Baabdullah et al., 2021; Leung et al., 2015).

This deficiency is addressed by the Technology-Organization-Environment (TOE) framework, which takes a more holistic approach and considers different dimensions of influence, thereby providing a more complete understanding of the organizational technology adoption process (Leung et al., 2015; Marzi et al., 2023). While acknowledging that technological issues should be of prime consideration, TOE also recognizes that adoption needs to consider both internal organizational and external environmental factors (Iranmanesh et al., 2023). With Ngah et al. (2022), as well as Zhu and Kraemer (2005), highlighting the framework's superiority as a flexible, adaptable, and holistic theory that more thoroughly facilitates an understanding of technology adoption, TOE has emerged as the predominant conceptual model of the factors influencing organizational technology adoption (Liu et al., 2020), and has been widely used across different organizational contexts, including with SMEs (Giotopoulos et al., 2022; Mkansi, 2022; Rakshit et al., 2022).

17.4 THE TECHNOLOGY-ORGANIZATION-ENVIRONMENT (TOE) FRAMEWORK

TOE framework is a theoretical model that helps decipher how organizations adopt and integrate technological advancements into their operations by scrutinizing the technological traits, organizational features, and environmental characteristics of the organization. At the conceptual level, the technological context entails examining the attributes of the technology in question to determine how well it fits and matches with the needs and strategic objectives of the business (Dadhich and Hiran, 2022), as well as its compatibility with current usage and potential future adoptions (Chau et al., 2021; Eze et al., 2018). By being aware of these technological aspects, organizations can better equip themselves to weigh the benefits and drawbacks of adopting a technology and make decisions about its implementation. The organizational context, in contrast, refers to characteristics and internal dynamics of the adopting organization that might influence the decision (Chau et al., 2021; Justino et al., 2022). Successful adoption can be optimized by considering how well organizations can understand, implement, and adapt to the technology based on their internal operations and capabilities (Nam et al., 2021). Finally, the environmental context considers key elements of the external business environment that could potentially affect the adoption decision (Chau et al., 2021; Justino et al., 2022).

While conceptually clear, TOE faces some challenges in terms of being operationalized, particularly in terms of what issues to consider and prioritize, especially in the context of SMEs in general and SMTEs in particular. Tornatzky and Fleischer's original 1990 model has been extensively tested, validated, and extended, and thus the resulting corpus of literature available offers a starting point as to what factors to consider when adopting technology. To this end, a systematic literature review was carried out, focusing on the subject areas of business, management and accounting, social sciences, economics, econometrics, and finance. The timeframe utilized was from 2004 to 2024, spanning a total of 20 years, with searches carried out in the SCOPUS database on the TOE framework and SMEs. Only articles in journals ranked A*, A, and B in the Australian Business Deans Council Ranking, or Q1 in the SCImago Journal Ranking, were considered, identifying 117 papers. Article titles and abstracts were manually reviewed to assess relevancy to the study's context, resulting in a database of 72 articles. Analysis of these studies identified a total of 47 relevant factors previously used in peer-reviewed research studies (16, 20, and 11 in the technological, organizational, and environmental context, respectively). Prioritizing these to factors that were cited four or more times allows the most frequently used determinants to be identified. These are summarized in Table 17.1.

17.5 ENHANCING TECHNOLOGY ADOPTION BY TOURISM FIRMS AND SMTES

As can be seen from Table 17.1, a wide variety of factors have been included in studies on understanding technology adoption. Prioritizing by number of times cited allows critical issues to be considered during the adoption process. These are summarized in the following sections.

17.5.1 TECHNOLOGICAL FACTORS

Within technological factors, relative advantage, compatibility, technological competence, and perceived usefulness emerge as key issues.

TABLE 17.1 Technology Adoption Determinants from Literature.

Category	Determinant	Description	Frequency in Prior Studies
Technological	Compatibility	Refers to alignment with the current values, experience, and needs of potential adopters.	25
Technological	Relative advantage	Pertains to the extent to which a new technology is perceived as superior to existing practices.	23
Technological	Technology competence	Ability to offer the technical assistance required to adopt a new technology, including processing appropriate technology systems, IT assistance, and a top-notch technical infrastructure.	20
Technological	Perceived usefulness	The belief or expectation that the technology will increase operational efficiency by reducing operating costs, improving customer service experience, distinguishing from rivals, or boosting marketing efficacy.	20
Technological	Complexity	Refers to the degree to which a technology is perceived as challenging to understand and implement.	14
Technological	Perceived ease of use	The belief or expectation that a specific system or technology will be easy to use and require minimal effort.	12
Technological	Cost	Assessing the anticipated costs of acquiring and implementing the technology.	9
Technological	Perceived risk	Refers to the unpredictability and possible drawbacks of applying a technology, which could include financial losses, mental stress, privacy violations, and technical challenges.	8
Technological	Security and privacy	Concerns related to data handling, data protection, data safety, and threat mitigation.	8
Technological	Measurement/ evaluation	Processes to assess effectiveness, particularly tangible outcomes like profitability and operational improvement.	6
Organizational	Organizational readiness	The preparedness of a company, especially in terms of its financial and technological resources, as well as the availability of appropriate skills, expertise, and other capabilities, to support IT adoption.	45

TABLE 17.1 *(Continued)*

Category	Determinant	Description	Frequency in Prior Studies
Organizational	Top management support	Backing from organizational leaders.	34
Organizational	Firm size	Size of an organization, typically in number of employees or sales turnover.	12
Organizational	Innovativeness	Organization's capacity to learn and combine new knowledge with existing expertise.	10
Organizational	Organization culture	The values, beliefs, conventions, and symbols of an organization.	4
Organizational	Business landscape	How the organization functions within its market, industry, and global context.	4
Environmental	Stakeholder pressure	Influence of external parties (e.g., rivals, clients, vendors, or the government) on an organization's actions.	42
Environmental	External support	Assistance, guidance, or expertise provided by external sources, such as government, consultants, and vendors.	20
Environmental	Customer insights	Collection and analysis of customers' needs, preferences, behaviors, and expectations regarding IT adoption.	8
Environmental	Trust	Assessing whether a technology is secure, reliable, and supported by strong relationships with stakeholders.	5
Environmental	Environmental dynamism	Refers to unpredictable changes in the external environment, including market trends, regulatory changes, technological advancement, and competitive dynamics.	5

Relative advantage refers to the extent to which a potential adoption is perceived to be superior to existing practices (Leong et al., 2023; Nam et al., 2021). When perceived as potentially adding more value than current methods, this positively influences adoption. Conceptually this is closely related to perceived usefulness, or whether the adoption being considered is forecast to improve productivity and performance, with a stronger perception positively influencing propensity to adopt (Collado-Agudo et al., 2023).

Compatibility, on the other hand, refers to how a new technology, system, or innovation is perceived as harmonizing effectively with existing systems and work practices (Maroufkhani et al., 2023). Where seen as high, this means that the potential adoption would be a good match with existing ways of doing things, making it more likely to be adopted and accepted. Related to this is perceived ease of use, or the likelihood that the adoption will be simple to understand and utilize, increasing the likelihood of adoption (Collado-Agudo et al., 2023). However, tourism businesses are challenged in both cases by the legacy nature of many existing systems, which tend to be proprietary in nature, with the result that they are both difficult to use and lack the interoperability needed to connect with today's newer generation, typically cloud-based, more open systems (Buhalis et al., 2023).

This legacy challenge is exasperated by the third most cited issue within the technological factors cluster, namely technology competence, which reflects an organization's ability to provide the necessary infrastructure and expertise to support the new adoption (Leong et al., 2023). As highlighted earlier, tourism organizations typically lack both a modern technological infrastructure as well as dedicated expertise to support technology operations. This, to some degree also drives complexity, or the degree to which the potential adoption is perceived as being challenging to understand and implement, and thus less likely to be adopted (Baig et al., 2023; Nam et al., 2021; Sharma et al., 2022).

17.5.2 ORGANIZATIONAL FACTORS

As with technological factors, examining adoption from an organizational perspective is multifaceted, with three major issues frequently cited. Most studies agree that the most critical organization issue for technology adoption is organizational readiness. This is strongly associated with employee proficiency, with a skilled and knowledgeable workforce as an asset, when considering the adoption of new systems within an organization (Low et al., 2022; Ngo et al., 2023). However, tourism organizations, particularly SMTEs, face considerable challenges in this regard as they typically lack specialized teams, with their small unit size and limited personnel providing few opportunities for division of labor or professional training (Buhalis, 1996). As a result, most lack both the dedicated personnel and the requisite specialized expertise, which hampers their awareness of new developments (Lutfi, 2022), and their ability to effectively exploit today's constantly evolving technology-based systems. Organizational readiness is also closely related to innovativeness, or the ability to support new ideas, experimentation, and creative processes, all of which help to create new products, services, processes, or competencies (Andrade-Valbuena and Llanos-Herrera, 2022). However, tourism organizations tend to be conservative in nature, typically suffering from a reluctance to embrace change (AlBar and Hoque, 2019), which negatively affects technology adoption.

A second key issue is the availability of appropriate support from senior management (Ali et al., 2023; Lutfi, 2022). Leading from the top helps improve the quality of adoption decisions by ensuring a strategic perspective, considering the overall long-term objectives of the organization. Top management support also helps smooth transitions by overruling the needs of individual functions or departments, as well as by ensuring access to appropriate resources (Hsu et al., 2019). However, leadership of this type tends to be lacking within many tourism organizations. Essentially family businesses typically lack professional management capable of thinking strategically and investing in appropriate technologies (Ben Aissa and Goaied, 2016). Instead, management's focus tends to be primarily operational, with lifestyle considerations often as important as driving profitability (Peters et al., 2019). As a result, top managements' capability and willingness, to lead digital transformation tends to be limited (Ghobakhloo et al., 2022).

A third organizational factor that undoubtedly affects adoption decisions is firm size (Yaseen et al., 2023). This has been shown to play a complex role in adoption, with larger firms tending to have more resources and capabilities available to support the evaluation and adoption processes (Salah et al., 2021), but at the same time suffering from strong organizational inertia that discourages change. Smaller firms, in contrast, typically have a scarcity of resources, operating on small margins and lacking the capital to be able to experiment with or invest in new technologies. At the same time, they also typically tend to be more agile, innovative, and adaptable, potentially facilitating the adoption process (Alshamaila et al., 2013).

17.5.3 ENVIRONMENTAL FACTORS

Prior studies on technology adoption prioritize two key environmental determinants. By far the most frequently cited, stakeholder pressure, refers to the influence exerted by third parties on an organization's decisions and actions. Such pressure can come from competitors, government, industry, partners, customers, or suppliers. For example, distribution partners further down the industry value chain may require organizations to make use of specific technology-based systems to receive reservations, handle reconciliation and payment, and work in partnership with them in an efficient manner. In such cases, they may mandate or even provide specific systems in effect, forcing adoption for anyone wishing to continue working with them (Hasani et al., 2017).

A second key environmental factor influencing adoption is the availability of assistance from third party sources. Such external support may come from government, technology experts, consultants, or even vendors (Chau et al., 2021), and can be a key driver of adoption, particularly for SMEs, which typically lack the expertise and other resources necessary to pursue adoption independently. Such additional help can therefore be highly beneficial, helping to drive adoption in situations where the organization would be incapable of exploring the options available on its own.

17.6 DISCUSSION, CONCLUSION, AND RESEARCH AGENDA

As can been seen from the above discussion, the complexities surrounding technology adoption in tourism are complex and interrelated. Despite the role that current and developing technologies could play in boosting efficiency and enhancing customer satisfaction, many tourism businesses lack the financial, technical, and expertise resources to be able to implement new systems successfully (Kuokkanen and Bouchon, 2021). And with their strong day-to-day operational focus, they also lack the managerial capacity to continuously monitor the multitude of options available; undertake comprehensive and valid evaluations of alternatives; as well as integrate innovative systems into their business processes (Stankovska et al., 2016). Such constraints reduce their ability to exploit emerging technologies, threatening resilience and competitiveness. Such challenges are not new and have acted as a brake on the tourism sector for decades. However, consumers' recent, COVID-19 motivated, stampede toward digital channels to aid in all aspects of their lifestyle has accentuated the challenge, making it more important than ever to embrace appropriate digital systems to enhance operations and customer service (Sigala, 2020).

The movement toward technology democratization may help address many of the aforementioned financial and expertise challenges (O'Connor, 2024a). Derived from the open-source movement, democratization refers to the growing availability of digital tools that are cheaper (or, in many cases, free), open (addressing the proprietary/compatibility challenge highlighted earlier), as well as more usable and easier to implement (addressing the challenge of expertise) (Andriole, 2022; Nuseir and Aljumah, 2020). Topical examples include WordPress, Google Analytics, and ChatGPT, which lower entry barriers and help empower organizations hitherto overlooked by the digital revolution to use technology to enhance performance, resilience, and agility (Stankovska et al., 2016). Democratized systems fit the classic pattern of disruptive innovation from *The Innovator's Dilemma.* Currently just "good enough" to get the job done, particularly when alternatives are expensive or require extensive technical expertise, democratized systems will grow in power and sophistication, as well as extend in terms of scope over time, providing tourism businesses with access to state-of-the art technology-based systems without significant financial or expertise challenges (O'Connor, 2024a).

The key remaining challenges tend to be organizational, rather than financial or technical in nature, and are deeply related to management awareness, bandwidth, and acceptability. Although technology has, and will become more affordable for the most part, consideration of its potential business utility remains off the priority lists of most owners/managers in the tourism sector. Lacking strategic vision, their predominantly operational focus leaves them blissfully unaware of the potential of new technology-based systems—with this absence of appropriate management capacity—limiting their ability to think strategically about developing technologies, business models, and distribution channels (Ruediger et al., 2012).

Addressing these organizational challenges requires a concerted effort to cultivate a culture of innovation within tourism businesses. External support, from governments, educational institutions, industry associations, and vendors is needed to build awareness and enhance organizational readiness by building digital literacy and capabilities, empowering both managers and employees with the necessary knowledge and skills to navigate technological advancements effectively (Ghobakhloo et al., 2022; Zamani, 2022). By fostering partnerships and knowledge-sharing initiatives, tourism businesses can streamline this learning process, thus facilitating the integration of cutting-edge technologies into their operations. In addition, proactively fostering strong leadership, as well as a culture of innovation within tourism businesses is crucial for driving digital transformation and aligning technology adoption with long-term strategic objectives. While in the short term, training programs and capacity-building initiatives can help empower existing managers with the skills and knowledge needed, eventually this challenge should fade away as younger, more digitally savvy managers gain prominence. In this way, as organizational challenges are gradually overcome, tourism businesses can surmount the current challenges of technology adoption to harness the transformative power of digital innovations more comprehensively, enhancing both operational efficiency and customer experiences, unlocking new avenues for growth and competitiveness, and positioning themselves for long-term success in an increasingly competitive digital world.

KEYWORDS

- **ingrained traditional practices**
- **organizational readiness**
- **perceived usefulness**
- **resistance to change**
- **stakeholder pressure**
- **technology adoption**
- **Technology-Organization-Environment framework**

REFERENCES

Abed, S. S. (2020). Social commerce adoption using TOE framework: An empirical investigation of Saudi Arabian SMEs. *International Journal of Information Management, 53*, 102118.

Abou-Shouk, M. A., Lim, W. M., & Megicks, P. (2016). Using competing models to evaluate the role of environmental pressures in ecommerce adoption by small and medium sized travel agents in a developing country. *Tourism Management (1982), 52*, 327–339. https://doi.org/10.1016/j.tourman.2015.07.007.

AlBar, A. M., & Hoque, M. R. (2019). Factors affecting the adoption of information and communication technology in small and medium enterprises: A perspective from rural Saudi Arabia. *Information Technology for Development, 25*(4), 715–738.

Ali, M. H., Chung, L., Tan, K. H., Makhbul, Z. M., Zhan, Y., & Tseng, M. L. (2023). Investigating blockchain technology adoption intention model in halal food small and medium enterprises: Moderating role of supply chain integration. *International Journal of Logistics Research and Applications*, 1–25.

Alsetoohy, O., Ayoun, B., Arous, S., Megahed, F., & Nabil, G. (2019). Intelligent agent technology: what affects its adoption in hotel food supply chain management? *Journal of Hospitality and Tourism Technology, 10*(3), 286–310.

Alshamaila, Y., Papagiannidis, S., & Li, F. (2013). Cloud computing adoption by SMEs in the north east of England: A multi-perspective framework. *Journal of Enterprise Information Management, 26*(3), 250–275.

Andrade-Valbuena, N. A. & Llanos-Herrera, G. R. (2022). Why are there discrepancies in the results of entrepreneurial orientation and its impact on a firm's performance?: A review of the literature. In R. Perez-Uribe, C. Salcedo-Perez, & A. Carvajal-Contreras (Eds.), *Handbook of research on organizational sustainability in turbulent economies* (pp. 315–334). IGI Global. https://doi.org/10.4018/978-1-7998-9301-1.ch017.

Andriole, S. (2022) Where did IT go? *International Journal of Technology Management, 89*(1–2), 1–138. https://doi.org/10.1504/IJTM.2022.123011.

Ashari, H. A., Heidari, M., & Parvaresh, S. (2014). Improving SMTEs' business performance through strategic use of information communication technology: ICT and tourism challenges and opportunities. *International Journal of Academic Research in Accounting, Finance and Management Sciences, 4*(3), 1–20.

Ayinla, K. O., & Adamu, Z. (2018). Bridging the digital divide gap in BIM technology adoption. *Engineering, Construction, and Architectural Management, 25*(10), 1398–1416. https://doi.org/10.1108/ECAM-05-2017-0091.

Baabdullah, A. M., Alalwan, A. A., Slade, E. L., Raman, R., & Khatatneh, K. F. (2021). SMEs and artificial intelligence (AI): Antecedents and consequences of AI-based B2B practices. *Industrial Marketing Management, 98*, 255–270. https://doi.org/10.1016/j.indmarman.2021.09.003.

Baig, M. I., Yadegaridehkordi, E., & Nizam Bin Md Nasir, M. H. (2023), Influence of big data adoption on sustainable marketing and operation of SMEs: A hybrid approach of SEM-ANN. *Management Decision, 61*(7), 2231–2253. https://doi.org/10.1108/MD-06-2022-0778.

Ben Aissa, S., & Goaied, M. (2016). Determinants of Tunisian hotel profitability: The role of managerial efficiency. *Tourism Management*, *52*, 478–487. https://doi.org/10.1016/j.tourman.2015.07.015.

Blut, M., Chong, A. Y. L., Tsigna, Z., & Venkatesh, V. (2022). Meta-analysis of the unified theory of acceptance and use of technology (UTAUT): Challenging its validity and charting a research agenda in the red ocean. *Journal of the Association for Information Systems*, *23*(1), 13–95. https://doi.org/10.17705/1jais.00719.

Buhalis, D. (1996) Enhancing the competitiveness of small and medium sized tourism enterprises. *Electronic Markets*, *6*(1), 1–6. https://doi.org/10.1080/10196789600000002.

Buhalis, D., O'Connor, P., & Leung, R. (2023). Smart hospitality: From smart cities and smart tourism towards agile business ecosystems in networked destinations. *International Journal of Contemporary Hospitality Management*, *35*(1), 369–393.

Buhalis, D., Harwood, T., Bogicevic, V., Viglia, G., Beldona, S., & Hofacker, C. (2019). Technological disruptions in services: Lessons from tourism and hospitality. *Journal of Service Management*, *30*(4), 484–506.

Chan, F. T. S., Yee-Loong Chong, A., & Zhou, L. (2012). An empirical investigation of factors affecting e-collaboration diffusion in SMEs. *International Journal of Production Economics*, *138*(2), 329–344. https://doi.org/10.1016/j.ijpe.2012.04.004.

Chatterjee, S., Rana, N. P., Dwivedi, Y. K., & Baabdullah, A. M. (2021). Understanding AI adoption in manufacturing and production firms using an integrated TAM-TOE model. *Technological Forecasting and Social Change*, *170*, 120880. https://doi.org/10.1016/j.techfore.2021.120880.

Collado-Agudo, J., Herrero-Crespo, Á., & San Martín-Gutiérrez, H. (2023). The adoption of a smart destination model by tourism companies: An ecosystem approach. *Journal of Destination Marketing and Management*, *28*, 100783. https://doi.org/10.1016/j.jdmm.2023.100783.

Chau, N. T., Deng, H., & Tay, R. (2021). A perception-based model for mobile commerce adoption in Vietnamese small and medium-sized enterprises. *Journal of Global Information Management (JGIM)*, *29*(1), 44–67.

Dadhich, M., & Hiran, K. K. (2022). Empirical investigation of extended TOE model on corporate environment sustainability and dimensions of operating performance of SMEs: A high order PLS-ANN approach. *Journal of Cleaner Production*, *363*, 132309. https://doi.org/10.1016/j.jclepro.2022.132309.

de Mattos, C. S., Pellegrini, G., Hagelaar, G., & Dolfsma, W. (2023). Systematic literature review on technological transformation in SMEs: A transformation encompassing technology assimilation and business model innovation. *Management Review Quarterly*. https://doi.org/10.1007/s11301-023-00327-7.

Eze, S. C., Olatunji, S., Chinedu-Eze, V. C., Bello, A. O., Ayeni, A., & Peter, F. (2019). Determinants of perceived information need for emerging ICT adoption: A study of UK small service businesses. *The Bottom Line (New York, N.Y.)*, *32*(2), 158–183. https://doi.org/10.1108/BL-01-2019-0059.

Gazzoli, G., Kim, W. G., & Palakurthi, R. (2008). Online distribution strategies and competition: Are the global hotel companies getting it right? *International Journal of Contemporary Hospitality Management*, *20*(4), 275–387.

Giotopoulos, I., Kontolaimou, A., & Tsakanikas, A. (2022). Digital responses of SMEs to the COVID-19 crisis. *International Journal of Entrepreneurial Behavior and Research, 28*(7), 1751–1772.

Ghobakhloo, M., Iranmanesh, M., Vilkas, M., Grybauskas, A., & Amran, A. (2022). Drivers and barriers of Industry 4.0 technology adoption among manufacturing SMEs: A systematic review and transformation roadmap. *Journal of Manufacturing Technology Management, 33*(6), 1029–1058.

Hasani, T., Bojei, J., & Dehghantanha, A. (2017). Investigating the antecedents to the adoption of SCRM technologies by start-up companies. *Telematics and Informatics, 34*(5), 655–675.

Huang, H. Y., Ku, E. C., & Chen, C. D. (2022). Cloud infrastructure enhancing product competitive advantage of tourism SMEs on online consumption values of tourists. *Business Process Management Journal, 28*(4), 1146–1163.

Hsu, Y. P., Chun-Yang, P., Pi-Hui, T., & et al. (2019) Managerial coaching, job performance, and team commitment: The meditating effect of psychological capital. *Advances in Management and Applied Economics, 9*(5), 101–125.

Iranmanesh, M., Lim, K. H., Foroughi, B., Hong, M. C., & Ghobakhloo, M. (2023). Determinants of intention to adopt big data and outsourcing among SMEs: Organisational and technological factors as moderators. *Management Decision, 61*(1), 201–222. https://doi.org/10.1108/MD-08-2021-1059.

Januszewska, M., Jaremen, D., & Nawrocka, E. (2015). The effects of the use of ICT by tourism enterprises. Zeszyty Naukowe Uniwersytetu Szczecińskiego. *Service Management, 16*, 65–73.

Justino, M. V., Tengeh, R. K., & Twum-Darko, M. (2022). A revised technology–organisation–environment framework for brick-and-mortar retailers adopting M-commerce. *Journal of Risk and Financial Management, 15*(7), 289.

Kuokkanen, H., & Bouchon, F. (2021). When team play matters: Building revenue management in tourism destinations. *Tourism Economics, 27*(2), 379–397. https://doi.org/10.1177/1354816620921250.

Leong, L. Y., Hew, J. J., Lee, V. H., Tan, G. W. H., Ooi, K. B., & Rana, N. P. (2023). An SEM-ANN analysis of the impacts of blockchain on competitive advantage. *Industrial Management + Data Systems, 123*(3), 967–1004. https://doi.org/10.1108/IMDS-11-2021-0671.

Leung, D., Lo, A., Fong, L. H. N., & Law, R. (2015). Applying the technology-organization-environment framework to explore ICT initial and continued adoption: An exploratory study of an independent hotel in Hong Kong. *Tourism Recreation Research, 40*(3), 391–406.

Liu, C., Hung, K., Wang, D., & et al. (2020). Determinants of self-service technology adoption and implementation in hotels: The case of China. *Journal of Hospitality Marketing and Management, 29*(6), 636–661.

Low, M. P., Seah, C. S., Cham, T. H., & Teoh, S. H. (2022). Digitalization adoption for digital economy: an examination of Malaysian small medium-sized enterprises through the technology–organization–environment framework. *Business Process Management Journal, 28*(7), 1473–1494. https://doi.org/10.1108/BPMJ-06-2022-0282.

Lutfi, A. (2022). Understanding the intention to adopt cloud-based accounting information system in jordanian SMEs. *International Journal of Digital Accounting Research, 22*.

Masood, T., & Sonntag, P. (2020). Industry 4.0: Adoption challenges and benefits for SMEs. *Computers in Industry*, *121*, 103261. https://doi.org/10.1016/j.compind.2020.103261.

Maroufkhani, P., Iranmanesh, M., & Ghobakhloo, M. (2023). Determinants of big data analytics adoption in small and medium-sized enterprises (SMEs). *Industrial Management + Data Systems*, *123*(1), 278–301. https://doi.org/10.1108/IMDS-11-2021-0695.

Marzi, G., Marrucci, A., Vianelli, D., & Ciappei, C. (2023). B2B digital platform adoption by SMEs and large firms: Pathways and pitfalls. *Industrial Marketing Management*, *114*, 80–93.

Mkansi, M. (2022). E-business adoption costs and strategies for retail micro businesses. *Electronic Commerce Research*, *22*(4), 1153–1193. https://doi.org/10.1007/s10660-020-09448-7.

Nam, K., Dutt, C. S., Chathoth, P., & et al. (2021). The adoption of artificial intelligence and robotics in the hotel industry: Prospects and challenges. *Electron Markets, 31*, 553–574.

Ngah, A. H., Thurasamy, R., Mohd Salleh, N. H., Jeevan, J., Md Hanafiah, R., & Eneizan, B. (2022). Halal transportation adoption among food manufacturers in Malaysia: the moderated model of technology, organisation and environment (TOE) framework. *Journal of Islamic Marketing*, *13*(12), 2563–2581.

Ngo, V. M., Pham, H. C., & Nguyen, H. H. (2023). Drivers of digital supply chain transformation in SMEs and large enterprises–a case of COVID-19 disruption risk. *International Journal of Emerging Markets*, *18*(6), 1355–1377.

Nuseir, M. T., & Aljumah, A. (2020). The role of digital marketing in business performance with the moderating effect of environment factors among SMEs of UAE. *International Journal of Innovation, Creativity and Change*, *11*(3), 310–324.

O'Connor, P. (2023a). Small- and medium-sized tourism enterprises and smart tourism: Tourism agenda 2030 perspective article. *Tourism Review*. https://doi.org/10.1108/TR-09-2022-0431.

O'Connor, P. (2023b). Chapter 14: Intermediation, disintermediation and reintermediation: Tourism distribution in the electronic age. In *Routledge handbook of trends and issues in global tourism supply and demand* (pp. 179–188). United States: Taylor and Francis.

O'Connor, P. (2024a). The democratization of tourism distribution: A horizon 2050 paper. *Tourism Review*. ahead-of-print. https://doi.org/10.1108/TR-12-2023-0852.

O'Connor, P. (2024b). Tourism enterprises and distribution: The effects of online food delivery platforms and OTAs. In R. Hallak & C. Lee (Eds.), *Handbook of tourism entrepreneurship: Research handbooks in tourism series*. United Kingdom: Edward Elgar Publishing Limited.

Omrani, N., Rejeb, N., Maalaoui, A., Dabic, M., & Kraus, S. (2022). Drivers of digital transformation in SMEs. In *IEEE transactions on engineering management* (Vol. 71, pp. 5030–5043). https://doi.org/10.1109/TEM.2022.3215727.

Pappas, N., Caputo, A., Pellegrini, M. M., Marzi, G., & Michopoulou, E. (2021). The complexity of decision-making processes and IoT adoption in accommodation SMEs. *Journal of Business Research*, *131*, 573–583.

Peters, M., Kallmuenzer, A., & Buhalis, D. (2019). Hospitality entrepreneurs managing quality of life and business growth. *Current Issues in Tourism*, *22*(16), 2014–2033.

Rakshit, S., Islam, N., Mondal, S., & Paul, T. (2022). Influence of blockchain technology in SME internationalization: Evidence from high-tech SMEs in India. *Technovation, 115*, 102518. https://doi.org/10.1016/j.technovation.2022.102518.

Rogers, E. M. (2003). *Diffusion of innovations*. Simon & Schuster.

Ruediger Kaufmann, H. A. N. S., Tsangar, H., & Vrontis, D. (2012). Innovativeness of European SMEs: Mission not yet accomplished. *Economic Research-Ekonomska istraživanja*, *25*(2), 333–360.

Salah, O. H., Yusof, Z. M., & Mohamed, H. (2021). The determinant factors for the adoption of CRM in the Palestinian SMEs: The moderating effect of firm size. *PLoS One, 16*(3), e0243355. https://doi.org/10.1371/journal.pone.0259344.

Sharma, S., Singh, G., Islam, N., & Dhir, A. (2022). Why do SMEs adopt artificial intelligence-based chatbots? In *IEEE transactions on engineering management* (pp. 1–14). https://doi.org/10.1109/TEM.2022.3203469.

Sigala, M. (2018). New technologies in tourism: From multi-disciplinary to anti-disciplinary advances and trajectories. *Tourism Management Perspectives*. https://doi.org/10.1016/j.tmp.2017.12.003.

Sigala, M. (2020). Tourism and COVID-19: Impacts and implications for advancing and resetting industry and research. *Journal of Business Research*, *117*, 312–321.

Stankovska, I., Josimovski, S., & Edwards, C. (2016). Digital channels diminish SME barriers: The case of the UK. *Economic Research-Ekonomska istraživanja*, *29*(1), 217–232.

Straub, E. T. (2009). Understanding technology adoption: Theory and future directions for informal learning. *Review of Educational Research*, *79*(2), 625–649. https://doi.org/10.3102/0034654308325896.

Venkatesh, V., & Bala, H. (2008). Technology acceptance model 3 and a research agenda on interventions. *Decision Sciences*, *39*(2), 273–315.

Venkatesh, V., Morris, M. G., Davis, G. B., & Davis, F. D. (2003). User acceptance of information technology: Toward a unified view. *MIS Quarterly*, *27*(3), 425–478. https://doi.org/10.2307/30036540.

Yaseen, H., Al-Adwan, A. S., Nofal, M., Hmoud, H., & Abujassar, R. S. (2023). Factors influencing cloud computing adoption among SMEs: The jordanian context. *Information Development*, *39*(2), 317–332. https://doi.org/10.1177/02666669211047916.

Zamani, S. Z. (2022). Small and Medium Enterprises (SMEs) facing an evolving technological era: A systematic literature review on the adoption of technologies in SMEs. *European Journal of Innovation Management*, *25*(6), 735–757. https://doi.org/10.1108/EJIM-07-2021-0360.

Zhu, K., & Kraemer, K. L. (2005). Post-adoption variations in usage and value of e-business by organizations: Cross-country evidence from the retail industry. *Information Systems Research, 16*(1), 61-84. https://doi.org/10.1287/isre.1050.0045

Index

D

U

V

W

www.ingramcontent.com/pod-product-compliance
Ingram Content Group UK Ltd.
Pitfield, Milton Keynes, MK11 3LW, UK
UKHW022159190926
475702UK00003B/114

* 9 7 8 1 7 7 9 6 4 4 7 6 3 *